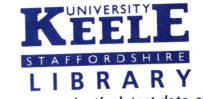

# THE CULTURAL USES OF PRINT
# IN EARLY MODERN FRANCE

ROGER CHARTIER

# The Cultural Uses of Print in Early Modern France

TRANSLATED BY
LYDIA G. COCHRANE

PRINCETON UNIVERSITY PRESS
PRINCETON, NEW JERSEY

*All Rights Reserved*
Library of Congress Cataloging in Publication Data will be
found on the last printed page of this book
Information on the original, French publication of these essays
will be found on the first page of each chapter

ISBN 0-691-05499-1

Publication of this book has been aided by the
Whitney Darrow Fund of Princeton University Press

This book has been composed in Linotron Granjon

Clothbound editions of Princeton University Press books
are printed on acid-free paper, and binding materials are
chosen for strength and durability
Paperbacks, although satisfactory for personal collections,
are not usually suitable for library rebinding

Printed in the United States of America by
Princeton University Press
Princeton, New Jersey

*For my father*

# CONTENTS

# LIST OF ILLUSTRATIONS

I AM GRATEFUL to the following institutions, which have permitted the reproduction of the illustrations in this book: the Bibliothèque Nationale, Paris, for figures 1-11, 13, 15, and 18-19; the Musée des Arts et Traditions Populaires, Paris, for figure 12; the Société Archéologique et Historique de Nantes for figure 14; the Musée des Arts Décoratifs, Paris, for figure 16; and the Rare Books and Manuscripts Division of the New York Public Library, Astor, Lenox and Tilden Foundations, for figure 17.

# ACKNOWLEDGMENTS

MY THANKS GO, first, to friends at Princeton University: to Natalie Davis, who first thought that these eight studies could make a book, and to Robert Darnton, who faithfully kept watch as the book gestated. They go next to Lydia Cochrane, who has translated my words with a care and intelligence that makes this her book as well as mine. I also thank the publishing houses of Promodis, Montalba, and Oldenbourg and the journals *Diogène, Annales E.S.C.,* and *Revue d'Histoire Moderne et Contemporaine* for permission to translate the texts which they originally published. My thanks also go to Miriam Brokaw and Joanna Hitchcock at Princeton University Press for overseeing the publication of this book and to Andrew Mytelka, who has given this work time and care.

Finally, I would like to say that all research benefits from dialogue and debate. All the essays gathered here were elaborated, discussed, and enriched in the framework of a variety of seminars and colloquies on both sides of the Atlantic. I am particularly indebted to the colleagues and friends who, over the years, have participated in my seminar at the École des Hautes Études en Sciences Sociales.

In the footnotes, Bibliothèque Nationale has been abbreviated as BN and Archives Départementales has been abbreviated as AD.

# THE CULTURAL USES OF PRINT
# IN EARLY MODERN FRANCE

# INTRODUCTION

. . . . . . . . . . . . . . . . . . . . . . . . . . . . . . . . . . . . . . . . . . . . . . . . . . . . . . . . . . . .

T HE EIGHT essays that compose this book, originally written and
published in French, concern cultural cleavages that marked
French society during the *ancien régime*, creating differences and tensions, oppositions and divisions. The book's coherence developed gradually as each successive study demanded the honing of concepts used
in previous ones, the rethinking of conclusions that turned out to be
less than definitive, and the opening up of other areas of research.
These eight texts ought therefore to be taken as successive steps toward
the definition of an approach that gradually claimed its own territory,
and also decided what was to be excluded from it. From one text to
another, a widening gap separated my approach from the axioms and
viewpoints most widely accepted by the definition of cultural history
(usually designated as French) that emphasizes a search for the texts,
beliefs, and acts that best characterize popular culture in French society
between the Middle Ages and the French Revolution.

This book has been constructed, then, primarily in opposition to this
now classic use of the notion of popular culture. This notion involves
three presuppositions: first, that it is possible to establish exclusive relationships between specific cultural forms and particular social
groups; second, that the various cultures existing in a given society are
sufficiently pure, homogeneous, and distinct to permit them to be characterized uniformly and unequivocally; and third, that the category of
"the people" or "the popular" has sufficient coherence and stability to
define a distinct social identity that can be used to organize cultural differences in past ages according to the simple opposition of *populaire*
versus *savant*. Long accepted without discussion—and perhaps un-
knowingly—these propositions posed problems for me. Where they
were thought to reveal strict correspondences between cultural cleavages and social hierarchies, I instead found evidence of fluid circulation, practices shared by various groups, and blurred distinctions.
There are many examples (in the present book as well) of "popular"
uses of motifs and genres and of objects and ideas that were never considered specific to the lower echelons of society. There are also many
instances of forms of and materials from a collective culture of the

greater mass of humanity from which the dominant classes or the various elites only slowly distanced themselves.

On the other hand, where a culture considered "of the people" had been identified and defined in terms of its literature, its religion, and its sociability—three terms to which the adjective "popular" was soon and enthusiastically affixed—my closer observation encountered mixed forms and composite practices in which elements of diverse origins found complex ways in which to intermingle. Each group of texts, beliefs, or modes of conduct that I considered attested to intricate cultural mixtures of discipline and invention, reutilizations and innovations, models imposed (by the state, the church, or the market), and freedoms preserved. "Popular" literature, "popular" religion, and "popular" sociability were thus not radically different from what was read, practiced, or experienced by men and women of other social strata. This means that it is illusory to attempt to set up such categories on the basis of the use, supposedly peculiar to each, of certain objects, codes of behavior, or cultural motifs.

Finally, where the very category of the "popular" identified a homogeneous social level to be grasped through its fundamental unity, a finer analysis of cultural practices brought differentiations to light. Thus I have preferred to set aside macroscopic divisions, which often define "the people" in *ancien régime* societies, by default, as all those situated outside the sphere of the dominant groups, and to inventory the many cleavages that divided prerevolutionary society. These cleavages functioned in deference to several principles (not necessarily superposable) to manifest oppositions or gaps that existed not only between men and women, city dwellers and rural folk, Catholics and Protestants, or masters and workers, but also between generations, crafts and trades, or city neighborhoods and country districts. Cultural history—in France, at any rate—has for too long accepted a reductive definition of society, seen strictly in terms of the hierarchy of wealth and condition. This view forgets that other differences, founded upon membership in a sexual category, a territorial population, or a religious group, were just as fully "social" and just as capable (perhaps more so) of explaining the plurality of cultural practices as was position on the socioprofessional scale—especially when judged in light of the one great opposition of dominators and dominated.

In this book I have attempted to profit from these preliminary reflections and, to begin with, to avoid as much as possible the use of the notion of "popular culture." All too frequently, this notion assumes from the outset that the basic problems posed by all examinations of a cultural object or a cultural practice—of defining the areas it covers and identifying the modalities of its use—have been resolved. It seems to me a poor methodology that supposes, a priori, the validity of the very divisions that need to be established. When, on the one hand, the concept of popular culture obliterates the bases shared by the whole of society and when, on the other, it masks the plurality of cleavages that differentiate cultural practices, it cannot be held as pertinent to a comprehension of the forms and the materials that characterize the cultural universe of societies in the modern period.

The essays that make up this book were also born of dissatisfaction on another level. Forms of speech and behavior of traditional culture, often called folkloric, have long been set in clear opposition to the innovative impact of the written word, which gradually penetrated this long-established cultural base, first in manuscript form and then through print. This has meant that these two modes for the acquisition and transmission of culture have been studied in isolation from each other. It has also encouraged the divergence of a methodology proper to historical anthropology, which attempts to locate within the societies of the *ancien régime* forms of expression and communication proper to preliterate societies, from a more classical interpretation of cultural history that focuses on the production, circulation, and utilization of texts. Formulated in these terms, this basic opposition fails to account adequately for the culture of the sixteenth to eighteenth centuries, when, typically, different media and multiple practices almost always mingled in complex ways. In this book I attempt to explore these complex connections. They can perhaps be reduced to a few, fundamental configurations. The first links speech and writings, whether the spoken word was set down in written form (as was the case in the composition of the *cahiers de doléances*) or, conversely, a text was grasped by certain of its "readers" only with the aid of someone reading it aloud. Thanks to the various social situations in which reading aloud occurred, there existed in prerevolutionary societies a culture dependent on writing, even among people incapable of producing or reading a written text. Full comprehension of that culture presupposes the view that access to the written word was a process much more broadly defined than simply the silent reading of an individual in isolation, literacy in its classic sense.

The second configuration is the relationships forged between written texts and actions. Far from constituting separate cultures, these two sets of phenomena were closely connected. To begin with, a great many texts had the precise function of disappearing as discourse and of producing, on the practical level, modes of conduct and behavior that were accepted as legitimate with respect to current social or religious norms. The guides to preparing for death and the civility books that are here studied are two examples of the sorts of texts and printed materials that aimed to impose behavior in conformity with the demands of Christianity or of *civilité*. In addition, the written word lies at the very heart of the most concrete and the most "oralized" forms of traditional cultures. This was true of rituals, which were often intensified by the physical presence of a central text, actually read aloud during the ceremony. It was also true in urban festivals, where inscriptions, banners, and signs bore a profusion of mottoes and slogans. There were, then, close and multiple connections between texts and human actions; each forces us to consider the practice of writing in all its diversity.

From the spoken word to the written text, from the written word to the act, from printed matter back to the spoken word: Such are a few of the trajectories that I shall attempt in this book to describe and to analyze, with the hope of restoring their full complexity to the various forms of expression and cultural communication. One notion has proved useful to an understanding of these phenomena: appropriation. It has enabled me to avoid identifying various cultural levels merely on the basis of a description of the objects, beliefs, or acts presumed to have been proper to each group. Even in *ancien régime* societies, many of these were shared by several different social groups, although the uses to which they were put may not have been identical. A retrospective sociology has long held that unequal distribution of material objects is the prime criterion of cultural differentiation. Here, this theory yields to an approach that concentrates on differentiated uses and plural appropriation of the same goods, the same ideas, and the same actions. A perspective of this sort does not ignore differences—even socially rooted differences—but it does shift the place in which this identification takes place. It is less interested in describing an entire body of materials in social terms (for example, designating books printed in Troyes and sold by peddlers as "popular" literature); it instead aims at a description of the practices that made for differing and strongly characteristic uses of the cultural materials that circulated within a given society.

There is thus something that seems insufficient in the statistical approach that for a time dominated cultural history in France and that was primarily intent on measuring the unequal social distribution of objects, discourses, and actions that provided data in chronological series. When this approach presumes oversimplified correspondences between social levels and cultural horizons and when it seizes thoughts and modes of conduct in their most repetitive and minimalized expressions, it falls short of the essential: the use made by the various groups or individuals of the motifs or forms they shared with others and the way in which they themselves interpreted these motifs and forms. The essays that follow are not intended to supply measurements and statistics. They merely serve to provide a preliminary indication of the extent and the range of the materials under consideration, for example the various genres of printed matter or the grievances expressed and fixed in written form on the eve of the Revolution. My primary aim is to reconstruct social and cultural practices, both as they were proposed in texts that dictated the norm to be respected (and sometimes even followed) and as they adapted to their own uses printed matter, festive and ritual formulas, and the rules imposed by the authorities.

To think of cultural practices in terms of the different ways in which they were appropriated also enables us to consider the texts, the words, and the examples that were aimed at shaping the thought and conduct of the common people: They were less than totally efficacious and radically acculturating. Such practices always created uses and representations not necessarily in accordance with the desires of those who produced the discourses and fashioned the norms. The act of reading simply cannot be divorced from the text itself, nor can the living experience of behavioral patterns be isolated from the prohibitions or precepts aimed at regulating them. Once proposed, these models and messages were accepted by adjusting them, diverting them to other purposes, and even resisting them—all of which demonstrates the singularity of each instance of appropriation. This means that several precautions need to be taken.

The first is that we must be careful not to confuse the study of texts with the study of the actions or thoughts that the texts were intended to produce. This warning may seem obvious, but the historian often forgets that he usually has available only discourses that dictate conduct to be imitated. This means that the history of practices must be based on their manifold representations—in literature and iconography, in statements of norms, in autobiographical accounts, and so forth. This is the perspective that must underlie the study of reading practices—solitary or collective, private or public, learned or simplistic—and that alone can help us comprehend the texts and books that publishers and printers of the sixteenth to the eighteenth centuries offered their readers. In order to understand the texts, themes, and forms of the *Bibliothèque bleue*, then, we also need to investigate the ways in which reading was originally practiced among people who did not belong to the extremely restricted world of fluent readers. It is no more adequate to note the statistical imbalance in the circulation of different genres of printed works than it is to thematically describe the catalogue of literature presumed to be "popular." We must grasp—as precisely as possible in spite of the limited documentation—the diverse ways in which readers of those now remote times encountered and manipulated the written word.

A second precaution: We must be careful not to accept without reservation the now consecrated time scheme that considers the first half of the seventeenth century to have been the period of a major rupture which pitted a golden age of vibrant, free, and profuse popular culture against an age of church and state discipline that repressed and subjected that culture. This view at one time appeared pertinent to the cultural evolution of France during the *ancien régime*. After 1600 or perhaps 1650, the combined efforts of the absolutist state to centralize and unify the nation and of the repressive church of the Catholic Reformation to acculturate the population were seen as stifling or inhibiting the inventive exuberance of the culture of an ancient people. By imposing new discipline, by inculcating a new submissiveness, and by teaching new models of comportment, church and state were alleged to have destroyed the roots and the ancient equilibrium of a traditional way of viewing and experiencing the world. The present book makes use of such a time scheme—and also of the view that the disqualification of popular culture was responsible for its disappearance—only with the greatest of prudence.

There are several reasons for prudence here. First, it is apparent that, when this schema contrasts the cultural splendor of the mass of men on one side of a watershed with misery on the other, it reiterates for the early modern period an opposition that historians have seen in other ages. In like fashion, in the twelfth century, a reordering of the theological, scientific, and philosophical domains that separated learned culture from folk tradition resulted in the censure of practices henceforth held to be superstitious or heterodox. This set apart the people's culture—*la culture des peuples*—as something dangerously seductive and menacing. A similar cultural watershed is supposed to have occurred in France during the half century that separated the wars of 1870 and 1914, a period devoted to freeing traditional cultures, peasant and "popular," from their enclaves (thus uprooting them) and to promoting a unified, national, and republican culture of modern stamp. Another such transformation is assumed to have occurred before and after the advent of today's mass culture, which, in this view, has used the new media to destroy an ancient, creative, plural, and free culture. Historiographically speaking, therefore, the fate of popular culture seems forever to be stifled, inhibited, and abraded, but at the same time ever to be reborn out of its decay. This perhaps indicates that the true problem is not to identify the decisive moment of the irretrievable disappearance of a popular culture. It is rather to consider for each epoch how complex relations were established between the forms imposed (sometimes more and sometimes less forcibly) and firmly established identities (sometimes allowed to blossom and sometimes held back).

This leads to yet another reason for not organizing our entire description of the cultures of the *ancien régime* in accordance with the rupture that is generally agreed to have taken place in the mid-seventeenth century. In point of fact, no matter how forcefully cultural models may have been imposed, they might nevertheless be received with reactions that varied from mistrust to ruse or outright rebellion. A description of the norms, disciplines, texts, and teaching through which absolutist, Counter-Reformation culture may have been intended to subject the population does not prove that the people were in fact totally and universally subjected. Quite to the contrary, we should assume that a gap existed between the norm and real-life experience, between injunction and practice, and between the sense aimed at and the sense produced, a gap into which reformulations and procedures for the avoidance of the model could flow. The mass culture imposed by those in power during those centuries was no more able to destroy particular entities and deep-rooted practices that resisted it than the mass culture of our own times. What changed, obviously, was the manner in which those entities and practices were expressed and by which they affirmed their existence and made their own use of innovations originally designed to curtail them. But accepting this mutation as incontestable does not necessarily oblige us to acknowledge a rupture in cultural continuity throughout the three centuries of the modern period. Nor does it force us to agree that, after the mid-seventeenth century, there was no place left for practices and thoughts other than those the churchmen, the servants of the state, or the makers of books wanted to inculcate.

This is why I have chosen to set aside the thesis of an abrupt break in the cultural history of the *ancient régime* and why I have preferred to use models capable of taking both continuities and divergences into account. The first of these models contrasts discipline and invention in various cultural forms and practices. These two categories are not to be taken as totally irreducible, nor as antagonistic. Used together, they show that all procedures intended to create constraints and controls actually implement tactics that mitigate their effects or subvert them. They also show that, conversely, there is no such thing as a completely free and original cultural product which uses none of the materials imposed by tradition, authority, or the market and which is not subject to the surveillance or censure of those who hold sway over things and words. The programs for festivities or the writing up of grievances are typical examples of this tension between freedoms constrained and discipline subverted. Overly simple theories of opposition between popular spontaneity and the coercion exercised by the dominant classes are simply inadequate to explain this phenomenon.

Discipline and invention, yes; but also distinction and dissemination. This second pair of linked notions is used in the studies that follow in order to propose a way of understanding the circulation of cultural objects and cultural models that does not reduce circulation to simple diffusion, usually considered to descend from the upper to the lower echelons of society. Processes of imitation and popularization are more complex and more dynamic: They need to be thought of as competitive efforts in which any instance of dissemination—whether granted or hard-won—was met with a search for new procedures for distinction. This can be seen in the career of the notion of *civilité*, defined both as a normative concept and as the conduct it demanded. As this notion was diffused throughout society by appropriation or inculcation, it gradually lost the esteem it had enjoyed among the very people whose social personality it described. They were then led to prize other concepts and other codes of manners. The same process can perhaps be seen in reading practices, which became increasingly differentiated as printed matter came to be less scarce, less often confiscated, and less socially distinguishing. For a long period, ownership of an object—the book—in and of itself signified social distinction; gradually, different ways of reading became the distinguishing factor, and thus a hierarchy among plural uses of the same material was set up. We need, then, to replace simplistic and static representations of social domination or cultural diffusion with a way of accounting for them that recognizes the reproduction of gaps within the mechanisms of imitation, the competition at the heart of similarities, and the development of new distinctions arising from the very process of diffusion.

One further word on the concept of culture itself, which up to this point I have used as if its definition were obvious and universally applicable. Let me make it clear that I do not use the term here in the sense that French historiography has generally assigned to it, which is to designate as cultural a particular domain of products and practices that is presumed to be distinct from the economic or social. Culture is not over and above economic and social relations, nor can it be ranged beside them. All practices are articulated according to the representations by which individuals make sense of their existence, and this sense, this meaning, is inscribed in their words, their acts, and their rites. This is why the mechanisms that regulate the working of society and the structures that determine relationships between individuals must be understood as the result—always unstable and conflictive—of relationships between the antagonistic representations of the social world. This means that our understanding of practices which serve to organize economic activity and which create ties among individuals must not be limited to their material ends or their social effects alone. All practices are "cultural" as well as social or economic, since they translate into action the many ways in which humans give meaning to their world. All history, therefore—whether economic, social, or religious—requires the study of systems of representation and the acts the systems generate. This is what makes it cultural history.

Describing a culture should thus involve the comprehension of its entire system of relations—the totality of the practices that express how it represents the physical world, society, and the sacred. This is an impossible and illusory task, at least for such complex societies as France during the *ancien régime*. Treating such complex societies presupposes, in my opinion, reliance on another approach, one that focuses on specific practices, particular objects, and clearly defined uses. Practices connected with the written word—that set down or produced the spoken word, cemented forms of sociability, or prescribed behavior; that took place in the *forum internum* or on the public square; or that sought to induce belief, persuade to action, or inspire dreams—offer a good entry into a society in which proliferating printed matter endeavored to establish a *modus vivendi* with traditional forms of communication and in which new social distinctions fractured a shared base. For the sake of convenience, I may occasionally refer to these practices as "cultural." But by no means do I hold such practices capable of being separated from the other social forms, nor do I intend them to be qualified or classified a priori within a specific domain designated as "cultural practices," as distinct from other, noncultural, practices.

These reflections are, essentially, the fruit of the case studies that follow, not the result of some fully coherent, preexistent program that has guided them. Thus it is possible that, in one or another particular analysis, I may ignore my methodological precautions or return surreptitiously to the very ways of thinking about culture—popular or otherwise—that these prefatory considerations have questioned. But it seems preferable to embrace these discordant elements rather than to eliminate the hesitations and afterthoughts of a methodology that, at each step of the way, was attempting to forge new tools for comprehension out of a dissatisfaction with earlier studies.

This means that there are two ways to read the present book. One way is to accept the order in which the essays have been arranged, the first four analyzing different aspects of the possible relations among words, texts, and modes of behavior and the second four concentrating on print culture, publishing strategies, reading practices, and books produced for the greatest number of readers. The second way would be to restore the chronological order in which these eight studies were written, not, to be sure, in the interest of reconstituting a personal itinerary, but rather because the evolution that can here be traced reflects the major trends in the writing of cultural history in France during recent years: at first swept along by an ambition to reduce cultural materials to numbers and serial data, then primarily interested in understanding usages and practices. I hope that, whatever route he chooses, the reader will not regret his journey.

....................................................................

# CHAPTER ONE

# Ritual and Print
# Discipline and Invention:
# The *Fête* in France from
# the Middle Ages to the
# Revolution

Aɴʏ historical reflection on the *fête* must depart from the observation of its actual conditions of existence, in order to understand the veritable "festive explosion" that has marked the historiography of this last decade. Although it is not specifically historical, the emergence of the *fête* (and in particular of the traditional feast) as a preferred subject of study leads one in effect to wonder why, at a given moment, an entire scientific class (in this case, French historians) felt attracted by a theme which until then was treated only by collectors of folklore. Seemingly, three reasons, which pertain as much to the recognized function of the historical discipline as to its internal evolution, may be cited. It is clear, above all, that the increased research into the traditional feast constituted a sort of compensation, in terms of understanding, for the disappearance of a system of civilization in which the *fête* had, or rather is considered as having had, a central role. Historical analysis has therefore been charged with explaining, in its idiom and with its technique, the nostalgia exuded by a present that has eliminated the *fête* as an act of community participation. On these grounds, it then becomes possible to rediscover one of the major functions assigned—implicitly or overtly—to history today: to restore to the sphere of knowledge a vanished world, the heritage of which contemporary society feels itself a rightful but unfaithful heir. That the process of understanding is difficult to separate from the fabrication of an imaginary

Originally written for the interdisciplinary conference *La Fête en Question*, held at the University of Montreal in April 1979, this essay was published in *Diogène* 110 (April-June 1980):51-71. Maria Antonia Uzielli's translation, for the English-language edition of *Diogène* (*Diogenes* 110:44-65), has been edited with the assistance of Lydia G. Cochrane.

past collectively desired is, in the end, insignificant, unless it is meant to underscore those things that, by being the most neglected by our present age, have become the most symptomatic of a world we have lost. The *fête*, evidently, is one of these.

On the other hand, the *fête*, at least as an object of history, has benefited from the rehabilitation of the specific event. After massive scrutiny of time's long courses and its stable flow, historians—particularly those of the *Annales* tradition—have turned their attention toward the event. In its transitoriness and its tension, it may in fact reveal, just as well as long-term evolution or social and cultural inertia, the structures that constituted a collective mentality or a society. The battle has been among the first to benefit from this reevaluation. Removed from narrative history, it can set up a suitable observation point for apprehending a social structure, a cultural system, or the creation of history or legend.[1] In the same manner, the festival has abandoned the shores of the picturesque and the anecdotal to become a major detector of the cleavages, tensions, and images that permeated a society. This is particularly evident when the *fête* engendered violence and the community was torn apart, as in Romans in 1580: "The Carnival in Romans makes me think of the Grand Canyon. It shows, preserved in cross section, the intellectual and social strata and structures which made up a *très ancien régime*."[2] The geological metaphor clearly illustrates a perspective in which the festive event is indicatory and the extraordinary is charged with speaking for the ordinary. Even when a *fête* does not generate excesses or revolt, it is amenable to this kind of approach. It always produces that singular albeit repeated moment when it is possible to grasp the rules of a social system, even though they are disguised or inverted.

A final reason has helped to focus historians' attention on the *fête*. It is, in effect, ideally situated at the nub of the debate that has dominated French historiography for the last ten years, the study of relations in the sphere of conflict or compromise between a culture defined as popular or folkloric and the dominant cultures. The *fête* is an exemplary illustration of this contest. To begin with, it is clearly situated at the crossroads of two cultural dynamics. On the one hand, it represents the invention and the expression of traditional culture shared by the ma-

---

[1] G. Duby, *Le Dimanche de Bouvines, 27 juillet 1214* (Paris, 1973), in particular 13-14.
[2] E. Le Roy Ladurie, *Le Carnaval de Romans. De la Chandeleur au mercredi des Cendres, 1579-1580* (Paris, 1979), 408. (Mary Feeney, trans., *Carnival: A People's Uprising at Romans, 1579-1580* [New York, 1979], 370.)

jority of people, and on the other, the disciplining will and the cultural plan of the dominating class. One can then quite rightly apply to the *fête* the analytic methods that Alphonse Dupront applied to the pilgrimage, which underline the tensions between the vital impulse of collectivity and the discipline imposed by institutions.[3] Furthermore, the "popular" festival was quickly looked upon by the dominant cultures as a major obstacle to the assertion of their religious, ethical, or political hegemony. Thus it was the target of a constant effort aimed at destroying it, curtailing it, disciplining it, or taking it over. The *fête* was therefore the stage for a conflict between contradictory cultural realities. Thus it offers a taste of "popular" and elite cultures at a moment of intersection—and not only through an inventory of the motifs which are supposedly their essence. The festival was one of the few scenes in which one may observe popular resistance to normative injunctions as well as the restructuring, through cultural models, of the behavior of the majority. From this the *fête* derives its importance for a history of mental attitudes that concerns the analysis of specific and localized cultural mechanisms.

Having thus acknowledged the reasons which have given the *fête* a priority in historians' work, it is possible, considering a well-defined period (France between the fifteenth and eighteenth centuries), to summarize the achievements of and problems posed by retrospective interpretation. In order to do this, a good method appears to be to consider a certain number of case studies, both original and borrowed. Finally, as a last preliminary, the great ambiguity inherent in the usage of the word *fête* must be kept in mind. Its apparently single meaning revolves, in fact, around manifold differences, often reflected through a series of oppositions: popular/official, rural/urban, religious/secular, participation/entertainment, etc. As it happens, these cleavages, far from aiding a clear typology of festive ceremonies, are themselves problematic, since nearly always the festival is a blend which aims at reconciling opposites.

On the other hand, *fête* carries in itself the definition—theoretical or spontaneous—with which each of us has invested the word. By blending memory and utopia, by affirming what the *fête* must be and what it is not, these definitions will certainly be highly personal and idiosyn-

---

[3] A. Dupront, "Formes de la culture des masses: De la doléance politique au pèlerinage panique (xviiie-xxe siècle)," in *Niveaux de culture et groupes sociaux* (Paris, 1967), 149-67.

cratic. Consequently, it becomes impossible to reconstruct the *fête* as a historical object with well-defined contours. In an attempt to halt this shifting, fleeting, and contradictory reality momentarily, we will accept here as *fêtes* all those manifestations which are described as such in traditional society, even though festiveness occurred outside the *fêtes* (and perhaps especially outside).[4]

THE FIRST and fundamental premise is that the traditional festival, far from being an established fact—capable of description within static limits—was, from the end of the Middle Ages until the Revolution, the object of many modifying influences which must, before anything else, be ascertained. Ecclesiastical censures were without doubt the oldest. The Church's condemnation of festivals and popular rejoicings supplied material for an uninterrupted series of texts from the twelfth to the seventeenth century. The literature of the *exempla*, which provided material for homilies, is the first example of those admonitions later relayed by the massive corpus of conciliar decrees, synodal statutes, or episcopal ordinances. From the end of the seventeenth century, the abundance of this material was such that it could serve as a basis for theological treatises responsible for transmitting Church tradition and entrusted with informing the priesthood—such as the two works by Jean-Baptiste Thiers.[5] These ecclesiastical interdictions were all the more important inasmuch as they were often adopted by civil authorities, *parlements*, and municipal councils. A typical example of this alliance among the organs of power was the struggle against itinerant festivals in the seventeenth and eighteenth centuries in the jurisdiction of the *parlement* of Paris.[6] These festivals, which were held on Sundays and holy days of obligation and were often associated with a fair marked by traditional rejoicings (dances and games), were banned by a decree of the *Grands Jours d'Auvergne* in 1665. Two years later, this

---

[4] M. de Certeau, "Une Culture très ordinaire," *Esprit* 10 (1978):3-26.

[5] J.-B. Thiers, *Traité des Jeux et des Divertissements* (Paris, 1696) and *Traité des Superstitions selon l'Écriture Sainte, les Décrets des Conciles et les sentiments des Saints Pères et des Théologiens* (Paris, 1679; 2d ed. in 4 vols., Paris, 1697-1704). On the latter text, see J. Lebrun, "Le *Traité des Superstitions* de Jean-Baptiste Thiers, contribution à l'ethnographie de la France du xviiᵉ siècle," *Annales de Bretagne et des pays de l'Ouest* 83 (1976):443-65, and R. Chartier and J. Revel, "Le Paysan, l'ours et saint Augustin," Proceedings of the Conference *La Découverte de la France au XVIIᵉ siècle* (Paris, 1980), 259-64.

[6] Y. M. Berce, *Fête et révolte. Des mentalités populaires du XVIᵉ au XVIIIᵉ siècle* (Paris, 1976), 170-76.

pronouncement was extended to the entire jurisdiction of the *parlement*. Further, during the last decade of the *ancien régime*, one finds this general ban extended by some fifty particulars. Everywhere the mechanism was identical: A complaint was deposited by the parish priest with the general prosecutor of the *parlement*, who then asked the local judges to open an inquiry. Often, if not always, his information resulted in a decree of interdiction. Such an organized and predetermined attack attests simultaneously to the intractability of the rural populace toward the injunctions of established authorities and to convergences between the Christianizing will of the clergy and the magistrates' efforts to enforce control over morals.

The objective of the Church was twofold: to obtain mastery over time and over peoples' bodies. The control of festive times was thus a point of primary confrontation between folk culture and the Church. Very early, as far back as the thirteenth century, the literature of the *exempla* revealed the deep conflict which enmeshed the cycles of Easter and Pentecost.[7] According to the folklore, that particular time of year was above all the time for those festivities that initiated youngsters into society, from the aristocratic tournaments to the dances of the *chevaux-jupons* in a popular environment. For the Church, however, this time of glorification of the Holy Spirit had to be for procession, pilgrimage, and crusade. This conflict for the possession of time occurred on a daily scale as well. The Church acted unceasingly to prevent nocturnal rejoicings and to eradicate the concepts which permitted such events. It tried to eliminate the partition between daytime, which belongs to the Church, and nighttime, the dominion of the people.

Aiming to discipline the flesh, the Church understood festive behavior according to the same categories which were conceived for the designation and description of superstitious conduct. Thus, a triple condemnation of the traditional *fête*: It was illicit, or even "popular" in the sense of Thiers's use when he suggested it as the opposite of catholic. Festive behavior, in fact, varied infinitely; it was not at all dependent upon ecclesiastical authority, but rather was rooted in specific community customs. It was therefore opposed, point by point, to the Catholic spirit which was universal, officially backed, equal for all. This theological condemnation was strengthened by a second, psychological

---

[7] J. C. Schmitt, "Jeunes et danse des chevaux de bois. Le Folklore méridional dans la littérature des *exempla* (XIII^c-XIV^c siècle)," *Cahiers de Fanjeaux* 11(Toulouse, 1976), 127-58.

one. For the Church, the popular *fête* was identified with excess and intemperance, with the irrational expenditure of body and wealth. It was situated, therefore, exactly opposite to authorized practices, which were necessary and carefully meted out. Finally, from a moral standpoint, the *fête* signified indecency and license. In it, the rules which formed the basis of Christian society were forgotten. Emotion was bestowed without control, modesty lost its standards, and the flesh let itself go without reverence for the Creator. Considered the abode of spontaneity, disorder, and dishonesty, the *fête* became, in the eyes of Christian moralists, the epitome of anticivilization. It combined, they felt, the different traits which tainted criminal practices as contrary to the true faith, to due propriety, and to Christian modesty. From all of this, it is not surprising that festivals have long been among the major targets of the Church's effort to Christianize the population.[8]

Strategies to censure the *fête* were diverse. The most radical tended to prohibit them—as, for example, in the case of the *Fête de Fous*, generally celebrated on the Feast of the Holy Innocents and characterized by the inversion of the ecclesiastical hierarchy, by the parody of religious ritual, and by manifold rejoicings (theatrical games, dances, feasts, etc.). A *fête* with strong religious connotations, unfolding essentially within the religious sphere, the *Fête des Fous* was the object of age-old condemnation, often reiterated and seemingly effective. In his *Traité des Jeux et des Divertissements*, Thiers reviews the texts that banned both the *Fête des Fous* and the Feast of the Holy Innocents. His series begins in 1198 with the decree of the Bishop of Paris and comprises three texts of the thirteenth century, seven of the fifteenth, and ten of the sixteenth.[9] Such persistence seems to have paid off, since the *Fête des Fous* disappeared at the end of the sixteenth century and by the mid-eighteenth century was already the object of history, but a history so far removed and strange that it was almost indecipherable: "The *fêtes* of which I undertake to recount the history are so extravagant that the reader would have difficulty in giving them credence were he not instructed on the ignorance and barbarism that preceded the renaissance of belles-lettres."[10]

[8] J. Delumeau, ed., *La Mort des Pays de Cocagne. Comportements collectifs de la Renaissance à l'âge classique* (Paris, 1976), 14-29.

[9] Thiers, *Traité des Jeux*, 440-51.

[10] J.-B. du Tilliot, *Mémoires pour servir à l'histoire de la fête des fous qui se faisait autrefois dans plusieurs églises*, cited in Y. M. Berce, *Fête et révolte*, 140.

Often this strategy of eradication was not possible and had to give way for compromises in which the festive apparatus passed under religious control. As in the case of the pilgrimage, the Church aimed at imposing its order on the spontaneous, at controlling popular liberty, and at extirpating its intolerable manifestations. Thus this is how one must understand the tenacious battle fought by the churches (both Protestant and Catholic) against dance, an essential element both symbolical and jocose of the traditional *fête*, which they saw as a practice possibly present in ceremonies of very different natures. Here again, Thiers cites various authorities to condemn dance as a school of impurity and weapon of the devil: "How few are those who, dancing or seeing others dance, will not bear within themselves some dishonest thought, will not cast an immodest glance, show an indecent posture, pronounce a lewd phrase, and, finally, will not form a certain desire of the flesh, which the Holy Apostle says?"[11] By deforming the body, dance distorts the soul and inclines it to sin. Thus it must not contaminate the authorized festivities.

A third clerical strategy was that of selectivity. The aim of Christianization was to separate the licit core of the *fête* from the superstitious practices deposited around it. A typical example of this perspective may be found in the religious discourse concerning the fires of Saint John.[12] The *fête* and its fires, which were meant to celebrate the

---

[11] Thiers, *Traité des Jeux*, 331-41. Like the dance, carnival masks are doubly to be condemned: They disguise the body of man and consequently blaspheme against his Creator. They authorize ribaldry of the most dangerous kind both for the good order of society and for its morals. As proof, two texts. First the synodal constitutions of the Diocese of Annecy (1773 edition): "We finally exhort Their Lordships the Archpriests, Parish Priests, and their Curates, especially in the towns and Cities, to eradicate the abuse of the masquerades which are nothing but a shameful relic of Paganism. To succeed, they must rise against it in their sermons and teaching, especially from Epiphany until Lent; they must demonstrate its absurdity and danger, showing the people that such disorder is injurious to God whose image is disfigured; that it dishonors the members of J.C. by lending to them burlesque and out-of-place characters; and that it encourages licentiousness by facilitating that which impairs modesty" (cited in R. Devos and C. Joisten, *Moeurs et coutumes de la Savoie du Nord au XIXᵉ siècle. L'Enquête de Mgr. Rendu* [Annecy and Grenoble, 1978], 120). Second the preamble of a decree of the Magistrat of Lille in 1681: "Considering that each year sometime before Lent such disorders and inconveniences occur, detrimental to the welfare of souls and the public good, caused by the licentiousness which many people of one or the other sex employ in going through cities masked or otherwise disguised ..." (cited in A. Lottin, *Chavatte, ouvrier lillois. Un Contemporain de Louis XIV* [Paris, 1979], 322).

[12] J. Delumeau, *Le Catholicisme entre Luther et Voltaire* (Paris, 1971), 259-61. (English

birth of the saint, were considered legitimate, but only on the condition that they would be strictly confined and controlled. The ceremony was to be brief; the bonfires had to be small to avoid any surplus or excess; the dancing and feasting which accompanied the fires were forbidden; and the superstitious practices which they engendered were prohibited. The fires of Saint John nourished, in effect, a great number of beliefs in which superstition was visible to the naked eye, since all were based on the illusive relationship that existed between a gesture (throwing grass on the fire, keeping the embers or the charcoal, going around the fire in certain turns or circles, etc.) and its supposed effects (to divine the hair color of one's future bride, to guarantee freedom from headaches or kidney pains for a whole year, etc.).[13] Between the licit festival and its superstitious and immoral perversion the dividing line was unclear, as is clearly witnessed on the local level by the difficult relationship established between communities and their parish priests.[14] Tolerance and condemnation lived side by side, as much to avoid open conflict, often litigious, as the intolerable infractions. Two cultures faced each other in the *fête*: one clerical, which aimed at organizing behavior to make of the *fête* an homage to God, the other, of the majority, which absorbed the religious ceremonial in an act of collective jubilation.

Although unquestionably the most constant and the most powerful, ecclesiastical pressure on the *fête* was not the only pressure brought to bear. Between 1400 and 1600, in fact, the urban festival (and especially the Carnival) had to face other interference as a result of growing municipal constraint. Everywhere municipal governments tried to curb the town *fête* by controlling its financing, its itinerary, and its program.[15] More and more, toward the dawn of modern times, the *fête* became supported by municipal finance and not only by the head of the

---

translation: *Catholicism between Luther and Voltaire: A New View of the Counter-Reformation* [Philadelphia and London, 1977].)

[13] These superstitions are reported in Thiers, *Traité des Superstitions*, 1:298 (1712 ed.) and 4:404 (1727 ed.).

[14] T. Tackett, *Priest and Parish in Eighteenth-Century France. A Social and Political Study of the Curés in a Diocese of Dauphiné, 1750-1791* (Princeton, 1977), 210-15, and D. Julia, "La Reforme posttridentine en France d'après les procès-verbaux des visites pastorales: ordre et résistances," in *La Società religiosa nell'età moderna* (Naples, 1973), 311-415, in particular 384-88.

[15] M. Grinberg, "Carnaval et société urbaine, xiv$^e$-xvi$^e$ siècle. Le Royaume dans la ville," *Ethnologie française* 3 (1974):215-43.

confraternity that traditionally organized it. Progressively, private charity gave way to public financing. Thus the municipality gained tighter control of the ceremonial itineraries and so granted a privileged place to certain locations which were the emblem of public identity and power (for example, Town Hall or the market place, occasionally even the municipal magistrates' residences). Thus also, the municipality began a more and more determined intervention in the elaboration of the festive program, which until then had been the exclusive responsibility of the organizing confraternities, the youth "kingdoms," or the *abbayes folles*.

This municipal control had an evident objective: to express, through the idiom of the *fête*, an ideology at once urban and secular. The composition of the processions is a prime example of this scope. They assembled, symbolically and in reality, all the principal corporations and guilds which composed the town, as in Metz in 1510 and 1511.[16] Assembling all hierarchically, the festival expressed the unity of the urban community. It also created an urban legend, which instilled the town's past with a prestigious history, ancient or biblical. In Metz on Torch Sunday, 1511, the eminent citizens disguised themselves to personify David, Hector, Julius Caesar, Alexander the Great, Charlemagne, and Godefroy de Bouillon, all of whom legitimated the power of the city and the authority of its oligarchy. The urban festival thus became a political tool that allowed the town to assert itself against the sovereign, the aristocracy, and neighboring towns. Through expenditure and ostentation, the *fête* demonstrated the town's wealth, and thus instituted a diplomacy of competition which was not without influence on the festive calendar. In order to authorize mutual assistance to the town representatives for the carnivals, the towns of Flanders and Artois in effect rescheduled their festivities. One can observe here how a political ideology is capable of inflecting, defining, or transforming ancient rituals to subvert their meaning.

Censured by ecclesiastical authorities and diverted by municipal oligarchies, the traditional *fête* did not therefore manifest itself except through the distortions progressively imposed on it by the authorities. It would seem impossible to rediscover, beneath these deformations and mutilations, an original base, appropriately "popular" or "folkloric." The raw materials of the *fête* in the sixteenth and seventeenth

---

[16] Ibid., 229-30.

centuries, as we understand them today, were always a cultural mix, the components of which it is not easy to separate, whether we attempt to organize them by dividing popular from official festivity or by tracing the change over time, in which dependence (on Church and municipal authorities) replaced an earlier spontaneity. That is why it has appeared legitimate to me to set down first the modifications effected on the festivals by the authorities rather than to attempt an illusory description of a festival supposedly free of doctrinal contamination. But this composite material is itself the object of a history which may perhaps be elucidated with a case study that focuses on the system of the *fêtes* in Lyons from the end of the Middle Ages to the Revolution.[17]

The scheme of this evolution is clear: It shows the succession from *fêtes* based in community participation to *fêtes* conceded to the populace. During the Renaissance the system of *fêtes* in Lyons was composed of two major elements: *fêtes* of all the citizenry and gregarious, spontaneous *fêtes*. The former presupposed the participation of the entire population of the town in the same rejoicing, even though this participation was hierarchical and occasionally conflictive. This was obviously the case of the religious festivals born of the Merveilles festival, which disappeared at the beginning of the fifteenth century, such as the pardons of Saint John's Day, the processions of Rogations, and the feasts of patron saints. This was also the case of the royal entries, such as the many into Lyons between the end of the fifteenth and the beginning of the seventeenth century: 1490, 1494, 1495, 1507, 1515, 1522, 1548, 1564, 1574, 1595, 1600, 1622—exactly twelve entries in 125 years, to which should be added all those that were not royal. Each triumphal entry presented a reciprocal spectacle: The citizens became spectators of the royal procession and the king and his court spectators of the urban procession, in which participated all the city dwellers, including artisans, assembled in corporations (until 1564) and by wards thereafter. The entry was also a plural festival par excellence, in which multifold elements overlapped: processions, cavalcades, theatrical games, *tableaux vivants*, fireworks, etc. The iconographic and scenographic material thus shown offered many readings, certainly as diverse as the different social and cultural groups, but at least unified within a ceremony that assembled the town together.

[17] The basic materials for such a study are collected in the catalogue *Entrées royales et fêtes populaires à Lyon du XVᵉ au XVIIIᵉ siècle* (Lyons, 1970).

The other essential component of the *fête* in Lyons of the sixteenth century was those *fêtes* which can be defined as "popular," on the condition that "people" not be too narrowly defined.[18] Some of these *fêtes*, taken in hand by the *confréries joyeuses*—in this case the twenty abbeys of Maugouvert—founded their activity upon close relationships within the neighborhood. The same was true of the charivari that ridiculed beaten husbands under the guise of a donkey ride. Organized by the world of artisans and merchants, these rejoicings were also spectacles that might be offered to the aristocratic visitors; such was the case with the cavalcade of 1550 and also with the one of 1566, which was to figure in the triumphal entry of the Duchess of Nemours.[19] On other occasions, the leading role belonged to the *confréries joyeuses* of the guilds, particularly that of the printers. The confraternity of La Coquille (The Typographical Error), which may also have been the organizer of donkey cavalcades (as in 1578), was responsible for the parodic processions which marked Shrove Sunday. Between 1580 and 1601, a half-dozen pamphlets "printed in Lyons by the Seigneur de la Coquille" attest to the vitality, in both merrymaking and criticism, of the group of printing guildsmen.[20]

The beginning of the seventeenth century, however, saw the breakdown of this system of festivals founded on popular participation or initiative. Two dates are symbolic historical turning points: In 1610, for the first time, the pamphlet printed on the occasion of the Shrove Sunday festival mentioned neither the *abbayes joyeuses* nor the confraternity of La Coquille; and in 1622, Louis XIII was the last to receive a triumphal entry in the old manner. The following ones, such as that of Louix XIV in 1658, were nothing more than simple receptions by the municipal authorities and did not imply the participation of the local population. The change brought about was therefore threefold. First of all, popular organizations (*abbayes*, confraternities), traditionally the organizers of the festivals, died away. Second, the *fêtes* of the urban population, the triumphal entries, and the religious ceremonies lost their force. A good index of this decline is a comparison of church ju-

---

[18] N. Z. Davis, "The Reasons of Misrule," in *Society and Culture in Early Modern France* (Stanford, 1975), 97-123.

[19] *Entrées royales et fêtes populaires*, 49-50. Two documents cited, one by Davis ("Reasons of Misrule," n. 70), the other in the Lyons catalogue (no. 22), permit one to see into one of these *confréries joyeuses*, which met in 1517 on the Rue Mercière.

[20] N. Z. Davis, "Printing and the People," in *Society and Culture*, 218.

bilees in Lyons in 1564, 1666, and 1734. From the sixteenth to the eighteenth centuries, the amount and the ostentatiousness of decoration in public celebrations seems to have grown in inverse relation to popular participation. Thirdly, the *fête*, conceded to the public and reduced to a display, became the norm. Thus, in the sixteenth century the artisans offered to the eminent members of society the spectacle of donkey cavalcades, but in the eighteenth century it was the authorities who offered fireworks to the populace. Over the passage of time, popular initiative vanished and the *fête* became standardized. Whatever the occasion, whoever the organizers—aldermen or lords-canon of Saint John—the ceremony was the same, reduced to a fireworks display in which the original meaning of the traditional bonfire—the *feu de joie*—was totally obliterated. The *fête* transmitted and instituted an order of separation in the city, which lost its consciousness as a unified citizenry in which each member participated at his own level.[21]

This evolution, detailed from the case of Lyons, can without doubt be generalized not only for the city, but also for the country. For example, the multiplication of rose festivals around 1770, following the Parisian discovery of the customary festivities in Salency, instituted in the village a form of *fête* provided as a spectacle, which aimed at supplanting traditional rejoicings.[22] Originating outside of the community and organized by aristocrats, ecclesiastics, or notables of the *parlement*, these *fêtes*, in search of a Christian Arcadia, had nothing to do with popular tradition, even though the elites, from having dramatized it, rediscovered the image of an ideal people, chaste and vigorous, simple and frugal, industrious and Christian. The anemia and displacement of the traditional *fête* entailed, in the eighteenth century, a double reaction. Popular emotions retreated to places the people could call their own, and, in turn, the *fête* became uniform and trite in its daily repetition. Provence, in the town as well as in the country, offers a good example of this evolution, which identified the *fête* more and more with a simple evening of dancing.[23]

[21] R. Chartier, "Une Académie avant les lettres patentes. Une Approche de la sociabilité des notables lyonnais à la fin du règne de Louis XIV," *Marseille* 101 (1975):115-20.

[22] On the rose festivals, W. F. Everdell, "The *Rosière* Movement, 1766-1789. A Clerical Precursor of the Revolutionary Cults," *French Historical Studies* 9, no. 1 (1975):23-36, and M. de Certeau, D. Julia, and J. Revel, "La Beauté du mort: Le Concept de 'culture populaire,'" *Politique aujourd'hui*, December 1970:3-23.

[23] M. Vovelle, *Les Métamorphoses de la fête en Provence de 1750 à 1820* (Paris, 1976), 84-90.

The other reaction was philosophical and invited thought on the *fête* to be invented. Many, in fact, criticized this artificial and dissociated *fête* (inevitably, the *fête* usurped by the authorities), whatever its modality was: "the eighteenth century is no longer capable of seeing in fireworks anything but the artifice of its rockets."[24] The new *fête* was radically different: patriotic, transparent, and unanimous. In his *Letter to d'Alembert*, Rousseau outlined the model of this ideal *fête* and at the same time constructed its political theory: "Drive a stake crowned with flowers into the center of a square, assemble the citizenry there, and you will have a *fête*. Do even better: have the spectators become the spectacle, render them actors, make each one see and love himself in the others, so that all will be better united." Etienne-Louis Boullée designed the architectural context for this *fête*, which rejects spectacle and abolishes all differences, in his project of a circus inspired by the Coliseum: "Imagine 300,000 people gathered as in an amphitheater, where none could escape the eyes of the multitude. From this arrangement would result a unique effect: The beauty of such an astonishing spectacle would derive directly from the spectators who are its unique components."[25] Utopian literature in its various forms thus became a privileged laboratory in which it was possible to outline the minutest details, circumstances, and regulations of those *fêtes* for which Rousseau and Boullée gave us the blueprint. From the *Code de la Nature* to the *Incas* of Jean François Marmontel, from the *Supplément au Voyage de Bougainville* to *L'An deux mille quatre cent quarante*, these texts build up a regenerated festival, pictured as a microcosm where the rules of a new social order are pedagogically recognized.[26] Before discussing the way in which the Revolutionary *fête* attempted to realize its utopia, however, we must make one final stop at the traditional *fête* in order to touch on some possible solutions to the problems it poses.

Working with historical material but also following those *fêtes* which are still alive today, ethnologists of traditional France have proposed a reading of the *fête* which accentuates its symbolic function. This approach is characterized by one trait: the particular importance

[24] M. Ozouf, *La Fête révolutionnaire 1789-1799* (Paris, 1976), 9. Forthcoming in English.

[25] These two texts are cited and commented upon by B. Baczko, *Lumières de l'utopie* (Paris, 1978), 244-49.

[26] Ibid., chap. 5, and J. Ehrard, "Les Lumières et la fête," in J. Ehrard and P. Viallaneix, eds., *Les Fêtes de la Révolution* (Proceedings of the Conference of Clermont-Ferrand, June 1974) (Paris, 1977), 27-44.

attached to the carnivalesque *fête* as the keystone of the whole festive system. There are two reasons for this.[27] On the one hand, the Carnival attracted to itself such other joyous celebrations (not necessarily of the same calendar period) as the charivaris, which in many ways (the food distribution, the wearing of masks, the festive justice) were reminiscent of the Carnival rituals.[28] Conversely, these Carnival rituals can be traced in festivals occurring outside the Carnival period, either in the festivities that clustered around Ascension Day and Pentecost or in summertime celebrations of parish patron saints' days. From an ethnological point of view, it is a primordial motive that structures the totality of actions and language. By staging the conflicts between opposites (night and day, winter and spring, death and life), the *fête* granted a new beginning to the calendar, to nature, and to man: "The *fête* pictures, mimes, and arouses a regeneration of time, of the world of nature, and of society."[29] The Carnival translated into its own multifold language the confrontation between extremes, and its efficacious ritual reestablished the order of the world every year.

This interpretation has, as its corollary, the treatment of all localized forms of Carnival rituals as so many signs responsible for showing the primordial motivations which underlay this order. Thus we must assemble in a general understanding the diverse elements which compose a *fête*: the wandering, the welcome, the judgment and death of King Carnival, the intrusion and immolation of the Wild Man (an effigy), and the passage of food and gas through the human body. Thus also we must draw together the infinitely varied living images, which, according to the time and place, gave tangible form to the Giant King or the Wild Man. Two very different approaches are possible. The historical approach stresses the universality of the categories at work in the Carnival festival. The Carnival therefore constituted the focal point of a veritable "popular or folkloric religion," both rustic and prehistoric, the mythical foundations and ritual expressions of which may be identified in diverse cultural systems.[30] Another point of view, which rejects this transcultural interpretation of the *fête*, draws attention

[27] D. Fabre and C. Camberoque, *La Fête en Languedoc. Regards sur le carnaval aujourd'hui* (Toulouse, 1977).

[28] D. Fabre and B. Traimond, "Le Charivari gascon contemporain: Un Enjeu politique," in J. Le Goff and J.-C. Schmitt, eds., *Le Charivari* (Paris, 1981).

[29] Fabre and Camberoque, *Fête en Languedoc*, 171.

[30] C. Gaignebet, *Le Carnaval* (Paris, 1974).

above all to the specific roots of the carnivalesque elements.[31] It is only within the bounds of a limited and homogeneous cultural space that symbolic interpretation takes on meaning, that ancient texts and contemporary observations are compatible, so that with good reason we may bring to light the diverse levels (historical, commemorative, liturgical) of interpreting a ritual. The regional or local differences in the embodiment of the central meaning of the carnivalesque practices counts more here than its supposed universality.

With this last interpretation, many connections emerge between ethnologists and historians. The latter, however, treat the *fête* in a different way. With its rituals, its actions, and its objects, it becomes a grammar of symbols that enables the articulation in a clear or implied manner of a political project (giving this phrase the broadest definition). As we have seen, between 1400 and 1600, the urban *fête*, remodeled by municipal oligarchies, became the expression of the community's unified ideology, which aimed to manifest its identity over rival authorities and, for this purpose, had to smooth over its internal divisions. This project was impeded to the extent that the *fête*, notwithstanding the will of leading citizens, left room for possible criticisms. A prime reason for this was that, regardless of municipal infringements and ecclesiastical censures, the *fêtes* essentially remained in the hands of youth and its institutions. This is, for example, the very evident case of Provence in the eighteenth century.[32] In fact, according to all religious and administrative documents of the seventeenth and eighteenth centuries, youth (including women) was one of the major figures of illegality. But the *fête*, and in particular the Carnival *fête*, dramatized (and thus it both expressed and displaced) the cleavages that split the community. Their expression is manifold since these cleavages were organized according to the opposition of sexes, the differences in age, the contrast between the married and single, and the differences in social status. Thus through the *fête*, under its mask and thanks to its parodic idiom, these distances and tensions may be considered, according to the case, to be deactivated or exacerbated. The idiom of the most turbulent age group and the "dramatization of differences" (Daniel Fabre), the *fête* remained resistant to the authorities' objective of uniformity.

[31] D. Fabre, "Le Monde du Carnaval," *Annales E.S.C.* 31 (1976):389-406 (about Gaignebet's book).

[32] M. Agulhon, *Pénitents et Francs-Maçons de l'ancienne Provence* (Paris, 1968), 43-64.

The *fête* may also occasionally have become the preferred setting of confrontation for two sociopolitical strategies. Thus in Romans in 1580 the factions of the plebeians and the leading citizens manipulated, each in its own way, the institutions, formulas, and codes of the *fête* to demonstrate to the general population their conflicting aims.[33] Both sides worked to distort the carnivalesque subject matter, one to denounce the intolerable patrician privileges (fiscal and political), the other to criticize the ridiculous pretensions of the people of Romans. Each one in control of its own festive institutions (*abbayes* and *reynages*), the opposite factions could engage in a war of symbols. On the artisans' side, resources were manifold: the rural rites of Saint Blaise's Day, the donkey parade, the rituals of affliction, and the sword dances. In the case of the elites, the handling of the festive elements was more limited, based as it was on the use of parody and role-reversal. With two *mises en scène* (or *mises en fête*), the social and political conflict escalated until it led to the slaughter of one of the factions (the artisans) by the other (the elite). Even when the outcome was not at all as tragic, the *fête* could provide an arena where, by means of different scenarios, fundamental conflict was expressed. This was the case at the Segovian *fête* of September 1613, where nobles and clothiers demonstrated, with the casts of characters and the organization of rival processions, their social and religious differences.[34]

Either as a symbol of unanimity or as an expression of dissensions, the *fête* could not but hold a prominent position in the Revolutionary code. Two fundamental studies—those of Mona Ozouf and Michel Vovelle—may perhaps enable us to conclude this survey of French *fêtes* between the fifteenth and eighteenth centuries by describing some of the major problems of the Revolutionary festival. But can one use the term *fête* in connection with festivity in the French Revolution? For a long time, the historiographic tradition considered the various Revolutionary *fêtes* in opposition to one another, as were the political trends they were intended to express. Always linked to a particular intention, always sustained by a definite faction, the *fête* of the Revolution could not be anything but political and partisan, reduced to the circumstan-

[33] Le Roy Ladurie, *Carnaval de Romans*; L. S. Van Doren, "Revolt and Reaction in the City of Romans, Dauphiné, 1579-1580," *The Sixteenth Century Journal* 5 (1974):71-100.

[34] Cf. E. Cros, *L'Aristocrate et le Carnaval des Gueux. Étude sur le "Buscón de Quevedo"* (Montpellier, 1975).

tial specification of its ideological framework. Ozouf has proposed another interpretation, which stresses the fundamental coherence of the Revolutionary *fête*. The comparative study of the most ideologically opposed *fêtes* (in 1792, the one in honor of the Swiss of Châteauvieux and the one in memory of Simoneau; the *Fêtes* of Reason and of the Supreme Being; and the *fêtes* which preceded and followed Thermidor) clearly shows a uniformity of intentions, conventions, and symbolisms. An ideal model of the *fête* has been established with the *Fête de la Fédération*: It was at the same time based on the ideal of gathering people together (although there were exclusions) and on the desire to dissolve the violence of real battle in a memorial oration. This festive model cut across the entire Revolutionary period, and although not only the political intentions but also the framework of processions and collective gestures changed, such a model regulated, in an unknown way, the functions and procedures of the Revolutionary *fête*. The unity of this original schema blurs what is too abrupt in the dichotomy often set up between popular and official *fêtes*, between spontaneity and institutionalization. In other respects, however, it brings understanding of why the same festive material (for example, that which derived from the carnival tradition) may have been employed for completely opposite ideological purposes.[35]

In the long history of the *fête*, what effect has this restored unity of the Revolutionary *fête* had? Two explanations here are perhaps complementary. First, it is evident that the Revolutionary *fête* irreversibly transformed the *fête* of the *ancien régime*. In Provence, a double change is easily identifiable.[36] After the Revolution, the *fête* lost much of its vigor. The rule was now one *fête* per year (instead of two or more), almost always held in August instead of between May and September. At the same time, the *fête* became mutilated: The profuse and complex system of the traditional *fête*, at once pious, professional, and municipal, gave way to a simpler one, almost always grafted onto a fair. By 1820-1830, the traditional *fête* had but partially regained its playful elements (races, contests, dances) and not at all retrieved its multifold significance. By trying to establish a new but short-lived system of *fêtes*, the Revolution brought to an end those evolutions that, since the eighteenth century (and possibly before), had begun to fragment the *fêtes* of earlier societies.

[35] Ozouf, *Fête revolutionnaire*, 108-14.
[36] Vovelle, *Fête en Provence*, 269-94.

It is certainly appropriate to add to the interpretation that depicts the Revolutionary *fête* as destructive of an ancient harmony another, which stresses its seminal value.[37] The Revolutionary *fête* was in fact creative, not because it survived the Revolution but because it was a major instrument in consecrating new values. More and better than discourses, it embodied and thus socialized a system of new values centered on the family, the fatherland, and humanity. From this point of view, the *fête* was the agent of a transfer of sacrality, doubtlessly because, through its heavily symbolic idiom, a persuasive and sensitive pedagogy, reiterated and communal, could be established.[38] The political manifestations of the *fête* may have been fleeting, but not the new values—domestic, civil, and social—which it was charged with rooting in hearts and in minds: "Let us attach morality to eternal and sacred principles; let us inspire man toward that religious respect for mankind, that deep sense of duty which alone can guarantee social happiness; let us nourish him through all our institutions; may public education be directed above all toward that goal. . . . There is a sort of institution which must be considered an essential part of public education. . . . I mean the national *fêtes*. Gather men together, you will make them better; because assembled men will try to please each other; and they will not be pleased but through that which makes them estimable. Give their assembly a great moral and political motif, and love for honest things will penetrate every heart along with pleasure, for men do not see each other without taking pleasure in it."[39]

THIS overall view of four centuries of the *fête* in France identifies it as a subject in which contradictory propositions get entangled. First of all, it was one of those rare events in which the powerful encountered the people; and, from the anthologies of superstitious practices to the travel journals, a complete literature on the subject flourished, which has multiplied "ethnological" observations on the festive customs of the population. But at the same time we see that authorities of every sort would not be satisfied until they had trimmed or subverted those ceremonies in which popular ignorance or deviance were most manifest.

[37] Ozouf, *Fête revolutionnaire*, 317-40.

[38] Baczko, *Lumières de l'utopie*, 280-82.

[39] Maximilien Robespierre, "Sur les rapports des idées religieuses et morales avec les principes républicains et sur les fêtes nationales, 7 mai 1794," *Textes choisis* (Paris, 1958), 3:175-76.

Commented on because it was popular and censured because it was popular, the traditional *fête* was always the object of a twofold desire of the elite, who wanted to preserve it as a point of observation and recollection and destroy it as a crucible of excess. A second uncertainty is added to this one. The *fête* has always, in effect, been considered, contradictorily, both a pedagogical device and a potential danger. From the Counter-Reformation Church to Robespierre and Saint-Just, from the medieval municipal oligarchies to the *philosophes*, the *fête*, on the condition that it be molded by and channeled through a device which would render it demonstrative, was depicted as something which could manifest (and thus disseminate) a plan, whether of a religious or a political nature. Hence its role as both a pastoral weapon and a civic institution. Domestication is, however, neither certain nor fully achieved, and the *fête* may, at any time, turn to violence against the established or the to-be-established order. Because the *fête* gives the leading role to those who are least integrated, because it can display through its idiom the tensions which rend a town, the *fête* is a threat to the community, for it can shatter that apparent and longed-for unity. Thus its uneasy control, its forever renewed censure. To say how the people experienced it, whether as a compensation or a deceit, would require a different approach, difficult to test because the anonymous mass leaves few statements. But perhaps it is not in vain to define the intentions and commentaries which the dominating class has deposited on the *fête* before being able to discover how the people handled their part of autonomous existence in this area of constant change.

# CHAPTER TWO

# Texts and Images
# The Arts of Dying, 1450–1600

*To the Memory of Michel de Certeau
and Eric Cochrane*

U NTIL recently, scholars interested in the history of attitudes toward death have shown a predilection for the corpus of materials
furnished by the waning Middle Ages. Emile Mâle, Johan Huizinga,
and Alberto Tenenti established the classical view that this period saw
the emergence and proliferation of macabre themes, in texts and visual
representations alike, reflecting a change in both the ways men thought
and the ways they felt. Emile Mâle was the first to inventory this new
iconography, which invented and disseminated visions of nude cadav-
ers (*transis*), dancing skeletons, and deathbed combats between angels
and demons.[1] The agonizing obsession with the *memento mori* we see
crystallized in sermons, poetry, frescoes, and engravings was one of the
basic motifs of collective sensitivity for men at the end of the Middle
Ages. Johan Huizinga read this obsession as a forceful depiction of
traits governing a mindset inclined to extremes of behavior, more sensitive to images than to rational argument, and, above all, worried
about death because it was tormented by salvation.[2] The works of Alberto Tenenti put this "religion of death," which dominated the minds
and wills of men, into the broader perspective of a Renaissance of gen-

This study was written in 1973–1974 for Pierre Chaunu's seminar on attitudes toward death between the sixteenth and the eighteenth centuries. It was presented as a
lecture (with Philippe Ariès and Daniel Roche) at Princeton University in 1976 and
was published that year as "Les Arts de Mourir, 1450-1600" in *Annales E.S.C.* 31
(1976):51-75.
    [1] E. Mâle, *L'Art religieux de la fin du Moyen Age en France. Étude sur l'iconographie du
Moyen Age et sur ses sources d'inspiration* (Paris, 1908; 5th ed., 1949), 347-89. (*Religious
Art in France: A Study of Medieval Iconography and Its Sources*, 3 vols. [Princeton, New
Jersey, 1978-1986].)
    [2] J. Huizinga, *The Waning of the Middle Ages* (London, 1924; Garden City, New
York, 1954), 138-50.

erous scope in the two centuries between 1450 and 1650.[3] In the fifteenth century, a new sensitivity, which both reflected and shaped the new visual forms, put death in the center of the picture. At the end of the century, this perception of death produced the text and the pictorial representations that expressed it most fully, the *Ars moriendi*, in Tenenti's words, a true "iconographic crystallization of Christian death." A balance seems then to have been struck: The dramatization of man's last moments to some extent subsided, and there was some degree of renewed interest in life, expressed as the humanist exaltation of the dignity of man and the Christian insistence on the need for a good life for a good death. Erasmus lies at the start of this evolution and Bellarmine at its end. This, roughly speaking, is the path Tenenti blazed for us.

Philippe Ariès now assumed the task of situating the "moment" of the waning Middle Ages within the long—extremely long—duration of Western attitudes toward death.[4] For Ariès, the macabre themes that had long been in the spotlight were merely the last throes of a movement which had begun in the eleventh or twelfth century and which had first brought about a change in the "Vulgate" of death established along with Christianization. Between the eleventh and sixteenth centuries, Western man, by means of representations of the Last Judgment, various *artes moriendi*, macabre images, and the individualization of tombs, gradually discovered the *speculum mortis* and underwent an apprenticeship in his own death, what Ariès called "la mort de soi." Man had previously felt familiarity with death and resignation before man's common fate, but a new attitude joined with the old (or substituted for it), emphasizing consciousness of self and individual death. The modern, Romantic period was to shift the emphasis to the death of others; still later, contemporary societies have expelled death as the supreme obscenity.

[3] A. Tenenti, "Ars moriendi. Quelques notes sur le problème de la mort à la fin du xvᵉ siècle," *Annales E.S.C.* 6 (1951): 433-46; idem, *La Vie et la Mort à travers l'art du XVᵉ siècle*, Cahiers des Annales (Paris, 1952); idem, *Il Senso della morte e l'amore della vita nel Rinascimento (Francia e Italia)* (Turin, 1957, 1977).

[4] P. Ariès, *Western Attitudes towards Death: From the Middle Ages to the Present* (Baltimore and London, 1974). See also his "Contribution à l'étude du culte des morts à l'époque contemporaine," *Revue des Travaux de l'Académie des Sciences morales et politiques* 109 (1966):23-34; "La Mort inversée. Le Changement des attitudes devant la mort dans les sociétés occidentales," *Archives européennes de sociologie* 8 (1967):169-95; and (published after this essay) *L'Homme devant la mort* (Paris, 1977) (*The Hour of Our Death*, trans. H. Weaver [New York, 1981]).

The present investigation of the arts of dying follows the trail blazed by those fundamentally important works, taking the *Ars moriendi* for its earliest limit and the proliferation of post-Tridentine literature on the subject as its terminal point. I hope to provide the first portion of an inventory of works on preparation for death in the modern period, which Daniel Roche has continued into the seventeenth and eighteenth centuries.[5] The same question can be put to this entire period of three and a half centuries: Had the models and forms worked out during the second half of the fifteenth century existed for centuries, or did the reformers—both Catholic and Protestant—forge new archetypes that gave an original cast to the age of French classicism? The answer obviously depends on an analysis of the 236 surviving works on preparation for death published in France from 1600 to 1798; it is nevertheless imperative to have a clear idea of our point of departure. First, this corpus of documents needs to be surveyed, with a pause to consider its finest flowering in the *Ars moriendi*. Next, the available quantitative data need to be gathered and analyzed to measure, inasmuch as is possible, the importance of works on the arts of dying in the general production and consumption of books between 1450 and 1600. Finally, we need to take a closer look at a few texts taken as exemplars to graph the curve of this evolving literature.

A good number of scholars—historians of *mentalités*, of religious attitudes, of art, and of book publishing—have shown an interest in the text and illustrations of the *Ars moriendi*. Before trying to introduce new data on its distribution, however, it is perhaps wise to recall what we already know about this work. First, the *Ars moriendi* is a text known in two versions, one longer and known as CP for its *incipit*, "Cum de presentiis," the other shorter and known as QS after its first words, "Quamvis secundum." The longer version is divided into six "moments": recommendations concerning the art of dying, the temptations that assail the dying, the questions to be asked of them, the prayers they should say, the proper behavior of those close to the dying man or woman, and the prayers that they should say. This is what nearly all the manuscripts and a majority of the typeset editions con-

[5] D. Roche, "La Mémoire de la Mort. Recherche sur la place des arts de mourir dans la librairie et la lecture en France aux xviie et xviiie siècles," *Annales E.S.C.* 31 (1976):76-112; M. Vovelle, *Mourir autrefois: Attitudes collectives devant la mort aux XVIIe et XVIIIe siècles* (Paris, 1974). Roche's article and my study are used in P. Chaunu, *La Mort à Paris, XVIe, XVIIe, XVIIIe siècles* (Paris, 1978).

tain. QS uses only the second section of the CP version, framing it between an introduction and a conclusion. It appears in woodcut editions and a small number of typeset editions. Thanks to the work of Helmut Appel,[6] Sister Mary Catherine O'Connor,[7] and Alberto Tenenti,[8] it is possible to trace the origins of this treatise. Its more remote sources are the chapters on death in the theological *summae* of the thirteenth and fourteenth centuries. Among its more immediate sources, works on the arts of dying that flourished at the turn of the fifteenth century, are the *Cordiale quatuor novissimorum*, the *Dispositorium moriendi* of Johannes Nider, and the third section of Gerson's *Opusculum tripartitum*. Following one traditional line, Tenenti attributes the text of the *Ars* to Cardinal Capranica, but Sister O'Connor proposes another hypothesis. Undoubtedly composed in southern Germany, since nearly a third (84 out of 234) of the surviving manuscripts are in Munich, and in all likelihood written during the Council of Constance on the basis of Gerson's treatise, the manuscript is perhaps the work of a Dominican from the priory of Constance. In this view, the text's dissemination was aided by the Fathers' return from the Council and by circulation among the houses of the Dominican order.

To judge by the inventory of surviving manuscripts, the *Ars* enjoyed wide distribution even in this first form. The catalogues of the great libraries list 234 manuscripts: 126 in Latin, 75 in German, 11 in English, 10 in French, 9 in Italian, and one each in Provençal and Catalan (plus one without indication of language).[9] Its diffusion was perhaps surpassed only by that of the *Imitatio Christi*, with some six hundred Latin manuscripts[10] that made it "the most widely read work in the

[6] H. Appel, *Die Anfechtung und ihre Überwindung in der Trostbüchern und Sterbebüchlein des späten Mittelalters nach lateinischen und oberdeutschen Quellen des 14 und 15 Jahrhunderts untersucht und mit der Anfechtungslehre Luthers verglichen* (Leipzig, 1938), 63-104 (on the *Ars*); idem, *Anfechtung und Trost im Spätmittelalter und bei Luther* (Leipzig, 1933).

[7] Sister Mary Catherine O'Connor, *The Art of Dying Well: The Development of the "Ars Moriendi"* (New York, 1942).

[8] Tenenti, *Il Senso della morte*, 80-107. R. Rudolf's *"Ars Moriendi": Von der Kunst des heilsamen Lebens und Sterbens* (Cologne, 1957) came to my attention after the completion of this study.

[9] O'Connor, *Art of Dying Well*, 61-112.

[10] Mgr. P. E. Puyol, *Descriptions bibliographiques des manuscrits et des principales éditions du livre "De Imitatione Christi"* (Paris, 1898), lists 349 Latin manuscripts, but J. van Ginneken, *Op Zoek naar der oudsten tekst en den waren schrijve van het eerste boek der Navolging van Christus*, Tekstvergelijkende Spoor-naspeuringen (Wetteren, 1929), 2, gives a figure of 600.

Christian world, the Bible excepted."[11] If we rely on this indication of the number of surviving manuscript copies, the *Ars moriendi* lies at approximately the same distribution level as a major political text like the *De Regimine Principum* of Giles of Rome (about 300 manuscripts),[12] a great literary success like the *Roman de la Rose* (about 250),[13] or a historical chronicle destined for a broad audience like the *Brute, or the Chronicles of England* (167 known manuscripts).[14] In contrast, I might note the small number of surviving manuscripts of Nicolas Oresme's translations of Aristotle: eighteen for the *Politics*,[15] ten for the *Economics*,[16] and six for the *De caelo* (*Le Livre du ciel et du monde*).[17]

The *Ars moriendi*, however, may easily have owed its enormous success with both the faithful of the fifteenth century and later historians to the impact of the eleven engravings that illustrated the shorter version, showing the path to a good death after the five diabolical temptations of loss of faith, despair, impatience, vainglory, and avarice had been vanquished by five angelic "inspirations." There are three traditions in the fifteenth century of this iconographic series, recently reexamined by Henri Zerner,[18] but it is impossible to establish a linear connection among them. They are the miniatures of the Wellcome Institute manuscript; the three groups of burin engravings attributed

[11] F. Rapp, *L'Église et la vie religieuse en Occident à la fin du Moyen Age* (Paris, 1971), 248.

[12] Information furnished by Jean-Philippe Genet.

[13] E. Langlois, *Les Manuscrits du "Roman de la Rose." Description et Classement* (Lille and Paris, 1910), lists 214 manuscripts and adds another 30 "whose current residence is unknown."

[14] F.W.D. Brie, *Geschichte und Quellen der mittelenglischen Prosachronik. The Brute of England oder The Chronicles of England* (Marburg, 1905), 1-5, lists 120 manuscripts in English, 43 in French, and 4 in Latin. (Also published as an introductory study to F.W.D. Brie, ed., *The Brut; or, The Chronicles of England* [London, 1906-1908].)

[15] Maistre Nicolas Oresme, *Le Livre de Politiques d'Aristote*, published from the text of Avranches Manuscript 223, ed. A. D. Menut, *Transactions of the American Philosophical Society*, n.s. 60, pt. 6 (1970):33-39.

[16] Maistre Nicolas Oresme, *Le Livre de yconomique d'Aristote*, French text from the Avranches Manuscript with original Latin version and English translation, trans. and ed. A. D. Menut, *Transactions of the American Philosophical Society*, n.s. 47, pt. 5 (1957):801-3.

[17] Nicolas Oresme, *Le Livre du ciel et du monde*, trans. A. D. Menut, ed. A. D. Menut and A. J. Denomy (Madison, Wisconsin, 1968), 32-36.

[18] H. Zerner, "L'Art au morier," *Revue de l'Art* 11 (1971):7-30, gives a recent bibliography on the subject and reproduces eleven miniatures from the manuscript of the Wellcome Institute of the History of Medicine and from the French translation of the *Ars moriendi* in its first woodcut edition.

to the Master ES, to the Master of the Flowered Borders, and to the Master of the Dutuit Garden of Gethsemane; and the woodcuts in both the thirteen series used in the twenty xylographic editions listed by Wilhelm Ludwig Schreiber[19] and the illustrations of the incunabula described by Arthur Mayger Hind.[20] It is not my intention to describe once again this sequence of illustrations that spring from the theme of the struggle for possession of the soul, as depicted in numerous miniatures in Books of Hours,[21] but rather to investigate the distribution and impact of these illustrations.

The *Ars moriendi* was perhaps the most widely circulated woodcut book, since it accounts for 15 percent of all surviving examples of the thirty-three texts published in the form of block books (61 out of 400 works).[22] Moreover, its circulation was not limited like that of the book. Engravings and *placards* (posters, handbills) assured it a wide distribution, particularly by giving the illustrations, which could be affixed to a wall, greater visibility. The Print Collection of the Bibliothèque Nationale in Paris has two woodcuts of this sort, probably Bavarian in origin and dated by Schreiber to 1465-1475.[23] On the left half of the first sheet (fig. 1) the engraver has placed a scene illustrating the good death in the middle register framed by the struggle between the five victorious angels (in the upper register) and the five defeated devils (at the bottom of the engraving). The right-hand portion (fig. 2) shows the Last Judgment. The engraving thus unites, by a singularly

[19] W. L. Schreiber, *Manuel de l'amateur de la gravure sur bois et sur métal au XV<sup>e</sup> siècle* (Leipzig, 1902), 4:253-313; A. Blum, *Les Origines de la gravure en France. Les Estampes sur bois et sur métal. Les Incunables xylographiques* (Paris and Brussels, 1927), 58-61, pls. 49-57; A. Hyatt Mayor, *Prints and People: A Social History of Printed Pictures*, The Metropolitan Museum of Art (New York, 1971; 2d ed., 1972), 23-25.

[20] A. M. Hind, *An Introduction to a History of Woodcut* (London, 1935), 1:224-30, supplemented for Italy by V. Massena (Prince d'Essling), *Les Livres à figures vénitiens de la fin du XV<sup>e</sup> siècle et du commencement du XVI<sup>e</sup> siècle* (Florence and Paris, 1907), 1:253-67; M. Sander, *Le Livre à figures italien depuis 1467 jusqu'à 1530* (Milan, 1942), 109-11.

[21] Mâle, *L'Art religieux*, 380-89; T.S.R. Boase, *Death in the Middle Ages: Mortality, Judgment and Remembrance*, (London, 1972), 119-26.

[22] O'Connor, *Art of Dying Well*, 114-15. The date of the first appearance of woodcut booklets has occasioned new controversies. See the reviews of the situation (with a bibliography of the works of L. Donati and A. Stevenson) in the catalogues of two recent expositions: *Le Livre*, Bibliothèque Nationale (Paris, 1972), 37, and *Les Incunables de la Collection Edmond de Rothschild. La Gravure en relief sur bois et métal*, Musée du Louvre (Paris, 1974), 32.

[23] See figures 1 and 2, described in Schreiber, *Manuel de la gravure*, 2:249-50 (Berlin, 1892) and 4:313-14.

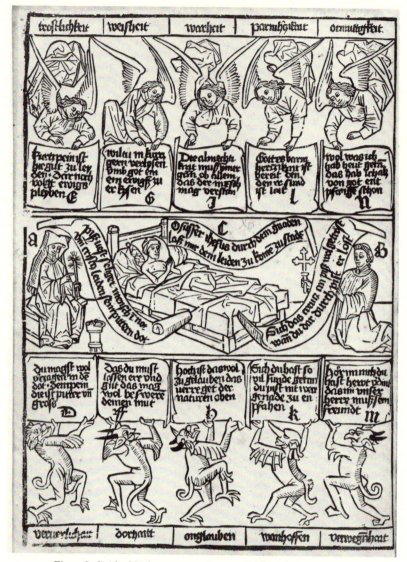

Fig. 1. Individual Judgment, c. 1465-1475 (Bibliothèque Nationale, Paris, Réserve des Imprimés, woodcut 37).

Fig. 2. Collective Judgment, c. 1465-1475 (Bibliothèque Nationale,
Paris, Réserve des Imprimés, woodcut 37).

efficient shortcut, the traditional image of Judgment as a collective sanction and the new idea of the judgment of each individual life based on resistance to temptation at the moment of death.[24] The second sheet teaches a similar lesson: Eternal life depends on one's attitudes facing death. Men and women who face death willingly will be crowned in Paradise by Christ, those who die without having done penance for their sins will be led to Purgatory, and those who have lived bad lives with no thought of death will be delivered to the Devil. Engravings of this sort, which were undoubtedly infinitely more numerous than the few that have come down to us, provided a major tool for mass pedagogy.[25]

The iconographic sequence of the five diabolic temptations, the five angelic "inspirations," and the good death by no means disappears with the increase in typeset books. It still illustrates the better part of the incunabula of the *Ars moriendi* in Latin and the vernacular tongues. German can serve as an example here. Out of 23 editions before 1500, 9 include the typical series of eleven woodcuts: In two cases they make up the entire illustration of the book; in three, pictures of a dying man receiving the last sacrament and of Saint Michael weighing souls are added; four others include these plus a fourteenth engraving representing confession.[26] In the sixteenth century, the editions published by Johan Weyssenburger in Nuremberg and, after 1504, in Landshut continued the successful career of this iconography. Reuse of the same woodcuts in different books further increased the audience for certain images. The depiction of the good death was one that proved of great importance, since it showed both the scene of the deathbed, anchored in this world, and the thoughts that should occupy the dying. Popularized by the woodcut booklets, this subject was often copied or imitated in fifteenth-century Germany. Among Augsburg printings, for example, were the *Büchlein des sterbenden Menschen* of Hans Münzinger, put out in two editions by Anton Sorg in 1480 and 1483; the *Mensch auf dem Totenbett* published by Johan Blaubirer around 1485; and the edi-

[24] On this duality, see Ariès, *Western Attitudes*, 29-39.

[25] With the aid of those who could read, the *placards* could have played the same role. See *Einblattdrucke des XV Jahrhunderts. Ein bibliographisches Verzeichnis* (Halle, 1914), no. 761, "Instrumentum continens modum disponendi se ad mortem" (Ulm, J. Zainer, ca. 1500) and no. 509, "Death Bed Prayers: O Glorious Jesu" (Westminster, W. Caxton, c. 1484).

[26] Figure for incunabula according to O'Connor, for the number of editions with illustrations according to Schreiber, *Manuel de la gravure*, 5:72-74 (Leipzig, 1910).

tions put out by Hanns Schönsperger in 1490 and 1494 of the *Versehung Leib, Seel, Ehrt und Gut*.[27] English practice of the early sixteenth century follows the same pattern. The deathbed scene is reproduced in nine of Wynkin de Worde's editions: in the *Ars Moryendi* of 1506, the *Arte to Lyve Well* of 1505 and 1506, the *Thordynary of Crysten Men* of 1506, the *Boke Named the Royall* of 1507 and 1508, the *Dyenge Creature* of 1507 and 1514, and the *Complaynt of the Soule* of 1519.[28]

The success of the *Ars moriendi* seems to have continued, in both illustrated and nonillustrated versions, until about 1530. Sister O'Connor's list, based on the *Gesamtkatalog des Wiegendrucke*, gives seventy-seven incunabula editions, and this figure is probably much lower than the truth.[29] Of these, the long version is more numerous than the short version by 51 to 26, a two to one ratio. Overall, vernacular editions outnumber the Latin 42 to 35, but editions published in Germany and France show, respectively, 16 Latin out of a total of 23 and 15 Latin out of 23. On the other hand, the vernacular triumphed in the Low Countries (5 editions out of 6), in Italy (13 out of 16), in Spain (4 out of 4), and in England (5 out of 5). The geographic distribution of these editions demonstrates the primacy of Paris (17 editions, or 22 percent of the total). Four other areas were prominent: northern Italy (14 editions), southern Germany and the Rhine valley from Basel to Cologne (also with 14), the city of Leipzig, where Kachelofen and Lotther accounted for 9 editions, and the Low Countries (6 editions). This distribution reflects that of printing itself, which guaranteed the lead taken by Paris and the German cities and gave northern Italy a dense network of printshops even before 1480,[30] the epoch of the great Rhenish and Flemish centers of spirituality.

The production of the *Ars* slowed down by the mid-sixteenth century. In England there were four editions, the last two of which were in 1506.[31] In Paris nine editions have been traced, five of which left the

[27] Ibid., nos. 4815, 4816, 4642, 5424, and 5425.

[28] E. Hodnett, *English Woodcuts 1480-1535* (Oxford, 1935), 188, no. 510, "A Dying Man in Bed."

[29] O'Connor, *Art of Dying Well*, 133-71. Tenenti, *La Vie et la Mort*, gives the figure of ninety-seven incunabula editions in a table (pp. 92-95), but does not describe them.

[30] L. Febvre and H.-J. Martin, *L'Apparition du livre* (Paris, 1958; 2d ed., 1971), 260-61 (map).

[31] A. W. Pollard and G. R. Redgrave, *A Short-Title Catalogue of Books Printed in England, Scotland and Ireland and of English Books Printed Abroad, 1475-1640* (London, 1926), 19.

presses between 1501 and 1510,[32] those of the Widow Trepperel and
Jehan Jehanot during the second decade of the century, and those of
François Regnault and Henri Paquot before 1550 (Regnault stopped
publishing in 1540 and Paquot in 1546). Only the edition of Nicolas
Bonfons appeared later, probably in the last quarter of the century.[33] In
Lyons there were two editions, one from Pierre Mareschal,[34] the other
from Jacques Moderne,[35] both before 1540. The same is true for the
editions in which the *Exhortation de bien vivre et de bien mourir* followed the *Grant danse macabre*. The *Ars* also survived in the North and
the East: in the North with the Swedish (Malmö, 1533) and Danish
editions (Copenhagen, 1570, 1575, 1577, 1580), and in the East with the
octavo-sized anti-Protestant versions printed by Adam Walasser in Di-
lingen (1569, 1570, 1579, 1583, 1603). Tenenti has clearly demonstrated
how, from the 1490s on, the *Ars moriendi* tended to shift, as it went
through its various adaptations and translations, toward a program for
right living that somewhat attentuated the tense concentration on
man's final hour.[36] The fact remains, however, that from the mid-fif-
teenth century to the mid-sixteenth century, one work and one series
of images circulated throughout the western world, constituting an ex-
ceptionally stable group of commonly held notions centering on the
death agony.

The years from 1530 to 1540 saw the decline of this "bestseller."
Around that period, two other major works on the preparation for
death, those of Clichtove and Erasmus, took over where the *Ars* had
left off. Clichtove's treatise, *De Doctrina moriendi opusculum necessaria
ad mortem foeliciter oppetendam preparamenta declarans et quomodo in
ejus agone variis antiqui hostis insultibus sit resistendum edocens*, was published in Paris in 1520. It went through eleven Latin editions between

---

[32] B. Moreau, *Inventaire chronologique des éditions parisiennes du XVIᵉ siècle, d'après les
manuscrits de P. Renouard* (Paris, 1972), vol. 1: 1501, no. 9; 1503, no. 7; 1504, no. 8; 1505,
no. 10; 1510, no. 14.

[33] BN, Paris, Réserve des Imprimés, Papiers Renouard; P. Renouard, *Répertoire des
imprimeurs parisiens, libraires, fondeurs de caractères et correcteurs d'imprimerie depuis l'introduction de l'Imprimerie à Paris jusqu'à la fin du XVIᵉ siècle* (Paris, 1965).

[34] H. Baudrier, *Bibliographie lyonnaise. Recherches sur les imprimeurs, libraires, re-
lieurs et fondeurs de lettres de Lyon au XVIᵉ siècle, publiées et continuées par J. Baudrier*
(Lyons, 1895-1921), 11:516.

[35] S. F. Pogue, *Jacques Moderne, Lyons Music Printer of the Sixteenth Century* (Geneva,
1969), 107-296 (bibliography of Moderne's publications): no. 67, *Le Livre nommé l'art
et science de bien vivre et de bien mourir*.

[36] Tenenti, *La Vie et la Mort*, 63-68.

that date and 1546 (seven in Paris and four in Antwerp),[37] then appeared in a French translation published in Rouen in 1553 entitled *Le Doctrinal de la mort extraict de ce que jadis en avoir escrit feu maistre Josse Clichtovus, traduict en langue vulgaire.* The great publishing success of the years 1530-1560, however, was Erasmus's *De praeparatione ad mortem*, which went through fifty-nine editions in Latin and in vernacular languages, counting both editions which gave the text alone and editions in which it followed the *Enchiridion.* In subsequent editions, Latin predominated with thirty-six editions spaced out between 1534 and 1563. Flemish followed, with eight editions between 1534 and 1566. French came next, with eight editions between 1537 and 1541 in two different translations, *La Préparation à la mort autrefois composée en latin par D. Érasme et maintenant traduite en français* (Lyons, 1537) and *Le Préparatif à la mort. Livre très utile et nécessaire à chascun chrétien. Adjoutée une instruction chrétienne pour bien vivre et soy préparer à la mort* (Paris, 1539, under the name of Guy Morin). Next in order came German editions, with three from 1534 to 1546, then Spanish, with three editions from 1535 to 1555, and finally one English edition in 1543.[38] Quite evidently, the book's distribution was limited to the second third of the sixteenth century; it nearly disappears after that period, to be found in only a handful of editions (seven in all) during the seventeenth century. One minor event, cited by Roger Doucet, gives a good indication of both the reception Erasmus's treatise met and the problems it caused. On 30 July 1535 the books of Marco de Erasso, a Milanese who was probably a student at the University of Paris, were inventoried. When the bookseller encountered Erasmus's work in Latin, he noted it but refused to appraise it "because it is suspect in faith."[39] What we can see in this brief "slice of life" is both the zeal of a particular milieu (the book, after all, had only appeared a year earlier) and the mistrust confronting humanistic novelties.

Beyond these two classics, the list of French and English works on the preparation for death in the sixteenth century is short. In France there were some ten titles, divided between books of instruction (*direc-*

[37] *Bibliotheca Belgica: Bibliographie Générale des Pays-Bas,* founded by F. van der Haegen, republished under the direction of M. T. Lenger (Brussels, 1964), 1:604-7. On Clichtove's work and its humanist leanings, see Tenenti, *La Vie et la Mort,* 68-70.

[38] *Bibliotheca Belgica,* 2:943-71. On this text, see Tenenti, *Il Senso della morte,* 122-27 and (more generally on the problem of death in Erasmus) 229-61.

[39] R. Doucet, *Les Bibliothèques parisiennes au XVIᵉ siècle* (Paris, 1946), 36-37.

*toires*) and books of meditations.[40] The works of Jean Columbi[41] and Pierre Doré[42] furnish examples of the first type; for the second there are those of the Protestant, Jean de l'Espine,[43] and the Jesuit, Father Richeome.[44] In England approximately the same number of titles appeared.[45] The first third of the century produced such works (generally anonymous) as the *Doctrynalle of Dethe*, published by Wynkin de Worde in 1498 and reprinted in 1534, and *A Treatise to teche a man to dye and not to feare dethe* (c. 1538). There was also the Erasmian text of Lupset, which was reprinted five times in ten years,[46] and in 1561 the enormously successful Calvinist treatise of Thomas Becon, which went through eleven editions in the sixteenth century and seven in the first thirty years of the seventeenth.[47] Finally, there was Edmund Bunny's Calvinist adaptation of the Jesuit Father Robert Parsons's treatise.[48]

After 1530, then, the *Ars moriendi* gave way to a discourse on death apparently more widespread but of less influence on the collective awareness. Before verifying this hypothesis by surveying quantitative data on book production, we need to linger a moment on the illustrations. The theme of the struggle between the angels and demons

---

[40] J. Dagens, *Bibliographie chronologique de la littérature de spiritualité et de ses sources (1501-1610)* (Paris, 1952); A. Cioranescu, *Bibliographie de la littérature française du XVIᵉ siècle* (Paris, 1959).

[41] R. P. Jean Columbi, *Directoire pour ceuls qui sont à l'article de la mort, extraict de la doctrine de Gerson, avec aucunes petites oraisons en rimes ajoutées* (n.p., n.d.).

[42] P. Doré, *La Déploration de la vie humaine avec la disposition à dignement recevoir le S. Sacrement et mourir en bon catholique* (Paris, 1554).

[43] Jean de l'Espine, *Traicté pour oster la crainte de la mort et la faire désirer à l'homme fidèle* (Lyons, 1558).

[44] P. Richeome, *L'Adieu à l'âme dévote laissant le corps avec les moyens de combattre la mort par la mort, et l'appareil pour heureusement se partir de ceste vie mortelle* (Tournon, 1590). There were six editions of this work in the sixteenth century and seven in the seventeenth.

[45] N. L. Beatty, *The Craft of Dying: A Study in the Literary Tradition of the "Ars moriendi" in England* (New Haven, 1970).

[46] T. Lupset, *A Compendious and a very fruteful treatyse teachynge the waye of Dyenge well . . .* (London). Editions appeared in 1534, 1535, 1538, 1541, and 1544.

[47] T. Becon, *The Sycke Mans Salue. Wherin the faithfull christians may learne both how to behaue them selues paciently and thankefully, in the tyme of sickenes and also vertuously to dispose their temporall goods, and finally to prepare them selues gladly and godly to die* (London). Editions appeared in 1561, 1563, 1568, 1570, 1572, 1574, 1577, 1584, 1585, 1594, 1596, 1601, 1604, 1607, 1611, 1613, 1631, and 1632.

[48] E. Bunny, *A Booke of Christian Exercise Appertaining to Resolution . . .* (London, 1584), an adaptation of R. Parsons, *The First Booke of the Christian Exercise appertayning to Resolution* (Rouen, 1582). On the latter text, see J. Driscoll, *Robert Parsons' Book of Resolution: A Bibliographical and Literary Study* (New Haven, 1957).

around the dying person, the focal illustration in the series, lasted longer in engravings than in the written texts.[49] It persisted throughout the century, for example, in the Hours published by the Widow Kerver and in a sequence of eleven plates engraved by Léonard Gaultier. In the 1542 edition of the *Heures de la Vierge à l'usage des Dominicains*, the quatrain

> Quant l'homme a vescu aage entier
> En ceste vallee miserable
> En esperant sans destourbier
> Dobtenir la vie perdurable

> (When man has lived his entire span
> In this valley of woe
> Hoping imperturbably
> To obtain eternal life)

serves as the legend to a picture (fig. 3) in which a dying man, attended by two persons and a priest administering the sacrament, lies beneath an image of Christ, whose hand is raised in blessing. Directly above the man, to the right of the viewer, an angel holds a phylactery bearing the words "Libera me Domine et Pone Me Iuxta Te," and at his feet there are three defeated devils. A window on the facing wall (to the viewer's left) opens onto a scene of a man digging a grave near a cross.[50] At the end of the century, Gaultier returned to the inspiration and even to the formal structure of the scenes in the *Ars moriendi* in some of his vignettes. The last five of a sequence of eleven engravings which illustrated a collection of religious and moral maxims on the human condition are devoted to death.[51]

> Apres les maux et douleurs temporelles,
> L'ame iouit des faueurs eternelles

> (After temporal woes and sorrows,
> The soul enjoys eternal favors)

reads the caption of one picture (fig. 4) illustrating the good death, which duplicates many elements found in the last illustration of the

[49] A. Linzeler, *Inventaire du Fond Français. Graveurs du XVIᵉ siècle* (Paris, 1932-1935).

[50] *Heures de la Vierge à l'usage des Dominicains* (Paris, Veuve Kerver, 1542), Iviᵛ. The woodcut can also be found in the editions of 1522 and 1569.

[51] L. Gaultier, *Suite de onze pièces* (BN, Paris, Réserve des Estampes), Ed 12 folio, nos. 140-44.

Fig. 3. The Moment of Death, with Angels and Demons, engraving from the *Heures de la Vierge à l'usage des Dominicains* (Paris: Veuve [widow] Kerver, 1542) (Bibliothèque Nationale, Paris).

Fig. 4. The Moment of Death, with Angels and Demons, engraving from Léonard Gaultier's *Suite de onze pièces* (late sixteenth century) (Bibliothèque Nationale, Paris, Réserve des Estampes, Ed 12 folio).

woodcut booklets. His family around him, the dying man is attended by a priest who offers him a candle with one hand and holds out a cross with the other. Meanwhile above him, his soul, pictured as a miniature person, is carried off by two angels, and at his feet defeated demons writhe in despair. The same theme inspires the next two plates in this series. One bears the legend

> Par oraison, par vœuz et par prière,
> L'homme est aydé en son heure dernière
>
> (By orisons, vows, and prayer,
> Man is aided at his final hour),

46

THE ARTS OF DYING

and shows the combat between angels and demons taking place in the presence of the Trinity and the Virgin, who stand at the dying man's bedside. The next scene depicts the angelic inspiration to good countering the temptation of avarice. Its legend reads:

> Ceux qui vers Dieu vont aux vrayes
> receptes,
> Sont consolez par ses Sacrez preceptes.
>
> (Those who turn to God for true earnings
> Are comforted by his holy precepts.)

The series ends, after burial, with a Last Judgment—

> Au jugement du grand seigneur et maistre,
> Tous les vivans et les morts doyvent estre
>
> (At the judgment of the great Lord and Master,
> All the living and the dead must be present)

—which echoes the woodcuts of the previous century that juxtaposed an eschatological vision of universal Judgment with a concern for individual salvation.

New themes, however, appeared along with the traditional ones. The first of two collections particularly appropriate to our purposes, *Les Simulachres et Historiées Faces de la Mort, autant elegamment pourtraictes, que artificiellement imaginées*, is a series of woodcuts by Hans Lutzelburger which copy works of Holbein.[52] These engravings take their iconography from the *danse macabre*, but the last illustration (fig. 5) is a *memento mori* of a new type. Under the words from Ecclesiasticus 1:13, "In whatever you do, remember your last days, and you will never sin," a new symbolism shows Death holding up a stone to break the hourglass, while the caption proclaims:

> Si tu veux viure sans peché,
> Voy ceste image à tous propos,
> Et point ne seras empesché
> Quand tu t'en iras à repos.
>
> (If you would live without sin,
> Look on this image at every opportunity,

[52] Baudrier, *Bibliographie lyonnaise*, vol. 5: Jehan II and François Frellon; R. Brun, *Le Livre français illustré de la Renaissance* (Paris, 1969), 73-76, 222; N. Z. Davis, "Holbein's Pictures of Death and the Reformation at Lyons," *Studies in the Renaissance* 3 (1956):97-130, the argument I follow here.

*Si tu veux viure sans peché,*
*Voy cesle image à tous propos,*
*Et point ne seras empesché:*
*Quand tu t'en iras à repos.*

Ds          Rom.

Fig. 5. *Memento mori*, engraving from *Les Images de
la Mort* (Lyons: Jehan Frellon, 1562)
(Bibliothèque Nationale, Paris).

And there will be nothing to impede you
When you go to rest.)

The first edition of *Les Simulachres*, put out in Lyons in 1538 by the
Treschel brothers, was the work not of Protestants, but of a group of
reform-minded and tolerant Catholics who at times had ties with Protestants though they never abandoned the Church of Rome. Two men
stand out in this milieu: Gilles Corrozet, a printer, bookseller, and man
of letters who composed the quatrains placed under the engravings,
and Jean de Vauzelles, an Erasmian priest and a prime mover in the
reform of public charity in 1531 who wrote the dedicatory epistle and

48

THE ARTS OF DYING

several essays interspersed among the engravings. As it first appeared, then, the work reflected the sensitivity of a group that resembled, in its inspiration and its faith, the circle working for urban reform. The work took on another meaning after 1539 when a journeymen's strike threw printing in Lyons into confusion and obliged the Treschel brothers to close their printshop. The wood blocks were sold to the Frellons, one of whom (Jean) was a zealous Protestant, and used for new editions that dropped Vauzelles's texts in favor of other, anonymous essays—"La Médecine de l'Âme" and "La Forme et manière de consoler les malades"—which were clearly Calvinist in inspiration behind their lip service to orthodox formulas. For the next thirty years the book was a great success, going through seven editions: three in French (1542, 1547, and 1562, this last by Symphorien Barbier when Protestants held Lyons), three in Latin (1542, 1545, and 1547), and one in Italian (1549).[53]

The resolutely Calvinist *Emblèmes ou devises chrétiennes* of Georgette de Montenay brought other motifs to the iconography of the preparation for death. The first edition, published in Lyons by Philippe de Castellas, dates from 1566, but there seems to be no surviving copy. In 1571 Jean Marcorelle, a Protestant printer, took up the book, which then went through several editions in Protestant countries, appearing in Zurich in 1584, Heidelberg in 1584, and La Rochelle in 1620.[54] A handful of the hundred vignettes, signed by Pierre Woeiriot, are devoted to the subject of death. On page 83, resistance by faith has taken the place of angelic inspiration for good (fig. 6):

> On voit asses combien grandes alarmes
> Satan, le monde, ont iusqu'ici liurez
> A tous Chrestiens: mais comme bons gendarmes
> Resistez forts par foy: car deliurez
> Serez bien tost de ces fols enyurez
> Du sang des saincts, qui crie à Dieu vengeance:
> Ainsi par foy Christ, vostre chef, suyurez.
> Voyci, il vient: courage en patience.

---

[53] Baudrier, *Bibliographie lyonnaise*, 5:259, mentions the edition of 1562 as being "the ninth and last," but he in fact lists only the eight editions, for which he repeats the description found in Brun, *Le Livre français*, 222.

[54] Baudrier, *Bibliographie lyonnaise*, 10:381-82; Brun, *Le Livre français*, 265; Tenenti, *Il Senso della Morte*, 278-81.

49

Fig. 6. Resistance by Faith, engraving from Georgette de Montenay,
*Emblèmes ou devises chrétiennes* (Lyons: J. Marcorelle, 1571)
(Bibliothèque Nationale, Paris).

(One can easily see what great battle
Satan and the world have until now made
On all Christians: but like good soldiers,
Resist, strong in faith: for delivered
You will soon be from the maddened fools
By the blood of the Saints, which cries to God for vengeance.
Thus by faith follow Christ, your chief.
See where he comes: take courage in patience.)

Fig. 7. Death Desired, engraving from Georgette de Montenay,
*Emblèmes ou devises chrétiennes* (Lyons: J. Marcorelle, 1571)
(Bibliothèque Nationale, Paris).

Page 89 has also omitted angels and demons: A man emerges from this
world to greet death (fig. 7). The words "Desiderans dissolvi" sur-
mount this scene, which is underscored by the verse:

> De grand desir d'aller bien tost à Dieu,
> Cestui se voit presque sorti du monde:
> Crainte de mort en son endroit n'a lieu,
> Ainsi qu'elle a au coeur sale et immonde.

51

La mort n'est plus au Chrestien sainct et monde
Qu'un doux passage à conduire à la vie
Et vray repos, où toute grace abonde:
Mais charité modere tell'enuie.

(From ardent desire to soon go to God
This man sees himself almost departed from the world.
Fear of death has no place in him
As in the sullied, unclean heart.
Death is to the holy and pure Christian
But a sweet path to lead life
To true rest, where all grace abounds.
But charity moderates such a desire.)

At first sight, then, the genre of preparation for death appears to
have evolved between 1450 and the end of the sixteenth century from
the massive presence of the *Ars moriendi* to the invention of new forms
that arose during a lull in the career of the *Ars*. The task that remains
is to attempt to verify this hypothesis by measurements. There are
fairly solid data for the age of the incunabula that allow us to evaluate
both the weight of religious titles within the total book production and
the importance of the *artes moriendi* within the production of religious
books.[55] My compilation covers the ten largest centers of book publishing in Europe.

Depending on the city, the proportion of religious books in the production of incunabula varies between 25 percent and 50 percent, but if
the Italian cities and Leipzig are ignored, the percentages rise and clus-
ter at between 40 and 50 percent, the average proposed by Robert Steele
and Father John Mary Lenhart.[56] The *Ars moriendi* in general accounts
for between 0.5 and 2 percent of religious books, with the exception of
Leipzig (thanks to the Kachelofen editions). This may seem modest,
but if we accept Tenenti's figure of ninety-seven editions and an average print run of five hundred copies per edition (as Lenhart estimates,
but this is far short of the truth concerning woodcut editions), this represents approximately fifty thousand copies. These are figures comparable to the *Imitatio Christi*, which was republished at least eighty-five

[55] J. M. Lenhart, "Pre-Reformation Printed Books: A Study in Statistical and Applied Bibliography," *Franciscan Studies* 14 (1935):76 (table).

[56] Ibid., 68, cites the figure given by Robert Steele in a series of articles that appeared
in *Library: A Quarterly Review of Bibliography and Library Lore* between 1903 and 1907.

| City | Total Editions | Religious Books | | Artes Moriendi | |
| | | Editions | Percent of Total | Editions | Percent of Religious Books |
| --- | --- | --- | --- | --- | --- |
| Venice | 3,754 | 974 | 25.9 | 4 (5) | 0.4 (0.5) |
| Paris | 2,254 | 1,063 | 47.2 | 17 (18) | 1.6 (1.7) |
| Rome | 1,613 | 465 | 28.8 | 1 (2) | 0.2 (0.4) |
| Cologne | 1,304 | 669 | 51.3 | 8 (16) | 1.2 (2.4) |
| Strasbourg | 980 | 561 | 57.2 | 2 | 0.4 |
| Milan | 962 | 226 | 23.5 | 1 (2) | 0.4 (0.9) |
| Lyons | 909 | 342 | 37.6 | 4 (6) | 1.2 (1.8) |
| Augsburg | 893 | 444 | 49.7 | 2 (4) | 0.5 (0.9) |
| Florence | 839 | 422 | 50.3 | 6 | 1.4 |
| Leipzig | 745 | 193 | 25.9 | 9 (7) | 4.7 (3.6) |

NOTE: For the *artes moriendi* books, when Sister O'Connor's results disagree with those of A. Tenenti, Tenenti is in parentheses.

times before 1500.[57] To the *Ars* should be added works for which I have not furnished data—those of Gerson, Molinet, Chastellain, and Castel,[58] as well as anonymous German and English works—which means that an admissible figure for works on preparation for death might amount to 3 to 4 percent of religious incunabula. This figure, which concerns an epoch of habitual reading about death's omnipotence, gives us a good basis of comparison by which to judge the impact of the Catholic Reformation. Daniel Roche has provided data for the seventeenth century which shows that in France alone preparations for death (which of course had changed in character) amounted to between four and five hundred thousand copies and made up from 7 to 10 percent of the production of books on theology. Bibliographic statistics thus permit us to put traditional data in perspective: The publication of works on preparation for death reached high points in the fifteenth and seventeenth centuries, but it was in the post-Tridentine period that this genre was most prevalent within religious literature.

Data are less certain for the sixteenth century. If we take Paris as our

[57] A. de Backer, *Essai bibliographique sur le livre "De Imitatione Christi"* (Liège, 1864), gives fifty-four incunabula publications in Latin, fourteen in Italian, eight in German, four in French, four in Spanish, and one in Polish.

[58] Tenenti, *La Vie et la Mort*, 60.

example,[59] the beginning of the century was marked by a stability in the share of the market enjoyed by works on the arts of dying. Between 1500 and 1510, printers in the capital published 1,656 editions, of which some 45 percent were religious books. Figures on theological works show three thresholds: The highest level, with some three hundred editions, belongs to books of hours; Bibles, missals, and breviaries come next, on the level of thirty to forty editions; and works on ritual and on the arts of dying—the *Ars* as well as the Gerson—belong on the lowest level with a dozen or so editions. Here we find the 1 percent of religious books on preparation for death. After the first decades of the century, works on the arts of dying become lost in a flood of publications. Let me give three examples. In Caen, 411 editions were published before 1560: thirty-one missals, twenty-two breviaries, but only one book on preparation for death, the *Esguillon de crainte divine pour bien mourir*, which came out of the Paris editions of the *Art de bien vivre et de bien mourir*.[60] Bordeaux produced 711 editions in the sixteenth century, not one of which was on preparation for death.[61] In Lyons 15,000 editions were published, thirty or more on death, among them Erasmus's work (six editions), the translation of Gerson, Columbi's *Directoire*, the *Exhortation de bien vivre et de bien mourir*, which followed the *Grant danse macabre* (four editions), and the *Simulachres et Historiées faces de la mort* (eight editions).[62]

Other, more indirect indications confirm this decline. First, there was an increasing gap between publications on preparation for death and the continued success of the *Imitatio Christi*, which had two hundred editions in the sixteenth century.[63] Second, there was the increase in Jesuit publications, which amounted to 20 titles on death between 1540 and 1620, 139 between 1620 and 1700, and 101 between 1700 and 1800.[64] Jean Polanco's *Methodus ad eos adjuvandos qui moriun-*

[59] Moreau, *Inventaire chronologique*.

[60] L. Delisle, *Catalogue des livres imprimés ou publiés à Caen avant le milieu du XVIᵉ siècle* (Caen, 1903-1904).

[61] L. Desgraves, *Bibliographie bordelaise. Bibliographie des ouvrages imprimés à Bordeaux au XVIᵉ siècle et par Simon Millanges (1572-1623)* (Baden, 1971).

[62] Baudrier, *Bibliographie lyonnaise*.

[63] De Backer, *Essai bibliographique*, gives for the sixteenth century sixty-eight editions in Latin, fifty-six in Italian, eighteen in French, seventeen in English, sixteen in Flemish, fifteen in German, six in Spanish, and four in Polish.

[64] C. Sommervogel, *Bibliothèque de la Compagnie de Jésus* (Paris, 1909), 10:510-19 (Tables de la Première Partie by P. Bliar).

*tur: ex complurium doctorum ac piorum scriptis, diu diuturnoque usu, et observatione collecta* was both the archetype and the most successful example of this Jesuit literature. This practical guide to the art of dying and helping others to a good death was significant for its small (duodecimo or sextodecimo) format. Eighteen editions appeared between 1577 and 1650, and this figure does not include editions in which this text followed other works.[65] Other publications worthy of note, of the same inspiration and for the same purpose, are the Latin works of José de Anchieta, *Syntagma monitorum ad juvandos moribundos*, and Jules Fatio, *Mortorium seu libellum de juvandis moribundis*, and, in the vernacular, the *Pratica de ayudar a morir* of Juan Baptista Poza (Madrid, 1619) and the *Modo de aiudar a ben morir als qui per malatia, ò per Justicia moren. Compost per lo P. Pedro Gil Doctor Theolec de la Compania de Jesus. Es utilissim per a tots los Parocos y Confessors, y Sacerdots ques emplean en profit de las Animas* (Barcelona, 1605).[66]

The sixteenth century was thus a low water mark for works on preparing for death, both in relation to the previous period, dominated by the *Ars moriendi* and the treatises it inspired, and in comparison with later years, when the number of titles increased sharply and regularly until the high point of the years 1675-1700. This does not mean that discourse on death was absent during the Renaissance, but that it chose other genres: meditations on Christ's Passion (in the minority), and prayers, poems, or consolations written on the death of an illustrious person (the majority). It is clear, even from Alexandre Cioranescu's listing, that religious literature during the latter half of the sixteenth century was almost totally absorbed in anti-Reformation controversy. And the preparation for death did not happen to be (at least not directly) one of the major points of dispute, as were confession or the Eucharist. The hypothesis of a relative decline in the arts of dying can thus be defended, but on the condition that we not forget two facts that work to attenuate contrasts. First, counts of titles or editions underrate the weight of literature which had broad distribution and high print runs. And second, many smaller published pieces, *placards*, and en-

---

[65] Ibid., 6:944, gives twelve Latin editions, one in German in 1584, and five in French, the first of which was published in 1599 under the title *Consolations très utiles, brièves et méthodiques pour bien et fructueusement consoler et ayder les Malades à l'article de la mort*.

[66] Ibid., 1:312 (J. Anchieta), 3:552 (J. Fatio), 3:1413 (P. Gil), 6:1135 (J. B. Poza).

gravings may have disappeared, and this sort of material for the most part escapes us for the sixteenth century.[67]

To estimate the rank of the arts of dying in literature, we have at hand only a few coherent bodies of material, a limited amount of data provided by Roger Doucet, and, above all, Albert Labarre's systematic study of Amiens. The Paris inventories published by Doucet indicate a tenuous but nevertheless real presence of works on preparing for death. Among the 101 works owned in 1499 by Nicole Gille, *contrôleur du trésor* and author of the *Annales et chroniques de France*, we find the *Art de bien mourir*.[68] In 1522 the bookseller Jehan Jehanot, husband of the widow Trepperel, had in stock five hundred "livres qui parlent de bien vivre," appraised at 35 *sous*, 6 *deniers*, which in all likelihood were copies of his edition of the *Art et science de bien vivre et de bien mourir*.[69] We find this same title, valued at 5 *sous*, in 1548 in the collection of Jean Le Féron, a lawyer at the *parlement* who owned a library of 783 titles,[70] and in 1555, with no appraised value, among the 280 works owned by the *marchand brodeur* (embroidered stuffs wholesaler) Pierre Valet, known as Parent.[71] Thus three inventories of private libraries give us three books on the art of dying. Still, it would be a mistake to jump to conclusions on the basis of this slim sampling, in which chance may have played a role, for the more thorough study undertaken by Alexander Herman Schutz of two hundred inventories in Paris fails to confirm this consistent presence of works on preparation for death.[72]

The same is true of Amiens, according to Labarre's study.[73] In that city, one estate inventory out of five between 1503 and 1576 contained books, but only 20 percent of them are described and identifiable (2,700 out of 12,300). In spite of its inherent limitation, this source can give us

---

[67] Almanacs and books of predictions of the sixteenth century say nothing on death and preparation for death, according to F. Ponthieux, "Prédictions et almanachs au XVIᵉ siècle" (master's thesis, Université Paris 1, 1973), supervised by Pierre Goubert.

[68] Doucet, *Les Bibliothèques parisiennes*, 87, no. 45.

[69] Ibid., 100, no. 117. The various titles directly concerning death make a total of 900 copies in a stock that included 53,475 volumes, or 1.7 percent.

[70] Ibid., 127, no. 246.

[71] Ibid., 167, no. 26.

[72] A. H. Schutz, *Vernacular Books in Parisian Private Libraries of the Sixteenth Century according to the Notarial Inventories* (Chapel Hill, 1955), bases his study on 220 inventories (listed, pp. 74-86) and describes 650 titles in vernacular languages (listed, pp. 31-73).

[73] A. Labarre, *Le Livre dans la vie amiénoise du seizième siècle. L'Enseignement des inventaires après décès 1503-1576* (Paris and Louvain, 1971).

a measure of the importance of religious works and set a hierarchy among them. Among books identified by title, 50 percent are works of theology. Within this category, books of hours, with 52 percent of the titles, make up the majority, followed at considerable distance by liturgical works (15 percent), books of piety (10 percent), treatises for the use of priests (10 percent), and Bibles (8 percent). Among the works of piety, books on preparation for death are far from numerous: There are two mentions of the *Cordiale de quatuor novissimis* (in 1518 and 1520), two of the *Art de bien vivre et de bien mourir* (1523 and 1541), one of *De Doctrina moriendi opusculum* (1531), one of the *Doctrinale mortis* of Raulin (1531), and three copies of Erasmus's work (in 1540, in the inventory of an *avocat au bailliage*; in 1553, in the collection of an *avocat du roi* attached to the *présidial* (district court of appeals); and in 1565, in the library of a parish priest who was a doctor of theology). In all, these represent 0.6 percent of religious books. The majority of the books of piety are hagiographies, in particular copies of Voragine's *Golden Legend*, which, with forty-five entries, comes close to equaling the fifty-three instances of complete Bibles.[74] When we can grasp readership by coherent survey techniques, therefore, the books read also reflect a certain decline of the arts of dying in the collective consciousness of men of the sixteenth century. This period was a low point lying between a high in which mass pedagogy focused on a dramatization of man's last moments and, after the Council of Trent, a program for the Christianization of all aspects of life and a socialization of customs and practices.

A closer look at a sampling of texts (but, thanks to the works of Tenenti and Ariès, without repeating what is now familiar ground) will make clear how works on preparation for death in the fifteenth and sixteenth centuries reveal commonly held feelings and collective practices. One characteristic that often crops up is the author's consciousness of sociocultural cleavages dividing the public he addressed. This was expressed in oppositions: between Latin and the vernacular language, between text and illustrations. In the *Art et science de bien vivre et bien mourir* of Nicolas Bonfons, a late edition which retained earlier traits (including gothic type), the "translator" of the *Ars moriendi* has this to say:

Cestuy livre j'ay regardé et considérant que à toutes gens de bien il est utile et convenable, pour ce que tous n'entendent pas com-

[74] Ibid., 189-95.

plétement le latin, l'ay voulu translater de latin en français au mieux que j'ay pu, afin que tous bons Chrétiens y puissent recréer leur entendement.

(I have looked at this book [i.e., the *Ars moriendi*], and, considering that it is useful and appropriate for all rightminded people [and] because all do not completely understand Latin, I have attempted to translate it from Latin into French as best I could, so that all good Christians can improve their understanding.)[75]

In 1513 an anonymous work appeared in Lyons published by the Arnoullets and entitled *Manière de faire testament salutaire*. The author ends his slim volume with these words:

Lequel j'ay faict en langue maternel pour l'amour de ma seur Renée et aultres personnes dévotes qui n'entendent point latin, affin qu'elles cognoissent comment elles doibvent faire leurs testamens, et mesmes comment il leur fault faire testament spirituel: c'est à savoir bien se préparer à la mort affin que par telle manière elles puissent parvenir à la gloire éternelle, laquelle nous veuille donner nostre seigneur dieu par sa bonté, clémence et miséricorde. Amen.

(Which [book] I have made in the mother tongue for love of my sister Renée and other devout persons who understand no Latin, so they may know how they should make their wills, and even how they should make their spiritual testament: that is, to know how to prepare themselves for death so that they can in this way come to eternal glory, which [we pray] our Lord God to give us through his goodness, clemency, and mercy. Amen.)[76]

The art of dying may well have been a text for clerics at the outset, but it soon aimed at universality in the mission of teaching Christian laity.

Even more than the vernacular language, it was the illustrations that took on this pedagogical function. This is explicitly stated as early as the first woodcut editions of the *Ars moriendi*:

Mais affin que ceste doctrine soit atous fructueuse et nulz nensoit fourcloz ains y aprendge salubrement morir tant clerz par la lettre comme par les ymages layz et clerz en cest miroir poront protinter

---

[75] *Art et science de bien vivre et bien mourir* (Paris, n.d.), Ki$^v$–Kii$^r$.
[76] *La Manière de faire testament salutaire* (Lyons, 1513), Dvii$^v$.

et les choses preterites et futures come presentes speculer. Qui dont veulle bien morir ces choses et subsequentes considere diligentement.

(But in order that this doctrine be fruitful to all and no one be excluded from learning how to die as well as the clergy, by the letter as by the illustrations, laity and clerics in this mirror will be able to profit from things past and future as well as speculate on those present. Thus anyone who would die well, let him diligently consider these things and those that follow.)[77]

The same theme is repeated with even greater clarity in the sixteenth-century adaptations of the work:

Mais afin que ceste matière soit fructueuse et vallable à tous, et que nuls ne soient exclus de la spéculation d'icelle; mais en icelle apprennent toutes gens de quelque estat qu'ils soyent à bien mourir, j'ai traicté et déduict ce livre en deux façons l'une a l'autre correspondantes. Premier en sermons, auctoritéz et parabolles pour servir aux gens clercs et lettrés, secondement en figures et ymages monstrant figurativement et devant les yeux ce que spéculativement par la lettre est dénoté. Et ay je faict pour servir aux laïques et gens non lettrés.

(But so that this matter may be fruitful and of value to all, and that no one be excluded from its speculations, but in it all people of whatsoever estate may learn that they must die well, I have treated and deduced this book in two manners corresponding one to the other. First in sermons, [citations of] authorities, and parables to serve the clergy and lettered people, second in figures and images showing figuratively and before their eyes what is meant speculatively by letters. And I have done so to serve the laity and the illiterate.)[78]

In a world in which Gutenberg had illumined only the very first stars in his galaxy and in which the old equations of clergy = literacy and laity = illiteracy were long in dying, the education of Christ's people must be by both words and images. This probably explains the emphasis in pastoral discourses on simple themes that were easy to develop

---

[77] *Art au morier*, introduction. I have followed the transcription given in Zerner, "L'Art au morier," 19-30.

[78] *Art et science de bien vivre et bien mourir*, Kiii$^r$.

and illustrate and the dramatization of the moment of death, even though this implied a risk of ignoring the Christian life since the entire drama seemed to be played out on the deathbed.

This is why early sixteenth-century texts insisted so forcefully on the need to prepare for one's death well before the decisive hour. Still, this injunction at first rested not on the hope that a Christian life might give but on the fears that crystallized around the "act of dying." The *Manière de faire testament salutaire* lists these fears: One must "dispose his soul and his affairs when he has wits and health and not wait until the article of death"[79] because anyone might die without full use of his reason, die unexpectedly, or die alone. There were three boons to pray for:

Qu'il plaise à dieu secourir à la dernière nécessité en telle façon que l'on ayt mémoire de dieu et de soy mesme en tel article et que l'entendement ne faille au besoing; qu'il plaise à dieu donner la grâce de bien et dévotement recepvoir à la dernière malladie et nécessité les saincts sacrements de l'eglise; qu'il plaise à dieu donner la grâce de mourir en compaignie de gens de bien, affin qu'ils aydent à l'heure de la mort tant par leurs oraisons que par bons advertissemens et exhortations.

(May it please God to come to our aid in our last necessity so that we remember God and ourselves at the point [of death] and that understanding not fail us in our need; may it please God to give [us] the grace of receiving well and piously in final illness and necessity the holy sacraments of the Church; may it please God to give [us] the grace to die in the company of good people, so they may aid us at the hour of death both by their prayers and by their good counsel and exhortations.)[80]

To be conscious of one's approaching end, to have the time to receive the last sacrament, to have clergy and laymen, kin and friends gathered around—these were the conditions for the best death. Philippe Ariès has traced a total reversal of these attitudes in contemporary Western societies, which idealize a quick death and make a daily occurrence of solitary death.[81] Another and more superstitious fear filters through these texts: Preparing for death perhaps hastens it. This can be seen in

[79] *La Manière de faire testament salutaire*, aiii[r].
[80] Ibid., bviii[v]–ci[r].
[81] Ariès, "La Mort inversée," 171-79.

the refusal to make a will ("others believe that they would soon die if they made their testament"[82]) or to receive the sacraments. The latter prompted René Benoist, who had been named bishop of Troyes two years before, to publish in 1595 his *Considérations notables pour les Chréstiens malades, contre les pernicieuses coustumes, et les diabolicques persuasions, de ceux qui ne veulent en leurs maladies recevoir les Sacremens qu'en l'extrémité. D'où vient la mort, de l'âme et du corps, en plusieurs.*[83]

Works on preparing for death spelled out, in a normative discourse that should not be taken for a simple transcription of actual practices, all the steps the Christian need take. The first of these, the *recordation et mémoire* of death, is also the prime reason for the existence of such texts. As the *Ars* puts it, "A quoi est très expédient que chacun l'art de bien mourir fréquente diligentement et pour pense sa mort et solution" (With which it is most expedient that each [person] frequent diligently the art of dying well to take thought for his death and [for his] release). Or the Bonfons edition: "Car c'est une des choses du monde qui plus incite la créature au salut de son âme que la cogitation de la mort" (For one of the things in this world that most incites [God's] creature to the salvation of his soul is thinking about death). Or Pierre Doré:[84] "La première préparation à la mort qu'il nous a aprinse est de souvent avoir la méditation et pensée de la mort" (The first preparation for death that he [Christ] has taught us is to often have meditation and thought on death). These contemplative exercises could be bolstered by attitudes that Doré highly recommends. First, frequent reading of a work on the art of dying to provide an occasion for and give food for thought on death:

Je conseille aux Chrétiens souvent lire et relire, car c'est le pain quotidien dont fault user durant le pélerinage de ce présent siècle, affin de parvenir au terme prétendu, en la cité de Jérusalem su-

---

[82] *La Manière de faire testament salutaire*, avi[r].

[83] Born in 1521, Benoist entered the priesthood in 1553 and was made *curé* of Saint-Eustache in 1568. He was supportive of the League at the start, but nevertheless remained faithful to Henry III and Henry IV, who named him Bishop of Troyes in 1593. The Pope refused him canonic investiture, however, because of a French translation of the Bible that was condemned in 1567. Benoist resigned his bishopric, returned to Saint-Eustache, and died in 1608. On him, see E. Pasquier, *Un Curé de Paris pendant les guerres de religion: René Benoist, le pape des Halles, 1521-1608* (Paris, 1913).

[84] P. Doré, *La Déploration de la vie humaine*. Doré was born around 1500 and was a preaching friar and doctor of theology. He preached at the court of Henry II and was the confessor of Claude de Lorraine, the first Duke of Guise. He died in Paris in 1559.

pernelle, où Jésus par sa miséricorde et conduite de sa grâce nous doint à tous à la fin aborder.

(I advise Christians to read and reread [this work] often, for it is the daily bread that must be used during the pilgrimage of this world, in order to reach the desired goal in the sempiternal city of Jerusalem, where Jesus by his mercy and the action of his grace, must at the end greet us all.)[85]

Should sickness strike, the faithful would do well to hearken to Christ's Passion:

Plusieurs bons Chrétiens en leurs maladies, font lire le texte de la Passion de nostre seigneur Jésus Christ, se reconfortant en la doulce mémoire de sa mort, s'appuyant sur les bras de la Croix où sont soutenus pour ne tomber en impatience.

(Many good Christians, in sickness, have the text of the Passion of our lord Jesus Christ read to them, taking comfort in the sweet recollection of his death, and leaning on the arms of the Cross, on which they are supported so they do not fall into impatience.)[86]

Finally, in health, but even more so if the end seems near, the sight of pious images should comfort the soul: "Pour ce met on au bout du lict du malade, la remembrance de la Croix de nostre Seigneur, où comme en mirouer devant ses yeulx se mire le pauvre malade" (For this reason have someone put at the end of the sick person's bed the remembrance of the Cross of our Lord, in which as in a mirror before his eyes the poor sufferer can see himself).[87]

A variety of acts were designed to prepare for death. Suffrages and other intercessory deeds, masses, charitable donations, and fasts, which could be stipulated by testament, were also (and perhaps essentially) practices of Christian life in thought of death. The *Manière de faire testament salutaire* emphasizes both the efficacy of the masses and prayers required by the dead person and the need for the living to make of them an exercise in preparation for death:

Le tiers poinct d'un testament concerne les suffrages par lesquels on peut ayder aulx âmes des trespassés, et y en a quatre manières,

[85] Ibid., aiii[v].
[86] Ibid., 144[r].
[87] Ibid., 176[v]–177[r] and 177[v].

c'est à savoir, messes, oraysons, aulmosnes, et jeusnes, par lesquels on entend toutes oeuvres labourieuses et afflictives du corps faictes pour le remède et salut des trespassés.

(The third point of a will concerns the intercessory deeds by which one can help the souls of the dead, and there are four sorts of these: masses, prayers, charitable donations, and fasts, all of which are understood as works laborious and afflictive of the body done for the relief and salvation of the dead.)

The text goes on to warn, however, that

C'est le plus seur et le plus prouffitable de faire dire des suffrages sa vie durant que de les laisser et ordonner par testament quand la personne a puissance et opportunité de ce faire. Il est tout manifeste que c'est le plus seur de faire soy mesme que de laisser à aultruy à faire après sa mort.

(It is surer and more profitable to have prayers said during one's life than to leave and order them by testament when the person has the means and occasion to do so. It is obvious that it is surer to do oneself than to leave to others to do after one's death.)[88]

The act of making a will is, however, essential. The organization of the *Manière de faire testament salutaire* parallels the typical structure of a will. The will also gives the work its religious meaning, since each article in the *testament commun* is echoed by a provision in the *testament spirituel*. The text is divided into six sections: the recommendation of the soul to God, to Our Lady, and to the saints in Paradise; the burial; the requests for intercessory prayers; the bequests, donations, and foundations; the debts and restitutions; and the choice of executors. Doré states, with Christocentric overtones, that the "testament should be made according to the order and manner of our Lord's, so that in all and by all his death will be a lesson for our own."[89] After confession and repentance, the dying person is to draft (or have someone draft) a text, for which Doré gives a model. An invocation is part of the first article:

Au nom du Seigneur Jésus, Amen. J'ai Chrystofle Doré recommandé mon âme à Dieu, et à la glorieuse Vierge Marie, et aux

[88] *La Manière de faire testament salutaire*, bvʳ.
[89] Doré, *La Déploration de la vie humaine*, 149ᵛ.

saincts et sainctes de la cour celestielle de Paradis: Priant mon
Dieu par le mérite de son fils Jésus et de sa Passion, avec l'intercession de sa mère, et touts les saincts, pardonner à mon âme, et la
colloquer lassus en son royaume éternel, Amen.

(In the name of Lord Jesus, Amen. I, Chrystofle Doré, have recommended my soul to God and to the glorious Virgin Mary and
to the saints of the celestial court of Paradise: Praying my God by
the merit of his son Jesus and by his Passion, with the intercession
of his mother and of all the saints, to pardon my soul and gather
it above into his eternal kingdom, Amen.)[90]

I might note that, in comparison to Parisian wills from the latter half
of the sixteenth century, this text is "advanced."[91] Along with elements
common to most testaments of the time (for example, the enumeration
at the beginning or the archaic concluding formula), it introduces
Christ's merits, a formula that can be considered a litmus test for the
Catholic Reformation. Seldom encountered before 1600, this motif
pervades Parisian testamentary style in the later seventeenth century.
The first article ends with the choice of a tomb, funeral arrangements,
and the founding of commemorative services and bequests ("Let annual or anniversary masses be said or distributions be made to the poor
in the churches each year or in some other way *obits* [anniversary
masses for the rest of the soul] be founded").[92] The second article is devoted to more worldly bequests, the payment of debts, and restitutions,
while the third, more original, is an admonition to the children "on the
example left us by our Lord, who gave a long sermon to his disciples
and Apostles shortly before his death."[93]

Then came the moment of the death agony. Modifications in the arrangements for this event can be read as reflecting shifts in popular sen-
sitivities. The *Ars moriendi* gives the model for the earlier period, when
death in public was a spectacle for the edification of the living and assured helping hands to the dying. Those present played a role of capital
importance during these last moments because they seconded—or
even supplanted—the dying person in the recitation of the proper
prayers to be addressed to God, to the glorious Virgin Mary, to the

---

[90] Ibid., 150[r].
[91] Chaunu, *La Mort à Paris*, 288-329.
[92] Doré, *La Déploration de la vie humaine*, 152[r].
[93] Ibid., 154[v]–155[r].

saints and angels, to the apostles, martyrs, confessors, and holy virgins. In the engraving in the *Ars* of the moment of expiration, center stage is occupied by the monk who offers the candle, but in the text, which makes no mention of the sacraments, the most fully developed figure is the faithful friend:

> Et come ainsi soit que le salut de la personne est et consiste en son definement de ce monde chacun se doit soingneusement pourveoir d'un bon dévot sochon féal et ydoine ami qui lui assiste en ceste nécessité et conforte à constance de vraie foy pacience devotion et perseverance lesmouvant et incitant à bon devot corage et adrechement de ceur a dieu la sus sa doulce mere et cetera. Et pour priant lui feablement en son agonie et trespas et apres par bonnes orisons et commendacions pour lequel lui peut moult valoir à sa saulvacion et est pour tel assistant au moritur chose de tresgrand merite come aussi voulroit qu'on feist pour lui.

> (And since the salvation of the person is and consists in his leaving this world, each man should make careful provision for a good, pious, and loyal companion and friend to assist him in this need and urge him to constancy, to true faith, patience, devotion, and perseverance, moving him and inciting him to devout courage and to direct his heart to God above, to his sweet mother, etc. And to pray for him loyally in his agony and his death and after by good orisons and recommendations, by which he can do much for his salvation and it is for such a helper of the dying a thing of great merit, as he would have someone do for him.)[94]

This image of a large gathering, in which the clerical presence is discernible but not dominant and the dying man or woman presides over the deathbed, is the motif that unites all the preparations. It is also presented as an ideal:

> On list d'ung bon hermite lequel cognoissant qu'il devoit mourir en bref, supplia estre receu en ung convent, et pource qu'on luy faisait refus à cause qu'il etait vieulx, il leur dist: ne craignez point que je vous face charge à cause de ma vielleisse, car je mourray de bref, et ainsi ne vous chargeray longtemps. On luy dist si sa mort était ainsi prochaine pourquoy il vouloit donc estre receu au con-

---

[94] *Art au morier*, "Bien utile conclusion de ceste salutaire doctrine."

vent, A, dist-il, le passaige de la mort est si très dangereux que je
ne le veulx point passer tout seul.

(We read of a worthy hermit who, knowing he must soon die,
begged to be admitted to a monastery, and when they refused him
because of his age, he said to them: Do not fear that I will be a
charge to you because of my great age, for I shall soon die and so
will not long be in your charge. They asked him, if his death was
so close at hand, why he wanted to be received into the monastery.
Ah, he said, the passage into death is so dangerous that I do not
want to pass through it all alone.)[95]

Receiving the sacraments is accepted as a foregone conclusion in the
QS version of the *Ars moriendi*, but is is described in detail in the vernacular versions:

Après que le patient a ésté adverty et interrogué, comme dit est,
on lui doit présenter et l'admonester de recevoir les Sacremens de
notre mère Saincte Eglise. Premiérement qu'il ayt en luy vraye
contrition de cueur d'avoir tant offencé Dieu. Secondement qu'il
face entière confession de bouche en tant qu'il luy sera possible,
avec volunté de faire pénitence s'il revient à santé, ou de prendre
la mort en gré s'il plaist à Dieu de luy envoyer, en espérant d'avoir
le Royaume de Paradis: non pas par les mérites de luy mais les
mérites de la Passion de notre sauveur Jesus Christ. Des autres sacremens pareillement comme du Saint Sacrement de l'autel, qui
est le viaticque des Chrestiens: lequel tout bon chrestien qui faire
le peut doit recevoir en la fin de ses jours. Combien que aucuns de
telles maladies soient malades qu'on ne leur ose donner de poeur
qu'ils ne le vomissent: mais à tout le moins on doit leur monstrer.

(After the patient has been warned and interrogated, as we have
said, one must present to him and admonish him to receive the
Sacraments of our mother, the Holy Church. First, may he have
true contrition in his heart for having so offended God. Second,
may he make full confession from his mouth inasmuch as this is
possible for him, with the desire to do penance if he returns to
health or to take death willingly if it please God to send it to him,
in the hope of experiencing the Kingdom of Paradise: not for his
own merits but for the merits of the Passion of our savior Jesus
Christ. The same holds true for the other sacraments, like the

[95] *La Manière de faire testament salutaire,* ci[r].

Holy Sacrament from the altar, which is the Christian's viaticum: All good Christians who can do so must receive it at the end of their days. Some are sick of diseases such that one dares not give it to them for fear they will vomit it, but at the very least one should show it to them.)[96]

The sixteenth century brought shifts in certain motifs of this scenario of the arts of dying. First of all, there was a growing desire to bring order to the deathbed scene, which led to fewer people being present. The aid of Christians was still considered necessary, but it could and should take place somewhere else than around the deathbed. Doré, for example, argued for a more discreet death by drawing a distinction between the proper place for the people of God, gathered in churches, and for the few persons present in the dying person's bedchamber:

La congrégation et assemblée des Chrestiens, assemblés en la foy et oraison est une arme espouventable à nos ennemis, qui sont les diables d'enfer. Pour ce on envoye es convents, églises et assemblées, des Chrestiens pour prier pour le languissant estant au traictz de la mort.

(The congregation and assembly of Christians, gathered by faith in prayer, is a weapon awesome to our enemies, who are the devils of Hell. Thus we send Christians to convents, churches, and assemblies to pray for the man languishing in the clutches of death.)[97]

He adds, however:

En telle sorte doibt faire l'homme qui s'en va mourir, deffendant que nul viene à luy (ainsi que faisait S. Augustin lisant les pseaulmes de David si ce n'est quand on luy baillait la viande ou la médecine), seulement à l'entour de son lit doibt avoir deux ou trois qui prient pour lui, ainsi qu'estaient les trois apostres nommés, quand nostre Seigneur sua sang et eau, priant au jardin d'Olivet.

(This is what the man on the point of death should do, forbidding anyone to approach him (as Saint Augustine did, reading the psalms of David except when they came to give him meat or med-

---

[96] *Art et science de bien vivre et bien mourir*, Kiii[v].
[97] Doré, *La Déploration de la vie humaine*, 170[v].

icine); he should have around his bed only two or three who pray
for him, like the three apostles named when our Lord was sweat-
ing blood and water, praying in the Garden of Gethsemane.)[98]

By the end of the century, the clergy had been promoted to a new
role, and now the *curé*'s presence at the deathbed pushed Christian aid
into the background. Two of the *Considérations* published by René
Benoist in 1595 demonstrate this change. Consideration Fourteen
states that the Christian who is stricken with illness

> s'addressera à celuy qui a la puissance de guerir son âme, luy re-
> mettant ses péchés et en luy ministrant les Sacremens, et en priant
> pour luy selon le devoir de sa vacation, qui est son Curé Pasteur
> hiérarchique immediat.

> (will address himself to the person who has the power to heal his
> soul by remitting his sins and administering the Sacraments and
> by praying for him according to the duty of his calling, his im-
> mediate hierarchical superior, his Priest and Pastor.)

Consideration Sixteen adds:

> que le premier recours soyt à son propre Pasteur, et à sa propre
> Eglise parochiale, pour plusieurs valables raisons, toutesfois il
> n'est mauvais mais souvent bien utile y adjouster les prières des
> personnes Religieuses et dévotes, tant régulières que séculières,
> qui doyvent compatir aux maladies, charitablement estant rede-
> vables à leurs bien-faicteurs.

> (although the first recourse should be to one's own pastor and to
> one's own parish church, for several valid reasons, still it is not
> bad, but often quite useful, to add the prayers of religious and
> pious persons, both of the regular [monastic] and secular clergy,
> who must sympathize when sickness strikes out of charitable
> gratitude to their benefactors.)[99]

Thus it is clear that the fifteenth and sixteenth centuries clung to
death as a spectacle, an attachment that loosened only when death became an event of the immediate family. Nevertheless, these centuries
saw some changes, at least on the level of normative texts such as these

[98] Ibid., 171[r].
[99] Benoist, *Considérations notables pour les Chréstiens malades*, 11, 13.

works on preparation for death. The move to limit the number of people present at the hour of death appears also in the iconography: Léonard Gaultier's engraving of a deathbed scene shows both fewer people and a higher proportion of women present.[100] To measure the change, this engraving should be compared with a similar scene as treated by the miniaturist of the Grimani Breviary, whose work dates from between 1480 and 1520.[101] The other change is in the emergence of the priest. The significance of this shift is ambiguous, since it crystallized superstitious fears that it was the priest who, by signifying the imminence of death, precipitated it. At the same time, however, the absence of the *curé* came to be felt as a painful solitude.

The study of attitudes toward death at the end of the Middle Ages and during the Renaissance consisted at first—thanks to works that have rightly become great classics—in the description of a sentiment scrutinized in iconographic motifs, literary representations, or expressions of religious sentiment. This led to the tracing of the essential outlines of the discourse on death among the *majores* (elites) as well as the images proposed for the teaching of the Christian populace. Today the history of death offers three ways to build on these gains. First, there has been an attempt to annex the sixteenth century, or at least its latter half, into a serial history of testamentary discourse using contrasting sites—for example, Paris. Second, we have learned from the work of Michel Vovelle of the pertinence of a massive, homogeneous, and broadly representative source. His regressive analyses have led us to an understanding of the construction phase and the apogee of a discourse, the destructuration of which he has clearly outlined in Provence. In a third context, death has become a fully legitimate object of study for a history whose aim is the quantification of facts pertaining to civilization. I have attempted here to use bibliographic statistics to establish a ranking of works on the arts of dying within the context of the distribution of printed works during the first century and a half of printing.[102] Other standards of measurement may prove feasible, but it seems possible to state, at least as a working hypothesis, that after the

[100] Gaultier, *Suite de onze pièces*, no. 140.

[101] Biblioteca Marciana, Venice, Grimani Breviary, fol. 449ᵛ, reproduced in Boase, *Death in the Middle Ages*, 121.

[102] I would like to thank the curators of the Service de la Réserve des Imprimés at the Bibliothèque Nationale, Paris, Mme Veyrin-Forrer, Mlle Baumeister, and MM. Labarre and Toulet in particular, for their unfailing aid.

high point of the years 1450-1530, the period of the *Ars moriendi*'s greatest success, works on preparation for death both diversified their argument and underwent a decline in the book shops. Another provi-
sional conclusion—an important one if it can be confirmed—is that
guides to a good death had a less important place within incunabular
religious literature than they did during the triumph of the Catholic
Reformation. A last trail to follow in the examination of these texts is
through an anthropologic investigation of the actions and practices that
they recommend or stigmatize. Followed in this direction, the history
of death might lead beyond a history of representations to ascertain the
differences or similarities that exist between injunctions that propose a
religious norm and actual behavior patterns, often superstitious, which
we know through their condemnation. The long term is obviously the
proper scale for such studies, but significant changes can be discerned
within a general model by consulting a more compact corpus of materials. Here, for example, we have noted trends toward greater order in
the last moments of the dying, then toward the takeover of this event
by the clergy—an evolution that found its endpoint in the rich discourse of the classical age.

# CHAPTER THREE

# From Texts to Manners
## A Concept and Its Books:
### *Civilité* between
### Aristocratic Distinction and
### Popular Appropriation

I SHALL try in this essay to trace the history of a notion—*civilité*—and at the same time to reflect on the historical operations that make it possible to do so—that is, to respect the conventions of *Begriffsgeschichte* (the history of concepts) and at the same time to explicitly formulate the difficulties encountered which the very nature of the concept under consideration probably increases. The first and most obvious difficulty doubtlessly lies in the impossibility of completely circumscribing the field of study. On the one hand, even if we stress the texts that contain the most common uses of the term (dictionaries, newspapers, memoires, manuals, treatises, etc.), the corpus they make up can never be complete or self-defined. On the other hand—and this is a more serious difficulty—any notion, *civilité* included, must be considered within a semantic field that is extensive, unstable, and variable. From the middle of the seventeenth century to the Revolution, there are several semantic contexts within which we encounter the word. First, the dictionary order of words by their roots provides *civil, civilisation, civiliser, civique* (in the expression *couronne civique*). Through this topographic and etymologic proximity alone, the notion has a double connotation: It is inscribed in the public space of the society of citizens, and it stands opposed to the barbarity of those who have not been civilized. It thus appears closely linked both to a cultural heritage that connects the western nations to the history of ancient Greece, the first

This essay was originally written for the *Handbücher politisch-sozialer Grundbegriffe in Frankreich, 1680-1820*, ed. R. Reichardt and E. Schmitt (Munich and Vienna: Oldenbourg, 1986), 4:7-50. This explains its genre (the history of one particular notion), the materials involved (widely diffused works attesting to the definitions or the usages of the term *civilité*), and its limits and aims, as described hereafter.

source of civilization, and to a form of society that presupposes the liberty of the subjects in relation to the power of the state. If civility is contrasted to barbarism, it is also the contrary of despotism. In a second semantic chain, both within and outside of the dictionaries, *civil* and *civilement* belong to a series of adjectives that designate social virtues. Chronologically speaking, this series began with *honnête* and was enriched by *poli, courtois, grâcieux, affable*, and *bien élevé*. It was reinforced by adjectives related to *civilisé*, such as *traitable* and *sociable*, and somewhat later (in the dictionaries, at least) it found an antonym in *rustique*. This group of near synonyms points to another more worldly and more exteriorized realm for *civilité*, in which what counts most is the appearance of certain manners of existence. A third set is comprised of notions—*honnêteté, bienséance*, and *politesse*—that are always compared to *civilité*, either because they seem acceptable equivalents or because they are contrasted to the term. The relation of *civilité* to these three notions—the latter in particular—is quite unstable. Sometimes it has been held in higher esteem than they, at other times lower. It is this immediate environment alone that I intend to consider at present because of the insuperable practical difficulties involved in any attempt to restore the whole of the open and changing semantic field of *civilité* as it refers to ethical notions (*morale, vertu, honneur*), to social designations (*cour/courtisan, peuple/populaire*), and to basic oppositions (*public/privé*). There is an unavoidable arbitrariness in setting limits: It is impossible to avoid isolating the notion under consideration—*civilité*—from the complex set of concepts which are linked to it at any given moment by meaning, etymology, or simple phonic association, and which are present (to varying degrees) in any author's mind when he defines the term.

A second difficulty involves the very conditions of the determination of meaning. The corpus of texts on which it is possible to work necessarily gives a preponderant place to normative statements that say what *civilité* is or should be. Some treat the uses of the word within the language (dictionaries, treatises on synonyms, or texts that question accepted definitions); others enumerate practices that illustrate civil behavior without necessarily using the term (such as the treatises which, from Erasmus to La Salle, outline a code of conduct). In both cases, the process of writing about the concept tends to construct an invarying and universal meaning, preexisting and existing outside all of the particular uses that are presumed to conform with that meaning. But, as we know, a historical recognition of the meanings of notions and of the words that designate them should neither strengthen nor accept as operative the tendency to neutralize the practical uses of terms. With each use, the determination of sense comes from without, from where the speaker or the writer's disposition or intention meets with a situation or a public: from a "market" in which the proposed statement takes on a meaning as it is weighed in relation to other statements and evaluated socially.[1] In the case of the term *civilité*, this interplay of usages and these practical definitions of meanings are obviously of decisive importance, since the notion that they express, correctly formulated and correctly embodied, is supposed to earn social distinction.

Each use of the word, each definition of the notion, then, sends us back to an enunciative strategy that is also a representation of social relations. To be sure, what is difficult is to make sure that in each instance we can reconstruct the practical relationship linking the writer, the readers he presupposes and for whom he is speaking, and the actual readers who, in the act of reading, create a meaning for the text. If we were totally rigorous, such a reconstitution would suppose that we could situate each formulation of the notion within the entire array of texts that produced it, either by imitation or by opposition to the received acceptations and delimitations of the term. It would also suppose that we could fix the position of every speaker or writer, without being overly schematic, within the social and literary space of his age. Finally, it would suppose that we are capable of defining the different audiences and the contradictory ways in which they received the proposed usages—and in the case of civility, usage has a practical as well as a linguistic meaning—conforming to them or rejecting them. The analysis that follows cannot possibly satisfy all these demands. Nevertheless, by positing the opposition between wide diffusion and social distinction as central to the analysis of *civilité*, I will attempt to show that it is this social dynamic of imitation on the part of some of the ways of speaking and behaving that others held specific to their social being on which the shifting meaning of these notions was constructed and by which they were realigned each time. The relations between *civilité* and *politesse*, which were reversed on several occasions, are a good illustration of this.

One last difficulty inheres in the very nature of the notion of *civilité*

---

[1] P. Bourdieu, *Ce que parler veut dire: L'Économie des échanges linguistiques* (Paris, 1982).

73

as it designates a group of rules that take on a reality only when actions put them into practice. Here *civilité* is always expressed in terms of what should be; it aims at taking the rules of discipline and the prohibitions it enumerates and collects and transforming them into automatic and unspoken mechanisms for the regulation of conduct. *Civilité* may well provide material for long treatises; it may well be the object of contradictory pronouncements; but it still must be eclipsed as discourse, explicit or implicit, in order to become a working code at the practical level for spontaneous, largely unconscious adaptations to the diverse situations that may confront the individual. This explains the particular status of texts that claim to teach supposedly legitimate behavior. Not only must they make norms explicit; they must also suggest devices for the inculcation of those norms. In one sense, such devices lie outside the texts and are dependent on their social applications, on where they are used (in the family, in the school), and on how they are appropriated (by individual reading or filtered through the discourse of teaching). In another sense, however, they are written into the text itself, which organizes its own strategies of persuasion and inculcation. Here too, analysis of the notion is powerless to reveal all of these social or enunciative devices. Since a direct grasp of the social uses of the texts is impossible, the best we can do is to circumscribe the areas— institutional or collective—for which their authors intended them. Then, rather than providing a complete breakdown of their rhetorical structure, we can describe some of the procedures the authors made use of in order to impose new meanings, for instance the contradiction between normative definitions and examples of usage or the creation of fictive uses to serve as examples. If we accept these limits, the study of an isolated notion such as *civilité* can perhaps be assured a greater pertinence.

### DICTIONARY DEFINITIONS: DIFFERENCES AND RELATIONSHIPS

In the mid-seventeenth century, the concept of *civilité* had long been used in the language and formed an accepted part of the intellectual baggage. One way to note its meaning and its most widely shared connotations is by comparing the definitions given in three dictionaries of the French language published within a span of fifteen years: the Richelet in 1680, the Furetière in 1690, and the *Dictionnaire de l'Aca-*

*démie* in 1694. The differences among them are obvious: Richelet understands *civilité* as a body of knowledge, a "science" complete with its own rules and its treatises; Furetière defines it as a set of practices, a "manner" of being in society, that the Academy's dictionary identifies with *honnêteté* and *courtoisie*. Thus one definition accentuates the normative, bookish content of *civilité*, which can be learned just as geometry can be learned; in the other definition, the accent shifts and *civilité* is perceived as a particular comportment or way of living different from other ways. This gives the two dictionary definitions widely differing social implications. Richelet does not specify the public to which the "science" of *civilité* is addressed. In contrast, the other two dictionaries suggest that it involves socially distinctive behavior, Furetière by stating that "peasants lack *civilité*" and the Academy by specifying that the social sphere of its exercise is that admired portion of society known as *le monde*. Thus the universality—or its potential at least—of a science that all can learn is contrasted with a behavior to which not everyone can accede.

There are several elements common to all three definitions, however, which show general agreement on what the notion contains. First, in all three dictionaries *civilité* appears close if not synonymous to *honnête* and *honnêteté*, which simply heightens the tension between a moral characterization of universal application and a socially distinctive comportment restricted to certain milieux. A second trait in common is that *civilité* is to be recognized not only in actions, but also in conversation. All three works emphasize a definition of *civilité* as the art of speech in society: Proof of *civilité* lies in knowing how to "say nothing that is not honest and appropriate" (Richelet) or to have "an honest manner of conversing in the world" (Academy). Thus the concept appears closely linked to the particular social practices characteristic of civilized society. Moreover, the plural, *civilités*, reinforces this "polite society" meaning of the term, since it refers back to the customs and intercourse of a code of courtesy recognized by the higher social circles. Finally, the three dictionaries all present *civilité* as something that can be taught and learned from early childhood. This accounts for their reference to pedagogically oriented works: "Children should be taught *la civilité puérile*" (Furetière) and "it is proverbially said of a man who fails to fulfill the simplest duties that he has not read *la civilité puérile*" (Academy).

## A First Backward Glance: The Legacy of Erasmus

Through both their differences and their similarities, the dictionary definitions of the end of the seventeenth century record an early direction taken by the notion of *civilité*. In the first place, they clearly no longer repeat an older meaning that was still alive in the sixteenth century and that defined *civilité*, or rather *civilités*, as the customs and habits characteristic of a given community.² Another meaning of *civilité* that had disappeared is "the manner, ordering, and governance of a city or community" to be found in Nicolas Oresme's translations of Aristotle of the end of the fifteenth century, which defined the contrary, *incivil*, as the inability to live in society.³ Finally, dictionaries of the classical period seem unaware of the new sense that the word had taken on after 1560: It was used by such writers as Étienne Pasquier, La Popelinière, and Guillaume Le Roy to express the notion of civilization itself as a process of wresting humanity out of primitive barbarity.⁴

The principal debt that is clearly discernible in the definitions of the end of the seventeenth century is to Erasmus's treatise, *De civilitate morum puerilium libellus*, and its various translations, adaptations, and imitations. Published by Johann Froben in Basel in 1530, the work met with immense success throughout Europe.⁵ The Latin text was quickly adapted, divided into sections and provided with notes (in 1531 in Cologne by Gisbertus Longolius), cast in the form of questions and answers (in 1539 by Reinhardus Hadamarius in Antwerp), and presented as selected extracts (in 1551, also in Antwerp, by Evaldus Gallus). The work was also quickly translated: in 1531 into High German, in 1532 into English, in 1537 into Czech, and in 1546 into Dutch. The first French translation, which introduced a new meaning of *civilité* into the

---

² For example: "Those who go to Germany, where the customs and the *civilités* are different from our own, when they return, are found vulgar [*grossiers*]" (François de La Noue, *Discours politiques et militaires* [Basel, 1587]).

³ On the older use of the term, see Huguet, *Dictionnaire de la langue française du XVIᵉ siècle* (Paris, 1932), vol. 2, which gives several examples of *civilité* in the sense of city dwellers' rights or the character of the citizen (in Seyssel's translations in particular). See also Littré, *Dictionnaire de la Langue Française* (Paris, 1863), vol. 1.

⁴ G. Huppert, "The Idea of Civilization in the Sixteenth Century," in A. Molho and J. A. Tedeschi, eds., *Renaissance Studies in Honor of Hans Baron* (De Kalb, Ill., 1971).

⁵ The fundamental study on Erasmus's treatise is H. de La Fontaine-Verwey, "The First 'Book of Etiquette' for Children: Erasmus's *De civilitate morum puerilium*," *Quaerendo* 1 (1971):19-30. This corrects A. Bonneau, *Des livres de civilité depuis XVIᵉ siécle*, published in the introduction of his translation of Erasmus's work (Paris, 1877).

French language, was published in Paris in 1537 by Simon de Colines in Pierre Saliat's translation under the title *Déclamation contenant le manière de bien instruire les enfants dès leur commencement, avec un petit traité de la civilité puérile et honnête, le tout translaté nouvellement de latin en français*. Erasmus's two pedagogical texts, the *Declamatio de pueris statim ac liberaliter instituendis* and the *De civilitate morum puerilium*, were thus brought together in one volume. A second translation appeared in 1558: Published by Robert Granjon, it was the work of Jean Louveau, a Protestant sympathizer who expurgated all references to the Roman church. It was republished in Antwerp in 1559 by Jehan Bellers under the title *La Civilité puérile, distribuée par petits chapitres et sommaires, à laquelle nous avons ajouté la Discipline et Institution des Enfants* (with the Protestant, Otto Brunfels, responsible for this second text). Granjon's edition introduced a basic innovation by printing Erasmus's text in a new typeface, the *lettre française d'art de main*, which imitated cursive writing and was later known as the *lettre de civilité*. There were several other French Protestant editions of Erasmus's work during the second half of the sixteenth century. It was freely imitated by Claude Hours de Calviac under the title *Civile honnêteté pour les enfants*, which, by its reversal of noun and adjective, indicates that the two terms were originally equivalent. (This work was published in Paris by Philippe Danfrie and Richard Breton.) It was republished that same year in Saliat's translation, purged of its "Roman infection" and accompanied by Mathurin Cordier's *Miroir de la jeunesse pour la former à bonnes moeurs et civilité de vie* (published in Poitiers by the Moynes brothers). A new adaptation, anonymous and of Protestant interpretation, was published in Paris in 1593 by Léon Cavellat.

Erasmus's work marks a fundamental moment in the history of the concept of *civilité*. On the one hand, thanks to its many Latin editions (at least eighty during the sixteenth century, at least thirteen during the seventeenth),[6] it offered all of learned Europe a unified code of conduct, the realization of which was to produce *civilité* in its new definition. On the other hand, by means of its translations and adaptations, it acclimated in vernacular languages a word and a notion that from that moment on designated an essential component in the upbringing of children. Following Norbert Elias's argument, the concept of *civilité*

---

[6] According to the list (undoubtedly incomplete) of the *Bibliotheca Erasmiana: Répertoire des Oeuvres d'Erasme*, 1st ser. (Ghent, 1893), 29-34.

received its particular stamp and its function in the process of the "civilization" of western society from Erasmus's work.[7] This slim volume
was both an interpretation of changes in comportment that had already
been effected and a definition of a new ideal; it is a good indication of
the needs of a time in which the traditional rules of chivalric society
were gradually yielding before the new demands that arose from a
denser social life and a closer interdependence among men. This is why
it differs so profoundly from medieval works on comportment at table,
which centered around one social event alone—the meal—and were
directed primarily at adults of chivalric circles.

In fact, even though Erasmus dedicated his treatise to the son of a
prince, he starts from the principle that the rules it contains are meant
for all, without distinction of status:

> To such as chance to be well born it is a shame not to be of like
> manners as their progenitors were. Whom fortune wills to be of
> common sort, of low blood, or uplanders [rustics] must labor the
> more to set themselves [up] with advancement of good manners
> in that [from which] fortune has disbarred them. No man can
> choose to himself father and mother or his country, but condition,
> wit, and manners any man may counterfeit.[8]

On several occasions Erasmus rejects the aristocratic models of the age:
"It is not good manners to let out the lips and make a boo or a bah,
although great men's sons (going through a multitude) do it. They
shall be pardoned as men in whom whatsoever they do is taken as man-
nerly, but I enform children."[9] Or: "To lean upon the table with both
elbows or one of them is pardoned to them that be weak and feeble by
reason of age or sickness: The same in courtiers delicious [delicate],
that think all things well that they do. It is to be forborne and not fol-

---

[7] N. Elias, *Über den Prozess der Zivilisation: Soziogenetische und Psychogenetische Un-
tersuchungen* [1939] (Frankfurt, 1978), 1:89-109. (*The Civilizing Process*, vol. 1, *The Development of Manners: Changes in the Code of Conduct and Feelings in Early Modern
Times*, trans. E. Jephcott [New York, 1978], 70-84.)

[8] I have used the French translation of Erasmus's work by A. Bonneau, recently republished with an introduction by P. Ariès (Paris, 1977). This passage can be found on
p. 106. The *De civilitate morum puerilium* was translated into English as early as 1540
with the subtitle: *A lytell boke of good maners for children, now lately compyled, put forth
by Erasmus Roterodam in latyne tong, with interpretation of the same in to the vulgare en-
glysh tonge, by Robert Whytington Laureate poete* ... (London). This passage is on p. D3.
Spelling has been modernized in this and subsequent quotations.

[9] Ibid.: French, 63; English, A6.

lowed."[10] Unlike the medieval *courtoisie, civilitas* defines what is proper, universally, for all men. And Erasmus adds that any variation connected to mores, which change according to time and place, is acceptable only in terms of what is in itself appropriate.

Erasmian rules of *civilité* are universal because they are based on an ethical principle: In every man, appearance is a sign of his being and behavior is a dependable indication of qualities of soul and mind. Good instincts, virtues, and intelligence have but one translation, which can be seen in bearing as in clothing, in behavior as in speech. Every chapter of *La Civilité puérile* is founded on equating the visible and the invisible, the outward and the intimate, and the social and the individual in this fashion. Body positions, facial expressions, comportment in church, at table, while gaming, in society, and even clothing, which is "the form and fashion of the body" and permits us to "conjecture the habit and apparel of the inward mind"[11] are thus not simply regulated by the demands of a life governed by relations with others (which might justify the existence of codes particular to each milieu); they have a moral value that leads Erasmus to consider them from an anthropological, not a social, point of view.

Although Erasmus's work marks a decisive moment in raising the threshold of modesty, in calling for controls on emotions, and in requiring the repression of impulses, it does not do so by referring to the lifestyle (actual or wished for) of a particular social group. It does all these things in order to teach morality to children. This turned *civilité* into an initial learning experience and Erasmus's treatises into textbooks for primary instruction—often for use in schools. This was already the case with Claude Hours de Calviac's free imitation of 1559, the complete title of which was *Civile honnêteté pour les enfants, avec la manière d'apprendre à bien lire, prononcer et écrire qu'avons mise au commencement*. It was even more true of the widely circulated editions of the Troyes printers, who coupled *civilité* with the rudiments of learning. One such work was published by Nicolas II Oudot in 1649 under the title *La Civilité puérile et honnête, pour l'instruction des Enfants. En laquelle est mise au commencement la manière d'apprendre à bien lire, prononcer et écrire. Revue, corrigée et augmentée des Quatrains du Sieur de Pibrac.*[12] In this way, *civilité*, childhood, good manners, the rudiments of learning, and elementary morality were tenaciously connected.

---

[10] Ibid., 80; B7.
[11] Ibid., 71; B3.
[12] The first Troyes edition of *La Civilité puérile et honnête* seems to have been Gir-

A SECOND BACKWARD GLANCE: THE LEGACY OF
*La Politesse Mondaine*

This first basis for references and usages in the late seventeenth century ran counter to another tradition that defined *civilité* as a part of proper social manners (*la politesse mondaine*).[13] During the first half of the century, the notion seems to have faded away: The word disappeared from titles, which emphasized instead the concepts of propriety (*Bienséance de la conversation entre les hommes*, 1617), honor (Antoine de Balinghem, *Le Vrai point d'honneur à garder en conversant, pour vivre honorablement et paisiblement avec un chacun*, 1618), or uprightness (Nicolas Faret, *L'Honnête homme ou l'art de plaire à la Cour*, 1630). These treatises share two characteristics. First, their models are Italian. The *Bienséance de la conversation* is a Jesuit adaptation for the use of their students of Giovanni della Casa's *Galateo*, which was published in 1558 and republished many times in French or bilingual editions. *L'Honnête homme* is directly inspired by Castiglione's treatise, *Il corteggiano*, and Stefano Guazzo's *La civil conversatione*. Second, these texts aim above all at drawing up rules for conduct in a specific social milieu—the court—and within a particular order of society—the nobility. As a result, these texts turned away from Erasmian universality to find their place in a literature that attempted, from the beginning of the seventeenth century on, to organize life at court and to inculcate new norms of comportment for gentlemen.[14]

When the notion of *civilité* reappeared, it bore some of these same marks, although it was not limited to the definition of courtly behavior alone. Antoine de Courtin's *Nouveau traité de la civilité qui se pratique en France parmi les honnêtes gens*,[15] a veritable bestseller that went through fifteen editions between 1671 and 1730, shows this clearly. In it, the author returned to the Erasmian tradition for this sort of litera-

---

ardon's of 1600. The Nicolas II Oudot edition is the second known and the earliest still available (BN, Paris, Res pR 117). See A. Morin, *Catalogue descriptif de la Bibliothèque bleue de Troyes (Almanachs exclus)* (Geneva, 1974), nos. 127-46 (pp. 67-74), no. 137 *bis* (p. 483).

[13] M. Magendie, *La Politesse mondaine et les théories de l'honnêteté en France au XVIIᵉ siècle, de 1600 à 1660* (Paris, 1925).

[14] Among others, Nerveze's *La Guide des Courtisans* (1606) and *Le Courtisan français* (1611) and Du Refuge's *Traité de la Cour* (1616).

[15] I have used the Amsterdam edition of 1708. For an English translation, see *The Rules of Civility: or, Certain Ways of Deportment Observed amongst all Persons of Quality upon Several Occasions* (London, 1685).

ture. The work is directed primarily if not exclusively at the "instruction of young people" and is founded on a moral definition of *civilité* that gives it universal application: "Civility proceeding essentially from Modesty, and Modesty from humility, which stands, like the rest of the Virtues, upon unshakeable Principles, 'tis certain, though Custom may change, Civility will not, and he will always be civil that is modest, and he will always be modest that is humble."[16] Linked in this way to a major Christian virtue—charity—*civilité* must necessarily concern every man, whatever his rank or quality. It is, in fact, what distinguishes man from the animals and what constitutes the quintessence of his nature: "Reason does naturally dictate, that the farther we keep from the practice of Beasts, the nearer we come to that perfection to which nature directs."[17]

In spite of these premises, however, *civilité*, according to Courtin, must be strictly regulated in conformity with the scale of social conditions—which brings us back to the inspiration of the treatises on *politesse mondaine*. For him, conformity to the rules of *civilité* implied exact observance of "four circumstances": "Our own age and condition. The quality of the person with whom we converse. The time. And the place of our Conversation."[18] Thus the manners and the postures to be assumed closely depend upon the status of the persons involved (young gentlemen should not have the same manners as members of the clergy or magistrates) and upon the relations existent between them. In fact, the same gestures, the same stance, take on a totally different value according to the rank or the relationship of the protagonists. On familiarity, for example:

Betwixt equals, if their acquaintance has been long, familiarity is commendable: if their acquaintance has been little, their familiarity ought to be less: but where there has been no acquaintance, it will be rude to be familiar. From an inferiour to a superiour, though their acquaintance has been great (without express Command) familiarity is indecent, but where there has been no acquaintance it would be brutish and insolent. From a superiour to an inferiour, familiarity is not only tolerable, but obliging.[19]

[16] Ibid.: French, 297; English, 300.
[17] Ibid., 13; 14.
[18] Ibid., 4; 4.
[19] Ibid., 15-16; 16-17.

In principle both Christian and universal, *civilité* thus differs in its execution, and it offers as many varieties of appropriate behavior as there are states or situations. This is what Courtin calls *contenance*, by which he means the agreement of "the good disposition within" with the "graceful comeliness without" or the "harmony of passion and the person with the thing, the place, and the time."[20] We should note that a similar tension between the universal and the particular underlies the definition of point of honor which follows that of *civilité* in the Amsterdam edition:

> Here are the different sorts of point of honor. The first, which is the point of honor according to nature, is common to all men. The second, which is the point of honor according to profession, is particular to each one of us. And the third, which is the point of honor according to religion, is common to all Christians.[21]

Courtin distinguishes seven "professions" or "employments," each of which must regulate its group conduct by norms particular to it: the prince, the magistrate, the man of war, the merchant, the artisan or the peasant, the clergy, and women.[22]

## "Baroque" *Civilité*, or the Tensions between Appearance and Existence

Interpreted according to social order, the notion of *civilité* thus came to have an ambiguous status during the seventeenth century. It quite naturally entered the heroic vocabulary to describe the ordinary conduct of royalty in tragedy. Corneille, who was fond of the word, bears testimony to this. *Civilité* reigns in obligatory relations between the great:

> Ne parlez pas si haut: s'il est Roi, je suis Reine,
> Et vers moi tout l'effort de son autorité
> N'agit que par prière et par civilité.

[20] Ibid., 224; 2, 286 ("For our outward behavior in general, that is best that declares the sincerity and uprightness of the Heart" and "Comity and Affability are the Ornaments of Converse, and declare one a lover of Mankind, and argue a good harmony and concord of the Passions").

[21] Ibid., 272 (French).

[22] Ibid., 264-66.

(Do not speak so haughtily: If he is a king, I am a queen,
and toward me all the effort of his authority
acts only by prayer and by civility.)[23]

Or, again:

> Non, non: je vous réponds, Seigneur, de Laodice;
> Mais enfin elle est Reine, et cette qualité
> Semble exiger de nous quelque civilité.

> (No, no: I can vouch for Laodice, my lord;
> but after all she is a queen, and that rank
> seems to demand some civility of us.)[24]

However—and this is a departure from the treatises of *civilité* that postulate a parallel between manners and feelings—*civilité* in Corneille does not necessarily indicate truth in sentiments. Princes owe courtesy to princes, but this courtesy can often be an appearance or a mask to disguise and deceive. In *Héraclius* it conceals the hatred and the resentment that Pulchérie feels for Phocas:

> J'ai rendu jusqu'ici cette reconnaissance
> A ces soins tant vantés d'élever mon enfance,
> Que tant qu'on m'a laissée en quelque liberté,
> J'ai voulu me défendre avec civilité.
> Mais puisqu'on use enfin d'un pouvoir tyrannique,
> Je vois bien qu'à mon tour il faut que je m'explique,
> Que je me montre entière à l'injuste fureur,
> Et parle à mon tyran en fille d'empereur.

> (I have to this extent requited
> The care with which thou boastest thou hast reared me,
> That as long as I have been left free
> Have courteously [with civility] declined to do thy will.
> But since thou usest now a tyrant's power,
> I see I must in turn explain my stand,
> Lay bare my whole heart to thy rage, and speak
> To my oppressor as an emperor's daughter.)[25]

---

[23] Laodice in *Nicomède* (1651), 1.2.148-50.
[24] Prusias in ibid., 2.4.736-38.
[25] *Héraclius* (1647), 1.2.109-16, in Lacy Lockert, trans., *Moot Plays of Corneille* (Nashville, 1959), 70.

Twenty years later, in *Othon*, similarly courtly manners clothe totally contrary sentiments in Camille, who loves Othon, and Othon, who does not return her love:

> Mais la civilité n'est qu'amour en Camille,
> Comme en Othon, l'amour n'est que civilité.

> (But all Camille's courtesy [civility] is love,
> While Otho's love is only courtesy.)[26]

*Civilité*, then, does not necessarily signify the agreement of "the good within" with the "graceful comeliness without," as Antoine de Courtin would have it. When it is a code of manners appropriate to the great, it can be a countenance that, far from expressing the entire individual, can dissimulate or disguise the intimate reality of his inmost sentiments.

This might lead to criticism of the notion. Far from being a sure indication of the qualities of a soul, *civilité* came to be understood as a possibly deceptive appearance or a purely conventional courtesy that conceals ill will. This can be seen in Molière. In *George Dandin*, the lesson of *civilité* that Madame de Sotenville gives her son-in-law cruelly underscored the social distance between the enriched peasant and the country gentry:

> Madame de Sotenville. Mon Dieu! notre gendre, que vous avez peu de civilité de ne pas saluer les gens quand vous les approchez!
> George Dandin. Ma foi! ma belle-mère, c'est que j'ai d'autres choses en tête, et . . .
> Madame de Sotenville. Encore! Est-il possible, notre gendre, que vous sachiez si peu votre monde, et qu'il n'y ait pas moyen de vous instruire de la manière qu'il faut vivre parmi les personnes de qualité?
> George Dandin. Comment?
> Madame de Sotenville. Ne vous déferez-vous jamais avec moi de la familiarité de ce mot de "ma belle-mère," et ne sauriez-vous vous accoutumer à me dire "Madame"?

> (Mad. de S. Good Heavens! son-in-law, it shows little civility not to bow when you come near people!

---

[26] Flavie in *Othon* (1665), 2.1.426-27, in Lockert, *Moot Plays*, 270.

Dan. Upon my word! mother-in-law, I have other things in my head, and . . .

Mad. de S. Again! Is it possible, son-in-law, that you know so little of what is proper? Is there no way of teaching you how to behave among persons of quality?

Dan. What do you mean?

Mad. de S. Will you never give up using towards me that word "mother-in-law," it is so colloquial: cannot you accustom yourself to call me "Madam"?)[27]

Dandin is unaware of the courtesy that an inferior owes his superior, to use Courtin's terms, and this very ignorance is the outward sign of his social and cultural condition. But, on the other hand, the Sotenvilles' *civilité* is entirely exterior, and it covers up their self-seeking interest (they have sold their daughter to someone whose money could be "found very useful in stopping many a large gap"), arrogance, and spiteful credulity. We find the same split between the appearance of manners and the real truth at another social level in *Le Bourgeois Gentilhomme*. For Monsieur Jourdain, blind to everything and ridiculed, nobility of condition and of customs must necessarily go hand in hand:

Que diable est-ce là! ils n'ont rien que les grands seigneurs à me reprocher; et moi, je ne vois rien de si beau que de hanter les grands seigneurs: il n'y a qu'honneur et que civilité avec eux, et je voudrais qu'il m'eût coûté deux doigts de la main, et être né comte ou marquis.

(What the devil is this? they are continually sneering at me about great seigneurs; while I can see nothing so fine as to frequent great seigneurs: they live in an atmosphere of honour and civility. To have been born a count or a marquis I would willingly have sacrificed a couple of fingers.)[28]

But Count Dorante's *civilité* is nothing but a mask for lies, deceitfulness, and scorn. Here again, there is total disagreement between seeming and being.

The treatises on *civilité* were quite conscious of this divergence,

---

[27] *George Dandin* (1668), 1.4, in A. R. Waller, trans., *The Plays of Molière* (Edinburgh, 1907), 6:13.

[28] *Le Bourgeois Gentilhomme* (1670), 3.14, in Waller, *Plays of Molière*, 7:177.

which undermined the notion itself. Antoine de Courtin, for example, devoted an entire chapter to the opposite of *la civilité*, which he defines not as *incivilité* but as false *civilité* or *la mauvaise civilité*. This bad *civilité* results from "two extreams into which we are in great danger to fall": excessive complaisance and excessive scruples. The second occurs when "we are too scrupulous and nice, making our selves Slaves to our suspicion, and disquieting our selves to that degree that we become ridiculous to other People by our formality and exactness." Such timorousness "implies meanness of Education, and savageness of Nature"; it runs counter to *civilité* which "ought to be free, natural, neither affected nor precise."[29] Even when it has been learned, *civilité* must keep the appearance of naturalness, and thus it serves to distinguish those in whom it seems to be an inherent trait of character from their favor-currying and clumsy imitators.[30] The other fault responsible for the degeneration of *civilité* lies in making "blind and superfluous Complements." *Civilité* in this case becomes flattery, which is a sure indication of "base and selfish minds."[31] Excessive *civilité* or an exaggerated politeness are thus sure signs of lowness and self-interest, not of gentility and respect. Obviously, Antoine de Courtin is trying here to preserve two of the underlying principles of the treatises on *civilité*: on the one hand, the parallel postulated between visible comportment, manners, and the qualities (or the flaws) of the soul, and on the other, the idea that true or just *civilité* cannot be the mask of an evil nature. When he concedes that an excess of *civilité* risks passing off a sentiment for something it is not and thus deceiving and abusing people, however, Courtin gives faithful expression to the uncertainty that infiltrated the notion during the second half of the seventeenth century, when its meaning was less clear than dictionary definitions might lead us to believe.

The concept of *civilité* stands at the very heart of the tension between appearance and existence that epitomizes baroque sensitivity and etiquette.[32] The *civilité* of the seventeenth century, poles apart from a con-

[29] Courtin, *Nouveau traité de la civilité*, 240-41 (English trans., 281-83).

[30] On an aristocratic naturalness that makes acquired manners pass for inborn, see Elias, *Über den Prozess*, 2:425-27 (*The Civilizing Process*, vol. 2, *State Formation and Civilization*, 312-15); P. Bourdieu, *La Distinction: Critique sociale du jugement* (Paris, 1979), 380-81.

[31] Courtin, *Nouveau traité de la civilité*, 239 (English trans., 282).

[32] P. Beaussant, *Versailles Opéra* (Paris, 1981), 22-28.

ception that perceived outward behavior as an exact and necessary translation of the disposition of one's inner being, is best understood as above all a social seeming. Every man must strive to be as he seems, and thus adjust his moral nature to the appearances demanded by his position in the world. A double danger threatens this unstable equation: Either the individual fails to act as his rank and the circumstances demand—and for this Antoine de Courtin coined the neologism *la décontenance*[33]—or he fails to have sentiments that conform with his visible behavior. Then *civilité* becomes pretense; it changes from a legitimate representation to a hypocritical mask.

If *civilité* posed a problem even for the treatises that claimed to codify its rules, it was also the object of critiques radical enough to make its very foundations crumble. For Pascal, for example, the human heart is always lying and the soul always inconstant:

> Man is then only disguise, falsehood, and hypocrisy, both in himself and in regard to others. He does not wish any one to tell him the truth; he avoids telling it to others, and all these dispositions, so removed from justice and reason, have a natural root in his heart.[34]

*Civilité*, like all other behavior in polite society, takes on the mask of a courtesy that is mere falsehood and trickery. The foundations on which it rests, which insist on an agreement between acceptable outward behavior and true sentiments, were thus undermined. On the other hand, manners are powerless to translate dispositions of the soul, which are inconstant and always changing: "Things have different qualities, and the soul different inclinations; for nothing is simple which is presented to the soul, and the soul never presents itself simply to any object. Hence it comes that we weep and laugh at the same thing."[35] Man's instability, a sign of his miserable condition, destroys the other requisite of *civilité*, which is to show the world the constancy of a naturally good character. At best, then, *civilité* can be little more than a custom, which, like other customs, "should be followed only because it is custom, and not because it is reasonable or just."[36]

[33] Courtin, *Nouveau traité de la civilité*, 230.
[34] *Penseés*, trans. W. F. Trotter (New York, 1941), no. 100.
[35] Ibid., no. 112.
[36] Ibid., no. 326.

## ORDER AND CHRISTIANIZATION: *Civilité* ACCORDING TO JEAN-BAPTISTE DE LA SALLE (1703)

Jean-Baptiste de La Salle was fully aware of the crisis that had struck the notion of *civilité* when he published *Les Règles de la Bienséance et de la Civilité chrétienne divisé en deux parties à l'usage des écoles chrétiennes* in Reims in 1703.[37] The preface explicitly declares that a "purely worldly and almost pagan" *civilité* must be distinguished from any *civilité* that can be called Christian. The former is founded on *l'esprit du monde* and is guided exclusively by a concern for reputation. It aims at obtaining a completely external sort of esteem by avoiding the ridicule that accompanies inappropriate deportment. La Salle rejects this urbane *politesse* and its motivations as they appeared in such treatises of the late seventeenth century as Ortigue de Vaumorière's *L'Art de plaire dans la conversation* (Paris, 1688), the Abbé Morvan de Bellegarde's highly successful *Réflexion sur ce qui peut plaire ou déplaire dans le commerce du monde* (Paris, 1688), or his *Réflexions sur le ridicule et sur les moyens de l'éviter* (Paris, 1696). In contrast to Pascal's radicalism, La Salle values *civilité* as more than simple decorum, provided that it is founded on "the spirit of the Gospel." Then it becomes a way of paying homage to God: Keeping a modest and decent bearing is to respect His perpetual presence; being civil and forthright with others is to render honor "to the members of Jesus Christ and to living Temples animated by the Holy Spirit." *Civilité* thus becomes both *honnêteté* and piety, and it concerns "the glory of God and salvation" just as much as it does social decorum.

For Jean-Baptiste de La Salle, as for those before him, this notion is founded in the relation between behavior and the soul manifested in that behavior. In complete conformity with the Erasmian tradition, one's "air" is taken as a sure index to one's "mind": "We often know, said the Sage, by what appears in a person's eyes what he has in the bottom of his soul, and how great is his goodness or his bad disposition."[38] But Christian *civilité* illustrates another, more fundamental relationship: Since man is a creature in the image of the Creator, the respect man owes himself and others is thus identified with the reverence

---

[37] I cite from the 1703 edition in the form of *Les Règles de la Bienséance et de la Civilité chrétienne. Reproduction anastatique de l'édition de 1703*, Cahiers Lasalliens 19 (Rome, n.d.).

[38] Ibid., 16.

toward God present in every being. Because of this, all human conduct must recall, in some way and in spite of its imperfection, the qualities of eternal God:

> Since [the Christian] is of high birth, because he belongs to Jesus Christ and is the child of God, who is the sovereign Being, he must have nothing and show nothing lowly in his exterior, and everything about him must have a certain air of elevation and of grandeur and must in some way reflect the power and majesty of God, whom he serves and who has given him his being.[39]

*Civilité* manifests and honors the divine perfections that are deposited in every man:

> Since we must consider our bodies as living temples, in which God wishes to be adored in spirit and in truth, and as tabernacles that Jesus Christ has chosen for his dwelling place, we must also, in view of these beautiful qualities that they possess, bear them much respect; and it is this consideration that must lead us most particularly not to touch them, and not even to look at them without an indispensable necessity.[40]

Speaking of the need for neatness in dress, La Salle repeats the same comparison:

> Negligence in clothing is a mark that either a person pays no attention to the presence of God, or that he has insufficient respect for Him; it also lets everyone know that he has no respect for his own body, which we must honor as the living temple of the Holy Spirit and the Tabernacle in which Jesus Christ has the goodness to accept often to take his rest.[41]

*Civilité* in La Salle, founded anew on "purely Christian motives" and therefore on universal motives, nevertheless returns—and with great rigidity—to the social distinctions that governed acceptable behavior in the treatises of urbane courtesy. The definition of Christian *bienséance* given in his preface is a good example of this. It begins by clearly equating deportment in the world and Christian virtue: "Christian *bienséance* is thus a wise and disciplined deportment that one dem-

---

[39] Ibid., 3.
[40] Ibid., 43.
[41] Ibid., 61-62.

onstrates in one's discourse and outward actions through a sentiment of modesty or respect, or of union and charity toward one's fellow man." But listen to the end: ". . . paying attention to the time, the place, and the persons with whom one is conversing, and it is this *Bienséance* toward one's fellow man that is properly called *Civilité*." This definition repeats, practically word for word, the "circumstances" of Antoine de Courtin. It also turns out to be close indeed to other, not necessarily Christian definitions, such as this one from a treatise that appeared in Amsterdam in 1689:

—What is *civilité*?
—It is an honest way of living one with another by which we render agreeably to each person, in [various] times and places, what is due him according to his age, his condition, his merit, and his reputation.[42]

In point of fact, Jean-Baptiste de La Salle quite scrupulously respects the social differences that determine conduct. Appearance must indicate not only the divine part of man of the qualities of his soul, but also his rank: "It is of no less consequence that the person who has a suit made consider his condition; for it would not be fitting that a pauper dress like a rich man, and that a commoner want to be clothed like a person of quality."[43] Furthermore, in each of the "common and ordinary actions" examined in the second part of the book, social distinctions are to guide people's behavior, at table as on promenade, during a visit as on a trip. Even as they claim to teach a modesty identified with the law of God and a sense of propriety that is sincerity and charity, La Salle's *Règles* are also a training in social order and an introduction to a world in which gestures of *civilité* are to express clearly understood social relations. It is not enough, then, to act in conformity with one's own condition; we must judge, in each situation, the respective social quality of other people so that differences between them can be respected accurately.

Jean-Baptiste de La Salle's treatise is an essential text in tracing the fortunes of the concept of *civilité*. Written explicitly for the use of schoolchildren in the classes of the Brothers of the Christian Schools (where they crowned the reading program), his *Règles* were also used

[42] *De l'Education de la Jeunesse où l'on donne la manière de l'instruire dans la Civilité comme on la pratique en France* (Amsterdam, 1689), 5.
[43] La Salle, *Les Règles de la Bienséance*, 60.

in other schools that imitated the Brothers' pedagogy. Republished many times during the eighteenth century,[44] these rules were perhaps one of the most efficacious agents for the implantation of elite models of comportment among the lower echelons of society.[45] While they Christianized the foundations of *civilité*, the rules also offered to a large juvenile audience from many levels of society norms of conduct that were new, constraining, and demanding.[46] What was important was to rein in what La Salle on several occasions refers to as "sensuality," to impose mastery of impulses and censure of affectivity on the greater part of the population. Understood in these terms, *civilité* deviates from the aristocratic use of the term, which confined it to the enunciation of the norms of a social appearance, and it becomes a permanent and general means of control over all behavior, even in private. There is little doubt that this difference in definitions reflected the lasting opposition between the elegance of the *hommes du monde*, of which only the judgment of their peers could approve, and an ethic, fashioned by pedagogues born of the middle class and taught among popular milieux, which strove to embody an all-powerful discipline, governing even men's solitude.

## *Civilité* in the Eighteenth Century: Diffusion and Decline

During the eighteenth century, the notion of *civilité* had a double and contradictory destiny. The charitable schools and books with large print runs spread the notion among broader and broader milieux, inculcating ideas both on how to live better and how to act in society. In the literature of the elites of this period, however, it came to be criticized, discredited, and stripped of its vitality. A double process was at work: The elite gradually abandoned the traditional signs of their distinction just as this increased dissemination led others to assume them.[47] The various editions of *La Civilité* published by the Troyes

[44] The collections of the Bibliothèque Nationale and of the Maison généralic of the Institut des Frères des Écoles Chrétiennes include twenty editions of La Salle's work, ranging in date from 1703 to 1789.

[45] Elias, *Über den Prozess*, 1:136. (*The Civilizing Process*, 1:101.)

[46] On the spread of the charity schools and on their clientele (almost exclusively drawn from the common people), see R. Chartier, M.-M. Compère, and D. Julia, *L'Éducation en France du XVIᵉ au XVIIIᵉ siècle* (Paris, 1976), 77-84.

[47] Elias, *Über den Prozess*, 1:135. (*The Civilizing Process*, 1:127.)

printing houses played an essential role in this diffusion.[48] After the Girardon edition of 1600 and that of Nicolas II Oudot in 1649, the little book took on its definitive form at the beginning of the eighteenth century, combining the text on *civilité*, which was approved 2 June 1714, with a treatise on orthography, approved 15 October 1705. Under the cover of these approvals, various permissions to publish were accorded: to Jacques Oudot's widow in September 1714, to Etienne Garnier in June 1729, to Jean IV Oudot in June 1735, and to Pierre Garnier in May 1736. (This last permission covered a half dozen editions by his widow and his son Jean.) All these editions bore the same title: *La Civilité pué-rile et honnête pour l'instruction des Enfants. En laquelle est mise au commencement la manière d'apprendre à bien lire, prononcer et écrire, de nouveau corrigée et augmentée à la fin d'un très beau Traité pour bien apprendre l'orthographe. Dressée par un Missionnaire. Ensemble les beaux préceptes et enseignements pour instruire la Jeunesse à se bien conduire dans toutes sortes de Compagnies.* The only difference was that in the Oudot editions *civilité* was "puérile et honnête," whereas in the Garnier editions it was merely "honnête." Editions of the beginning of the nineteenth century—those of Sainton in 1810, of the Widow André in 1822, 1827, and 1831, or of Baudot—bore nearly the same title.

One of the Widow Garnier's editions of *La Civilité honnête* can serve as an example for them all.[49] Here the notion is founded in religion. On the one hand, the constraining rules of *civilité* are there to correct, as far as possible, the sinful nature of man:

The Education of Youth is assuredly of the greatest consequence after the corruption of our nature through the sin of our first Father. Man is so miserable that he produces nothing but evil on his own. Thus it is not enough to teach nothing evil to Children or to show them no bad examples to make them good; we must uproot in them all that is worthless.[50]

On the other hand, as with Jean-Baptiste de La Salle, *civilité* is held as a Christian virtue, not a worldly one:

---

[48] In 1781, Garnier the Elder had more than 3,500 copies of *La Civilité puérile et honnête* in stock, either ready for sale "in sheets and not assembled" or in press (Archives Départementales de l'Aube, 2E, 3 January 1781).

[49] BN, Paris, R 31 784, no. 127 of Alfred Morin's catalogue.

[50] Ibid., 5.

The reading of this book will not be useless to you, my dear Children; it will teach you what you owe to God, at least concerning your outward actions, and it will instruct you in the manner in which you must comport yourselves with your fellow man to render him all the duties of *civilité* to which Christian charity obliges you.[51]

Defined in this manner, a training in *civilité* relies on a dual pedagogy: parental upbringing ("Thus, Fathers and Mothers, you see your indispensable obligation to take great care of your Children: . . . make them learn the rules of proper behavior and make them practice them") plus the imitation of examples ("Still, you must note, my dear Children, that the shortest route to becoming an *honnête homme* is to haunt *honnêtes gens* and to pay attention to their ways of acting, because examples have much more effect on our minds than words").[52]

The Troyes editions of *La Civilité*, which circulated like the other titles of the *Bibliothèque bleue* in hundreds of thousands of copies, aimed at inculcating, recognizing, and encouraging the imitation of the appropriate gesture. They taught people both how to conduct themselves without scandal and how to find their place on the social scale. From the Nicolas II Oudot edition of 1649 through the editions of the eighteenth century, there is a clear increase in the importance given to social differences in the definition of acceptable deportment. In the middle of the seventeenth century, the Troyes editions of *La Civilité* showed traces of the Erasmian model, the organization of which they followed, treating successively bearing and dress, comportment in church, meals, encounters and conversations, games, and bedtime ritual. A century later, the book opened with the two obligations held to be fundamental: toward God and toward superiors—fathers and mothers, masters and mistresses, the clergy, the elderly, and "persons constituted in dignity." Furthermore, the text molded its precepts on several occasions to the social position of the protagonists: "Faults against *honnêteté* are all the graver when the persons you offend are considerable or are close to you" and "Pay heed to the persons with whom you converse: make it your business to know their conditions and to study their humors." Similarly, another chapter is entitled "The

[51] Ibid., 3.
[52] Ibid., 6, 4.

manner of Qualifying the persons to whom one Speaks, and the proper Closing of Letters." In its most widely circulated editions, then, *La Civilité* stressed social distinctions, which had in all instances to be correctly decoded and carefully respected. The book enabled those of humble extraction to comprehend the code of behavior that had expressed, from the beginning of the seventeenth century onward, the inequality of social conditions and power relations[53] and that, correctly interpreted, assigned every man to his rightful place.

As *civilité* was taught to the people, it lost status in the eyes of the elite. First of all, its meaning shrank to become equated with the urbanity necessary to encounters, visits, and conversations. In his *Synonymes français*, Gabriel Girard defined the word in terms of the circumstance of the encounter: "We are civil in the honors we render to those whom we happen to meet." Thus he distinguishes *civilité* from *honnêteté*, which is the observation of the rules of life in society, and from *politesse*, which should rule all ordinary relations with one's fellow men.[54] In point of fact, the most common usage of the word here refers to the consideration required between persons who are not on familiar terms and who respect the conventions of social exchange. Thus Jean Buvat reported gravely in his *Journal*: "This [Turkish] ambassador was lodged with his retinue at the mansion for ambassadors extraordinary in the rue de Tournon, where, after he had been escorted to the apartment reserved for his use, he reaccompanied M. le Maréchal d'Estrées to his carriage, by which he observed the same *civilité* practiced in France between distinguished lords."[55] And thus the *Journal* of Charles Collé reported ironically: "It is said that an officer was recently attacked as he returned from dining by a man in a dressing gown with a pistol in his hand. Unable to resist this urgent *civilité*, the officer gave up his sword, his tobacco case, and his watch."[56]

Throughout the century, when *civilité* retained a positive sense it was understood merely as a "social virtue" that made commerce between men agreeable. In his *Dictionnaire philosophique* Chicaneau de

[53] On the political utilization of etiquette and good manners, see O. Ranum, "Courtesy, Absolutism and the Rise of the French State, 1630-1660," *Journal of Modern History* 52 (1980):426-51.

[54] G. Girard, *Synonymes français, les différentes significations et le choix qu'il en faut faire pour parler avec justesse* (3d ed., 1740), 221-22.

[55] J. Buvat, *Journal de la Régence, 1715-1723*, ed. E. Compardon (Paris, 1865), 221.

[56] C. Collé, *Journal et mémoires sur les hommes de lettres ... 1748-1772*, ed. H. Bonhomme (Paris, 1868), 1:117.

Neuville defined the word thusly: "It consists in mutual regard, which usage and the difference in ranks and conditions have established. *Civilité* is also the demonstration of our sentiments, obliging toward our peers by means of our gestures and our bearing."[57] Fifteen years later, Father Joseph-Romain Joly proposed a variation on the same theme:

> *Civilité* is an ease or a good grace with which we receive those who come to us and we approach persons with whom we wish to converse. This virtue makes us take on an agreeable and modest countenance, without pride and without affectation. Those who make a point of being civil graciously salute those who greet them, show them a serene face, answer them softly, and speak to them with an affable air, avoiding all sharp or biting rejoinders, and by this means they attract the confidence of everyone.[58]

*Civilité* here is completely detached from any reference to qualities of the soul or the divine in man and is understood simply as an urbane virtue and a condition for an agreeable social life, since the enjoyment of all depends on the affability and the good temper of each. In this minimal sense, *civilité* came to be identified with the patience toward others necessary to tolerable relations among men: "Let us suffer one another mutually; this is what constitutes true *civilité*," Father Joly concludes.

Shrunken in certain texts to the urbanity indispensable to meetings and conversations, the term is completely depreciated in others. We can see this in the entry of the *Dictionnaire de Trévoux*, which ran unchanged in the editions from 1723 to 1743. At first sight, the definition of *civilité* could not be more classical: It is a "forthright, soft-spoken, and polite manner of acting and conversing together." The terms are the very same as those in dictionaries of the end of the seventeenth century and will still be found in the 1777 edition of the *Dictionnaire de l'Académie*. When we read the twelve examples given, however, we see that the notion can no longer be reduced to this first positive and normative statement, which generalizes the neutralized sense of the term. Two of the citations criticize excessive *civilité*, which tends to importune others or attract bothersome people. In seven others, the very foundations of *civilité* itself are undermined. It no longer appears as the

[57] D. P. Chicaneau de Neuville, *Dictionnaire philosophique, ou introduction à la connoissance de l'homme* (Lyons, 1756), 45.

[58] Father J.-R. Joly, *Dictionnaire de morale philosophique* (Paris, 1771), 1:147.

sincere expression of a naturally good character, but is guided by an interest in one's reputation ("*Civilité* is often merely a desire to pass for polite and a fear of being regarded as a wild and ill-mannered man"—Abbé Esprit); by a desire for reciprocity ("*Civilité* is a desire to receive the same and to be esteemed polite in certain occasions"—La Rochefoucauld); by a self-seeking interest ("It is quite difficult to distinguish flattery from *civilité* in society's politeness"—Scudéry); or, at the very least, by the enjoyment of a superior position ("Those who have been raised to the first ranks should lower themselves in some manner by their *civilités*, in order to enjoy their preeminence"—Malebranche). "To pass for," "being regarded as," "to be esteemed": *Civilité* does not belong—or no longer belongs—to the order of truth, but to that of reputation. It has no inherent identity, but is defined by the regard and the judgment of others. And, as it happens, those others are not perfect and are easily deceived by masks: "*Civilité* is certain jargon that men have established to hide the bad sentiments they have for one another" (Saint-Evremond); "*Civilité* is nothing other than a continual commerce of ingenious lies for mutual deceit" (Fléchier); "How many secret hatreds are covered by the appearances of an affected *civilité*!" (Fléchier). Only three examples of usage run counter to this depreciated meaning of a self-seeking, dissimulating, hypocritical *civilité*. The first, which is the oldest in date, still retains something of the notion's positive qualities: "*Civilité* is like beauty; it begins and ties the first knots of society" (Montaigne). The two other examples show only the weakened sense that likens respect of *civilité* to pleasure in social commerce: "*Civilité* has augmented among us as, little by little, *politesse* has entered into it" (de Caillières); "The true *esprit du monde* has discovered the art of introducing a certain familiar *civilité* that makes society agreeable and convenient" (Saint-Evremond). In contrast to the first definition given above, the uses of the term *civilité* cited by the Jesuits of the *Dictionnaire de Trévoux* illustrate, for the most part, the discrediting of a notion that, for them, had lost its ethical roots and its religious backing. Being and seeming were now totally separated, and when *civilité* was equated with an amiable courtesy that demanded no authenticity of feeling, the rupture was complete.

### *Civilité* Reformulated

The article in the *Encyclopédie* entitled "Civilité, Politesse, Affabilité," written by the Chevalier de Jaucourt, records this shrinkage and depreciation.[59] *Civilité* here is merely a "portion" of courtesy, actuated negatively (the fear of being regarded as ill-mannered) and shaped by the social condition of those who respect or should respect it ("the greater number" or "persons of an inferior condition" in contrast to "those of the court"). *Civilité* is thus characteristic of the lowest echelon of two parallel hierarchies: that of the estates and that of manners. Jaucourt makes clear the double process of diffusion and discrediting that had changed the usage of the term: *Civilité*, with its tight, constraining network of precepts and prohibitions, had been imposed on a growing number of milieux. By this same token, it had lost its value as a distinctive feature of "the better people," who had turned away from it and, rejecting its tiresome formalism, defined a different and freer code of conduct known as *politesse*. The *Encyclopédie* acknowledges that *civilité* has been inculcated among "the greater number" and that is had become a norm for conduct among the people. It shows that this social depreciation, expressed through a criticism of useless and tiresome formalities, had led persons of quality to define another model, the spontaneous nature of which agreed better with the value aristocrats put on "natural," unstudied manners.

In Jaucourt's text, the description of this change of direction is accompanied again by a portrayal of hypocrisy that attacks *civilité* and *politesse* alike: "Without necessarily emanating from the heart, they give the appearances of [doing so] and make man seem outwardly as he should be inwardly." The concept of *civilité*, however, if recast and reformulated, can rise above its accepted usages, which confine it within the world of deceiving appearances and usurped reputations. Jaucourt continues: Two conditions define *civilité* "taken in the sense that one should give to it," not the sense of the present times. The first demands that marks of respect and the regard due others must be rooted in the truth of inner feeling. The second, less traditional and taken directly from Montesquieu (*L'Esprit des Lois*, Bk. 19, chap. 16), is to consider the obligations of *civilité* as a visible expression of the reciprocal dependence that connects men one to another. Following Montesquieu, Jaucourt ends his article by citing China as a perfect example of a country in which *civilité*, manifested as the fundamental social bond, had been regulated and imposed by the legislator. This citation of a state in which the laws, customs, and manners had been merged in

[59] *Encyclopédie ou Dictionnaire raisonné des sciences, des arts et des métiers* (Paris, 1753), vol. 3.

a common code represents the most radical attempt to recast the concept of *civilité*. It also brought it back to something approaching its original, communitarian, and political meaning as *civilitas*.

In point of fact, there were some who tried to restore the validity of this much decried notion on the basis of the two conditions stated in the *Encyclopédie* article. François Vincent Toussaint, for example, took as his point of departure the criticism (which had become common) of a hypocritical *civilité* and reversed its terms:

> In vain do clowns, and cynics, declaim against civility; in vain do they represent it, as an imposing, hypocritical commerce, which serves only to mask our true sentiments. Let them really have, as they ought, that affection in their hearts, which well-bred people express by reciprocal signs; then their civility will not be imposture.[60]

Admitting that sentiment no longer always agrees with manners ought not to present *civilité* as an artificial "assortment of grimaces";[61] quite to the contrary, it should legitimize the necessity for *civilité* since "affecting outwardly virtuous dispositions is to confess that one ought to have them in his heart." To be sure, the rules of *civilité* formed for Toussaint "a ceremonial, agreed upon and established by mankind." It was a set of arbitrary signs that varied from one nation to another and were in no way based on reason. Thus we are far from the normative tradition that, from Erasmus to La Salle, used prohibitions and injunctions to define the right gestures, the appropriate attitudes, and the obligatory deportment that was universally applicable to inclinations and the manifestation of sentiments alike. But here it is not the code itself that is determined by necessity, but the respect of a code, whatever it might be; for it is this subjection to usage that is capable of arousing the virtues that it is supposed to manifest. People should have "that affection in their hearts which well-bred people express." Having once expressed the soul, *civilité* here has become a practical training in morality. Therefore the social defense of "well-born people," whose authority and dignity risk being weakened by the devaluation of the

---

[60] The citations in this paragraph are from F. V. Toussaint, *Les Moeurs* [1748] (Amsterdam, 1760), 384-87, and quoted from the English translation: *Manners: Wherein the Principles of Morality, or Social Duties ... are Described ...* (2d ed., London, 1751), 255.
[61] P. A. Alletz, *L'Esprit des journalistes de Trévoux* (Paris, 1771), 1:427.

notion that designates their manner of being, must be based on a restoration of an ethical nature.

The rehabilitation of the concept of *civilité* was based on the same text of Montesquieu that Jaucourt had used. Cited with varying degrees of exactitude, the comparison between *civilité* and *politesse* found in the *Esprit des Lois* became a commonplace during the last decades of the century: "*Civilité* is in this respect preferable to politeness. Politeness flatters the vices of others, and *civilité* keeps us from bringing our own to light. It is a barrier that men place between one another to keep from corrupting each other" (19:16). Taken over in the *Encyclopédie* article, this passage can be found in many other works, for example in the *Encyclopédie des pensées, maximes, réflexions sur toutes sortes de sujets* of Pons Augustin Alletz, published in 1761 (p. 72), or in the *Dictionnaire critique de la langue française* of Father Jean-François Féraud, which appeared in 1787 (1:454). This passage met with success mostly because it reversed the relationship that usage had established between *civilité*, discredited because of its widespread diffusion, and *politesse*, exalted as the new norm for aristocratic behavior. Furthermore, it gave clear expression to the connection between control of individual emotions and the proper order of society. By concealing and censuring the vices of human nature, *civilité* is not, as its detractors believed, a deceitful mask for immorality; rather, it fulfills the indispensable function of policing morals. Positively, it signifies the interdependence of men in society; negatively, it prevents the contagion of corrupt mores. In this way, the passage from Montesquieu designated with great acuity the social space in which *civilité* operated: The tightening of men's interdependence, linked to an increased differentiation of social functions, implied a newfound mastery of everyone's conduct and the powerful self-control of individual manifestations (here, the exhibition of vices) that threatened to weaken the fabric of community.[62] Even though *civilité* does nothing to modify the nature of sentiment and cannot make man better in his heart, it is nevertheless necessary, since by imposing severe inner constraints, it guarantees disciplined social relations protected from violence and corruption.

Obviously, the figure of Jean-Jacques Rousseau stood behind both the attempt to rehabilitate the idea of *civilité* and the continued success

---

[62] For this reading of the Montesquieu passage according to Norbert Elias's categories, see Elias, *Über den Prozess*, 2:316-17. (*The Civilizing Process*, 2:232-34.)

of Montesquieu's text. Rousseau, in fact, was disturbing in more ways than one. First, he discredited the usages of urbane society and the pronouncements of opinion, which were worthless when judged by the standard of natural human sentiments; and second, he himself, in his conduct as well as in his books, showed precious little respect for the code of good manners. In Book 4 of *Émile*, the young pupil's entry into the world is the decisive moment of a confrontation between polite society's accepted rules for living and a natural behavior inspired by the heart and by reason.[63] Rousseau contrasts, term for term, the conventions and customs that make society misjudge Émile, who is held to be maladroit and ignorant, with the truth of sentiments (goodness, frankness, good will, etc.) that, in return, morally discredit the pretense of "the world." Rousseau's critique is sweeping: He at once strikes at the root of pedagogical habits (a "stock of precepts" is worthless in comparison with the free blooming of a virtuous nature), the customs of "proper" society ("Émile will be, if you like, an agreeable foreigner" in a society that holds norms he refuses to recognize), and the hierarchies of convention ("No one could be more attentive to every consideration based upon the laws of nature, and even on the laws of good society; but the former are preferred before the latter, and Émile will show more respect to an elderly person in private life than to a young magistrate of his own age").

Rousseau, who did so much to destroy the notion of *civilité* as it was understood by the society of his time, was himself viewed as the very picture of an uncivil man. Louis Sébastien Mercier, among others, echoed society's judgment of a man who, like Émile, "cares too little for the opinions of other people to value their prejudices." In volume 11 of his *Tableau de Paris*, Mercier evokes Rousseau in these terms:

> The debt of *civilité* that everyone owes his fellow man is thus evident. An author of our own times who has long failed to pay this tribute brought on himself universal enmity, and the sharp darts of his criticism worked more against himself than the fine shafts of his writings worked to do him honor. He should inconvenience himself a little in his pronouncements to avoid inconveniencing others.[64]

[63] J.-J. Rousseau, *Émile ou De L'Éducation* [1762] in his *Oeuvres Complètes* (Paris, 1969), 4:665-70. (*Émile*, trans. B. Foxley [New York, 1966], 300-304.)

[64] L. S. Mercier, *Tableau de Paris, Nouvelle édition* (Amsterdam, 1782-1788), 11:188-89.

It is precisely this social utility of the notion of *civilité* that Mercier treats on the chapter he devotes to the question in volume 1 of his work (pp. 302-303). Here *civilité*, qualified as an "ingenious lie," is praised for facilitating agreeable encounters and for censuring "petty and vile passions." As a social virtue, it does not in the least presuppose moral qualities or psychological dispositions in those who practice it. Thus a gap is set up between the familiar sphere, where traits of character are known in their true forms, and the social sphere, where internalized constraints dictate civilized conduct: "When people meet, they show their better side, and the hideous surface of their character will be unveiled in the domestic scene, before eyes that have become accustomed to it or are made to withstand this trial." For the division within the individual, torn between impulse and constraint, affect and censure, there is a corresponding division that delegates to the conscience all that must remain hidden in social intercourse. Far from receiving moral condemnation, appearance is here esteemed for the same social advantages as fine dress: "A light robe thrown over morality is thus perhaps as necessary as clothing is to man's physique."

## Founding a Republican *Civilité*

With the Revolution, this sort of justification of *civilité* was no longer acceptable, and the texts that defended the notion now based it on totally different values. First, however, the relation between *civilité* and *politesse* needed to be completely reformulated. This is what Pierre-Louis Lacretelle does, for example, when he examines *politesse* in the *Dictionnaire de l'Education*, added to the fourth volume of Charles-Joseph Panckoucke's *Encyclopédie méthodique*.[65] This text, which appeared in 1791, proposed a totally new demarcation between the senses of *politesse*, considered here as a language, and *civilité*, held to be a disposition of the mind and the heart, a "virtue which is the first and the most charming of all the social virtues." While *civilité* supposes unvarying and universal sentiments—a "general good will" to be found, at least in theory, in all men—*politesse*, which is the expression of this *civilité*, varies with time and place, depends on national customs, and dictates conventional gestures of no intrinsic necessity. Thus to teach *ci-*

---

[65] C.-J. Panckoucke, *Encyclopédie méthodique ou par ordre de matières*, vol. 4, *Logique et métaphysique* (Paris, 1791), 694-98.

*vilité* is not to inculcate arbitrary manners, which all will discover through usage, but to inscribe the sentiments of humanity in the heart of the child:

> To tell you my thoughts freely, as long as children do not act from stubbornness, pride, or some other evil principle, it matters little how they take their hats off or how they bow and curtsy. If you can teach them to love and respect other men, they will find a way, when they have reached the right age for it, to show it obligingly to all men, according to the manners to which they have become accustomed.[66]

Detached from the network of obligations and prohibitions that had characterized it, *civilité* is seen here as a major virtue, a guarantee of and emanation from all other virtues, since it presupposes respect of others, good will, modesty, and beneficence. Its opposite, for Lacretelle, is no longer bad manners but a series of vices that produce *incivilité*: "the natural ferocity that makes a man pitiless toward other men," "scorn or lack of respect," "the critical spirit" that leads to mockery or contradiction, the "overnicety that is shocked at the least thing." From this point of departure, Lacretelle proposes a radical break with traditional education, substituting the ideal of a training in virtues, which will always find adequate expression in words, for the rote repetition of gestures held to be appropriate but that imply no necessary reality in the sentiments they are supposed to manifest. Thus *civilité* becomes basically moral instruction.

It was on this foundation that a *civilité républicaine*, totally different from the *civilité* that dictated the manners of the old society, struggled toward definition during the revolutionary years. The first difference between the two was that the new *civilité* presupposed and fostered liberty. Louis-Marin Henriquez described *civilité* in these terms in a treatise published in Paris in Year III entitled *Principes de la civilité républicaine destinés à l'enfance et à la jeunesse sous les auspices de J.-J. Rousseau*. The work is presented in the form of conversations between a father, Ariste, and his two children, Prosper and Adèle:[67]

[66] Ibid., 697.

[67] This selection is from pp. 39-40 (BN, Paris, R 38 384). L.-M. Henriquez, Professor at the *collège* of Blois, published in Year II his *Épitres et évangiles du républicain pour toutes les décades de l'année à l'usage des jeunes sans-culottes*, a work that won a prize in Germinal of Year IV in a competition for elementary school textbooks decreed by the

Ariste. *Civilité*, which insists on a reciprocal regard that, like natural law, prescribes that we do nothing to others that we would not want them to do to us, *civilité*, I say, leads man to want and to maintain his liberty.

Prosper. Papa, the men who lived before liberty, didn't they know *civilité* at all?

Ariste. I could answer you yes without fear of being mistaken. In a despotic regime *civilité* is constrained and virtues are rare. A few men, however, console nature for the disgrace into which their fellow men are plunged.

True *civilité*, inseparable from liberty, is equally inseparable from equality. Again in Year III, citizen Gerlet opens his *Civilité républicaine* in this fashion: "The level of Equality in no way excludes the regard that men owe to one another."[68] Four years later, in another *Civilité républicaine*, this time from the pen of Chemin, there is a distinct contrast between the inegalitarian etiquette of a society divided into orders and the natural morality of the age of equality:

> In the age in which men esteemed one another and were esteemed only by their power, their rank, or their wealth, a good deal of study was needed to know all the shades of deference and courtesy to be observed in society. Today there is only one rule to follow in the intercourse of life, which is to be free, modest, firm, and loyal with everyone.[69]

law of 9 Pluviôse Year II. In Year III he published both his *Civilité républicaine* and his *Histoires et morales choisies pour chaque mois de l'année républicaine* (according to J. Morange and J.-F. Chassaing, *Le Mouvement de réforme de l'enseignement en France, 1760-1798* [Paris, 1974], 121-27).

[68] Citizen Gerlet, *La Civilité républicaine contenant les principes d'une saine morale, un Abrégé de l'Histoire de la Révolution et différents traits historiques tirés de l'Histoire romaine, suivis d'un vocabulaire de la Langue Française. Ouvrage essentiellement utile et agréable aux jeunes Citoyens de l'un et l'autre sexe, et propre à leur faire aimer et pratiquer les vertus* (Amiens, Year III). (Institut Pédagogique National, Paris, 40213 *bis*.)

[69] Chemin, *La Civilité républicaine contenant les principes de la bienséance puisés dans le monde, et autres instructions utiles à la jeunesse* (Paris, Year VII). Neither the Bibliothèque Nationale nor the Institut Pédagogique National has a copy of this booklet, but it is described and cited in C. Nisard, *Histoire des livres populaires ou de la littérature de colportage depuis l'origine de l'imprimerie jusqu'à l'établissement de la Commission d'examen des livres de colportage* (2d ed., Paris, 1864), 394-95. The author is probably the same as the Chemin *fils* who published in Year II an *Alphabet républicain* and *L'Ami des jeunes patriotes ou catéchisme républicain dédié aux jeunes martyrs de la liberté* (see Morange and Chassaing, *Le Mouvement de réforme*, 136).

The obligations of republican *civilité*, then, were in no way to be governed by differences of condition or position, but only by natural inequalities based on age or degree of kinship.[70]

Based in liberty and in conformity with equality, this recast *civilité* was at last to reconcile qualities of soul with outward appearances. The discovery of this accord, which the old, artificial, and deceitful *politesse* had failed to achieve, underlies all the exchanges between Ariste and his children.

> Adèle. Papa, tell us what *civilité* is . . .
> Ariste. My children, it is a virtue that establishes a pleasurable, honest commerce among men and that communicates through polite manners, without falsehood and without affectation. Not only does it compose a citizen's outward appearance; it also guides his soul and makes a social being of him.[71]

Henriquez states, in a typically Erasmian formula, that one's face must be clean because it is "the symbol of the soul." He adds, however, in a more revolutionary vein, that the forehead should remain uncovered because "a free man should have a clear [brow]." Moreover, the virtues that *civilité* demands—frankness, temperance, vigilance, justice, etc.—are the virtues that strengthen a republican nation, a nation that "recognizes no head other than itself and no other power than that of the people, and of which all the institutions are directed to the general good." As with Lacretelle, *civilité* is raised here to the status of the republican virtue *par excellence*, embracing all other virtues essential to the new form of government.

In all these works on the *civilité républicaine*, the ultimate guarantee of the new morality is a Supreme Being, whose existence is asserted in opposition to atheists and doubters. Gerlet, for example, states: "A secret and sweet penchant brings us to admit a Supreme Being, to love our fellow man, to respect old age, to educate the young well, to esteem virtue, to honor merit, in short, to hate vice." In another passage Gerlet repeats the images found in La Salle's *Règles*:

> We model ourselves after [the Supreme Being] toward ourselves and toward our fellow men: first, toward ourselves, by respecting

---

[70] A similar reorganization according to age classifications and familial roles marked festivities. See M. Ozouf, *La Fête révolutionnaire 1789-1799* (Paris, 1976), 223-33 (forthcoming in English).

[71] Henriquez, *Principes de la civilité*, 7-8.

our own body, which is like a vessel in which God has enclosed our soul, the image of his Divinity. We take pleasure in adorning our body with virtues, in making it a temple worthy of our soul, [so that] this emanation of his Divinity need not blush at its dwelling place.[72]

Henriquez's God derives from Rousseau rather than from Christianity: The existence of a Supreme Being "sovereignly and infinitely perfect in its virtues and in its works" and the immortality of the soul are the principles of a natural religion that founds republican morality. The works on *civilité* of the revolutionary period thus share the deism of two other groups of moralizing works: republican catechism manuals, which abounded in Years II and III,[73] and patriotic almanacs, which also spread a Rousseauean defense of a natural and civil religion.[74] But works on *civilité* were far outweighed by these other works, as if the word remained a prisoner of its former meaning and the genre was confused with the manuals of etiquette for the society that had been abolished.[75] The few texts that do exist, however, clearly show a desire to revolutionize the notion by giving it a new definition that was republican and deist, egalitarian and moral, free and natural.

The old formalities were firmly refused. For Lacretelle, as we have seen, how a man raised his hat or bowed was of little importance, and true *civilité* had nothing to do with the rules and precepts that previously codified it. Traditional etiquette was rejected just as firmly in the political sphere. One good example of this can be seen in an article in the *Révolutions de Paris* of January 1792 entitled "The *Incivilité* of the Executive Power."[76] The author of the article denounces the king's poor reception, in the Tuileries, of a deputation from the National Assembly that was bringing him a decree to sign: "Only one panel of the door was opened, and the orator was practically the only one admitted

---

[72] Gerlet, *La Civilité républicaine*, 12-13.

[73] Morange and Chassaing, *Le Mouvement de réforme*, 169-72, cite nine printed works and ten manuscripts in Years II and III entitled *catéchisme* and destined for the primary schools.

[74] G. Gobel and A. Soboul, "Audience et pragmatisme du Rousseauisme: Les Almanachs de la Révolution (1788-1795)," *Annales Historiques de la Révolution Française* 234 (1978):600-40. The authors list 81 patriotic almanacs of various tendencies.

[75] I might also cite *La Véritable civilité républicaine* (Paris, Year III) of citizen Prevost (Institut Pédagogique National, Paris, 40214, unfortunately lost).

[76] *Révolutions de Paris, Adressées à la Nation et au District des Petis Augustins*, no. 133 (21-28 January 1792):179-80.

into the prince's *cabinet*; the rest waited outside the door." Such conduct, a "marked *incivilité*," was to be condemned, above all, because it was an outward sign of the power relations of the *ancien régime* rather than of relations between the representatives of a sovereign people and a delegated, salaried king: "Must we advise our representatives that a national assembly is not a *parlement*, nor a *Cour des Aides*, nor a *Chambre des Comptes*, and that it is essential that our deputies remain equal to the high charge we have given them?" For the journalist of the *Révolutions de Paris*, the previous forms of etiquette, defined and imposed by the will of the monarch, were no longer acceptable and had to be rejected as the relics of a humiliating dependence. Abolishing the ceremonial that had regulated public life meant the definitive destruction of one of the means by which the absolutist state, from Richelieu onward, had "forced sovereign courts to its will, broken the officers, subjected peoples."[77] The new political equilibrium demanded other practices and a different public *civilité*, one that precluded "for one minute leaving kings with the idea that the people are dependent on them."

## 1800–1820: Popular Civilities and Bourgeois Proprieties

By the beginning of the nineteenth century, very little of this aspiration to a revived *civilité* remained in the notion as it circulated. First of all, the booklets on *civilité* for mass distribution were identical to those that the Troyes printing houses had published in the previous centuries.[78] In a great many cities, *La Civilité* was republished with its text largely unchanged since the approval of June 1714. Modifications were minor: Occasionally a new title was proposed (as in the case of the volumes printed in Lille during the Empire entitled *Nouveau traité de la Civilité Française pour l'instruction de la jeunesse chrétienne*) or the *lettre de civilité* typeface—now difficult to read—was abandoned in favor of roman characters. In certain cities there was a tradition, somewhat in-

---

[77] See Ranum, "Courtesy, Absolutism and the Rise of the French State."

[78] For the beginnings of an inventory, which describes the collection of the Bibliothèque Nationale, see M. Calais, *Répertoire bibliographique des manuels de savoir-vivre en France* (Conservatoire National des Arts et Métiers, Institut National des Techniques de la Documentation, 1970, typescript).

dependent of the Troyes version of the work, that continued into the beginning of the nineteenth century. In Rouen, for example, printers republished under the title *La Civilité honnête en laquelle est mise la manière d'apprendre à bien lire, prononcer et écrire, et mise en meilleur ordre qu'auparavant* a text approved in 1751 that shortened, retouched, and reorganized a version originally published in the mid-seventeenth century by Nicolas II Oudot. Similarly, several new editions of La Salle's *Règles* were printed for the use of both boys' and girls' Christian schools. Between 1804 and 1820 twenty editions emerged from the presses of Paris, Rouen, Reims, Evreux, and Charleville.[79] It is undeniable, then, that during the first two decades of the nineteenth century this longstanding material spread, perhaps on an unprecedented scale and both inside and outside of the schools, the most classical form of a Christian notion of *civilité,* which was founded on and respectful of an inegalitarian idea of social order.

During the same period, normative definitions of the term returned to the mid-eighteenth-century meanings that had lost their validity. Thus Benoît Morin, in his treatise on synonyms published in 1802, reestablished a strict hierarchy that subordinates *civilité* to *politesse*. *Civilité* is inferior to *politesse* from three points of view: socially, since "a man of the people, even a simple peasant, can be civil," whereas *politesse* is particular to the man of the world; culturally, since *civilité* is compatible with a bad upbringing, while *politesse* presupposes an excellent upbringing; and morally, since *civilité* is nothing but a conventional ceremonial compared to the fineness of sentiment and delicacy of mind characteristic of the polite man.[80] The equilibrium between the two notions achieved by texts like Montesquieu's and Lacretelle's and by the works on republican *civilité* was thus totally reversed. Faced with the wide circulation of the notion of *civilité* among the people, *politesse* was once more valued as a means of distinction, now based on an equivalence, given as self-evident, among natural qualities, cultural mastery, and social superiority.

To be sure, some texts, faithful to Rousseau, pleaded that training in *civilité* should be above all moral instruction:

---

[79] According to the list of the principle known editions given in La Salle, *Les Règles de la Bienséance*, iii-xii.

[80] B. Morin, *Dictionnaire universel des synonymes de la langue française* (2d ed., Paris, 1802), 290-94.

We must never separate the principles of morality from the rules of *civilité*: Each lesson in *politesse* that we give children must correspond to a moral rule and be based on it . . . for any rule of *civilité* that does not have a moral principle at its base and is the fruit of caprice or of some singularity becomes a vain superfluity.[81]

The majority of the manuals that determined to break with the precepts and the antiquated language of the Troyes text and its imitations, however, had no such point of view. *Civilité* was defined in the new manuals as a set of rules that made relations between men agreeable and easy. Thus we return to the restricted, minimal sense of *civilité* of the beginning of the eighteenth century, which saw it as an urbane virtue that facilitated life in polite society. This is what we see in the small volume published in 1812 in which Madame de Sainte Lucie leads the conversations. "My children," she states, "*civilité* is the manner of acting and speaking in the world with *honnêteté* and *bienséance*. . . . It forces men to give one another outward signs of esteem and good will, which maintain pleasantness and peace among them."[82] Attention is concentrated on these "outward signs" that are to be made—or withheld—in society. Abandoning the ethical and civic ambitions of the revolutionary years, *civilité* henceforth is understood as the code of good manners necessary in the world and as the nomenclature of the "usages of good company."[83] Thus for the entire century *civilité* was established as identical with bourgeois propriety.

Between the sixteenth and the nineteenth centuries, then, the history of the notion of *civilité* was one of shrinkage and increasing insipidity. In spite of several attempts to find a new base for the concept or to reformulate it—for example at the end of the *ancien régime* or during the Revolution—it gradually lost the ethical and Christian status of its beginnings and came to signify no more than training in and respect for the manners appropriate to social relations. In two sorts of texts—booklets on usage that enumerated precepts without necessarily defining them and collections of ideal definitions that situated the term

[81] Dubroca, *La Civilité puérile et honnête à l'usage des enfants des deux sexes. Nouvelle édition* (Paris, n.d. [early nineteenth century]), 43-44.

[82] Madame de Sainte Lucie, *Civilité du premier âge* (Paris, 1812), 6-7 (BN, Paris, R 19189).

[83] *Civilité en estampes, ou Recueil de gravures propres à former les enfants des deux sexes à la politesse et aux usages de la bonne compagnie* (Paris, n.d. [early nineteenth century]) (BN, Paris, R 31781).

among such closely related notions as *honnêteté*, *politesse*, and *biensé-ance*—the definition of *civilité* as discipline predominated. Cut off more and more from its foundations in anthropology, religion, or politics, *civilité* delineated for some (the greater number) the elementary rules on how to behave in society. For others, it represented conduct that gave immediate access to *savoir-vivre*. Caught between seeming and being, between the public and the private, between imitation and exclusivity, the concept of *civilité* followed an itinerary, from Erasmus to the Restoration treatises, that tells of a desire, which may or may not have been realized, to install constraints always thought of—and always rejected—as discriminatory.

# CHAPTER FOUR

# From Words to Texts
## The *Cahiers de doléances*
## of 1789

THERE are few collections of documents that have been more thoroughly investigated than the statements of grievances drawn up for the convocation of the Estates General in 1789. The first systematic reading of these documents was made in the latter part of 1789, when a three-volume *Résumé Général* of the *cahiers de bailliage* (the final step in the reporting process) attempted to give an accurate picture of the grievances as they were submitted at Versailles.[1] After their political urgency had passed, the *cahiers de doléances* were approached in two different ways. Some have used them to draw up an accurate picture of the kingdom more somber than the one reflected in official administrative documents. As the title of Edme Champion's short study of 1897 indicates,[2] this mass of grievances sanctioned a somewhat dismal description of the state of France on the eve of the Revolution. In this view, the various reports, taken in the aggregate, seem to reveal the real situation in the kingdom, and the *cahiers* are used, basically, as a document of social history. In contrast to this "objective" reading of the *doléances*, which takes them at face value as true statements, the second approach takes the *cahiers* as omens of things to come. There is, in fact, a great temptation to read these texts, written in March or April of 1789, in light of the events of the following summer. Neither Cochin

This study was originally published in *Sozialgeschichte der Aufklärung im Frankreich*, ed. H. U. Gumbrecht, R. Reichardt, and T. Schleich (Munich: Oldenbourg, 1981), 2:171-99. It appeared in French in the *Revue d'Histoire Moderne et Contemporaine* 28 (1981):68-93. It owes much to the study carried on at the École des Hautes Études en Sciences Sociales by François Furet, Julien Brancolini, Maria Flandrin, and Edna Lemay. My thanks to François Furet for permission to use results of this collective research, in part unpublished, in this chapter.

[1] *Résumé Général ou Extrait des Cahiers de Pouvoirs, Instructions, Demandes et Doléances, remis par les divers Bailliages, Sénéchaussées et pays d'États du Royaume, à leurs Députés à l'Assemblée des États Généraux ouverts à Versailles le 4 mai 1789, par une Société de Gens de Lettres*, 3 vols. (Paris, 1789).

[2] E. Champion, *La France d'après les cahiers de 1789* (Paris, 1897).

nor Tocqueville escaped this temptation to retrospective history; both viewed the *cahiers* as predictive, either because they saw them as profoundly imbued with subversive ideology or because the accumulated demands for reform reached the point where they brought on the ruin of the existing order. In this view, the *cahiers de doléances*—and indeed the entire eighteenth century—are read in terms of a predestined outcome, the Revolution.

My interests lie elsewhere. Taking my cue from recent studies that have focused on the 1789 *cahiers*, I see them as documentary material particularly appropriate to a study of opinion. My aim is not only to draw up an inventory of the ideas most widespread at the time and a listing of the major preoccupations found in the *cahiers*; I also intend to investigate the ways in which those ideas were expressed and written down. The *cahiers* provide an extraordinary opportunity to do so, both through their number (nearly thirty thousand) and their hierarchical structure. Since every assembly at every level of the consultation process was to report its own grievances, the *cahiers* give a highly fragmented picture of opinion, permitting distinctions between the rural areas (in the *cahiers des paroisses*) and the cities (in the *cahiers* of guild and communal groups, of *habitants libres*, and of cities) and also between the *assemblées primaires* and the *assemblées des bailliages*, both secondary and principal.[3] This massive but highly differentiated corpus lends itself to two sorts of questions: First, can the *cahiers* provide pertinent data on the cultural stratification of French society at the end of the eighteenth century? Second, do they reflect the language or the ideas of the Enlightenment? And if so, to what extent and with what reservations? In order to answer these questions, we first need to define, in cultural terms, the social groups that were most influential during this referendum process and that, more often than not, had a hand in the writing of the *cahiers primaires*, the first round of reports. We then need to inventory these reports on the basis of their form, their content, and their vocabulary before we can test two fundamental hypotheses: First, the *cahiers* from cities and towns differed from the ones drawn up in the country; and second, at the level of the *cahiers de bailliage*, the grievances of the nobility and of the bourgeoisie closely resembled one another.

---

[3] A fundamental work on the procedures for the soliciting and the drawing up of the *cahiers* is A. Brette, *Recueil des documents relatifs à la convocation des États Généraux de 1789*, 4 vols. (Paris, 1895-1915).

ANY ATTEMPT to interpret the 1789 *cahiers* sends us back to a prior question, however: Under what conditions were they drawn up? Even more important, precisely what groups took charge of writing the reports (since they controlled the procedures for their solicitation)? Exceptional cases apart, the majority of men had little voice in the *cahiers primaires*; we hear instead what Alphonse Dupront has called "a state of confrontation, in reality extraordinary, between what was set down in writing and the grievance that in all probability was spoken or expressed in terms different from those of its written version and, at the least, differently endured."[4] Who were these "translators," then, and what did they translate? A detailed examination of the mechanisms of the referendum may offer a tentative answer to this dual question.[5]

At all levels of the consultative process, one social group appears predominant: the royal or seigneurial *officiers* (officials and officeholders) and men of the law—lawyers, notaries, and attorneys. In the first place, these were the ones who often presided over village council meetings (the *communautés*) in rural areas. Altogether, the legal profession accounted for 98.5 percent of the presiding officers of such assemblies in the *bailliage* of Orléans, 90 percent of those in the *sénéchaussée* of Draguignan, and 77 percent of those in the *bailliage* of Troyes. This overwhelming preponderance conformed with article 25 of the electoral law of 24 January 1789, which stipulated that every primary assembly must be presided over by the local judge or, failing that, by a public official. It is interesting to note that this injunction was interpreted differently from one place to another. Often it was followed to the letter, as in Troyes or Draguignan, where such presiding officers were for the most part seigneurial officials, for example judges, *procureurs fiscaux* (seigneurial prosecutors), *baillis*, or *prévôts*. In other places the legal profession predominated, as in Orléans, where sixteen notaries, seven attorneys (*procureurs*), and two lawyers (*avocats*) presided over nearly 90 percent of the rural assemblies. In still other places, for example in the *bailliages* of Rouen and Nancy, the *communautés* ignored the royal

---

[4] A. Dupront, "Formes de la culture de masses: De la doléance politique au pèlerinage panique (xviiᵉ-xxᵉ siècle)," in *Niveaux de culture et groupes sociaux*, Acts of the colloquy held on 7-9 May 1966 at the École Normale Supérieure (Paris and The Hague, 1967), 150.

[5] F. Furet, "Les États Généraux de 1789. Deux bailliages élisent leurs députés," in *Conjoncture économique, structures sociales. Hommage à Ernest Labrousse* (Paris and The Hague, 1974), 433-48.

decree and designated their own presiding officer (*syndic or consul*) as president of the assembly. This gesture of mistrust of seigneurial authority does not seem to have been the rule, however, and the leadership of rural assemblies was generally taken on by men of law (*robins*). Thus in the *bailliage* of Salers in Haute-Auvergne (to pick one example), of thirty-four primary assemblies held between 3 March and 16 March, twenty-three were presided over by the local judge, seven by a royal notary, two by royal *officiers*, one by a burgher, and one by the *syndic* of the municipality.[6]

The presidential role brought many advantages to these officeholders and men of the legal professions, particularly when they held multiple presidencies. Cases of doubling up abounded. To cite two examples: In the *bailliage* of Baume in Franche-Comté, the *juge châtelain* (judge of the seigneurial court) of the Blamont district presided over nineteen assemblies, the royal notary of Servin presided over eleven, and the notary of Bonnétage ten.[7] In the *bailliage* of Orléans two university professors who served as the *baillis* of two abbeys in that city between them presided over nine assemblies.[8] These multiple presidencies usually occurred within one seigneurial jurisdiction and were the result of one person's accumulation of several juridical offices. When this was the case it obviously assured the legal profession's control over the drawing up of the peasants' *cahiers*. This has made it possible to pinpoint the role of certain "rural intellectuals" (to use Georges Lefèbvre's expression) in the writing of the *doléances*[9] and to investigate the role of the presidents in the circulation of model *cahiers*. The seigneurial *baillis* were the most active in this connection, both by presiding over several assemblies and by mobilizing their officeholding allies (local judges, *procureurs fiscaux, prévôts*). Hence the distribution of models often followed the geographical contours of the seigneury. Such was the case in Vendeuvre, for example, a seigneury situated to the east of Troyes. Here we can identify a series of fifteen related *cahiers* all inspired by the *bailli*, the lawyer Gilbert-Charles Vanier, who

---

[6] A. Poitrineau, "Les Assemblées primaires du bailliage de Salers en 1789," *Revue d'Histoire Moderne et Contemporaine* 25 (1978):419-41, table 2.

[7] M. Gresset, *Le Monde judiciaire à Besançon de la conquête par Louis XIV à la Révolution Française (1674-1789)* (Thesis, Université de Lille III, 1974) (Lille, 1975), 122.

[8] Furet, "Les États Généraux," 436, n. 2.

[9] G. Lefèbvre, *Les Paysans du Nord pendant la Révolution Française* (Paris, 1974), 335, cites five lawyers, two notaries, one *bailli*, one postmaster, one court clerk, and one doctor as having much to do with the drafting of rural *cahiers* in the north of France.

chaired only five parish assemblies himself, but could count on the co-operation of the other presidents, seigneurial agents subordinate to him. The circulation of a common model, however, does not mean that related *cahiers* were necessarily identical: In the group of fifteen *cahiers* from Vendeuvre, only 7 percent of the articles can be found in all the *cahiers*, 25 percent do not even appear in the model, and the majority of the articles in the original model (68 percent) appear in only some of the *cahiers*.

The control that officeholders and men of the legal professions exercised over the 1789 consultation (hence over the preparation of the *cahiers*) can be found at the level of the *assemblées de bailliage* as well, where, on the lowest level of the electoral process, such men made up a good part of the parishes' deputies. As the following table shows, the peasants often chose them as their representatives at meetings of the Third Estate. Here we see the proportion of officeholders and men of the legal and liberal professions, first as a percentage of the *comparants*—the participants in the primary assemblies—whose profession is known, then as a percentage of the deputies from the rural communities, in five *bailliages*.

In Troyes and in Draguignan the proportion of *robins* may have been even higher, since the *syndics* and the *consuls*, who made up, respectively, 21 percent and 17 percent of rural deputies, included many men who exercised a juridical profession. Their overwhelming influence—contested only by the *laboureurs* (independent farmers)—was the case in all or nearly all of France.[10] In the maritime provinces of Flanders, for example, twenty community assemblies chose their *bailli*

| Bailliage | Percentage of comparants | Percentage of rural deputies |
|---|---|---|
| Rouen | 4 | 12 |
| Orléans | 1.5 | 13.5 |
| Château-du-Loir | 4 | 27 |
| Troyes | 7 | 28 |
| Draguignan | 4 | 45 |

[10] In the French part of the Vexin, large-scale farmers (*fermiers*) and independent farmers (*laboureurs*) took over leadership in the rural areas. See J. Dupaquier, "Structures sociales et cahiers de doléances. L'Exemple du Vexin français," *Annales Historiques de la Révolution Française* 194 (1968):433-54.

as their representative;[11] in the *bailliage* of Salers in Auvergne, more than 35 percent of the eighty-two rural deputies were of the legal professions, royal notaries, or lawyers.[12] The preponderance of the *robins* was further increased when rural deputies were cut back to one-fourth of their original number between the primary and secondary assemblies, as stipulated in article 23 of the electoral law. This is what happened in the *bailliage secondaire* of Salers, for example, where, after the reduction, ten notaries, ten lawyers, two royal officeholders, and one *bourgeois* were the only remaining representatives of the rural *communautés* at the assembly of the Third Estate of the *bailliage principal* of Saint-Flour.[13] The deputies to assemblies of the *bailliages principaux* were also cut down in number when they had *baillages secondaires* as well, or if there were more than two hundred deputies from the rural *communautés*. The *bailliage* of Troyes fell into the first category, and the number of its country deputies was cut down from 628 to 167. This drastic reduction was accompanied by a shift in social status that favored the *petits notables*: The number of legal professionals, seigneurial and royal officeholders, and members of the liberal professions, who accounted for 28 percent of the rural deputies of known profession, later rose to more than one-third of the delegation.[14]

When these nonpeasant representatives of the peasant world arrived at the assemblies of the entire *bailliage*, they met the deputies of the cities, a comfortable majority of whom came from the ranks of officialdom. Officeholders and members of the legal and liberal professions accounted for 40 percent of the deputies at Rouen, 42 percent at Troyes, and 67 percent at Nancy. It is hardly surprising, after the *bailliages secondaires* and then the *bailliages primaires* had met, that this group controlled the commissions charged with writing up the *cahiers* for both the *bailliages principaux* and the *grands bailliages*. In the *bailliage principal* of Nancy, five out of twelve drafters of *cahiers* were public officials or men of the legal professions, as were twelve out of twenty in Orléans, fifteen out of twenty-four in Troyes, and thirteen out of fourteen in Draguignan. I might note, however, that men from the bigger cities by no means monopolized the drafting process, since commissioners elected from country areas and small towns remained in the majority.

[11] Lefèbvre, *Les Paysans du Nord*, 329.
[12] Poitrineau, "Les Assemblées primaires," 437.
[13] Ibid., 438.
[14] Furet, "Les États Généraux," 145.

(In Orléans, for example, only seven drafters of *cahiers* came from the city.) This majority nevertheless reflected a nearly total delegation of power to the *robins*. The same preponderance can be seen in the drafting of the final *cahiers*: In Orléans the final draft was the work of sixteen commissioners, seven from the area of the *bailliage principal* and nine from secondary *bailliages*. Eleven of them were officeholders or lawyers. In Troyes three out of the ten commissioners were seigneurial officeholders, two were lawyers, and four were mayors or *échevins* (city councilmen). Furthermore, these *cahiers de bailliage* were often imitated from those of the principal city of the region, where they were the work of commissions in which officeholders, judges, and lawyers were in the majority—as in Orléans, Toulouse, and Besançon—or were equal in number to the *négociants* (wholesale merchants)—as in Rouen or Troyes. In Toulouse, for example, the *cahier* of the *sénéchaussée*, drawn up by a commission that included many lawyers, directly imitated that of Toulouse itself, which was drawn up by a lawyer, Alexandre Augustine Jamme, who had close connections with members of the *parlement*.[15]

It is clear, then, that on all levels the referendum was solidly in the hands of the legal profession. Such men oriented, shaped, and transmitted the peasants' complaints; they were active in the drafting of city dwellers' demands; they gave the commoners' *doléances* their final form. The *cahiers* are profoundly marked by the culture of judges and holders of public office. Furthermore, the national assembly chosen as an outcome of this electoral process reflected the sway that law held over society in France under the *ancien régime*. Even though, as François Furet has shown, the election of deputies at the level of the *bailliage* contains some surprises in favor of men whose presence (at least overtly) was not very evident in the electoral process, the assemblies overwhelmingly chose men of the law, judges or lawyers. Among the Third Estate's 648 deputies to the Estates General, 151 were lawyers (23 percent) and 218 held offices in the judicial system (34 percent), to which fourteen notaries and thirty-three deputies who held municipal offices should be added.[16] All in all, nearly two-thirds of the future members of the Constituent Assembly came from the social milieux

[15] L. Berlanstein, *The Barristers of Toulouse in the Eighteenth Century (1740-1793)* (Baltimore and London, 1975), 154-55.

[16] E.-H. Lemay, "La Composition de l'Assemblée Constituante: Les Hommes de la continuité?" *Revue d'Histoire Moderne et Contemporaine* 24 (1977):344-48.

that had the greatest influence in the drafting of the *cahiers*. Office-holders on the level of the *bailliages* and the *sénéchaussées* give a perfect illustration of the predominance of the provincial men of law, whose hands wielded the pens and whose voices were heard: 127 such men were elected deputies of the Third Estate, making up nearly one-fifth of the deputation, which means that one *officier de bailliage* out of twenty was chosen to sit at Versailles.[17]

The problem that arises next is to describe in cultural terms this group, which, if it did not dictate the contents of the *cahiers*, was at least in a position to give them form and written expression. One good method for sketching this cultural portrait might be to test the hypothesis proposed by Alphonse Dupront. For Dupront, "the *cahiers* were drafted by people who knew how to write, thus who were witnesses to or heralds of an opinion that expressed itself in writing and had been formed by writing, [an opinion] proper to the society of liberal and legal professions, of local officeholders, even of *régents de collège* [professors in secondary schools], which represented the final, provincial stratum of an enlightened bourgeoisie."[18] In this view, the drafters, taken collectively, belonged to a "society of intermediaries" that constituted the lowest base of the world of the Enlightenment. The recent increase in works of sociocultural history exploring eighteenth-century France gives an opportunity to test this hypothesis, at least in part, and to grasp the chief characteristics of the culture of the men—non-noble *officiers*, lawyers, legal practitioners—who mostly controlled the process of referendum and election and who gave the *doléances* formal expression.

A first trait shared by all or nearly all of these men was the cultural matrix provided by the *collège*. Retrospective sociological studies of school attendance have shown, in fact, that the sons of officeholders and of members of the legal and liberal professions made up a large proportion of the enrollment of the *collèges*. In Avallon in the decade from 1760 to 1770, to cite one example, 35 percent of the students, from both inside and outside the city, came from these milieux. If we look just at the city, it is even clearer that the liberal and legal professions led to the privilege of learning: One-third of the students had parents in these groups, a percentage equal to that of sons of the nobility or sons

[17] P. Dawson, *Provincial Magistrates and Revolutionary Politics in France, 1789-1795* (Cambridge, Mass., 1972), 186-87.

[18] A. Dupront, *Les Lettres, les sciences, la religion et les arts dans la société française de la deuxième moitié du XVIIIᵉ siècle* (Paris, 1964), 1:44.

of the merchants and the *bourgeois*.[19] Professional continuity in the family was strong in these circles, and it is clear that the majority of the sons of officeholders or lawyers who had gone through the *collège* entered the world of law in their turn. Toulouse provides a typical example of this: Two-thirds of the *avocats* and *procureurs* of the city admitted to the bar between 1750 and 1789 were the sons of *avocats, procureurs*, officeholders, notaries, or court clerks (*greffiers*).[20]

Within the legal profession, however, we can see differences, arising from their formative years, in the culture of the men who drafted the *cahiers*. Notaries and *procureurs* usually had not gone through the university: After the *collège* they were apprenticed for a number of years with a law practitioner, sometimes a lawyer or a judge.[21] The *avocats*, on the contrary, had attended the university for a minimum of three years and had obtained their *licence en droit*.[22] If the students in Dijon can be taken as typical, there were two groups among *avocats* who held law degrees: sons of lawyers (in Dijon 54 percent of the law students whose fathers were lawyers became lawyers themselves) and sons of *procureurs* and notaries (in Dijon 56 percent of such students were admitted to the bar). I might also note that a minority of lawyers' sons gained access to the world of administrative office either in the *bailliages* or in the *parlements*.[23] Thus we can attempt a portrait of the lawyers who drafted the *cahiers* in 1789. They had received a classical education and, in some cases, university preparation in jurisprudence. Most of them were heirs of a family tradition in the law. A great many of them managed to use their university degrees for upward social mobility, for, by means of their *licence*, the sons of practitioners could become *avocats* and the sons of lawyers could become *officiers*.

But does this mean that these men as a group represented "the final stage in the popularization of the ideas of the philosophy of the Enlightenment"?[24] Without bringing up once more the formidable prob-

[19] These percentages were calculated according to table 1 (p. 14) and table 4 (p. 18) in W. Frijhoff and D. Julia, *École et société dans la France d'Ancien Régime. Quatre exemples: Auch, Avallon, Condom et Gisors* (Paris, 1975).

[20] Berlanstein, *The Barristers of Toulouse*, table II-1 (p. 35).

[21] Gresset, *Le Monde judiciaire à Besançon*, 252-56.

[22] Ibid., 257-59.

[23] R. L. Kagan, "Law Students and Legal Careers in Eighteenth-Century France," *Past and Present* 68 (1975):59 (table 5); R. Chartier and J. Revel, "Université et société dans l'Europe moderne: Position des problèmes," *Revue d'Histoire Moderne et Contemporaine* 25 (1978):373-74.

[24] Dupront, *Les Lettres*, 45.

lem of a definition of the Enlightenment, it might be useful to look at the extent to which men of law shared in the intellectual sociability of the age. Judges and administrators held assured places in learned societies, particularly in the provincial academies, where they accounted for 51 percent of lay, non-noble full members and 28 percent of associate members. In nineteen out of the thirty-three provincial academies (including the two in Toulouse), men of legal and administrative circles made up more than half of the Third Estate academicians.[25] The better part of this group were *officiers de bailliage* (and presiding officials of other lower courts) and *avocats*. This unequivocally attests to the participation in the most prestigious provincial intellectual institutions of the upper levels of the social group that played a decisive role in the drafting of the *cahiers* of 1789.

The picture is the same in the Masonic lodges, but with two important nuances. In the lodges of the thirty-two cities with academies, non-noble officeholders, administrative officials, and lawyers made up 33 percent of bourgeois Masonic membership (a percentage roughly equivalent to that of the same social and professional groups in all categories of academic recruitment).[26] Beginning with the 1770s, the *robins* abandoned the more traditional associations (the penitential confraternities in particular) to join Masonic lodges. Toulouse offers striking confirmation of the general model that Maurice Agulhon has crafted for all of Provence.[27] Among Toulouse lawyers practicing in 1785, 36 percent of those admitted to the bar before 1770 belonged to a penitential confraternity and only 19 percent were Masons. Among those admitted to the bar after 1770, however, the proportions are reversed: 29 percent of the lawyers were Masons and 7 percent penitents.[28] It should be noted, however—and this was a prime difference between Masonic and academic membership—that the Masonic lodges even included men from the humbler levels of the legal profession, welcoming modest practitioners, *procureurs*, and notaries as well as officeholders and lawyers. Such men, spurned by the learned societies, found the lodges excellent places for making acquaintances and ex-

[25] D. Roche, *Le Siècle des Lumières en province. Académies et académiciens provinciaux, 1680-1789* (Paris and The Hague, 1978), 1:239-43; 2:406-407 (table 30).

[26] Ibid., 1:267.

[27] M. Agulhon, *Pénitents et Francs-Maçons dans l'ancienne Provence* (Paris, 1968), 165-211.

[28] These percentages were calculated according to table V-1 (p. 129) in Berlanstein, *The Barristers of Toulouse*.

changing opinions. Fairly often, however, the Masonic lodges were highly selective in their recruitment and no widespread social mixing occurred. One example of this was in Lyons, where in 1782-1783 legal practitioners gathered in one of the city's lodges, *La Bienveillance*, the twenty-seven members of which included thirteen *procureurs*, three notaries, and six other legal practitioners. The *avocats*, who in fact were few among the Masons of Lyons, preferred the company of the no-tables and wealthy merchants in the *Grande Loge Provinciale*.[29] A sim-ilar cleavage can be seen in Toulouse, but there it separated two groups of *avocats*. Some of the *avocats* of the *parlement* penetrated the aristo-cratic lodges (like the lodge of *La Parfaite Amitié*, where members of the *parlement* were in the majority), while others controlled the other lodges. (They made up two-thirds of the membership of *La Paix*, for example, and one-half of *Les Vrais Amis*.) Lawyers attached to the lower courts and legal practitioners had to be satisfied with the mer-chants' lodge.[30] An analysis of Masonic recruitment thus shows that the group largely responsible for drafting the *cahiers* was also deeply in-volved in that triumphantly successful form of sociability at the end of the century. It also suggests—as does an examination of the school cur-ricula—that legal circles were not a homogeneous milieu, but were subject to two sociocultural cleavages, one separating officeholders and *avocats* from practitioners, the other distinguishing between lawyers of the sovereign courts and those of the courts of lower jurisdictions.

It is not enough to note their participation in "enlightened" institu-tions in order to understand to how great an extent the social milieux that generally controlled the drafting of the 1789 *cahiers* were open to ideas. Men of a culture that had been nourished and shaped by the written word, the *robins* of the Third Estate were also readers whose tastes should be inventoried. A study of their libraries seems to offer a useful approach, but it soon reveals its limits: The picture we get is of a group of men whose books, for the most part, were professional. In Toulouse between 1770 and 1793, for example, in only one among fif-teen inventories of lawyers' estates or inventories of possessions confis-cated during the Revolution are less than 80 percent of the books on

---

[29] R. Chartier, "L'Académie de Lyon au xviiiᵉ siècle. Étude de sociologie culturelle," *Nouvelles Études Lyonnaises* (Geneva, 1969), 183-89; Roche, *Le Siècle des Lumières*, 2:439-50 (table 46), concerning Lyons.

[30] Berlanstein, *The Barristers of Toulouse*, 126; Roche, *Le Siècle des Lumières*, vol. 2, table 46, concerning Toulouse.

jurisprudence.[31] Moreover, the Enlightenment seems to have penetrated this milieu only timidly. The *Encyclopédie* rarely appears among the books listed in Besançon libraries, and the same is true for all of Diderot.[32] There are some indications, however, that this is not the whole story. In Toulouse, a *Lettre des avocats au Parlement de Toulouse à Monseigneur le Garde des Sceaux sur les nouveaux édits*, signed in 1788 by twenty-five lawyers, cites the *Encyclopédie* and Gabriel Bonnot de Mably. Moreover, a Besançon "bookbinder and billiard keeper" named Fantet kept a number of prohibited books in a "secret closet": philosophical works such as *De l'Esprit* or *Le Contrat Social* and titillating books like *Le Sopha* or *Les Égarements de Julie*. When he was arrested in 1766, Fantet was let off lightly by the *parlement* of Besançon, which permits us the supposition that legal professionals may not have been completely absent among his clientele.[33] Perhaps estate inventories, which did not describe all the books in the possession of the deceased, tell us only part of the truth concerning the reading habits of men of the legal professions. According to Robert Darnton's studies, this is assuredly the case.

It is clear, to begin with, that the *Encyclopédie* had a much wider circulation than it was long thought to have had. Even considering just the six editions based on the text assembled by Diderot, at least 11,500 copies were distributed in France before 1789, more than half of them in the Geneva and Neuchâtel quarto editions. Some of the Yverdon editions of the *Encyclopédie*, with a total press run of 1,600 copies, should be added to this total, as well as the 5,000 copies of the *Encyclopédie méthodique* published by Panckoucke.[34] All in all, then, nearly fifteen thousand copies of the *Encyclopédie* reached French readers before the Revolution. As it happens, men of the legal professions were well represented among them. In Franche-Comté, where there is information on the majority of the subscribers to the quarto edition of the *Encyclopédie*, men of legal and administrative circles accounted for 56 percent of the 137 Third Estate subscribers, distributed equally between Besançon and the other cities of the region.[35] Although it did not figure

---

[31] Berlanstein, *The Barristers of Toulouse*, 96-97.

[32] Gresset, *Le Monde judiciaire à Besançon*, 1091.

[33] Ibid., 1088-89.

[34] R. Darnton, *The Business of Enlightenment. A Publishing History of the Encyclopédie, 1775-1800* (Cambridge, Mass., and London, 1979), 36-37.

[35] This percentage calculated according to figures 6 and 7 of ibid., 287-94.

prominently in library inventories, then, the *Encyclopédie* enjoyed a wide distribution in Franche-Comté. This example seems to be applicable throughout the kingdom, and members of the legal and liberal professions were doubtless among the principal readers of the Enlightenment's most famous book. It is more difficult to ascertain the lowest social limits of its distribution, but it is reasonable to surmise that the many *cabinets de lecture* that opened their doors during the two last decades of the *ancien régime* contributed much to opening up the public to philosophical works, and hence to the *Encyclopédie*.[36] Although proof is unavailable, it is legitimate to suppose that during the 1780s the provincial bourgeoisies and the legal profession made up a good part of a clientele eager for scandalmongering chronicles, political lampoons, anticlerical satires, and works of pornography.[37] The most radical literature of the Enlightenment reached provincial France in this erotico-political form to a much greater extent than is apparent from a perusal of official bookstore account books or library catalogues. The men who drafted the 1789 *cahiers* certainly were not strangers to such a cultural movement as this, and it is a good bet that *robin* commoners were often to be found among the readers of this literature that forged the image of a despotic and depraved monarchy.

A final problem: To what extend did non-noble members of the legal professions participate in the *sociétés de pensée* and in the committees, which by the end of 1788 had launched a campaign in support of the demands of the patriotic party for doubling the representation of the Third Estate, for the per capita vote, and for the exclusion of nobles and seigneurial agents from the assemblies of the Third Estate? If we can take Burgundy as typical, lawyers were among those most active in this political battle over the form of the convocation of the Estates. A twenty-man committee in Dijon, on which lawyers had a clear majority, elaborated a "patriotic" political platform and imposed it on the entire province, winning over successively the corporate bodies and community assemblies of Dijon, the *échevins* of Dijon and the other cities

[36] The *cabinet littéraire* opened by Nicolas Guerlache in Metz offers one example of this. See R. Darnton, "The World of the Underground Booksellers in the Old Regime" in *Vom Ancien Régime zur Französischen Revolution. Forschungen und Perspektiven*, comp. E. Hinrichs, E. Schmitt, and R. Vierhaus, ed. A. Cremer (Göttingen, 1978), 442-51.

[37] R. Darnton, "Trade in the Taboo: The Life of a Clandestine Book Dealer in Prerevolutionary France" in P. J. Korshin, ed., *The Widening Circle: Essays on the Circulation of Literature in Eighteenth-Century Europe* (Philadelphia, 1976), 11-83.

and towns, and finally the villages. Since it had been decided that elections would take place by *bailliage* and not within the framework of the provincial Estates, the Dijon lawyers, having won the day, called a meeting of the Third Estate of the city on 22 February, fifteen days before the meeting of the city's electoral assembly and a month before that of the Burgundian *bailliages*. The assembly charged an eight-man commission with drafting *projets de mandats*. Of the eight commissioners, six were *avocats*, one was a *procureur*, and one a doctor, and all had been active in the patriotic campaign since December 1788. These *projets de mandats* provided a thorough outline for a *cahier*, and they circulated widely among the parish assemblies.[38] Two facts, however, suggest qualifications to the thesis of the lawyers' close connection to the patriotic party and the strong influence of such models. First, it is clear that members of the bar in Burgundy were divided. Lawyers were active in the *parlement* party as well, and they had the support (for example in the *bailliage* of Semur-en-Auxois) of the Masons, the municipal governments, and some of the *officiers de bailliage*. The entire legal profession did not by any means rally to the more radical positions. Furthermore, the committees' manipulation of the referendum had its limits. The Dijon lawyers' outline for a *cahier*, however well known and circulated, does not seem to have very closely inspired the 133 *cahiers* of the *bailliage* of Semur-en-Auxois, and in any event it was unable to impose its form on even the most enlightened *cahiers* of the juridical district.[39] Although it is clear that the patriotic party invented a new mode of political operation and a new form of legitimacy during the winter of 1788-1789,[40] it is more doubtful that its influence on the referendum found expression in the bulk of the written *doléances*.

Before passing on to study the contents and the vocabulary of the *cahiers*, it is perhaps useful to summarize what has been established thus far. First, we can state that one social group, the *légistes*, appears to have had a decisive role during the referendum of the spring of 1789. This group usually drafted the *cahiers* in the cities and in the *bailliages* (both primary and secondary), as evidenced by the membership of the

[38] On the electoral campaign in Burgundy, see A. Cochin and C. Charpentier, "La Campagne électorale de 1789 en Bourgogne" [1904], republished in A. Cochin, *Les Sociétés de pensée et la démocratie moderne. Étude d'histoire révolutionnaire* (Paris, 1978), 166-204; and R. Robin, *La Société française en 1789: Semur-en-Auxois* (Paris, 1970), 229-53.

[39] Robin, *La Société française*, 283-94.

[40] F. Furet, *Penser la Révolution Française* (Paris, 1978), 58-61, 234-43.

drafting commissions. Its influence was no less strong in the assemblies of the rural *communautés*, even though this is more difficult to pinpoint. The mechanism of the drafting of the *cahiers* in rural areas is not always clearly discernible, but it seems that more often than not it was the president of the assembly who gave final form to the complaints of the inhabitants of the area, which were then written down by a clerk. As we have seen, in most of the *bailliages* the seigneurial judges presided over these assemblies, which means that the president was often a man of the legal profession and a city dweller, since a great many of the offices of judge, *juge châtelain*, and *procureur fiscal* were in the hands of city lawyers or notaries. In the region of Besançon, for example, forty-five seigneurial jurisdictions were divided among fifteen *avocats* and five *procureurs* and notaries of the city; in Toulouse, onetenth of the lawyers of the *parlement* and more than half of the lawyers attached to the *présidial* court were seigneurial judges. The lawyers' juridical sway over the rural assemblies was occasionally reinforced by an economic control, since many of these men either owned lands outright or enjoyed *rentes constituées* from the area. Thus the *cahiers* in rural areas were, as a general rule, the result of a compromise between the collective expression of the assemblies' participants, an order and form given to this expression by the jurist president, and a final written form imposed by the clerk. The leadership by the legal professions seems to have been threatened under only two circumstances: first, when the parish priest, at the demand of the inhabitants of the village, replaced the official who normally would have presided over the assembly; and second, when the community assembly imposed one of its own, in general its *syndic* or *consul*, as president. These two cases aside, the *cahiers* bear the imprint of juridical culture. This culture—and this is the second conclusion we can draw—seems to have been divided between a professional culture, connected with the practitioners' formative years and with social practice, and a decided openness toward the ideas of the century, as seen in their participation in new forms of sociability and their acquaintance with "philosophical books." At this point another question arises: Which of these two cultural views was more influential in the drafting of the *cahiers*? Do the written style and the contents of the 1789 grievances reflect the Enlightenment? Or, on the contrary, do they merely formulate common complaints in a juridical and administrative language?

The very presentation of the *cahiers primaires* brings a partial answer to this question. Most of them, in fact, present the *doléances* by dividing them into categories, separating them into articles, or, more rarely, organizing them under headings. In the *bailliage principal* of Montbrison, for example, 60 percent of the surviving *cahiers* are organized into articles.[41] The majority of the *cahiers* so organized (forty-nine out of seventy) simply number their grievances, generally using "premièrement" or "primo," "2º," "3º," and so forth; occasionally one sees "première doléance," "seconde doléance," "troisième doléance," and so forth. Another twenty-one *cahiers* use the words "article" or "item," most of the time in abbreviated form: "art. 1ʳ," "art. 2" or "2ᵉ," etc. In Forez, only two *cahiers* replace numerical order with a presentation by headings: somewhat sketchily in Saint-Marcel-de-Felines ("Salt," "Measures," "Seigneurial rights"), more carefully worked out and thought through in Cleppé ("Domains of the Crown," "Estates General," "General Assemblies," "Ministers," and so forth). In a handful of *cahiers* in which each grievance is introduced by an ordinal number ("1º," "2º," etc.), the complaints and propositions are grouped either in two sections ("Specific Observations" and "General Observations and Demands"), as in the case of Sainte-Colombe, or in three ("Complaints and Grievances," "Remonstrances," and "Advise and Means"). The three *cahiers* so structured come from community assemblies in which the same man, a royal notary named Jacques Moncigny, presided. The texts show little variation from one *cahier* to another, except that in Saint-Christo in the Fontanès region there is a significant addition to the "Remonstrances" section: "10º finally that the laborer gather the fruit of his toil in peace." This seems to show traces of the expression of community sentiment grafted onto a previously drafted text. The *cahiers* that are not presented in an ordered manner (in the *bailliages* of both Montbrison and Semur-en-Auxois)[42] show wide variation: Some express the peasants' complaints in a manner that approaches the free flow of speech; others (as in Chalmazel, where the *cahier* is obviously the work of the elected deputy, the lawyer Recorbert) offer an enlightened and reform-oriented prose that avoids the straitjacket of an organization by articles. What we can learn of the organization of *cahiers* in Montbrison

[41] This analysis is made possible by the recent publication of the *cahiers* of Forez in E. Fournial and J.-P. Gutton, *Cahiers de doléances de la province de Forez (Bailliage principal de Montbrison et bailliage secondaire de Bourg-Argental)* (Saint-Étienne and Montbrison, 1974-1975), 2 vols.

[42] Robin, *La Société française*, 289-90.

seems to be applicable throughout France, although *cahiers* arranged by article seem to have been in even greater majority elsewhere: In the *bailliage principal* of Rouen 150 out of 154 *cahiers* are arranged in this manner, as are 116 out of 133 in Semur-en-Auxois.[43]

The consistency of this mode of presentation has an obvious connection to a dual tradition. The first part of this tradition is notarial, since notaries customarily enumerated and described goods in statements of last wishes. The second is administrative, rooted in the ordered structure of edicts and ordinances and reinforced by practices, new in the eighteenth century, of numbering and classifying. A comparison of the form of the *cahiers* of 1614 with those of 1789 illustrates how deeply analytical and orderly writing habits had penetrated in a century and a half. In 1614 the text remains poorly organized even when it appears to be separated into articles. The presentation of the grievances is not well articulated, and the text lacks the ordinal numbers that make most of the 1789 *cahiers* so easy to read. Thus how the *cahiers* are presented is one good way to measure the progress of an administrative writing style within the milieu of the jurists who controlled the drafting of such documents both at the beginning of the seventeenth century and the end of the eighteenth. The very operation of giving written form to grievances obviously had certain effects. Jack Goody's remarks on the construction of lists in ancient societies are perhaps applicable here, inasmuch as the interposition of the better educated in 1789 was above all a process of "drawing up lists"—and the numbering of them—of the communities' complaints and proposals. According to Goody, by the very nature of the process, the drawing up of a list cannot ever be a pure translation of the spoken word, but is always a task involving reorganization and transformation. Lists "do not represent speech directly. Or rather they stand opposed to the continuity, the flux, the connectedness of the usual speech forms, that is, conversation, oratory etc., and substitute an arrangement in which concepts, verbal items, are separated not only from the wider context in which speech always, or almost always, takes place, but separated too from one another."[44] The application of this analysis to the listing of *doléances* suggests two remarks. First, it is obvious that the process of giving formal organization to the *doléances* represents a working over of their contents,

---

[43] Dupront, "Formes de la culture," 154; Robin, *La Société française*, 289.

[44] J. R. Goody, *The Domestication of the Savage Mind* (Cambridge and New York, 1977), 81.

since ordered transcription reformulates, accentuates, and divides in a new way what has been said. Consequently, the change that the peasant grievances underwent by the pen of the jurists was not primarily the result of an ideological warp but the inevitable effect of a shift from one system of communication to another. It is because of the very formality of the *cahiers* that collective spoken expression—contaminated perhaps by writing—changed into another sort of discourse, the rules of which were those of written culture.

Does the notarial and administrative organization of the *cahiers* indicate the influence of the Enlightenment? Did the officeholders and lawyers, pens in hand, introduce the ideas of the century into the mass of the primary *cahiers*? A first way to answer such a question might be to conduct a thematic survey of the *doléances*, grouping under the heading "values and rights" grievances inspired by an enlightened ideology: denunciations of arbitrary power, demands for individual rights, and the need for a declaration of rights guaranteeing the sovereignty of the Nation, civil equality among citizens, individual liberties, and the right to property. This was the method used in the investigation directed by François Furet of all the grievances from four *bailliages* (Rouen, Orléans, Troyes, and Nancy). This study found, first of all, that such propositions were generally few: In no assembly, rural or urban, primary or on the *bailliage* level, did they represent more than 5 percent of all *doléances*. To be sure, the proportion of such propositions was higher—but only slightly so—in urban *cahiers* than in rural ones, as we see in the following table.

Other investigations conducted with approximately the same criteria confirm the limited proportion of demands directly inspired by philosophical literature. Such demands represented only 3.2 percent of

PROPORTIONS OF "ENLIGHTENED" GRIEVANCES

| *Bailliage* | Rural *cahiers* | *Cahiers* from urban groups | *Cahiers* from the city |
|---|---|---|---|
| Rouen | 2.4% | 3.5% | 3.5% |
| Orléans | 0.8% | 1.7% | 2.1% |
| Troyes | 0.8% | 2.4% | 1.2% |
| Nancy | 1.4% | — | 4.6% |

the grievances in Paris *extra muros*,[45] 3.2 percent in the woodlands of Houlme and the plain of Argentan,[46] and 1.1 percent in the *bailliage* of Salers.[47]

Contrary to what might be expected, the *cahiers* of the Third Estate on the *bailliage* level were not the most open to demands concerning personal values and individual rights. These demands appear in general proportionally fewer times than in the urban *cahiers* or, at best, are on a par with them. The *cahiers* from the four *bailliages* that figure in the investigation carried on at the École des Hautes Études en Sciences Sociales illustrate the situation on the level of the *bailliage*, with 2.9 percent of the grievances falling under the heading of "values and rights" for the *cahier* from the *bailliage* of Rouen, 2 percent for that of Orléans, 0.4 percent for that of Troyes, and 3.1 percent for that of Nancy. In Normandy, the *cahiers* from the *bailliages* of Falaise and Exmes, considered together, show a proportion of 3.3 percent of "enlightened" grievances, which is identical to the percentage we find in the *cahiers primaires*.[48] Within this category, grievances show some variation between the city and the country. In rural areas, it is sometimes the denunciation of arbitrary powers that heads the list (*bailliages* of Troyes and Nancy) and sometimes the affirmation of fundamental rights (*bailliages* of Orléans and Rouen). In the cities, on the other hand, the expression of and demand for individual rights always comes first. The *cahiers de bailliage* once again occupy a middle position between rural and urban demands. This painstaking statistical analysis of the *doléances* gives full confirmation to Daniel Mornet's conclusion in his 1933 survey of the *cahiers*: "To tell the truth, 'ideas' have little place in them, and even less philosophical ideas."[49]

The *cahiers* seem timid if we compare them with the ideas of the Enlightenment, as summarized in the nineteenth and twentieth centuries and probably as early as the revolutionary period.[50] They are more con-

---

[45] I. Janeau and A. Lefèvre, *1789: Les Cahiers de doléances du tiers état de l'élection de Paris hors les murs*, Mémoire de l'École des Hautes Études en Sciences Sociales, 1977, typescript.

[46] J.-C. Martin, "Les Doléances de 1789 dans le bocage de Houlme et la plaine d'Argentan," *Le Pays Bas-Normand* 3 (1977):17-23.

[47] Poitrineau, "Les Assemblées primaires," 436.

[48] Martin, "Les Doléances de 1789," 95.

[49] D. Mornet, *Les Origines intellectuelles de la Révolution Française* (Paris, 1933), 454.

[50] Aside from Daniel Mornet's classic study, see I.A.O. Wade, *The Structure and Form of the French Enlightenment*, vol. 1: *Esprit Philosophique* (Princeton, 1977), 313-

cerned with the criticism and reform of institutional detail than with an affirmation of the new values the century had forged. Does this remain true if we shift our point of comparison forward to the set of ideas and sweeping reforms of the first phase of the Revolution (from the decrees of 4-14 August 1789 to the Constitution of September 1791)? By comparing a sampling of 741 *cahiers* to an "ideal *cahier*" comprising all revolutionary measures, George Taylor has measured the degree of revolutionary consciousness and political radicalism of the demands formulated in 1789.[51] His conclusions are unequivocal: An overwhelming majority of the *cahiers primaires* were far removed from the ideal *cahier*, since 70 percent of those drawn up by rural parishes or urban corporations and guilds demanded no modification of the mechanisms of government and no redistribution of sovereignty. Even when they are generalized to refer to the whole of the kingdom, these grievances remain local and fragmented; at best, some *cahiers* allude to the question of the per capita vote in the Estates General. Although extremely weak in the *cahiers primaires*, political radicalism increases with the level of the *cahiers* and with the size of the cities involved. The *cahiers* expressing a desire to see true legislative power (not just fiscal power) given to the Estates General, for example, represent 5 percent of the *cahiers primaires* of parishes and guilds, but 60 percent of the *cahiers* in the *bailliages* containing few city dwellers, 68 percent of the *cahiers* from sections in Paris, 82 percent of the *cahiers* from cities, and 90 percent in highly urbanized *bailliages*. The correlation between radicalism and urbanization is reiterated in George Shapiro and Philip Dawson's analysis of the *cahiers de bailliage*: The higher the population of the principal city in a *bailliage*, the more the *cahier* of the Third Estate in that *bailliage* favored equality among citizens and the more strongly it prefigured the decree of 4 August and the Declaration of the Rights of Man.[52] There is still an enormous gap between the contents of the *cahiers* and what would later be the Revolution in action. On the one hand, as George Taylor demonstrates, the immense majority of the *ca-*

---

434 ("Politics"); and J.-M. Goulemot, "De la polémique sur la Révolution et les Lumières et des dix-huitièmistes," *Dix-Huitième Siècle* 6 (1974):235-42.

[51] G. V. Taylor, "Les Cahiers de 1789: Aspects révolutionnaires et non révolutionnaires," *Annales E.S.C.* 28 (1973):1495-1514.

[52] G. Shapiro and P. Dawson, "Social Mobility and Political Radicalism: The Case of the French Revolution of 1789" in W. O. Aydelotte, A. G. Bogue, and R. W. Fogel, eds., *The Dimensions of Quantitative Research in History* (Princeton, 1972), 159-91, esp. table 6 (p. 184).

*hiers* proposing a new distribution of power founded their arguments not in the political philosophy of the Enlightenment, but in an appeal to the traditional authority of the Estates. On the other hand, even the most radical and the most enlightened *cahiers* formulated only very partially the revolutionary transformations later carried out by the Estates General and the Constituent Assembly. At best we find only half the statements and demands of the "ideal *cahier*" in the most innovative of the actual *cahiers*—those of the Third Estate in *bailliages* of high urban population.

If the *cahiers* of the Third Estate were organized according to the writing habits of notaries and administrative officials; if they were by and large inhospitable to the political philosophy of the Enlightenment; and if they offered little hint of the tumultuous events to come during the summer of 1789, were the bulk of them to any extent written in the new vocabulary of the age? The question deserves to be raised, since it is known that the vocabulary of the Enlightenment circulated well beyond the texts that propagated its philosophical ideology.[53] Exploration of the semantic universe of the *cahiers* has followed one of two routes: All occurrences of a series of words designated as root words have been mapped (there are seventy-four such words in the matrix set up by Alphonse Dupront).[54] Or, alternately, all words of more than two letters in a given section of *cahiers* have been analyzed (for example, in Régine Robin's study of eight *cahiers* of cities and towns in the *bailliage* of Semur-en-Auxois[55] or in André Burguière's analysis of three *cahiers* from trade guilds and corporations in Reims[56]). These investigations differ in their methods but concur in their findings. The vocabulary characteristic of the Enlightenment appears only very sporadically in the texts of the *cahiers*. In the sampling from the *bailliage* of Semur-en-Auxois, the words *instruction* and *raison* appear

[53] J.-M. Goulemot, "Pouvoirs et savoirs provinciaux au xviiie siècle," *Critique* 397-398 (1980):603-13.

[54] Dupront, "Formes de la culture," 166.

[55] Robin, *La Société française*, 294-98. The index she establishes for these eight *cahiers* contains seventeen thousand words.

[56] A. Burguière, "Société et culture à Reims à la fin du xviiie siècle: La Diffusion des 'Lumières' analysée à travers les cahiers de doléances," *Annales E.S.C.* 22 (1967):303-39. The forty *cahiers* of the guilds and corporations of Reims are analyzed, and the terms designating individuals, power, and collectivity are codified. Three *cahiers* (those of the election officials, the mirror makers and upholsterers, and the tailors and secondhand clothes dealers) are subjected to a systematic inventory of vocabulary.

only eight times, *luxe* and *préjugés* three times, *éducation* twice, and *lumières, bonheur,* and *progrès* only once.[57] In Reims, although *lumières* is repeated seven times in the *cahier* of the mirror makers' and upholsterers' guild, *bonheur* appears only five times, *instruction* four, *humanité* twice, and *progrès* not at all.[58] Furthermore, certain words that seem to indicate the new vocabulary, such as *constitution* or *liberté*, are used in their older senses. The verdict is unequivocal: "Overwhelmingly, the vocabulary of the Enlightenment, in active ferment for thirty years, had not reached the world of petty *robins*, judicial officeholders, ordinary people in the liberal professions, rectors, professors, and bourgeois (even of the smaller cities that were more rural than urban) who penned or gave form to" the *cahiers*.[59]

The vocabulary of these men was one "of juridical structures and juridical decrees, worked out within the framework of the institutions of the French monarchy for at least two centuries."[60] For the most part this vocabulary used traditional terms to designate administrative areas, social estates, the procedural aspects of the referendum, and the institutions to be reformed. In the small towns of the *bailliage* of Semur-en-Auxois, the ten most frequent nouns were (with the exception of the highly neutral word *nombre*): *articles* (226 occurrences), *état(s)* (139), *droit(s)* (62), *impôt* (59), *ordre(s)* (51), *députés* (44), *majesté* (42), *assemblée(s)* (38), *juges* (33), and *province* (29).[61] Even the vocabulary of denunciation and political reform belonged much more to a traditional language than to the lexical innovations of the century. This was true of the word *abus*, which was omnipresent in 1614 and 1789 and used with just as much force at both times. It was also true of the vocabulary defining society in political terms. In Burgundy, the word *habitants* was still more frequently used than *citoyen*, and *royaume* more often than *nation*. In Reims, *nation* was much used in the *cahiers* of the guilds—except in those of the poorest guilds, which remained faithful to the older term *peuple(s)*—but it was used in a passive sense with no implied demand for power; it simply transferred to a new vocabulary the traditional relation of subordination to royal authority.[62] The word *citoyen*

---

[57] Robin, *La Société française*, 314.
[58] Burguière, "Société et culture à Reims," table 6 (p. 336).
[59] Dupront, "Formes de la culture," 158.
[60] Ibid.
[61] Robin, *La Société française*, 315.
[62] Burguière, "Société et culture à Reims," 328-29 and table 8 (p. 339).

also found tradition difficult to shake off. In many texts it seems to reach a compromise with its apparent opposite, *sujets*; in others it remains mired in the vocabulary of the society of estates, as in the expression "ordres des citoyens," which is, literally speaking, self-contradictory.[63] Thus older vocabularies still dominated most of the 1789 *cahiers*, and traditional meanings even more so.

Thus far we have been treating the *cahiers* as an all-inclusive corpus, hence as an undifferentiated whole in which the *cahiers primaires* of the rural community assemblies and the guilds enjoy numerical superiority. When the *cahiers* are studied for their differences, however, it is soon clear that they offer an excellent vantage point for observing the cultural stratification of French society on the eve of the Revolution. Does a recognition that, overall, the *cahiers* were not particularly open to the diction and the themes of the Enlightenment necessarily mean that they were totally homogeneous? Some scholars have seen the basic distinctions as geographical. After studying the *cahiers de doléance* of three hundred parishes in what is now the *département* of the Sarthe, Paul Bois drew up a map comparing demands in that area aimed at the nobility and the clergy. In the western part of the region there were many such demands, expressed in bitter terms, but in the southeast they were few and tepid, so that their distribution curiously resembles that of the Chouan insurrection, which was received favorably where antinoble and anticlerical grievances had been strong and was rejected, even violently, where this was not the case.[64] In much the same way that it radicalized a desire for reform that was still embryonic in 1789, the crisis of the Revolution totally upset the traditional tendencies of the rural world. Farther to the west things seem to have been different. When Charles Tilly compared the *cahiers* of Mauges, a bastion of the Vendée insurrection, with those of Val-Saumurois, which remained republican, he found correlations between the conservatism of the *cahiers* and later counterrevolution and between critical and reforming zeal and later attachment to the Revolution.[65] Although these two studies reach contradictory conclusions, they are based on the same presupposition. In Charles Tilly's words: "the Grievances represent compromises among multiple points of view. . . . As such, they are val-

[63] Dupront, *Les Lettres*, 56.

[64] P. Bois, *Paysans de l'Ouest. Des structures économiques et sociales aux options politiques depuis l'époque révolutionnaire dans la Sarthe* (2d ed., Paris, 1971), 91-97.

[65] C. Tilly, *The Vendée* (Cambridge, Mass., 1964, 1976), 177.

uable evidence of the public political position to which the sum of all its internal forces brought the community."[66] Thus were formed geographically homogeneous clusters, which can be measured on a scale of antiseigneurial radicalism. Within these clusters there was agreement on grievances, and the differences between more strictly peasant *cahiers* and those influenced by the urban environment became less clearly defined.

The gap between rural and city grievances is nevertheless a hypothesis that remains fundamental to Tocqueville's interpretation. For Tocqueville, "the spirit of the Revolution" changed as it passed from city to village. "All that was generalization and abstract theory in the minds of the middle classes here took on fixed and precise forms. The city was preoccupied with rights, the country with needs."[67] Can an affirmation of this sort be tested? The overall analysis of the grievances in the *bailliages* of Rouen, Troyes, Nancy, and Orléans suggests a preliminary response. A look at the rural grievances concerning the distribution and organization of power leads to three conclusions. First, this category represents a relatively modest proportion of all demands, ranging from as low as 12 percent in Rouen to as high as 18 percent in Nancy. Second, a notable part of these grievances concerned the organization of municipalities (this headed the list in Rouen and Orléans), focusing on a desire to give fiscal powers to the municipalities that were set up in 1787. Third, demands concerning the Estates General and the Provincial Estates were closely connected to questions of taxation. The demand that elected assemblies consent to and apportion taxes in fact provided a base for all the other propositions concerning the composition, the frequency of meeting, and the operation of the Estates. There are marked differences, however, in the *cahiers* from the cities. Demands concerning powers vary considerably—from 6 percent in Troyes to 42 percent in Nancy—and the content of the grievances and their relative weight differ from those in the countryside. Demands concerning the municipalities disappear, proposals concerning the Estates, both Provincial and General, lose their strictly fiscal character, and (except in Troyes) the proportion of constitutional demands augments; in Rouen and Nancy, for example, it doubles. Urban political

[66] Ibid.
[67] A. de Tocqueville, *L'Ancien Régime et la Révolution*, vol. 2: *Fragments et notes inédites sur la Révolution* (Paris, 1958), 126.

grievances thus freed themselves from their fiscal roots to become formulated more abstractly.

Grievances concerning social order show the same sort of cleavage
between city and country *cahiers*. Demands of this type appear in approximately the same proportions in country and city—they represent
between 13 and 22 percent in rural *cahiers* and between 17 and 22 percent in the cities (Nancy excepted)—but they concerned realities in the
city very different from those in rural areas. A good half of the demands in rural *cahiers* concern seigneurial rights and tithing—the *dîme*.
In the country areas of the *bailliage* of Troyes, for example, complaints
directed at the seigneurial system and the *dîme* make up 12.4 percent
of all complaints but nearly two-thirds of all grievances than can be
classified as aiming at "traditional society." Eighty-two percent of the
parishes list demands concerning the seigneurial institution. The pre-
rogatives held most shameful were those pertaining to seigneurial justice, which accounted for 16.3 percent of such demands. Next came
hostility to seigneurial rights and dues in general, attacked both in
principle and for their manner of exaction (11.4 percent). This was followed, in order, by a rejection of the *terriers* (land use registers) and the
role of the *feudistes* (feudal law specialists) (11.1 percent); complaints
about the *cens* (recognitive land rent) (9.2 percent), hunting rights, and
the right to keep a dovecote (7.4 percent); and grievances about the
*banalités* (obligatory use of the lord's mill, ovens, winepress, and so
forth) (5.9 percent), personal servitude and the *corvée* (obligatory manual labor) (5.7 percent), and the *lods et ventes* (the lord's dues on sales of
peasant tenures) (3.7 percent). This scale of detestation is not much al-
tered if we consider the overall frequency of appearance of these grievances: Juridical procedures head the list (criticized by more than half
the parishes), followed by the *cens* (41 percent of parishes), the *corvées*
(25 percent), hunting rights (24 percent), the *terriers* (23 percent), and
the *banalités* (22 percent). The *cahiers* illustrate three different attitudes
toward such rights. The first attitude, in the majority, calls for reform.
Forty-five percent of the cases speak of "buying back" the rights,
"transferring" them, "reforming," "diminishing," or "simplifying"
them. On a lesser scale, 32 percent of the cases are simple complaints
that propose no solution, and only 21 percent of the cases express a clear
desire to abolish such rights. The demand to abolish rights appears frequently in only three areas: the *corvées* (more than half of the demands
call for a simple elimination of this right), the hunting rights, and the

*banalités*—which perhaps gives an indication of the true hierarchy of peasant hatred in Champagne at the eve of the Revolution. Similarly, the rejection of the *dîme* as it was collected may account for only 1.7 percent of grievances, but it was mentioned in nearly one out of two *cahiers* (114 out of 250). Criticism of the *dîme*, however, did not necessarily imply a desire for its elimination. Only fifteen *cahiers* in the *bailliage principal* called for simple abolition; the others complained of the abusive exactions of the *dîme*, of the misdeeds of the *décimateurs* (tax collectors), or of the tax rate, or else they proposed that the sums collected be transferred (80 percent said to the parish priests and vicars, 11 percent said to public aid, 5 percent said to public instruction, and 4 percent said to the state). Or they called for the suppression of particular *dîmes*, such as the feudal *dîme*, the *dîme novale* (tithe on newly cleared land), or of extraordinary collections of the *dîme*. More than mounting anticlerical feeling, what the 1789 *cahiers* reveal here is the population's aspiration to participate in decision making. The overwhelming majority of parishes did not question the principle of the *dîme*; the community assemblies simply wanted a say in how it would be levied and what it would be used for.

Grievances followed a totally different order in *cahiers* from the cities. Complaints against seigneurial rights and tithing waned as the urban drafters focused on two favorite targets: the Church, attacked for its system of benefices (which perhaps expresses the bourgeoisie's hunger for land), and the privileges of birth or condition, combatted in the name of an equality viewed in terms of fiscal equity and access to rank and office by merit alone. The *cahiers de bailliage*, which stood halfway between the seigneurial world of the rural *cahiers* and the special demands of the larger cities, generally leaned toward the latter, but they left room for discourse on seigneurial rights. This general model, which was established through the scrutiny of tens of thousands of grievances from the four *bailliages* chosen as the sample, is echoed in more strictly local studies. Three familiar traits appear around Houlme and Argentan. First, one-fourth of the grievances from these areas concern the social order; second, demands aimed at seigneurial rights and the *dîme* head the list in the rural areas; and third, to the contrary, the *cahiers de bailliage* concentrate on criticism of the system of benefices.[68] Thus quantified analysis verifies Tocqueville's intuitive understanding

[68] Martin, "Les Doléances de 1789," 17, 34, 95.

of the cities' grievances as "general and abstract" and of the country's complaints as directed at more particular and familiar objects.

Not only was the order of priorities different in city and country; within rural areas some *cahiers* reflected, if not the peasants' writing, at least their voices, while others, although drawn up by rural communities, took the urban type for their model. These two groups of *cahiers* differ in many ways, as Régine Robin's semantic analysis of the *cahiers* of the *bailliage principal* of Semur-en-Auxois demonstrates.[69] The "peasant" *cahiers* are almost always written in the present indicative or the imperfect indicative; *cahiers* from small towns or their nearby villages prefer the subjunctive, the future indicative, or the imperative. Thus the first group's recital of woes and its description of a state of affairs felt to be insupportable contrasts with an impulse toward reform expressed in proposals or demands for a new order in the second group. The vocabulary used to express demands (as studied in the *cahiers* from the *bailliage* of Rouen) clearly demonstrates the gap separating these two modes for the formulation of grievances. The peasant *cahiers* use terms that refer to the sovereign's pleasure (*prier, solliciter, supplier*), but the urban *cahiers* use words that assert collective rights to impose change (*requérir, réclamer, exiger*).[70]

The two sorts of rural *cahiers* are just as opposed in what they say as they are in how they say it. In the peasant *cahiers*, complaints are usually concrete and particular, directed at a designated adversary (one particular seigneur, a certain city, one abusive act or another), and are couched in strongly emotional terms. Occasionally they are introduced by an avowal of the writer's limitations, as in Ohain (Flanders), where a grievance is prefaced with the phrase, "with very little acquaintance with affairs of state and limiting themselves to the objects particular to them. . . ."[71] Similarly, in Dracy-les-Viteaux (Burgundy): "Occupied every day in the hard labors of the country, we are cognizant of our insufficiency and we feel keenly that we are incapable of discussing the important matters that will occupy the Estates General."[72] And in Férréol (Forez): "The inhabitants of the village of Férréol leave to the big

---

[69] Robin, *La Société française*, 273-94; R. Robin, "Histoire et linguistique: Premiers jalons," *Langue Française* 9 (1971):47-57.

[70] D. Slatka, "L'Acte de 'demander' dans les 'cahiers de doléances,'" *Langue Française* 9 (1971):58-73.

[71] Lefèbvre, *Les Paysans du Nord*, 334.

[72] Robin, *La Société française*, 403.

cities the care of discussing the major interests of the province . . . thus they will limit themselves to the matters that touch them directly."[73] Indeed, it is the *cahiers* based on the urban model that propose a global view of society and of the nation, a view supported by a network of verbs in which the complementary terms *supprimer* and *établir* are key notions and by a network of adjectives and adverbs that evoke universality through frequent use of such words as *général, aucun,* and *tous.*

The *cahiers primaires* thus show two strongly contrasting modes and levels of expression that divide along rural/urban lines. This cleavage exists not only between *cahiers* from peasant communities and those from the cities, but also between two families of rural *cahiers,* distinguished by a greater or lesser geographical and/or cultural distance from the bigger cities. Differences between these two types appear in the content and the relative importance of the various grievances as well as in their vocabulary and syntax. We can identify two cultural levels. On one, a mediating scribe writes at the prompting of the peasants, so his text carries a vision of the world and a manner of speaking that in part are not his; on the other, drafters with legal or administrative training fashion a discourse of reform as they see fit.

Once again Tocqueville gives us a hypothesis to be tested: As seen in the *cahiers de bailliage* of the two orders, the grievances of the bourgeois and the nobles closely resembled one another. Tocqueville says:

> Not only did the provinces resemble each other more and more, but in each province the men of different classes, at least all those who ranked above the common people, became more and more alike, despite the differences of rank. Nothing shows this more clearly than the reading of the 'instructions' [the *cahiers*] presented by the different orders in 1789. Those who drew them up differed profoundly in their interests, but in everything else they showed themselves alike.[74]

Tocqueville later explains what he meant by "everything else" (*tout le reste*). "But fundamentally all men of rank above the common people were alike: they had the same ideas, the same habits, they followed the same tastes, they indulged in the same pleasures, they read the same

---

[73] Fournial and Gutton, *Cahiers de doléances de la province de Forez,* 1:125.

[74] Tocqueville, *L'Ancien Régime et la Révolution,* vol. 1 (Paris, 1954), 144. (M. W. Patterson, trans., *De Tocqueville's "L'Ancien Régime"* [Oxford, 1933, 1962], 84.)

books, they spoke the same language. They only differed in their rights."[75]

It would require a systematic comparison of all the *cahiers de bailliage* of the Third Estate and of the nobility to confirm or refute Tocqueville's proposition. Sasha R. Weitman has attempted such a comparison, working with the 209 *cahiers* of the Third Estate and the 173 *cahiers* of the nobility that survive.[76] Resemblances between the two groups are many. They advance, to begin with, a common demand for individual rights: 67 percent of the *cahiers* of the nobility and 60 percent of those of the Third Estate demand that the recognition of individual liberties be included in the drafting of the Declaration of Rights. Seventy-three percent of the noble *cahiers* and 74 percent of the Third Estate *cahiers* favor freedom of the press; 40 and 31 percent, respectively, favor *habeas corpus*; and 66 and 74 percent, respectively, call for the abolition of the *lettres de cachet* (warrants for arbitrary imprisonment). These very similar figures speak clearly of a common fondness for individual liberty, as the English had defined it, guaranteed by law.

Likewise, agreement can be found on a number of measures aimed at setting up a new political order and defining a new equilibrium between the monarchy and civil society. There was agreement, first, on measures to enhance political representation: Regular meetings of the Estates General were demanded in 90 percent of the noble *cahiers* and 84 percent of the bourgeois; ministerial responsibility, respectively, in 73 and 74 percent; and requiring the Estates' consent for taxation in 81 and 82 percent. The two groups also agreed on the establishment of a constitution: 64 percent of the noble *cahiers* and 57 percent of those of the Third Estate demanded a constitution as a precondition to any fiscal concessions. Both groups, moreover, conceived of such a document as giving written form to the customary and latent constitution of the kingdom—not as a new creation, which was demanded by only 21 percent of the *cahiers* of the nobility and 28 percent of those of the Third Estate. To end the list, the two groups also agreed on the need to found a new juridical order by a total recasting of the judiciary (70 percent of

[75] Ibid. (Patterson trans., 87.)

[76] S. R. Weitman, "Bureaucracy, Democracy and the French Revolution" (Ph.D. diss., Washington University [St. Louis], 1968). For a summary of his findings see G. Shapiro, J. Markoff, and S. R. Weitman, "Quantitative Studies on the French Revolution," *History and Theory* 12, no. 2 (1973):163-91. I make use here of the figures given by Weitman in tables 6-1 (pp. 317-19), 6-2 (pp. 345-49), 6-3 (pp. 391-93), and 6-4 (pp. 402-406).

the noble *cahiers* and 79 percent of the bourgeois) and on the need for a reform of criminal laws and the penal code (demanded by 68 and 75 percent of the noble and bourgeois *cahiers de bailliage*). If there were shades of difference between the demands of the nobility and the Third Estate, they show in the differing weights given to the various grievances concerning the state. The Second Estate emphasized reforms to limit and place checks on the monarchy, whereas the Third Estate accentuated measures to reduce diversities of practice and to bring rational order to the mechanisms of government, hence to make the exercise of royal power more efficient once it was placed on a par with the authority of the nation.

The *cahiers* of the nobility and those of the Third Estate also concurred on matters regarding the organization of society. Both groups declared that property is a sacred right to be included in the Declaration of Rights (the proposition figures in 56 percent of the noble *cahiers* and in 46 percent of the bourgeois ones). Above all, they proclaimed the need for equality of taxation, which meant the abolition of fiscal privileges and the participation of all, each according to his abilities, in the necessary levies. Here, 86 percent of the *cahiers de bailliage* of the Third Estate favored equality before taxes, but so did 71 percent of those of the nobility. Thus the Second Estate appears to have been less nervous about its ancient privileges, and all the more so since many of its *cahiers* also renounced the judicial or economic privileges they had enjoyed. The two differed, however, concerning seigneurial rights and jurisdictions: 64 percent of the *cahiers* of the Third Estate demand the abolition of the first and 50 percent the disappearance of the second; among the nobles these percentages are, respectively, 6 and 9 percent. This perhaps illustrates the difference of "interests" of which Tocqueville spoke. The gulf between the two estates ought not to be exaggerated, however, since few noble *cahiers* explicitly demand that seigneurial rights and jurisdictions be maintained (only 12 percent and 9 percent of all *cahiers*). The prevailing attitude among the nobles is thus a silence that is difficult to interpret but is perhaps equivalent to a renunciation.[77]

Everything therefore seems to confirm Tocqueville's interpretation, except for one reservation that seems to reveal noble egotism: their po-

[77] At least this is the hypothesis of S. R. Weitman, "Bureaucracy, Democracy and the French Revolution," 387, and Dupront, *Les Lettres*, 47.

sition on the question of the vote in the Estates General. Things are clear on the Third Estate side, where 84 percent of the *cahiers* come out in favor of a per capita vote and 6 percent for a vote by estates. A survey of the noble *cahiers* (ignoring shades of difference) shows them far from sharing that stance: Only 16 percent accept a vote by head, but 68 percent demand a vote by orders. The ideological consensus between the Second and the Third Estates during the essential debate before the meeting of the Estates thus seems to have broken down. A more detailed examination of the wording of such demands in the nobility's *cahiers* (such as Guy Chaussinand-Nogaret's study)[78] may, however, lead us to modify this judgment. In point of fact, only a minority of the noble *cahiers* (41 percent) expressly demand a vote by orders; an almost equal number (39 percent) demand a per capita vote or would accept it if the Estates so decided or if the general interest required it; and 20 percent of these *cahiers* come out for a mixed vote, by order for certain questions and by head for others. Even on a problem as decisive as the voting procedures of the Estates, therefore, the position of the nobility is more complex and divided than it might seem, which once again takes us back to Tocqueville's judgment of the nobility's *cahiers*: "The most striking feature of the *cahiers* of the nobility," he says, "is the perfect harmony which exists between these noblemen and their age. They are imbued with its spirit and speak its language."[79]

As it happens, the *cahiers* of the nobility are indeed by far the more "enlightened," if by that we mean they show a marked attention to the rights of the individual and offer a liberal set of proposals for the reform of the monarchy. The heading "value and rights" accounts for 18.3 percent of the 4,953 grievances traced by Guy Chaussinand-Nogaret in the *cahiers* of the nobility he has analyzed,[80] or nearly ten times more than in the *cahiers de bailliage* of the Third Estate, where the heading accounts for 2.9 percent of the total in Rouen, 2 percent in Orléans, 0.4 percent in Troyes, and 3.1 percent in Nancy. If to these proposals in favor of the rights of man we add others concerning equality among citizens or portraying a limited and well-controlled monarchy, then more than half the *cahiers* of the Second Estate contain grievances

---

[78] G. Chaussinand-Nogaret, *La Noblesse au XVIII^e siècle. De la Féodalité aux Lumières* (Paris, 1976), 187-92.

[79] Tocqueville, *L'Ancien Régime et la Révolution*, 1:300. (S. Gilbert, trans., *The Old Régime and the French Revolution* [Garden City, N.Y., 1955], 271-72.)

[80] Chaussinand-Nogaret, *La Noblesse*, 206-16.

that define a new social and political order. Of all the *cahiers* of the nobility, the ones from Paris were perhaps the most open to the new values of the age: The affirmation of the rights of man appears in 14 percent of their demands, and liberal and constitutional reform of the state in 36 percent.[81] Even though the *noblesse d'épée* played a leading role in the Parisian nobles' assemblies, these meetings were inspired by a reforming radicalism as lively as that discernible in the *cahiers* of the sixty districts of the Third Estate.[82] Furthermore, just as the *cahiers* of the nobility were more "enlightened" in the capital than in the provinces, they also showed more openness to new ideas in the *pays d'élections* (provinces governed by royal *intendants*) than in the *pays d'états* (governed by Provincial Estates). Seventy-two percent of the former demanded the recognition of individual liberty, 79 percent liberty of the press, 75 percent fiscal equality, and 71 percent the drawing up of a constitution before any vote on taxes. Sixty-five percent were favorable to the abolition of privileges, and 64 percent to a reorganization of the state. The percentages obtained from the *cahiers* in the *pays d'états* on these same questions are in every case lower, giving, respectively, 61 percent, 65 percent, 67 percent, 56 percent, 49 percent, and 47 percent.[83] The fundamental role that Tocqueville attributes to administrative centralization in the shaping of a homogeneous and egalitarian public opinion is thus confirmed by this comparison of noble grievances from regions of a well-established state presence and those from provinces less directly subject to royal power.

There are two ways to interpret the conformity of opinion between the Third Estate and the nobility that we have seen in the *cahiers de bailliage*. First, this agreement relied on a common cultural practice, forged and tested throughout the century. Learned societies and *sociétés de pensée* provided particularly good opportunities for encounters between the orders. It was not just a thin layer of enlightened aristocrats and intellectual bourgeois who met one another, but a large cultural class that drew many of its members from the ranks of both the provincial nobility and the bourgeoisie of talent and service. There were 6,400 members of provincial academies in the century as a whole,

[81] M. Flandrin, "La Noblesse parisienne face à la convocation des États Généraux en 1789," *Acta Poloniae Historica* 36 (1977):95-100.

[82] Taylor, "Les Cahiers de 1789," 1509.

[83] Weitman, "Bureaucracy, Democracy and the French Revolution," tables 7-1 (pp. 474-77), 7-2 (pp. 506-13), 7-3 (pp. 553-56), and 7-4 (pp. 575-81).

and, in its last two decades, more than ten thousand Freemasons entered the lodges of the Grand Orient in the academic cities alone, which leads us to estimate that there were nearly fifty thousand Masons in the whole of France.[84] These data help us to appreciate the extent of a provincial milieu which, although it cannot be designated as universally "enlightened," was nevertheless capable of thinking in terms of governmental procedures and was dedicated to the accumulation of knowledge, to progress through the exercise of its proficiencies, and to working for the public good. Whether or not it is legitimate to put this collective enterprise under the heading of "Enlightenment" is, in the last analysis, of little importance. One thing is certain, however: It was in these shared intellectual interests that the future framers of the *cahiers de bailliage*, nobles and bourgeois alike, forged their reforming aims. The short-term *conjoncture* of the crisis brought on by a power vacuum during the summer of 1788 reinforced and gave a more directly political dimension to this century-old intellectual preparation. The pamphlets that came out at that time, like certain official acts, expressed all the demands that would later appear in the *cahiers de bailliage*. Even if we consider no more than the fifteen texts examined by Beatrice Hyslop, it is clear that the new social and political order that the *cahiers* later demanded had already found a place in people's minds. Thirteen out of these fifteen texts demand fiscal equality; twelve demand liberty of the press; eleven, the Estates' vote on taxes; ten, regular meetings of the Estates; nine, the recognition of individual liberty; and nine, the doubling of the Third Estate representation and per capita voting in the Estates.[85] In this brief but lively ideological incubation period, ideas grew full-blown to transform what might have been nothing more than a catalogue of administrative reforms into an innovative political discourse. This cross-fertilization between, on the one hand, a shared experience with utilitarian thought, ongoing for a century or more and placed under the control of the state, and, on the other, a radicalized public opinion, formed during the summer of 1788 and nour-

---

[84] Roche, *Le Siècle des Lumières*, 2:149 (table 38).

[85] B. Hyslop, *A Guide to the General Cahiers of 1789 with the Texts of Unedited Cahiers* (New York, 1936), 66-67. The fifteen texts analyzed are the Arrêt du Parlement of 5 December 1788; Necker's report; the deliberations of the Third Estate of Rennes of 1788; the *Instructions* of the Duke of Orléans; pamphlets by d'Antraigues, Bergasse, Condorcet, La Revellière, Mirabeau, Petion de Villeneuve, Rabaut Saint-Etienne, Servan, and Target; the *Avis aux bons normands* of Thouret; and *Qu'est-ce que le Tiers État?* of Sieyès.

ished by what Tocqueville calls "abstract and literary politics," brought
to the *cahiers de bailliage* a taste for detailed administrative reform and
an emotional dynamism aiming at, in the words of Alphonse Dupront,
"a society of happiness and eternity."

Do THE *cahiers* show that Enlightenment notions had widespread circulation in France during the eighteenth century? The answer to such
a question is more complex than it might seem. It is obviously negative
concerning the *cahiers primaires*: They use a juridical and notarial writing style to express the complaints of the mass of men caught in an
unendurable day-to-day existence. Neither by their vocabulary nor by
their contents do the rural *cahiers* give any echo of the preoccupations
central to the political literature of the century. Is this to say, however,
that the *robins*, officeholders, and lawyers, who more often than not
drafted them, in no way participated in the new ways of thinking and
speaking? Many indications lead us to think that the low and middle
levels of the world of legal professionals populated the new associations, the Masonic lodges in particular, and provided readers for Enlightenment ideas either through the *Encyclopédie* or in more popularized forms. If the *cahiers primaires* fail to express this enthusiasm for
innovation, this may perhaps be due to the practical conditions that
governed their fashioning. These men of law presided over the assemblies, they perhaps shaped the grievances, and they certainly put them
into order, but they did not dictate them. Peasant speech is almost
never heard exactly as it was pronounced, but it nevertheless constrained the mediating hand that held the pen. In a situation of this
sort, the drafter depended more on his professional culture than on his
possible attraction to the new ideas in order to give written form, under
the supervision of the community assembly, to collective grievances.

On the level of the *cahiers de bailliage* the situation changes. Here the
men trained in the legal professions had more freedom to impose their
views since they generally controlled the commission charged with
drafting the reports. This explains why, even though the language for
the most part remained that of jurisprudence and administration, more
weight was given to general and abstract demands. It explains the expectations of a new political order, the definition of new relationships
between the king and the nation, and the piling up of proposals for reform. Although they fail to reflect the more audacious aspects of eighteenth-century thought, the *cahiers de bailliage* of the Third Estate,

which inherited a tradition of utilitarian thought and benefited from the political radicalization of the summer of 1788, reflect a thought that contains noticeable echoes of the values and ideals of the Enlightenment. Does this mean that the bourgeoisies of the cities, great and small, were the only groups that embodied the new thought? When we read the grievances of the nobility we see that this was far from true. The nobles' *cahiers*, which rivaled or surpassed those of the Third Estate in "enlightenment," attest to the favorable reception of reforming ideas by the Second Estate. From this point of view, they represent the point of arrival for a century of shared reading and common intellectual pursuits—which does not, however, signify identical interests. The *cahiers* are thus doubly the "testament of the *ancienne société française*": first, because they show proof that the bourgeoisie of talent and service and an urbanized nobility met on common cultural grounds; and second, because they give expression to a determination that the peasantry had already attained, translated into a style that was not yet its own.

# CHAPTER FIVE

# Publishing Strategies and
# What the People Read,
# 1530–1660

ANY history of publishing must necessarily also be a history of the diffusion of printed matter. There are several reasons for this. First, it is clear that publishing strategies depend largely upon the extent and the character of the public that constitutes the bookmaker's potential clientele at any given moment in history. The decision to print a particular text and the choice of format and press run respond primarily to the prospective market—or at least to the publisher's idea, accurate or inaccurate, of that market. On the other hand, the circulation of printed matter modifies a cultural equilibrium. When the printing profession proposed a new instrument for knowledge and entertainment, multiplied the possible uses of the written word, and instigated new forms of social exchange, it transformed the cultural practices and cultural concepts of those into whose hands its products fell. Elsewhere Elizabeth L. Eisenstein has surveyed the profound changes that the growing recourse to the printed word brought to the intellectual habits and mental equipment of learned culture.[1] I intend to take up a different problem, and a difficult one: the diffusion of the book and of other forms of printed matter among people of social strata other than the elites of wealth, power, and culture. Can we detect, in the century (broadly speaking) from the first third of the 1500s to the middle of the 1600s, a "popular" familiarity with printed matter, which offered a new and immense market to the printing profession and profoundly transformed the culture of the mass of men? An answer to this question would obviously lead to a more accurate evaluation of what it has become customary to call "popular culture" and a

This essay originally appeared in *Histoire de l'édition française*, ed. H.-J. Martin and R. Chartier (Paris: Promodis, 1982), 1:584-603. Like the three studies that follow, it was used in a seminar at the Newberry Library, Chicago, in April 1985.

[1] E. L. Eisenstein, *The Printing Press as an Agent of Social Change: Communication and Cultural Transformations in Early Modern Europe* (New York and London, 1979); idem, *The Printing Revolution in Early Modern Europe* (New York and London, 1983).

clearer grasp of the editorial choices made by the printer-bookdealers—or certain of them—of the early modern period.

## "The People" as Readers

Were sizable numbers of the general populace among the owners and buyers of books in the sixteenth and seventeenth centuries? The answer to such a question first requires a definition of the notion of "popular classes." I shall consider "popular" readers, by default, as all those who belonged to none of the three "robes" (to borrow Daniel Roche's expression)—the black robe of the clergy, the short robe of the nobility, or the long robe worn by an array of officeholders great and small, lawyers and attorneys, men of letters, and medical doctors. This means that those identified as "of the people" were peasants, journeymen and masters in the crafts and trades, and merchants, including the retired merchants often designated as "bourgeois." It is not an easy matter to ascertain whether such people were familiar with printed matter, and so far only a limited number of urban sites have offered an opportunity to study this.

### Amiens, 1503–1576

First among these is Amiens in the sixteenth century,[2] for which Albert Labarre's meticulous study gives us an excellent picture of who owned books in this middle-sized city (it had perhaps 20,000 inhabitants). It is clear that book owners were in the minority: Out of 4,442 extant estate inventories from the years 1503-1576, only 887 mention books—20 percent, or one inventory out of five. Within this small society of book owners, merchants and artisans seem to cut a fairly fine figure: 259 merchants owned books, as did 98 artisans or craftsmen, representing 37 and 14 percent, respectively, of the total of those whose inventories list books and whose profession is given. It is clear, then, that from the first century of their existence printed books (which far outnumber manuscripts in the Amiens inventories) were not the exclusive privilege of the prominent members of society, but reached a population of modest readers on the lower end of the professional and social scales.

This conclusion, however, calls for several reservations. First, the proportion of inventories that mention books turns out to vary greatly

---

[2] A. Labarre, *Le Livre dans la vie amiénoise du seizième siècle. L'Enseignement des inventaires après décès 1503-1576* (Paris and Louvain, 1971).

according to differences in social category. It is highest in the medical profession, where 94 percent of doctors owned books (although the total number of inventories is only 34). It remains high for the legal profession (where 73 percent of the inventories mention books), the nobility (72 percent), and the clergy (also 72 percent). According to Labarre's data, only an estimated 11.6 percent of merchants and artisans, considered together, owned books, with no apparent difference between the two groups.[3] Within the merchant and artisan population, then, only a small minority managed to own a book. Furthermore, the distribution of these books was far from even: The merchants of Amiens, who made up 37 percent of the book owners whose professions are known, held only 13 percent of all the books owned, and the artisans, who accounted for 14 percent of book owners, held only 3 percent of the books. Other data attest to the limited size of the "libraries" on the lower end of the social scale. Whereas the average number of books owned is 37 for the legal professions, 33 for doctors, 23 for the clergy, and 20 for the nobility, it is only 6 for merchants and 4 for the trades. The ownership of one book is the norm among craftsmen and tradespeople; this is true for 53 percent of artisans' inventories which mention books, and also for 44 percent of merchants' inventories listing books. On the other end of the scale, only sixteen merchants and only two artisans—a *déchargeur de vin* (wine distributor) and a cabinetmaker—owned more than twenty books. Although ordinary people are not completely absent from the list of city dwellers who owned books in the sixteenth century, the example of Amiens clearly shows that only a small fraction of them did so and that for this extreme minority a book remained a rare possession, unique or to be owned in very limited numbers.

One last remark concerning the uneven distribution of books in the world of artisans and craftsmen in Amiens: Among the 98 who owned

[3] Ibid., 129. The percentage of inventories listing books under the grouped category of merchants and artisans is calculated by means of the hypothesis that the proportion of inventories without professional identification is the same for inventories with books as for the whole of the inventories (or 21 percent). This allows us to obtain the total (not given by Labarre) of the inventories with or without books for merchants and artisans. If we accept the notion that figures for the merchants and for the artisans are the same in the two sets of data (inventories mentioning books and total inventories), or 72.5 percent merchants' inventories and 27.5 percent artisans' inventories, we can then arrive at a percentage of inventories mentioning books for each of these categories: 11.6 percent in both cases.

books, three groups seem to have been particularly disadvantaged—tillers of the soil residing within the walls, people of the foodstuffs trades, and masons, only 6, 6, and 3 of whose inventories, respectively, mention books. Woodworkers (15 inventories with books), metalworkers (10), leatherworkers (10), and workers of hides and harnesses (10) seem to have been more familiar with printed matter. The textile trades—serge workers and wool combers—seem well represented (22 inventories with books), but there were so many of them in the city that this figure must correspond to a fairly small percentage of book owners among them. The hierarchy among Amiens book owners parallels the hierarchy that Natalie Zemon Davis has established concerning the ability to sign one's name in Lyons during the 1560s and the 1570s. Here, the metalworkers, leatherworkers, and textile workers lead the list, followed by the building trades, alimentary trades, and farmers.

### Paris, 1601–1670

In Paris between 1601 and 1670, merchants and artisans represented a smaller proportion of book owners than in Amiens a century earlier. Henri-Jean Martin's sampling of four hundred estate inventories has shown that artisans and merchants, taken together, accounted for 16 of the 187 (8.6 percent) inventories for the period 1601-1641 that mention books and whose proprietors' social status is given and 13 out of the 175 (7.4 percent) inventories for the period 1642-1670.[4] If to this we add the "bourgeois de Paris," often retired merchants, the share grows, but it remains far below what it was in the Amiens inventories: 15.5 percent before 1641 and 13.7 percent after that date. If few Parisian merchants and artisans possessed books at all, they also owned few books each: Between 1601 and 1641, when the average total of all book owners' collections varies between 101 and 500 titles, ten Parisian merchants' and artisans' inventories out of sixteen show fewer than 26 titles. This remained true in the following period (1642-1670), where 7 merchant and artisan "libraries" out of 13 show fewer than 26 books. For example, the 1601 inventory of one master glazier on the Place Maubert mentions only four books, and in 1606 a draper also owned no more than four books.[5]

---

[4] H.-J. Martin, *Livre, pouvoirs et société à Paris au XVIIᵉ siècle (1598-1701)* (Geneva, 1969), 1:492.

[5] Ibid., 1:516-17.

## Grenoble, 1645–1668

Grenoble offers an opportunity for one last survey of an urban area, thanks to the publication by Henri-Jean Martin of the account books kept by the bookseller, Jean Nicolas, between 1645 and 1668.[6] What we find here is the purchase, the visit to the shop for the purpose of acquiring a book, to be paid for later. Among Nicolas's 460 clients whose social status or profession can be traced, merchants and craftsmen number only 49, or 10.7 percent. Furthermore, it should be added that some of these, who lived outside Grenoble, are listed only as subscribers to the *Gazette* and that others in fact were themselves booksellers (although not noted as such) who would subsequently resell the books they ordered from Nicolas. Thus Nicolas's Grenoble clientele, strictly speaking, was made up of only twenty-two merchants and seven master craftsmen. Aside from four of these customers who acquired more than ten titles each, they bought on a small scale: Six merchants and six artisans bought only one book and eight merchants and the remaining artisan, a master goldsmith, bought only two or three. The four exceptional merchant customers were a M. Brun (eleven purchases, two of which were for his sons), the *traiteur* (restaurant owner) Milleran (eleven purchases), a wealthy Protestant merchant, Eliza Julien (eighteen purchases), and the apothecary Jacques Massard, a Protestant as well and socially on the borderline between commerce and medicine (twenty-one purchases). Thus the account books of Grenoble confirm the Parisian estate inventories: In the seventeenth century, merchants and to an even greater extent artisans seldom bought books, and when they did, they bought few works.

## The Books Bought and Owned: The Supremacy of Religion

But what did they buy? The books that sixteenth-century merchants and artisans in Amiens owned were for the most part religious books, and particularly Books of Hours. These account for 6 percent of the total number of the books contained in the inventories, but in the collections of the craftsmen this share rises to 15 percent. Furthermore, Books of Hours were often the only sort of book owned: 124 merchants

[6] H.-J. Martin and M. Lecocq, *Livres et lecteurs à Grenoble. Les Registres du libraire Nicolas (1645-1668)* (Geneva, 1977), 1:137-265, "Les clients des Nicolas."

out of 259 (or 47.9 percent) had nothing else in their "library." Ninety-one of them owned one, 23 two, 7 three, 1 four, and 2 five. Among the artisans, 32 out of 98 (or 32.7 percent) show a similar pattern: 28 owned one, 3 owned three, and 1 five. Next in order after the *livres d'heures*, but fewer in number, came copies of the *Golden Legend* (a dozen among the merchants, ten among the artisans), Bibles (seven and five, respectively, and all in French it seems), breviaries, and missals. The religious book was predominant, then, by a wide margin, and it left little room for other books. The only coherent group of books that could compare with the religious books was what the inventories call books of "pourtraicture," which were collections of models, patterns, and illustrations used in the exercise of a trade. Such books appear in the inventories of two painters, two manuscript illuminators, two glaziers, one bin-maker, one cabinetmaker, one mason, one armorer, and three goldsmiths. The reading matter of merchants and artisans, as we see in the Amiens inventories, had limited horizons: profession and religion. It was quite obviously the latter that created the most demand, liturgical books in particular. The Books of Hours, which contained liturgical texts and fragments of Scripture, were the chief form of this pious literature. They were printed in enormous quantities, as the stock records of Parisian booksellers attest. In 1528 Loys Royer's warehouse contained 98,529 Books of Hours out of a total stock of 101,860 books; in 1545 Guillaume Godard had 148,717 out of a total stock of 263,696 books, all liturgical. Thus the Book of Hours provided a basic market for the publishing profession in the sixteenth century, since it satisfied a clientele of "notables" as well as a "popular" clientele for whom it was the most usual, and often the only, purchase. Both social levels are clearly visible in the appraisals of this sort of book that survive from Amiens: 43 percent of the Hours were worth less than eighteen *sous*, 42 percent between one and four *livres*, and 15 percent between four and twenty *livres*. We should add that these inventory prices, which usually concerned bound books, are a poor indication of the purchase price for an unbound Book of Hours, which was generally less than one *sou*, making it the cheapest book available and quite within the possibilities of even the most impecunious readers.[7]

In mid-seventeenth-century Grenoble, religious works obviously had an important place in Jean Nicolas's sales to the twenty-two mer-

---

[7] See Labarre, *Le Livre dans la vie amiénoise,* 164-77.

chants and seven artisans of the city who frequented his shop, representing a third of the books delivered to them (42 titles out of 124). This proportion is higher than that of religious books in Nicolas's total sales, which stands at 23 percent. Bibles, liturgical books (Hours, breviaries, missals), books of piety (for example the *Consolations de l'âme fidèle* of the Protestant minister, Drelincourt), and apologetic literature were the works most frequently acquired by these readers of modest social status, both Catholic and Protestant. Next, with 25 titles, were books or single sheets for classroom use, bought for youngsters enrolled in the *collèges*: ABCs, grammars (Despautère's among them), and the Latin classics. This confirms that *collèges* during the *ancien régime* recruited from a range of social levels, welcoming not only the sons of notables but also those of merchants (although we might note that no artisan here bought any schoolbooks other than ABCs). Outside these two larger categories, purchases were scattered and reflected personal tastes and interests, reserving a place (albeit limited) for contemporary literature (Guez de Balzac, Corneille, and the novelists), for history (with four buyers for Louis Videl's *Histoire du Connestable de Lesdiguières*), for *occasionnels*, and for *mazarinades* (such as the political pamphlets or songs published during the Fronde). Although the merchants and artisans of seventeenth-century Grenoble seem to have had somewhat more curiosity than their equivalents in Amiens a hundred years earlier, the fact remains that more than half the books they bought were destined either for their religious guidance or the education of their sons. The "popular" clientele reflected in Nicolas's account books thus does not seem to have required books to be published specifically for its use. (For example, there was not one merchant or artisan among the twenty-eight people who bought almanacs.) As with the Book of Hours in the sixteenth century, however, this clientele formed a part of the market for books with large press runs—books of piety or schoolbooks.

## The Specific Reading Matter

The estate inventories from Amiens and the account books from Grenoble enable us to draw several conclusions. First, they confirm the notion that "popular" readers formed only a minority of the public for books, a minority that more often than not purchased or owned only a few titles. Moreover, these documents do not show that these readers—the humblest on the social scale—had expectations specific to them as a group. They did not read all that the notables read—far from it—

and the books that they owned or acquired were not reading matter they could call their own. Liturgical works, books of piety, schoolbooks, and even the books of "pourtraicture" (a category that included works illustrated by Alberti or Holbein as well as pattern books) were products of the printers' art that reached a market in which several groups shared. Thus it would seem, as we make a first approach to the question, that a specifically "popular" book-reading public did not exist in the sixteenth and seventeenth centuries. This seems to imply that all strata of society related to the printed word in identical ways. It also seems to imply the absence of an exclusive market available to a printer-publisher who might want to limit his activities to large press runs of works designed to be sold at modest prices to a public of merchants and artisans (although not exclusively to them). Such conclusions raise two questions, however, that must be answered. First, can we limit our understanding of the popular relationship to the book to its possession as documented in estate inventories or booksellers' account books? And second, must we interpret the relationship to "print culture" (in Elizabeth Eisenstein's phrase) exclusively in terms of book ownership, whether sold by a bookseller or appraised by notaries and court functionaries? In the sixteenth and seventeenth centuries, doubtlessly more so than earlier, a relationship with the written word did not necessarily imply individual reading, reading did not necessarily imply possession of books, and familiarity with the printed word did not necessarily imply familiarity with books. A good part of the activities of printing and publishing follow from propositions such as these, so what we need to do now is bolster them.

## The Uses of Print

In the cities, the people's utilization of the printed word could be collective when it was "mediated" through someone reading aloud. This was most likely to occur in three socially defined places, which corresponded to three experiences basic to the life of the people. First, there was the workplace and the shop, where the master craftsman and his workers could consult the books of familiar techniques to guide them as they worked. In the Amiens inventories such works are often anonymous: "ung livre concernant le mestier de hucher où sont emprins plusieurs patrons" (a book concerning the bin-maker's trade in which several patterns are printed), "ung livre où sont plusieurs pourtraictz

servant au mestier de menuisier" (a book in which there are several illustrations serving the cabinetmaker's art), and "huit volumes où sont
emprins plusieurs pourtraictz" (eight volumes in which there are several printed illustrations). In Grenoble, Nicolas noted the sale of an
*Arithmétique* to one Rose, a potter, and a *Praxis medica* to Massard, the
apothecary. Printers in the seventeenth century devoted some of their
activities to these books of technical reference, which were often written by a master craftsman. Among other illustrations of this are *La Fi-
delle Ouverture de l'art de serrurier* and *Le Théâtre de l'art de charpentier*,
both written by Mathurin Jousse, "master locksmith in the city of La
Flèche," and published in 1627 by a printer of that city, Georges Gri-
vaud.

### In the City: Collective Utilization of
### Printed Matter

A second setting for the collective use of printed matter was the religious assembly held in the cities, and occasionally in the country villages as well, by proselytizing Protestant missionaries. Because it aimed
at reaching even the humblest men and women, even the illiterate who
had access to the written word only through speech, the Reformation
depended on these conventicles, where listeners, teachers, and learners
united by faith gathered to sing psalms and read the Gospel aloud.
Such gatherings depended on the clandestine commerce in books
printed in Geneva and brought into the kingdom of France by peddlers and dry goods sellers. Three such men, Jehan Beaumaistre, Hector Bartholomé, and Pierre Bonnet, are listed among the clients of Laurent de Normandie, a Geneva bookseller who furnished them with
Bibles, psalmbooks, and pamphlets of John Calvin.[8] In the cities affected by the Reformation, Protestant worship services (as best we can
picture them in spite of their secrecy) were one of the places in which
training in group reading took place, as they brought together men and
women, the literate and the illiterate, and the faithful of different
professions and of different parts of the city. Such services show that
the Protestant community had already achieved a certain coherence
and also that they served to initiate men and women into the reading

[8] H.-L. Schlaepfer, "Laurent de Normandie," in *Aspects de la propagande religieuse*
(Geneva, 1957), 176-230.

of the Holy Writ.[9] In the cities of Flanders and of Hainaut, it was gatherings such as these that prepared the way for the storm of iconoclasm in the summer of 1566: In private houses, empty buildings, or barns at the city gates, the faithful of the new cult sang psalms and read the Gospel. Their books came to them through peddlers who bought their stock in Antwerp. In Lessines, a small town to the east of Tournai, for example, one eyewitness remarked concerning the Protestant assemblies: "No distribution of books took place. . . . [The participants] had bought the better part of these psalmbooks in this city, to which a co-religionist came now and then from Antwerp, selling such books right in the marketplace."[10] The printed word was read and commented on by ministers and preachers; it was owned and handled by the faithful; it permeated the entire religious life of Protestant communities. For them, the return to the true faith was inseparable from entry into the civilization of the printed word.

The third setting for the use of printed matter in common was the *confréries joyeuses*—festive associations of a craft or neighborhood—in which printed broadsheets and booklets to accompany their festivities were written, circulated, and read.[11] In Lyons, the merrymaking confraternity of the printers' journeymen, called La Coquille (The Typographical Error), took charge of providing this printed matter. First, they took part in the donkey cavalcades organized by the Abbayes de Maugouvert (Abbeys of Misrule), neighborhood-based associations that made fun of henpecked husbands. The brothers of La Coquille had their place in the parade and exhibited "certain mottoes, printed in Latin and in French." They also distributed written accounts of the proceedings in printed anthologies, for example, the *Recueil faicte au vray de la chevauchée de l'asne faicte en la ville de Lyon et commencée le premier jour du mois de septembre 1566* or the *Recueil de la chevauchée faicte en la ville de Lyon, le dix-septième de novembre 1578*. The print workers' confraternity was also active during Carnival, when they put out brochures such as *Les Plaisants devis des supposts du Seigneur de la*

[9] N. Z. Davis, "The Protestant Printing Workers of Lyons in 1551," in *Aspects de la propagande religieuse*, 247-57; idem, "Women on Top" and "Printing and the People" in her *Society and Culture in Early Modern France: Eight Essays* (Stanford, 1975), 124-51 and 189-226, respectively.

[10] Cited by S. Deyon and A. Lottin, *Les "Casseurs" de l'été 1566. L'Iconoclasme dans le Nord* (Paris, 1981), 19-20.

[11] N. Z. Davis, "The Reasons of Misrule" in her *Society and Culture*, 97-123; *Entrées royales et fêtes populaires à Lyon du XVe au XVIIIe siècles* (Lyons, 1970), 46-59.

*Coquille* (The Joking Sayings of the Henchmen of the Lord of the Typo), which gives the text of the parodic exchanges that supposedly took place between the three henchmen of this festive dignitary as he led the parade on the Sunday before Mardi Gras. In Lyons texts "printed by the Seigneur de la Coquille" are extant for the years 1558, 1581, 1584, 1589, 1593, 1594, and 1601. Thus there was an entire category of printed matter—and we might add that similar materials accompanied the triumphal parades of the Abbaye des Conards in Rouen and the Carnival parades in the cities of Languedoc—which incontestably indicates a highly familiar form of acculturation to the written word, worked out and deciphered in common and read by those who could read to those who could not.

## In the Countryside: Veillées *without Books*

We have no systematic studies of country areas comparable to the studies of the Amiens inventories, but there are several things that we can say about them. In the countryside, collective access to the printed book could occur in two modes, one community-oriented and the other seigneurial. The first was the *veillée*, when country folk gathered on winter nights to work, talk, and enjoy one another's company. On such an occasion, someone who knew how to read would read aloud—that is, would select parts of a book that a peddler had brought to the village, would comment on them, and perhaps translate them. Of course, we should avoid exaggerating the role of these village gatherings in the diffusion (even mediation) of printed matter, at least as far as the sixteenth and the seventeenth centuries are concerned. Peasant *veillées* appear in documents when they were condemned by synodal statutes and ecclesiastical ordinances, but such evidence is, in the last analysis, fairly scarce and fairly late. Furthermore, this evidence alludes to games, dances, or work accomplished in common, but not to the reading of books. The protagonists of such gatherings in literary works were above all rustic "notables."[12] It is in these terms that Noël du Fail, in his *Propos rustiques de Maistre Léon Ladulfi Champenois* (Lyons, 1548),

[12] See two fundamental articles on this question, with which I concur: H.-J. Martin, "Culture écrite et culture orale, culture savante et culture populaire dans la France d'Ancien Régime," *Journal des savants*, July-December 1975:225-82; and J.-L. Marais, "Littérature et culture 'populaire' aux XVIIᵉ et XVIIIᵉ siècles. Réponses et questions," *Annales de Bretagne et des Pays de l'Ouest* 87 (1980):65-105, which somewhat modifies Robert Mandrou's perspective in his *De la culture populaire aux XVIIᵉ et XVIIIᵉ siècles. La Bibliothèque bleue de Troyes* (Paris, 1964, 1975).

describes a *veillée* in the house of Robin Chevet, in which the master of the house sings and tells tales:

> Often after supper, his stomach stretched like a drum, drunk as Pataut, he liked to chat with his back to the fire as he cut hemp or remade his boots to the current fashion (for a proper man usually adjusts to all fashions), singing most melodiously—for he sang well—some new song, while Jouanne, his wife, on the other side answered him in like manner as she spun. The rest of the household was working, each on his own task, some mending the thongs of their flails, the others making teeth for rakes, scorching faggots to reconnect (possibly) the wagon axle broken by an overload, or making a stick whip out of medlar wood. [When they were] thus occupied with their various tasks, goodman Robin, after imposing silence, would begin a fine story about the time when the animals talked (it was just two hours before); of how Renard the fox stole a fish from the fishmongers; of how he got the Washerwomen to beat the Wolf when he was learning how to fish; of how the Dog and the Cat went on a voyage; about the Crow which lost its cheese when it sang; about the fairy Mélusine; about the Werewolf; about Asnette's hide; about fairies and how he often spoke with them familiarly, even at vespers as he passed through the hedgerows and saw them dancing near the Cormier fountain to the sound of a red leather bagpipe.

Note that there is nothing here to indicate that Robin read. The stories he tells belong to the oral tradition, but he may perhaps have found some of them in a book. It is clear that here, however, he is reciting by heart to his wife and his household:

> And if by chance one of them fell asleep, as such things happened when he was telling these old tales (to which I often listened), master Robin would take a piece of straw lit at one end and would blow through the other at the nose of the sleeper, making a sign with his free hand that no one was to wake him. Then he would say, " 'Struth! I've gone to so much trouble to learn these and I'm breaking my head here so that everybody will keep at his work, and they don't even deign to listen to me."[13]

[13] Noël du Fail, *Propos rustiques de maistre Léon Ladulfi Champenois*, Contes français du xvie siècle, Bibliothèque de la Pléiade (Paris, 1965), 620-21.

In the first chapter of this work du Fail gives a marvelous sketch of four village readers, who are the narrators of his "Rustic Tales." They do not participate in any *veillée*, however. Quite to the contrary, they remain apart, "under a spreading oak tree," during a village celebration. There is Anselme, "one of the rich men of this village, a good *Laboureur* [independent farmer] and a fairly good little notary for these parts"; there is Pasquier, who has hanging from his belt a "large hunting pouch containing Spectacles and a pair of old books of hours"; there is master Huguet, a former schoolmaster become "a good viticulturist," but who "cannot but bring us some of his old books on feast days and read to us as much as we let him, for example from a Shepherds' Calendar, from Aesop's *Fables*, from the *Roman de la Rose*"; and there is Lubin, "another very rich man," who looks over master Huguet's shoulder as he reads "from his book."[14] There is not the slightest allusion here to the peasant *veillée*, but there is evidence of the circulation of books and the practice of reading aloud among those who were above the common people of the village. Mentions of reading taking place at the peasant *veillées* are thus very rare indeed, if not nonexistent, for the century between the reigns of Henry II and Louis XIV, which makes me strongly doubt that the *veillées* contributed much to the penetration of printed matter into the country.

## Seigneurial Reading

Did the relationship between the lord and his peasants contribute any more to the spread of printed matter? Here we have direct evidence. Gilles Picot, Lord of Gouberville, writes on 6 February 1554: "It is raining without cease. [My men] were in the fields, but the rain chased them off again. In the evening, all through vespers, we read in *Amadis de Gaulle* about how he vanquished Dardan."[15] We know that this Norman gentleman read and that books circulated—given, lent, or exchanged—among his friends. Thus in November 1554, "a copy of [Justinian's] *Institutes* in which there is written [about] a Pythagorean wheel" is given to him by the parish priest of Beauficet, and during the same month, "being in Valognes, I returned to M. Jehan Bonnet the

[14] Ibid., 607-608.
[15] *Un Sire de Gouberville, gentilhomme campagnard du Cotentin de 1553 à 1562*, pub. A. Tollemer, intro. E. Le Roy Ladurie (Paris and The Hague, 1972), 203-11; M. Foisil, *Le Sire de Gouberville. Un Gentilhomme normand au XVIᵉ siècle* (Paris, 1981), 80-81, 231-34.

*Promptuayre des Medales* that he had lent me some time ago; and he gave me back the writings of Pierre Messye, which I left with my host to lend to M. de Hémesvez." (This last was a work by the Spanish author Mexia, translated into French by Claude Gruget.) In 1560, someone brought him from Bayeux "an almanac of Nostradamus," a previous edition of which is mentioned on 29 October 1558, when Gouberville declares: "I had [my men] begin to sow wheat at La Haulte-Vente. Nostradamus said in his almanac that this was a good day for plowing." In November 1562, Lieutenant Franqueterre returned "a prognostication of Nostradamus, and I returned to him the receipt that he gave me for it"; this illustrates both Gouberville's prudence and the high price attached to books, still precious objects. Some medical and surgical books should be added to this list of his readings, along with Machiavelli's *Prince* and the *Quart Livre* of Rabelais, lent to him by the priest of Cherbourg, who was at the time staying at Mesnil-au-Val. Gouberville seems to have himself read these books that he so often notes as having been lent or borrowed. The allusion to *Amadis*, read aloud one rainy evening, is unique in the entire journal, which is not much in a text that speaks of the daily occupations of five thousand days. Although Gouberville's chronicle is evidence that seigneurial reading could possibly have been an oral medium for the diffusion of the printed word, it also speaks of its infrequency by what Gouberville failed to record. In the city there seem to have been numerous and various occasions for those unable to read to encounter the printed word. The same was certainly not true of country areas, where, all that has been said of the *veillée* notwithstanding, reading aloud was the exception.

## Printed Matter in the City: Images and Texts

At least in the cities, then, there existed a relationship to printed matter somewhere between the individual's reading of a book, an activity that takes place privately, within the reader's *forum internum*, and the simple hearing of a written text, which occurs, for example, when listening to a sermon. In the workshop, in the dissident churches, in the festive confraternities, writing in typographic form was close at hand, even for those unable to read. Manipulated in common, by some taught, by others deciphered, printed matter was profoundly integrated into the life of the community, and it made its mark on the culture of the mass of city dwellers. By the same token, it created a public—therefore a market—that reached beyond those who knew how to read and beyond the readers of books alone. In point of fact, the relationship with the written word for most city dwellers between 1530 and 1660 was not one that involved books, or at least not the sort of books valuable enough to be kept a lifetime and appraised in one's estate. The "typographic acculturation" of the urban population depended on other more modest and more ephemeral material. This material accounted for a large part of printers' activities, and in all its forms it offered both text and image, although in highly varying formats and proportions. It is difficult to draw a clear distinction between the *image volante* (flysheet picture) and the *placard* (political broadsheet), between the *placard* and the *canard* (satirical or sensational news sheet), and between the *canard* and the slim volumes of the *Bibliothèque bleue*, as there were multiple transitional forms between each genre. The *image volante*, the typographic genre at first sight farthest from written culture, gives one example of this. These flysheet pictures always contain printed written material, giving titles, captions, and commentaries, as we can see, for instance, in the images made for trade-oriented or religious confraternities.[16]

### *The* Images Volantes

Always printed on large format sheets, the confraternity images combined picture and text. In some of them, the focus is on the engraved design; in others, for example the *placards* of pardons and indulgences or the listing of confraternity membership, the printed text is more important. But a vignette usually accompanies the text of such pieces; in turn, the large pictures left space in increasing amounts to writing—to a presentation of the tutelary saint or event that gave the *confrérie* its name and a mention of the church where it was founded; to a prayer in the patron saint's honor; and to notes on the history or statutes of the confraternity. As one image from the Confrérie du Saint-Sacrement states, this material could always be "read" two ways: "Whoever keeps this writing in a place where it can be read and whoever reads it—or, not knowing how to read, bows his head reverently—will earn plenary

---

[16] J. Gaston, *Les Images des confréries parisiennes avant la Révolution* (Paris, 1910), particularly his introduction, xv-lvi.

Indulgence."[17] Such pictures were for both private and public use. Every year, when dues were payable, all the brothers received a copy to paste on a wall of their bedroom or workshop. Some statutes made this obligatory, for example the Confrérie du Saint-Sacrement of Rueil stipulated that the brothers "will have in their house an image that represents this mystery." When the patron saint's feast day was celebrated, the images were distributed throughout the city and posted in the church. The carpenters, who belonged to the Confrérie de Saint-Joseph based in the parish of Saint-Nicolas-des-Champs, "have a High Mass sung, with Deacon, Subdeacon, and Chapter as well, with organ and carillon, [with] tapestries hung outside and inside the church *along with the images of the confraternity* on which it is marked that King Robert, thirty-seventh king of France, was the founder, and [with] the Bulls of Indulgence which were accorded in the month of March of the year 1665 by Pope Alexander VII." (Emphasis added.) These images provided prayers and pious formulas, they gave the names of the confraternity's masters and churchwardens, and they offered tangible or figurative form to the object of common devotion (the Holy Sacrament, the Rosary, the patron saint). They fed the piety of both those who could and those who could not read. One can imagine that their familiar presence at the center of daily life was an introduction to written culture for those to whom the schoolhouses of the city had failed to teach their ABCs.

Some of these images were printed from plates that remained the property of the confraternities. For example, the carpenters' *confrérie* in Saint-Nicolas-des-Champs, which we have already encountered, owned "two copper plates which serve to print the Images that are given to the confraternity" and "one large cooper plate which was made in 1660." But more often than not the confraternities turned to specialized *imagiers*, engravers, and printers. In Paris the printshops of the Rue Montorgueil controlled the market up to the end of the sixteenth century, producing large woodcuts for wall mounting. Later the lead passed to the copperplate engravers of the Rues Saint-Jacques and Saint-Jean-de-Latran, who also published illustrated books. Although religious images long constituted the greater part of the *imagiers'* work, the confraternities' orders obviously represented only a part of their activities. According to studies made of the prints in the Bibliothèque

[17] BN, Paris, Réserve des Estampes, 19.

Nationale collection, religious subjects accounted for 97 percent of the woodcuts put out by the printshops of the Rue Saint-Jacques at the end of the fifteenth century, 80 percent of those at the end of the sixteenth century, and close to 50 percent of those at the beginning of the seventeenth century.[18] There are several remarks that need to be made about this production of religious images—which must be considered as a form of "publishing," as attested by the bookseller-printers' annoyance at the proliferation of picture prints with texts. First, about its extent: Each plate lent itself to multiple reprintings and could serve for an extremely long time. The images extant thus represent only an infinitesimal portion of those that circulated and were pasted to walls, affixed to bedsteads, hung over mantels, closed in strongboxes or drawers, or buried with the dead. On the other hand, the religious image evolved: The large-format woodcuts, which often were printed in series and sometimes were colored by hand, gave way to smaller copperplate engravings that could also serve as illustrations for books of the same format. This double use of the print—as a flysheet and as a plate in a book—is, moreover, only one instance of the multiple reuse of such engravings, and confraternity materials give many examples of this. The same picture could be printed with different titles and texts for different confraternities, when a new text was not simply glued onto leftover stock.

## Secular Prints

Dominated by religious imagery in the sixteenth century, print production included more and more secular subjects during the seventeenth century. Religious pictures account for 48 percent of extant prints from the beginning of the century, but only 27 percent of those of the midcentury. The leading secular use was political. During the Wars of Religion, and particularly during the League, a war of images paralleled the war of pamphlets. Such pictures turned pious imagery to political ends (for example, by juxtaposing a crucifixion scene with a view of the funeral bier of the Duke of Guise and his brother the Cardinal of Lorraine) and often relied on the contrary political uses of a given iconographic motif (for example, the cooking-pot turned upside down). They circulated widely, were carried and brandished during

[18] P. Chaunu, *La Mort à Paris XVIe, XVIIe et XVIIIe siècles* (Paris, 1978), 279-82 and 337-44.

processions, and were "hawked, preached, and sold publicly in Paris in all places and streets of the city," as Pierre de l'Estoile writes in the introduction to his collection of such images. Henry IV grasped the importance of the printed image. For one thing, in 1594 he ordered the burning of all such pieces concerning the League; in addition, he had printed an entire series of propaganda pictures bearing his portrait or celebrating his royal deeds. The success of the printsellers of the Rue Saint-Jacques was obviously due in part to their enrollment in the service of monarchical glory, which brought redoubled orders for prints to illustrate books of propaganda or to be distributed as flysheets.

Fig. 8. Prints as political propaganda: Henry IV curing the king's evil (scrofula) in *Comme le Roy Tres-chrestien Henry IIII . . . touche les écrouelles*, copperplate engraving by Pierre Firens, Paris, c. 1605 (383 x 392 mm) (Bibliothèque Nationale, Paris).

After political imagery, pictures for entertainment, both satirical and moralizing, account for the next sizable group of nonreligious prints. During the first half of the seventeenth century two themes overshadowed all others: the process of aging and relations between men and women. This last theme appeared in various forms, for example in portrayals of two imaginary beasts, Bigorne, well nourished with "bons hommes," and Chiche-Face (France), dying of hunger for lack of "bonnes femmes," or in the portrait of Lustucru as a cephalic surgeon, putting women's heads back on wrong side out. In this sort of imagery (which includes the various series of Lagniet's *Proverbes* published between 1657 and 1663) as in the political engravings, the text takes up less space than in the religious prints. It is often limited to a title and an explanatory or moralizing commentary in verse placed under the picture, which was usually oblong in form. Writing never disappeared completely, however, and, as with the devotional images, the prints that aimed at amusing or persuading did their part to further the entry of the urban populace into the culture of the printed word.[19]

## Placards

Among the *canards* and *occasionnels*, those that were printed on the recto side alone of a large-format sheet differed little (aside from their subject matter) from the larger engravings. But this format was rare among the *canards* (which presented news of extraordinary happenings), at least among those extant. The inventory of Jean-Pierre Seguin lists only seven of these from between 1529 and 1631.[20] All—with the exception of one not illustrated—have the same layout: From top to bottom of a lengthwise sheet (unlike satirical images, which were generally horizontal), they bear a title, made to be seen and cried, then a woodcut and a descriptive text of ten to twenty lines. Image and text concurrently describe celestial prodigies (*Le Pourtraict de la comète, Qui est apparue sur la ville de Paris depuys le Mercredy 28e Novembre 1618, jusques à quelques jours ensuivans* [Paris, M. de Mathonière, 1618]); the evil deeds of witches and sorcerers (*Mort et trespas de Monseigneur le Prince de Courtenay, par la malicieuse Sorcellerie d'un misérable Sorcier qui depuys fut exécuté* [n.p., n.d.]); or monstrous creatures, as in the two

[19] *Cinq siècles d'imagerie française* (Paris, Musée National des Arts et Traditions Populaires, 1973). (*French Popular Imagery: Five Centuries of Prints*, trans. and adapted by P. S. Falla and S. Lambert [London, 1974].)

[20] J.-P. Seguin, *L'Information en France avant le périodique. 517 canards imprimés entre 1529 et 1631* (Paris, 1964), nos. 252, 410, 461, 465, 466, 467, and 472.

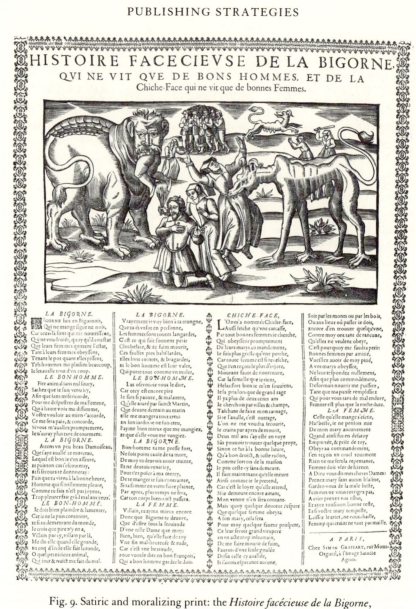

Fig. 9. Satiric and moralizing print: the *Histoire facécieuse de la Bigorne*, copperplate engraving published in Paris by Simon Graffart, c. 1600 (Bibliothèque Nationale, Paris).

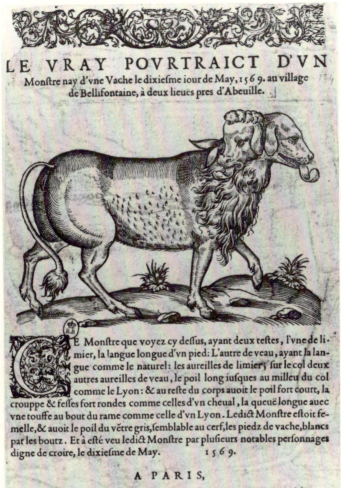

# LE VRAY POVRTRAICT D'VN

Monſtre nay d'vne Vache le dixieſme iour de May, 1 5 6 9. au village
de Bellifontaine, à deux lieuës pres d'Abeuille.

E Monſtre que voyez cy deſſus, ayant deux teſtes, l'vne de limier, la langue longue d'vn pied: L'autre de veau, ayant la langue comme le naturel: les aureilles de limier, ſur le col deux
autres aureilles de veau, le poil long iuſques au milleu du col
comme le Lyon: & au reſte du corps auoit le poil fort court, la
crouppe & feſſes fort rondes comme celles d'vn cheual, la queuë longue auec
vne touffe au bout du rame comme celle d'vn Lyon. Ledict Monſtre eſtoit fe-
melle, & auoit le poil du vêtre gris, ſemblable au cerf, les piedz de vache, blancs
par les boutz. Et à eſté veu ledict Monſtre par pluſieurs notables perſonnages
digne de croire, le dixieſme de May.        1 5 6 9.

## A PARIS,

Par Iean Dallier Libraire, demeurant ſur le Pont ſainct Michel à
l'enſeigne de la Roſe blanche.

Fig. 10. A *placard* describing a monster born in a village near
Abbeville published in Paris by Jean Dallier in 1569
(height: 287 mm) (Bibliothèque Nationale, Paris).

*canards* of identical layout printed in Chambéry in 1578 by F. Poumard (the *Briefz discours d'un merveilleux monstre né à Eurisgo, terre de Novarrez en Lombardie, au moys de Janvier en la présente Année 1578. Avec le vray pourtraict d'icelluy au plus prez du naturel* and the *Vray pourtraict, et sommaire description d'un horrible et merveilleux monstre, né à Cher, terre de Piémond, le 10 Janvier 1578. A huit heures du soir, de la femme d'un docteur, avec sept cornes, celle qui pend jusques à la sainccture & celle qui est autour du col sont de chair*).

Some of the *occasionnels* that were related to political events took up the same formula and were printed on the recto of one sheet (allowing them to be posted). For example, in 1642 *Le Pourtraict de Monseignr le Cardinal de Richelieu sur son lit de parade, avec son Épitaphe* was printed in Paris by François Beauplet. Folio *occasionnels*, which bore a longer text than the *images volantes* but, unlike the *placards*, were illustrated, were a transitional form between one typographic format and another. They were destined for an ephemeral life, but they could also reach people who did not buy them. Less immediately "popular" because they had written texts alone, the *placards* still could bring sustenance to the culture of the generality of men, since, when posted on the city walls, those who could read could share them with those who could not. This was surely what reformers hoped for when in 1534 they plastered the walls of Paris with a *placard* attacking the mass written by Antoine Marcourt and printed by Pierre de Vingle; both fled to Geneva. It was also in an attempt to influence popular opinion that in January 1649 the Queen and Mazarin, residing in Rueil, ordered a *placard* posted in Paris, the text of which was later printed in the form of a *libelle* (pamphlet) entitled *Lis et fais* and distributed secretly in the city by the Chevalier de La Valette on the night of 10-11 February.[21] In the sixteenth and the seventeenth centuries, then, the printing profession gave wide diffusion to an abundance of typographic materials designed to be posted on or pasted to the walls of houses and churches, bedrooms and workshops. These materials appeared in a variety of forms that almost always permitted a double reading—of text and image. Thus it is beyond doubt that printing profoundly transformed a culture that, until then, had been deprived of contact with the written word. A change of this importance, which made the printed word familiar and neces-

[21] H. Carrier, "Souvenirs de la Fronde en U.R.S.S.: Les Collections russes de Mazarinades," *Revue historique* 511 (1974):27-50, and particularly p. 37.

sary to a full comprehension of the images offered to view, was quite probably decisive for the introduction of literacy in urban areas, a literacy that was both significant and precocious and that in due time created a "popular" market for the book.

## Canards

If the estate inventories show no signs of this market as late as the mid-seventeenth century, it is perhaps because humbler people found sustenance in reading matter of so little value that it did not merit appraisal. As early as the 1530s, this would have been true of the *canards* distributed by urban *colporteurs* (peddlers), those "porte-paniers" or "contre-porteux" of which Pierre de l'Estoile spoke. Some of these *canards*, as we have seen, were printed in folio format and could be posted like the *placards*, but the majority of them were quarto or octavo booklets of only a few pages. Among the *canards* extant, according to Jean-Pierre Seguin's study, nearly 60 percent have between thirteen and sixteen printed pages and are composed of either one octavo signature (the most prevalent formula) or two quarto signatures. Thirty percent of surviving *canards* are shorter than this, with seven or eight printed pages (one quarto signature or half an octavo signature). A few, approximately 5 percent, have as many as twenty-two or twenty-four printed pages (three quarto signatures or one and one-half octavo signatures). The publication of such booklets seems to have grown with the passage of time, since, among those studied, 4 percent were printed between 1529 and 1550, 8 percent between 1550 and 1576, 22 percent between 1576 and 1600, and 66 percent between 1600 and 1631. These percentages may not be accurate for all *canards*, however, because of the higher chances of preservation for the seventeenth-century pamphlets.

Between 1530 and 1630, the publication of *canards* was above all in the hands of the booksellers and printers of Paris and Lyons. Paris produced more than half of the pieces preserved (55.3 percent) and Lyons nearly a quarter (22 percent). In Paris, the printers who put out the greatest number of *canards* did not specialize in the production of low-cost books for a "popular" audience, but on occasion they put their presses to work printing materials of low price and wide appeal. Three of these printers accounted for nine titles or more: Abraham Saugrain (14 titles), Fleury Bourriquant (12), and Antoine du Breuil (9). For each of these men, the printing of *canards* was one activity among others: Bourriquant also put out political lampoons and mathematical texts and Breuil printed travel accounts and collections of poetry. In Lyons the market for *canards* was dominated by one printer, Benoît Rigaud, who printed nearly one quarter of the *canards* put out in that city. For him, the publication of *occasionnels* was part of a business centered on the printing of inexpensive books (which does not mean books destined for one public alone) such as almanacs and books of predictions, songs and poetry, and official acts and decrees.

In one out of four *canards* the text was accompanied by a woodcut, usually small in size and of extremely varied origins. The same wood block, retouched or not, might serve for several publications, and a monstrous serpent in Cuba could easily be transformed into a dragon flying through the Paris sky.[22] The principle of reutilization seems to have been fundamental to the commerce in *canards*, since not only the picture but the text as well could be used more than once. Indeed, the same account could be repeated some years apart with changed names and dates, as in the case of one text that originally described the death of Marguerite de la Rivière, executed in Padua in December 1596, then the death of Catherine de la Critonnière, executed in that city in September 1607, then once again the death of Marguerite de la Rivière, still executed in Padua, but this time in December 1617, and finally the death of the same heroic Marguerite, executed in Metz in November 1623.[23] Seguin notes five other examples of such reutilizations involving two, four, or six *canards* published by one printer or by different printers. Pierre de l'Estoile on several occasions also mentions *canards* that were "rescratched" (*regrattées*): "On that day [16 June 1608] criers were hawking the *Conversion d'une Courtizanne vénitienne*, which was a rescratched piece of nonsense, for every year three or four of them are made." Or, two years later: "Today [13 March 1610] they were hawking the following piece of nonsense as new, although it is rescratched and out of fashion, the *Discours prodigieux et espouvantable de trois Espagnols*, which bears a false date and was made out of pity to warm up the poor peddlers, who are in dreadful straits, by the printer Ruelle, who told me so this very day and brought me one."[24] But even without considering these publications that were camouflaged as novelties, the texts of most *canards* were written by dipping into a limited repertory of plots and a restricted number of narrative formulas. Among the 517

[22] Seguin, *L'Information en France*, nos. 462 and 237.
[23] Ibid., nos. 14, 15, 16, 17.
[24] Cited in ibid., 23-34.

Fig. 11. A *canard* concerning the celestial phenomenon
that appeared above Paris in 1531 (height: 130 mm)
(Bibliothèque Nationale, Paris).

*canards* listed by Seguin from between 1530 and 1630, six themes account for more than thirty publications apiece: crimes and capital ex-
ecutions (89 publications), celestial phenomena (86 publications, to
which we might add 8 concerning the visions of the Grand Turk),
magic spells and diabolic possessions (62 publications), miracles (45
publications), floods (37 publications), and earthquakes (32 publications). Next in order come sacrileges, monstrous births, thefts, and
lightning damage.

The *canard* was aimed at the literate, since the text predominated
even if pictures were still present, and it fed the imaginations of city

dwellers with accounts of things out of all proportion to daily life—moral aberration, the inclemency of the elements, the supernatural, the miraculous, and the diabolic. With large press runs, the *canards* (along with the almanacs) undoubtedly constituted the first series of printed texts in booklet form destined for the greatest number and the most "popular" of readers—which does not mean, of course, that their buyers were all artisans or merchants, nor that reading them produced the same effect. Pierre de l'Estoile attests to the taste of the urban elites for such literature, but he also proves that such groups regarded with some detachment these "pieces of nonsense," "frivolities," "imbecilities," and "idlers' amusements," which only the naive and the credulous could believe.

### The Origins of the Bibliothèque bleue

The printers of Troyes had a part, limited to be sure, in the market for *canards*. Nicolas du Ruau printed two *canards*, one in 1584 and another in 1586. At the beginning of the seventeenth century the Oudots published a few more, Jean Oudot in 1605 and 1609 and Nicolas I Oudot in 1608 and 1610. Perhaps because of the success of these inexpensive books, and perhaps also because Paris printers controlled their publication, Nicolas Oudot had the idea of producing similar works, but slightly heftier and of a different content, for the same large public. In 1602, reutilizing woodcuts of various origins that had been set aside after the triumph of copperplate engraving, using old type, and printing on paper of mediocre quality made by paper mills in Champagne, Nicolas Oudot began to publish inexpensive slim volumes that soon were spoken of as "blue booklets" (*livrets bleus*), referring perhaps to the color of their paper or cover stock.[25] From his address on the "rue Nostre Dame, au Chapon d'Or couronné" until his death in 1636, he put out 52 such publications, which we can inventory thanks to the catalogue prepared by Alfred Morin.[26] Chivalric romances, with 21 titles, make up close to half of this production. The list of heroes he resuscitated is long: the noble and mighty Hector, the Chevalier Geoffroy Longtooth, the Lord of Lusignan, Doolin of Mayence, Maugis d'Aygremont and his son Vivien, Morgant the Giant, Artus (Arthur) of

[25] On the Oudots see L. Morin, "Les Oudot imprimeurs et libraires à Troyes, à Paris, à Sens et à Tours," *Bulletin du Bibliophile* (1901):66-77, 138-45, 182-94.

[26] A. Morin, *Catalogue descriptif de la Bibliothèque Bleue de Troyes (almanachs exclus)* (Geneva, 1974).

Brittany, the Four Sons of Aymon, Gallien, Alexander the Great, Olivier of Castille and Artus of Algabre, the knights Milles and Amys, Guérin Mesquin, Ogier the Dane, the Prince Meliadus, Mabrian, king of Jerusalem and India, and—one woman among all these doughty knights—Helen of Constantinople. The second group of inexpensive booklets printed by Nicolas Oudot was composed of saints' lives. There were ten titles in all, recounting the lives of saints Susanna, Catherine, Claude, Nicholas, Augustine, Roch, Reine, and Helena, to which should be added a "Life, Death, Passion, and Resurrection" of Jesus Christ and a *Vie des trois Maries*, which bears an authorization date of 1602 and reuses seventy-five woodcuts originally used in Books of Hours published in Troyes in the sixteenth century by the Lecoqs. Unlike the chivalric romances, which surpassed one hundred and sometimes two hundred pages and were mostly in quarto format, the saints' lives were slim booklets generally printed in one octavo signature. Finally, the new publishing formula that Nicolas Oudot had invented enabled him to give wider circulation to texts taken from learned literature, for example a half-dozen French tragedies with subjects similar to those of the chivalric romances. There was little else aside from these three categories: a few works of religious edification, a New Testament, a guide to the royal roads of France, two editions of *Mélusine*, and one edition of the *Vie généreuse des mercelots, bons compagnons et boesmiens*, a picaresque novel in miniature.

Thus it is clear that, from the start, the "Bibliothèque bleue" was above all a publishing formula appropriate to the distribution of strongly different texts. Nicolas Oudot used this formula to print three general types of texts. First, there were the medieval romances, which elite culture in the sixteenth century had discarded and which had therefore been abandoned by the more "ordinary" avenues of publication. Second, there were the texts that belonged within the traditional store of hagiographic literature. And third, there were certain titles from the learned literature that found their "pocket book edition" in the Troyes booklets. Oudot's son Nicolas II, born of his second marriage (to Guillemette Journée), continued this activity, adapting it to his tastes, first at the address of the "Sainct Esprit rue du Temple" and, after 1649, at his father's old address, the "Chapon d'Or couronné." Nicolas II devoted a portion of the forty-two works he was to print between 1645 and 1679 to the same sorts of texts as his father: chivalric romances (with a republication of *Gallien restauré* and the two volumes of *Huon de Bordeaux*); hagiographic and pious literature (with a *Life* of Saint Julien, a *Grande dance macabre des hommes et des femmes*, and, in 1679, *La Grand Bible des Noels tant vieils que nouveaux*); and literary texts (with an edition of *Polyeucte* and one of Mairet's *Sophonisbe*). Still, most of Nicolas II's efforts went into using the format that his father had established to publish texts that his father had missed. Heading the list were books of instruction and apprenticeship (17 titles): the *Civilité puérile et honnête pour l'éducation des enfants*; model conversation books (the *Cabinet de l'Éloquence française* and the *Fleurs de bien dire*); practical and technical books (the *Cuisinier français* of La Varenne and the *Maréchal expert*); medical advice (the *Médecin charitable enseignant la manière de faire et préparer en sa maison avec facilité et peu de frais les remèdes propres à toutes maladies* and the *Opérateur des pauvres, ou la fleur d'opération nécessaire aux pauvres pour conserver leur santé et soy guérir à peu de frais*); and, finally, astrological works (the *Palais des Curieux où l'Algèbre et le Sort donnent la décision des questions les plus douteuses et où les songes et les visions nocturnes sont expliquées selon la doctrine des Anciens*, the *Miroir d'Astrologie Naturelle*, and the *Pronostications generalles* of Commelet, published in five successive and different editions). Nicolas II Oudot also devoted a good deal of space to the burlesque works that were so characteristic of the mid-seventeenth century; he published, for example, the *Fantaisies de Bruscambille*, the *Oeuvres burlesques* of Scarron and their sequels, the *Tracas de Paris en vers burlesques*, and an adaptation of the French translation of the *Buscón* of Quevedo. Finally, he introduced (albeit timidly) the pious literature of the Catholic Reformation into the catalogue of the "Bibliothèque bleue" by publishing the *Sept trompettes spirituelles pour resveiller les pecheurs et pour les induire à faire pénitence* of Barthélemy Solutive, a Recollect Franciscan. The second generation of the Oudots, faithful to the format of the earlier publications, enlarged the range of the texts they published, distributing at low cost fashionable literature, guides to the new spirituality, and booklets that taught practical knowledge and savoir-faire. From one Nicolas Oudot to the other, the corpus of Troyes publications broadened its base as the accompanying table shows.

Thus in the span of seventy years the basic repertory was established among the genres from which Troyes publishers were to draw for the next two centuries.

|                 | Religion | Fiction  | Instruction |
|-----------------|----------|----------|-------------|
| Nicolas I Oudot | 15 works | 36 works | 1 work      |
| Nicolas II Oudot| 6 works  | 19 works | 17 works    |

### Competitors of the Oudots

Nicolas Oudot and his son were not the only printers in Troyes who published slim blue books during the first two-thirds of the seventeenth century. Several of their fellow printers picked up the formula, beginning with their own circle of relatives. Jean Oudot the Elder and his son Jean Oudot the Younger printed several works of this sort. For the former, there were the two *canards* already mentioned and a *Histoire de France avec les figures des rois*; for the latter, there were an *Exposition des Evangiles*, the *Histoire de Valentin et Orson*, and the *Prédictions et pronostications generalles pour dix-neuf ans* of Pierre Delarivey. In January 1623 another Troyes printer, Claude Briden, sold the younger Jean "stories on wood, copper, lead, and others serving to print novels" for one hundred *livres*, due at Easter, and Oudot's promise to print such works as Briden would request, to equal a sum of 150 *livres*. Another Oudot, Jacques, whose printshop was also on the Rue Notre Dame, published two collections of predictions attributed to Jean Petit, the *Prédictions generalles pour l'an MDC.XLII* and the *Prestations perpétuelles du nombre d'Or ou cicle lunaire*, along with a *mazarinade*, the *Conférence agréable de deux paysans de Saint Ouen et Montmorency*—further proof of the flexibility of the form that Nicolas Oudot had invented.

Beside the various Oudots, there were three other printers who published similar inexpensive books: Edme Briden, at the address of "la rue Notre Dame à l'enseigne du Nom de Jésus" (5 works), Yves Girardon (8 works, nearly all reprinting texts already published), and Jacques Balduc (2 works). As we can see, none of these printers offered serious competition to Nicolas Oudot and his son, who had the production of the low-cost book well in hand. Still, this production was modest in comparison to what it would become in the next two centuries. All in all, the works published by the two Nicolas Oudots and their rivals total 116 editions, not even one-tenth of the 1,273 editions of the *Bibliothèque bleue* listed by Alfred Morin.[27] In the first seventy-

---

[27] Morin's catalogue comprises 1,226 items. The total number of 1,273 published

five years of the existence of the editorial formula they had invented—
which survived for two and one-half centuries—the Troyes printers
gradually built up the full range of genres that they could distribute,
but at this time the number of titles and editions within each genre was
still limited.

This statement perhaps calls for one reservation, since it fails to take
into account one genre of publishing in Troyes that does seem to have
produced multiple editions during the first three quarters of the seventeenth century: the almanacs. As early as the beginning of the century, many Troyes printers were bringing almanac writers under contract, particularly since Nicolas I Oudot had plunged into the
production of the chivalric romances and had no interest in almanacs.
Louis Morin cites several of these contracts, which stipulated both parties' obligations. The author was to provide the text of the almanac annually for six, eight, or ten years, and it was his responsibility to obtain
the necessary permission from the civil and ecclesiastical authorities.
The printer promised the annual payment of a certain sum of money,
sometimes also promised to give the author a number of copies of the
almanac, and occasionally agreed to insert the astrologer's portrait in
the work. Agreements of this sort were made in 1616 between Jean
Berthier and Pierre Varlet, "master writer enrolled [at the guild] in
Troyes, professor of mathematics, geometry, and arithmetic"; in 1618
between Pierre Sourdet and Louis de la Callère, "astrologer from
Champagne"; and in 1620 between Jean Oudot the Elder and Pierre
Patris, known as Pierre Delarivey.[28] The production of almanacs paralleled that of the *Bibliothèque bleue* titles, and as the number of almanacs increased, two sorts of conflicts arose. The first was among the
printers of Troyes, which was the case, for example, in 1623 when
Claude Briden and Jean Oudot the Younger signed an agreement concerning the printing and distribution of their almanacs. The second
was between Troyes printers and competitors from other cities. In 1635
the same Claude Briden quarreled with a printer in Autun, Blaise Si-
monnot, who was printing Pierre Delarivey's almanac without Briden's permission. Notarized agreements settled or dispelled possible
conflicts in these cases, as they did in 1630 when the same Briden sold
Louis Dumesgnil the right to print and distribute Pierre Delarivey's

works is obtained by subtracting the numbers with no corresponding items and the
numbers eliminated and by adding the "*bis*" and "*ter*" numbers from the catalogue and
its supplement.

[28] L. Morin, *Histoire corporative des artisans du livre à Troyes* (Troyes, 1900), 244 ff.

almanac in the jurisdiction of the *parlement* of Rouen for a period of ten years in exchange for an annual payment of 60 *livres*, payable in stock from his bookstore.

It was toward the middle of the seventeenth century, however, that the production of Troyes almanacs reached its highest point.[29] On the one hand, there were several printers who never put out books in the *Bibliothèque bleue* format, but who published almanacs regularly, alone or in association with other printers. This was the case for Denis Clément, Jean Blanchard, Edme Adenet, Eustache and Denis Regnault, Edme Nicot, Léger Charbonnet, and Gabriel Laudereau. On the other hand, Nicolas II Oudot, who had always published some works on astrology and prognostication in the *Bibliothèque bleue* format, printed an increasing number of almanacs until his retirement in 1679. Very significant among these was, in 1657, the first "popular" edition of the *Grand calendrier et compost des bergers*, which had already been published in the sixteenth century in Troyes (in 1510, 1529, and 1541), but in editions in no way similar to those of the *Bibliothèque bleue*. Moreover, every year Nicolas II Oudot added new almanacs to those he already printed, which culminated in the publication of thirteen different almanacs in 1671, twelve in 1672, and still eight in 1673. The tangle of these various editions has not yet been unraveled, but it is certain that they constituted a considerable production demanding the combined efforts of a growing number of astrologers, real or fictive, dead or alive, whether faithful or episodic contributors. Through the titles of the almanacs published by Nicolas II Oudot we can trace a good twenty of such authors, who either worked for him exclusively or whom he shared with other publishers. The publication of almanacs must be distinguished from that of the blue booklets, if for no other reason than because a greater number of printshops were involved. Almanacs gave the kingdom of France its most widely distributed books, and they provided the Troyes booksellers with one of the most dependable bases of their prosperity.

### The City Clientele

It is no easy task to trace those who read these booklets that were printed in such large numbers, first in Troyes and then in other cities (Rouen for example), nor is it easy to ascertain just what they read, par-

[29] E. Socard, "Étude sur les almanachs et les calendriers de Troyes (1497-1881)," *Mémoires de la Société Académique d'Agriculture, de Sciences, Arts et Belles-Lettres du Département de l'Aube* (1881):217-375.

ticularly since our observation has to end with the years 1660-1670. There are two propositions, however, that seem possible to advance. In the first century of its existence the *Bibliothèque bleue*, including the almanacs, seems to have reached a public that was essentially urban. That the low-cost books of the Oudots and their imitators were sold by peddlers must not lead us into error. Seventeenth-century sources on book peddling, found particularly in the royal ordinances, derived exclusively from responses to an urban activity that it was necessary to supervise and occasionally to restrict, since it was in competition with bookstore sales and encouraged the distribution of prohibited books.[30] The book peddler was thus an urban figure, and his stock included a jumble of *occasionnels* and official publications, almanacs and blue booklets, pamphlets and gazettes. The following extract and painting demonstrate this. The text dates from 1660 and, in satirizing the *merciers'* (sellers of small wares) packs, it describes them for us. They

> carry here and there almanacs, little ABCs, Gazettes ordinary and extraordinary, legends and little romances of Mélusine, of Maugis, of the four sons of Aymon, of Geoffroy Longtooth, of Valentin and Ourson, [books] to chase away boredom, worldly songs, dirty and nasty, dictated by a filthy wit, *vaudevilles* [satiric songs], villanelles, court airs, and drinking songs.[31]

Thus peddlers carried a heterogeneous stock of different forms of literature to satisfy different cultural expectations, all printed in small sizes and limited numbers, with paper bindings and low prices. Similar remarks could be made based on figure 12, a painting of the beginning of the seventeenth century. It shows a peddler selling the *Almanach pour l'an 1622* by P. Delarivey, "young astrologer of Troyes"; *Le Siege de La Rochelle. Année 1623*, printed in Rouen; an *Edict du Roy pour les monnoyes*; an *Advis donné pour la Réformation des prestz*, printed in Normandy in 1623; *La Prinse de Clérac* by "Monseigneur, the Duke Delboeuf"; *La Fuite du Compte Mansefe[l]d et de levesque Dalbestrad en Hollande* of 1623; and, stuck in the peddler's hat, *La Reception du prince de Galle en Espaigne*, also in 1623. Here again we see a mixed stock, including *occasionnels*, one official document, and an almanac. There is

---

[30] R. Chartier, "Pamphlets et gazettes," in Martin and Chartier, *Histoire de l'édition française*, 1:405-25.

[31] D. Martin, *Parlement nouveau* ... (Strasbourg, 1660), cited in Marais, "Littérature et culture 'populaire,'" 70.

Fig. 12. *Le Colporteur* (The Peddler), c. 1623, by an anonymous painter of the
French School of the seventeenth century (oil on canvas, 850 x 720 mm)
(Musée des Arts et Traditions Populaires, Paris).

nothing, of course, to indicate with absolute certainty that that extract
and this image show us urban peddlers, but the absence of contemporary regulations on the rural peddling of books, along with the inclusion in the peddler's packs of works known to have been read in the
cities (for example, the *occasionnels* or the *Gazette*), make it reasonable
to suppose so. It was perhaps only in the eighteenth century that peddling escaped the confines of the cities to carry the little blue booklets—
and the prohibited books and books normally sold in urban stores—
into the small towns and villages that had no bookstores.

Another indication of the city distribution of materials printed by Troyes printers lies in the agreements they made with booksellers in the capital. Nicolas I Oudot was the first to try out a formula of this sort with the Parisian bookseller Jean Promé. In 1627 he printed a *Nouveau Testament de Nostre Seigneur Jésus Christ*, which was reprinted in 1635. Alfred Morin has found a copy of this work in which, pasted over the original title, an engraved title gives the address, "À Troyes, et se vendent à Paris, Chez Jean Promé rue Frémentel au petit Corbeil 1628."[32] In 1670 it was Nicolas II Oudot who noted a Parisian outlet for one of his almanacs, the *Almanach pour l'an de Grâce mil six cens soixante dix*... by M. Chevry of Paris, "King's Engineer" and "Mathematician in ordinary ... of Monseigneur the Duke d'Orléans." The book bears the legend, "À Troyes, et se vend à Paris chez Nicolas Oudot" (one of Nicolas II's sons, who had settled in Paris in 1664 and had married one of the widow Promé's daughters).[33] During the last third of the seventeenth century, the booksellers Antoine Raffle and Jean Musier were to sell the booklets from Troyes on a large scale, but it is clear that from the start the printers of the *Bibliothèque bleue* had considered the Parisian market essential and had worked to conquer it through their associates among the booksellers and by means of the peddlers. This recalls the practices of the printers of Paris and Lyons, who, in the sixteenth century—even before Nicolas Oudot—had directed a large part of their activity to the printing and sale of inexpensive editions; these titles were to furnish the Troyes printers with part of their stock in trade. The most important of these predecessors of the Oudots were, in Paris, the Trepperels, Jean Janot, and the Bonfons and, in Lyons, the Chaussards, Claude Nourry (the publisher of Rabelais), and Benoît Rigaud.[34]

## Shared Reading

Distributed particularly well in the cities, the literature of the *Bibliothèque bleue* was not only read by humble folk there. This is the second statement that can be risked about its distribution before the eighteenth

---

[32] "[Printed] at Troyes, and sold in Paris at the store of Jean Promé, Rue Frémentel, at [the sign of] the little Basket." A. Morin, *Catalogue descriptif*, nos. 822, 823.

[33] Socard, "Étude sur les almanachs," 280-81.

[34] Martin, "Culture écrite et culture orale," 232, 244; J.-P. Oddos, "Simples notes sur les origines de la Bibliothèque bleue," in *La "Bibliothèque bleue" nel seicento o della letteratura per il popolo* (Bari and Paris, 1981), 159-68.

century. It seems certain insofar as the almanac is concerned, a book that all society shared in reading. Book collections that survive attest to this, as do account books and mentions in literature like those in the *Histoire comique de Francion*, the *Caquets de l'accouchée*, and the *Fortune des gens de qualité* of Jacques de Caillières and the theater of Molière.[35] By its very nature the almanac was open to a plural readership, for it provided a written text for those who knew how to read and signs or images to be deciphered for those who did not. It gave information to some about the schedules of the courts and the markets; it told others about the weather to be expected, offering predictions and horoscopes and precepts and advice in its dual language of illustration and writing.[36] A book to be used and to be used in multiple ways, the almanac intertwined signs and written text like no other book. It seems the quintessential book for a society still unequally used to the written word and in which many different relationships with print undoubtedly existed, ranging all the way from fluent reading to halting decipherment. The same might be said for the blue booklets, although to a lesser degree since their texts were accompanied by only a few images.[37] The limited indications that can be found of how such books were read in the seventeenth century perhaps permits us a two-part hypothesis. On the one hand, these books were present in a society of readers that comprised neither the *petit peuple* of the cities nor the clientele of the learned book, but a world of semiliterate people—petty nobles, city burghers, and merchants either active or retired—who were fond of the old-fashioned works and the humorous or practical volumes that constituted a good part of the Troyes printers' stock in trade. On the other hand, in the world of the urban trades, such books were capable of the same collective manipulation as other texts, since they could be read in common in the workshop or in the roistering confraternity. Before the rise of rural peddling, before the increase in literacy, and before the scorn of society's notables consigned it to the popular classes, such must have been the first public for the *Bibliothèque bleue*.

[35] Marais, "Littérature et culture 'populaire,' " 83-84; Martin, *Livre, pouvoirs et société*, 1:538.

[36] G. Bollème, *Les Almanachs populaires aux XVIIᵉ et XVIIIᵉ siècles. Essai d'histoire sociale* (Paris and The Hague, 1969).

[37] G. Bollème, *La Bibliothèque bleue. Littérature populaire en France du XVIIᵉ au XIXᵉ siècle* (Paris, 1971); idem, *La Bible bleue. Anthologie d'une littérature "populaire"* (Paris, 1975).

## Publishing Strategies and Cultural Gaps

The years from 1530 to 1660 marked a decisive stage in the history of publishing in France.[38] Although illiteracy remained widespread—even in the cities, which were much in advance of the country areas around them—and although individual ownership of many books remained the privilege of the elites, it was during this century (broadly understood) that a "popular" market for the printed word was established. The groundwork for such a market had doubtlessly been prepared by the circulation of an entire set of materials that, since the block books, had brought together image and text and had made the written word familiar even to those unable to read. This new relationship with the printed word cannot be separated from the social relations that lay at the heart of all forms of popular sociability—work-connected, religious, or festive. Far from supposing, at least at first, any withdrawal into one's inner self, the circulation of printed texts depended strongly on the community bonds woven among the *petit peuple* of the cities. Popular receptivity to printed matter did not create a literature specific to the popular audience; it meant that the humblest of citizens handled texts that were also read by "notables" great and small. This was what happened with the almanacs, with the *canards*, and with the blue booklets. In Paris and Lyons in the sixteenth century and in Troyes in the seventeenth, printers devoted the better part of their activities to publishing these slim volumes that cost little and had a great number of buyers. In so doing, however, they created or reinforced cultural gaps that until then had been little or not much felt.

The first of these gaps was between the cities and the countryside. In rural areas, traditional culture left little room for the printed word, and books were rarely owned and rarely handled. In the cities, however, acculturation to printing happened on an almost daily basis because books were present, because the walls bore images and *placards*, and because people had frequent recourse to writing. The cultural universe on one side of the city walls became increasingly different from the cultural universe on the other side, and this led to scorn from within and hostility from without. In a world based on oral commu-

---

[38] See the two fundamental articles already cited, by N. Z. Davis ("Printing and the People") and H.-J. Martin ("Culture écrite et culture orale"), which suggest the hypotheses we follow here. See also my "La Circulation de l'écrit," in *Histoire de la France urbaine*, vol. 3: *La Ville classique* (Paris, 1981), 267-82.

nication and the gesture, the cities became little islands of another culture, a culture based on writing and typography, in which all or nearly all the urban population directly or indirectly participated. And thereafter all other cultures were to be measured by this new culture that rested on the newest of the aids to communication, and all other cultures came to be deprecated, rejected, and denied.

To this first gap, the "popular" diffusion of printed matter and of the book added another. The new forms of publishing that had produced the low-cost booklets did not make equal use of all available texts. For the most part, they contributed to the distribution of texts that did not belong or that no longer belonged to the printed culture of the elites. This is why medieval texts and works of an outdated piety found their most widespread distribution at a time when learned readers had abandoned them. Likewise, works claiming to decipher the universe and the future and books giving advice on *savoir-vivre* multiplied at just the moment when the notables began to disdain them. We can see traces, then, of an opposition, which was to prove lasting, between two sorts of texts: those that provided food for thought for the wealthiest or the best-educated members of society and those that fed the curiosities of the common people. Even though these two sets of works did not have two radically different publics in the seventeenth century—as we have seen, there were many occasions for shared reading—it nevertheless remains true that they characterize two sorts of material that the printers published, aimed at clienteles, circulations, and uses that were not the same. These contrasting intentions can be read in the material aspect of the book. For one group the book is a noble object, well-made, leatherbound, and to be carefully preserved; for the other, it is an ephemeral and roughly made thing. By its form and by its text, the book became a sign of distinction and a bearer of a cultural identity. Molière is a good example of this sociology *avant la lettre* that characterizes each milieu by its books. For him, the presence of the "blue" tales or of an almanac was all that he needed to portray a cultural horizon that fell between that of the humble and that of the learned. "Popular" printing's success thus had complex significance. In part, it was the recovery under a new guise and for the use of a new public of texts that had had their rightful place within the culture of the elites before falling into disgrace. But it also contributed to the decline in status of the books that it offered. In the eyes of the lettered, such works became reading unworthy of *their* status when they entered the province of the vulgar herd. It was not that editorial strategies created a progressive broadening of the book-reading public; rather, they created, and to an unsuspected extent, systems for gauging differences. Such systems categorized the products of the printing trade in cultural terms, thus fragmenting the market into clienteles presumed to be discrete and establishing new cultural frontiers.

# CHAPTER SIX

# Urban Reading Practices, 1660–1780

O NCE a book is written and comes off the presses, it can be used in a multitude of ways. It is generally made to be read, to be sure, but there are multiple modes of reading, varying with the time, place, and milieu. For too long the manifold usage of books and the diversity of reading habits have been masked by an overly strict sociological analysis of the unequal distribution of books. Moreover, it has been forgotten that printed matter is set—always—within a network of cultural and social practices that give it its meaning. Reading is not an invariable in history, even in its most physical manifestations; rather, it is an activity, individual or collective, produced on each occasion by a form of sociability, by an idea that people have of knowledge or of leisure, or by a conception of individuality.

Thus it is that in the cities of France between the middle of the seventeenth century and the end of the *ancien régime* several styles of reading came into being, along with several different ways to use printing. Before attempting to reconstruct these styles and uses, let me offer a precaution and state an organizing principle. The precaution first: We must not forget that the production of printed matter was not restricted to the publishing of books—far from it. This fact had a good deal of importance for printers, who often made their living more from the city's daily demands than from book printing. It was just as important to readers, particularly (but not exclusively) among humble folk, for whom reading was not necessarily book reading, but might be deciphering, each in his own way, the varied pieces of religious or secular printed matter that one could either own or encounter posted or distributed in the city. The principle of organization next: The central tension between the area of the private self and areas of collective activities can serve as a focus for both the acquisition of data and the out-

This study appeared in *Histoire de l'édition française*, ed. H.-J. Martin and R. Chartier (Paris: Promodis, 1984), 2:402–29. It is in part founded on materials gathered and analyzed by Daniel Roche, and the French version bears both his name and mine.

line of research. For too long, the circulation of printed matter has been seen in terms of individual ownership and defined by the study of private collections. In fact, access to books in the seventeenth and the eighteenth centuries was not in the least limited to purchase and individual ownership, since it was precisely in these centuries that growing numbers of institutions, from the public library to the *cabinet de lecture*, offered opportunities for collective use of books. What we need, then, is a diptych: one panel to portray the private geography of the book, the different traditions of reading, and the actions that were taken to preserve books; the other to illustrate the various forms of public reading during the *ancien régime*.

The tension between the private and the public areas also affected reading practices themselves (and I take as public all the areas or practices other than the individual and private). A study of representations of reading in literature and iconography can help us to more firmly grasp the contrast between the two styles of reading, the one in the *forum internum*, the other geared to familial sociability, literate company, or chance encounters in the public realm. Thus what we need to examine is the pertinence of this sort of division, which pleads implicitly for the unique character of reading in urban, as opposed to rural, areas. Nor should we forget that the culture of the people, even where their familiarity with printing is concerned, was not always public, and that until fairly late reading, even among the dominant groups in society, remained a collective and open social exercise.

## Private Ownership of Books

A first way to grasp the society of readers in cities between 1660 and 1780 is through a serial study of estate inventories. The use of this source, however, requires some caution. The inventorying of estates was in no way obligatory, hence such documents inform us about only a part of the population. Furthermore, the description of owned books is often extremely incomplete, concentrating on works of a certain worth and appraising those of minimal value by lots or bundles. The significance of the owned book remains uncertain as well: Was it personal reading matter or an inherited keepsake? Was it a working aid or a valued object that was never touched? Was it a bosom companion or an attribute of social appearances? The dry entries of the notarial style give us little help here. In sum, it is clear that all the books people read were not books they owned. There were a good number of places in which public reading was possible in eighteenth-century cities, from the bookseller's *cabinet* to the library. There was also an extensive private circulation of books lent or borrowed among acquaintances as well as group readings in drawing rooms or at gatherings of literary societies. Estate inventories thus cannot tell us the whole story. Nevertheless, by the massive amount of data they provide, they offer an opportunity for preliminary categorization, and they permit us to test comparisons and to sketch evolving changes.

A first thought that comes to mind is to ask to how great an extent books were actually present, as seen in the percentage of estate inventories that mention at least one book. In the cities of western France (Angers, Brest, Caen, Le Mans, Nantes, Quimper, Rennes, Rouen, and Saint-Malo), this figure is 33.7 percent for the eighteenth century as a whole,[1] while in Paris it was 22.6 percent for the decade 1750-1760.[2] Thus there is a noticeable gap between the provinces and Paris, which is even greater if we compare the same figure for Paris with the 36.7 percent of the nine western cities for 1757-1758. How are we to explain that less than a quarter of Parisians owned a book at the same time that more than a third of the inhabitants of the cities of the Loire Valley, Normandy, and Brittany did so? Does this indicate that more negligent notarial practices existed in the capital, in which less elegant books—books of piety or practical techniques, for example—were ignored as worthless precisely because they were so abundant? Or should we put the blame on the nonchalant habits of a population more familiar with books and thus less inclined to keep them or put them away carefully? Or should we conclude that, for the mass of Parisians, the culture of printing did not involve the privately owned book but the *canard* and the *libelle* (pamphlet), which were discarded when they had been read, the *placard* and the poster, which were deciphered on the street corner, or the portable book? As we can see, the lower percentage of book owners in Paris is no reason to jump to the conclusion that Parisians were backward.

[1] J. Queniart, *Culture et sociétés urbaines dans la France de l'Ouest au XVIIIᵉ siècle* (Paris, 1978), 158. The total number of inventories studied was 5,150 (spread among four periods: 1697-1698, 1727-1728, 1757-1758, and 1787-1788), of which 1,737 mention books.

[2] M. Marion, *Recherches sur les bibliothèques privées à Paris au milieu du XVIIIᵉ siècle (1750-1759)* (Paris, 1978). The total number of inventories studied was 3,708; 841 mention books.

Did the physical presence of books increase as the eighteenth century progressed? Most assuredly, if we can take the cities of the west as typical. Estate inventories that mention books account for 27.5 percent of total inventories in 1697-1698, 34.6 percent in 1727-1728, and 36.7 percent in 1757-1758, but only 34.6 percent in 1787-1788 (exactly the same percentage as sixty years earlier).[3] Growth was not constant, nor was it the same everywhere. While in certain places book ownership grew throughout the century (as in Angers, Rouen, or Saint-Malo), in others the last decades of the *ancien régime* were marked by notable reductions, which of course influence the totals. Thus in Rennes the percentage of book owners dropped by 10 percent and in Caen by 9 percent. In Nantes and Brest, the proportion of book owners declined from midcentury on. Demographic changes, which transformed the population structure of certain cities, may have accounted for such variations, as may geographically limited economic conjunctures or fluctuations in literacy. Taken together, these variations demonstrate that the culture of print in the eighteenth century did not spread in a linear and continuous manner; once book ownership reached a first threshold, socially speaking, it underwent advances and retreats, and conquests were followed by periods of stagnation.

### The Hierarchy of Books and the Hierarchy of Conditions

If book ownership varied from one city or one time to another, it also varied according to social status. Let us look at three examples, first among them Paris. In a sampling of two hundred inventories drawn up between 1665 and 1702, 16.5 percent come from artisans, merchants, or bourgeois, 32.5 percent come from officeholders and *gens de robe*— lawyers, magistrates, doctors—and 26 percent come from noblemen and courtiers—proportions that differ, of course, from their relative numerical importance in the city.[4] In the middle of the eighteenth century, the percentage of inventories mentioning books varies greatly according to the different social categories. At the top of the scale, there are six groups in which more than one inventory out of two describes books: writers and librarians (100 percent), professors (75 percent), lawyers (62 percent), the clergy (62 percent), officers of *parlement* (58

---

[3] According to Queniart, *Culture et sociétés urbaines*, 163-71.

[4] H.-J. Martin, *Livre, pouvoirs et société à Paris au XVIIᵉ siècle (1598-1701)* (Geneva, 1969): 2:927.

percent), and nobles at the court (53 percent). At the other end of the scale are the groups in which less than 15 percent of the inventories list books: merchants (15 percent), journeymen and salesclerks (14 percent), master craftsmen (12 percent), and those in the minor trades (10 percent). Domestic servants (19 percent) and the *bourgeois* of Paris (23 percent) cut a better figure.[5] The difference between one group and another easily varied, as in the case of domestics and salaried workers. Around 1700 domestic personnel owned more books: 30 percent of their inventories mention books owned, as against only 13 percent of the journeymen and *gagne-deniers* (lowest-paid workers). Eighty years later the gap has considerably closed: 40 percent of the domestics have books, but so do 35 percent of salaried personnel.[6] As the century wore on and books became more available and less of a novelty, the *petit peuple* of Paris grew more familiar with them.

The example of Paris suggests two general rules that suffer few exceptions:

1. The higher the average wealth of all people in any given social category, the higher will be the proportion of its members who own books.
2. Within any category, the proportion of book owners increases with the scale of wealth.

As an illustration of this, at midcentury only 5 percent of Parisian merchants whose fortunes amounted to less than 8,000 *livres* owned books, as compared to 28 percent of those over that level of wealth. Members of *parlement* show a similar gap at a different social and economic level: 42 percent of those with fortunes below 30,000 *livres* owned books, compared to 64 percent of those wealthier.[7]

Social status and wealth also determined the number of books each individual owned. During the second half of the seventeenth century in Paris, the threshold of one hundred works was rarely reached by merchants or bourgeois, whereas one out of every two noblemen had such collections, and as a rule all libraries of *gens de robe* were at least

[5] Marion, *Recherches sur les bibliothèques privées*, 94.

[6] D. Roche, *Le Peuple de Paris. Essai sur la culture populaire au XVIIIᵉ siècle* (Paris, 1981), 217.

[7] These percentages are calculated according to the data furnished by Marion, *Recherches sur les bibliothèques privées*, 76-79.

this large.[8] In 1780 the number of works owned by the common people of Paris—salaried and domestic workers—surely indicates relatively easy or tight circumstances. Those best off—that is, those with greater than average wealth—in each category owned twice as many books on average as the others among the domestics (28 to 12) and three times as many as the others among the salaried workers (24 to 6).[9]

Lyons in the second half of the eighteenth century offers a second example. Cultural discontinuities are clearly reflected in the varying presence of books: 74 percent of the estate inventories of officeholders and members of the liberal professions mention them, followed by 48 percent for the bourgeois, 44 percent for the nobility, 42 percent for merchants and shopkeepers, and only 21 percent for manual workers and artisans. Collection size parallels this first scale: The average number of books owned by members of the wealthiest group—lawyers, magistrates, and the liberal professions in general—was 160, but among the least fortunate—the artisans and workers—it was 16, a ratio of ten to one.[10] Among the "popular" classes, then, books remained rare even though literacy was making progress: In Lyons on the eve of the Revolution 74 percent of the silk workers were able to sign their marriage contract, and the same was true of 77 percent of the cabinetmakers, 75 percent of the bakers, and 60 percent of the shoemakers.[11] At a time when all commerce, even at the lowest level, was carried on by means of credit, and in a city in which silk workers did piecework, the acquisition of the skills of reading and writing were absolutely necessary, since it was only with such skills that a worker could keep an account book to show a client or a book of finished piecework to compare with the merchant's records. But it is obvious that this does not imply a high level of book ownership. Owning a book indicated something like a second and infinitely more restrictive cultural threshold. Parisian inventories of the mid-eighteenth century confirm this: 60 percent of people who owned writing materials (a writing desk, ink, pens) owned no books.[12]

In one last example, the cities of western France allow us to trace this evolution for a hundred years or more. The most spectacular change,

[8] Martin, *Livre, pouvoirs et société*, 2:927.

[9] Roche, *Le Peuple de Paris*, 218.

[10] M. Garden, *Lyon et les lyonnais au XVIIIe siècle* (Paris, 1970), 459 (based on a survey of 365 inventories for the years 1750, 1760, 1770, and 1780).

[11] Ibid., 311, 351-52.

[12] Marion, *Recherches sur les bibliothèques privées*, 116.

which came between the end of the seventeenth century and the 1750s, was an increase in the percentage of inventories that list books. This is true at all levels of wealth, but it is particularly apparent at the upper and lower ends of the economic scale. In inventories valued at less than five hundred *livres*, book owners grew from 10 to 25 percent; in those valued at five hundred to one thousand *livres*, they grew from less than 30 percent to more than 40 percent; in those worth fifteen hundred to two thousand *livres*, the change was from 30 to 55 percent; and in those valued at more than two thousand *livres*, book owners increased from 50 to 75 percent. The final thirty years of the *ancien régime* put a halt to this attainment of the privately owned book, since on all levels of wealth the proportion of inventories that mention books declined, occasionally sharply, as in the case of moderately wealthy people (between one thousand and fifteen hundred *livres*), where the figure for inventories mentioning books fell from 50 to 32 percent.[13] Since this decline was less marked at the bottom end of the scale, the discrepancy between the worst off and the moderately prosperous was much reduced by the end of the 1780s. Translated into social terms, this evolution points to two changes. On the one hand, we can see the penetration of the book into artisan and merchant milieux, either over the entire century (as with the woodworking trades) or until a peak in the 1750s which was followed by a decline (as with the textile and clothing trades and the merchants). On the other hand, the size of the collections owned by the "notables" increased. Between the end of the seventeenth century and the 1780s, average library size among the *bourgeoisie à talents* grew from the one-to-twenty-volume bracket to the twenty-to-one-hundred-volume bracket; among members of the clergy, it grew from the twenty-to-fifty-volume size to the one-to-three-hundred-volume size; and among nobles and major officeholders, it expanded from the one-to-twenty-volume size to more than three hundred volumes each, on average.[14] It is clear, then, that collections grew and that the number of texts available for the private perusal of library owners increased as the century progressed—which quite possibly affected the way they read.

### Traditions of Reading: The Urban Clergy

In French cities between 1660 and 1780, several different reading traditions, characteristic of the various sociocultural groups, either arose,

---

[13] Queniart, *Culture et sociétés urbaines*, fig. 26.
[14] Ibid., figs. 38, 29, 34.

continued, or changed direction. First, there was the tradition of the urban clergy. There were considerable differences in reading habits between Paris and the provinces (in this case, the cities of the west of France). Collections were much larger in Paris, but religious books overall accounted for a smaller part of them. According to a scrutiny of forty catalogues of the sales of libraries belonging to Parisian canons, abbés, and parish priests, theological works accounted for 38 percent of their collections between 1706 and 1740, 32.5 percent between 1745 and 1760, and 29 percent between 1765 and 1790.[15] In the cities of western France between 1697-1698 and 1787-1788, there is a discernible decrease in religious books, but they remained at a higher level than in Paris, passing from 80 to 65 percent.[16] We should note that in book production, as revealed by permissions to publish, works on theology declined sharply between 1723-1727 and 1784-1788, dropping from 34 to 8.5 percent.[17]

The holdings of ecclesiastical libraries, which were more conservative in the provinces than in Paris, recorded the progress of the Catholic Reformation, becoming increasingly homogeneous in centering around a few major sets of works. From the mid-seventeenth century on, the library of the *bon curé* grew noticeably weightier. Aside from the Bible and the catechism of the Council of Trent written by Carlo Borromeo (and often French catechisms as well), he now had to own the commentaries and homilies of the Fathers and Doctors of the Church—Saints Thomas and Bernard in particular—works on moral theology useful to his ministerial duties (confession manuals, works on points of conscience, the reports of ecclesiastical conferences), and uplifting religious works (the *Imitation of Christ*, the *Guide des Pécheurs* of Luis de Grenada, François de Sales's *Introduction à la vie dévote*).

Both the broadening and the growing uniformity of the urban clergy's reading matter were the result of tenacious efforts on the part of the ecclesiastical authorities. The possession and the reading of a certain number of books, required by seminary regulations, strongly recommended in synodal statutes and episcopal ordinances, and indispen-

---

[15] C. Thomassery, "Livre et culture cléricale à Paris au xviiie siècle: Quarante bibliothèques d'ecclésiastiques parisiens," *Revue Française d'Histoire du Livre* 6 (1973): 281-300.

[16] Queniart, *Culture et sociétés urbaines*, fig. 33.

[17] F. Furet, "La Librairie du royaume de France au xviiie siècle," in G. Bollème et al., eds., *Livre et Société dans la France du XVIIIe siècle* (Paris and The Hague, 1965), 1:3-32.

sable for participation in ecclesiastical conferences, became obligatory for all priests.[18] Rectory libraries gradually conformed to these injunctions, acquiring the books recommended in the synodal statutes or drawing on the lists of books furnished by the diocesan printer at the suggestion of episcopal ordinances. This explains the presence of a "Summary of Library [materials] for clergymen, which can be found in the shop of Jacques Seneuze, Printer to the Monseigneur, with the most just prices" that was appended to the *Statuts, ordonnances, mandemens, règlements et lettres pastorales* of the Bishop of Châlons-sur-Marne in 1693. This printer proposed for the edification of the clerics of the diocese "the proper books for all those who aspire to the ecclesiastical state or who are in the greater or lesser seminary, and [he] also sells all the proper books for the divine service, according to both the Roman usage and [that of] the diocese of Châlons." His list gives eighty-three titles, the prices for which ranged from ten *sous* for a *Curia clericalis* to fifteen *sous* for *La Pratique de la cérémonie de la messe* to the thirty-nine *livres* he asked for the thirteen volumes of the *Missionnaire Apostolique*. A good 15 percent of these titles cost less than two *livres* (among them, the *Catéchisme du Concile*), however, and half of them cost eight *livres* or less. Insistent encouragement and accessible prices probably go far to explain the expansion of clerical libraries. This expansion had a dual result. First, it served to differentiate clearly between generations among the clergy, opposing clerics prepared after 1660 (in the era of the seminaries) to those who preceded them. Second, it minimized differences between clerics of the city and of the country, since all their libraries, modeled on the bishops' ideal lists, closely resembled one another.

Differences persisted, however, in the provinces between the libraries of the canons and those of the parish priests and between the provincial and Parisian clergy. These differences can be seen most clearly in the place occupied by nonreligious books in their libraries. In the capital, history had a place equal to that of theology: 32.5 percent of works listed between 1706 and 1740, 28 percent between 1740 and 1760, and 31 percent between 1765 and 1790. Moreover, in a sign of modernity, Latin works declined as the century progressed, shrinking from 47 to 27 percent of all titles, while subscriptions to various peri-

---

[18] D. Julia and D. McKee, "Les Confrères de Jean Meslier. Culture et spiritualité du clergé champenois au xviie siècle," *Revue d'Histoire de l'Église de France* 69, no. 182 (1983):61-86.

odicals increased. In its upper ranks, the clergy did not exist in cultural isolation closed to all innovation, but it shared in the culture of the other urban elites.

### Reading among the Nobility

Identifying the reading habits of the Second Estate is not an easy task.[19] More than for the other social groups, scrutiny of estate inventories here presents uncertainty. The life of a noble was divided between his city *hôtel* and his rural residence, his library was often willed as an undifferentiated whole or excluded from his common property, and books were objects of little value in comparison to other sorts of cultural goods, which were present in great number. This easily explains why the absence of books in the inventories of noblemen does not necessarily mean that they were in fact nonexistent. Hence prudence is called for when we deal with data pertaining to aristocratic book ownership. These data show that a sometimes sizable number of nobles had no library. This was true for the larger cities. In Paris in the mid-eighteenth century only 44 percent of noble estate inventories mention books.[20] The figure is exactly the same, 44 percent, for Lyons during the second half of the century.[21] It was also true for smaller cities: In Brittany, a clear majority of the nobles seem not to have had a library worthy of the name.[22] In the cities of the west of France, however, the proportion of noble inventories that list books, higher than anywhere else, is on the order of 78 percent at the end of the seventeenth century and 79 percent on the eve of the Revolution.[23] Even if this source minimizes noble ownership of books, it is still true that a large part of the Second Estate did not own books. The (relatively) impecunious state of widows, younger sons, and the "poor" nobility perhaps explains this, but another reason lies in the easy access nobles had to the collections of relatives, protectors, and administrative offices, which could have rendered the assembling of a personal library unnecessary.

Within the nobility, there was a marked contrast between the fam-

---

[19] A preliminary summary is given in D. Roche, "Noblesse et culture dans la France du xviiie siècle: Les Lectures de la noblesse," in *Buch und Sammler. Private und öffentliche Bibliotheken im 18. Jahrhundert* (Heidelberg, 1979), 9-27.

[20] Marion, *Recherches sur les bibliothèques privées*, 94.

[21] Garden, *Lyon et les lyonnais*, 459.

[22] J. Meyer, *La Noblesse bretonne au XVIIIe siècle* (Paris, 1966), 1166.

[23] Queniart, *Culture et sociétés urbaines*, 226.

ilies "of the robe," who held juridical or financial offices, and the families "of the sword," who held military charges or titles. In the cities of the west of France, the gap between the two was great at the end of the seventeenth century: 45 percent of the inventories of squires and knights bear no mention of books in contrast to less than 5 percent of the high officeholders. This gap narrowed as the eighteenth century progressed but it never disappeared, leaving the *robins* with a consistent advantage of 5 to 10 percent. Collection size is another sign of this advantage. For the titled nobles, the number of books owned remained stable—between one and twenty titles—for the three samplings (1697-1698, 1727-1728, 1757-1758), whereas for the officeholders it changed from the twenty-to-one-hundred-title bracket in 1697-1698 to the one-to-three-hundred-title bracket in 1727-1728 and 1757-1758. On the eve of the Revolution, half of the libraries of the *robins* had more than three hundred volumes, which was true of only one-fourth of the libraries of the titled nobles.[24]

The study of the contents of the nobles' libraries leads to two conclusions. First, it confirms the existence of opposing cultural traditions within the aristocracy. And second, it shows long-term shifts in the reading habits of the Second Estate. Reading habits among the nobility of the western cities, taken as a whole, show three basic changes (see table 1). First we see a long-lasting increase in the proportion of religious books, which stretched over the entire first half of the eighteenth century, but was followed by a sharp decline in the thirty years that preceded the Revolution. Provincial noble culture was slow to be receptive to the literature of the Catholic Reformation, then brutally de-

TABLE 1. THE LIBRARIES OF THE URBAN NOBILITY
OF WESTERN FRANCE

|  | 1696–1697 | 1727–1728 | 1757–1758 | 1787–1788 |
|---|---|---|---|---|
| Religion | 17% | 28% (21%) | 36% (24%) | 11% |
| Antiquity | 22% | 17% | 13% | 6% |
| Literature | 15% | 17% | 24% | 44% (30%) |
| History | 19% | 18% | 21% | 22% |

NOTE: The percentages in parentheses do not include certain highly specialized libraries that distort the overall percentages.

[24] Ibid., fig. 34.

tached itself from its former religious fidelities. The abandonment of traditional works (Fathers of the Church, Roman law, ancient history, Greek and Roman literature), on the other hand, was regular and continuous, indicating a progressive detachment from the wholly classical culture of the *collège*. Finally, among all nobles, the predominant readings became not the arts and sciences, the strong rise of which was connected with increases in book production as a whole, but belles-lettres. Literature surpassed history after the midcentury, an incontestable sign of the success of the new genres among the traditional elites.

The traditional elites were by no means a homogeneous group, however, as the example of Paris attests (see table 2).[25] They did share one trait: History, particularly French history, accounted for a large part of their reading. That category led the list among the dukes and peers of the realm and among the members of the *parlements*, and it was almost on a par with literature among the tax farmers. The aristocracy shows a strong originality in this, since works on history never accounted for more than 20 percent of book production, as the registry of permissions to publish shows. Even though the various groups of nobles did not

TABLE 2. THE LIBRARIES OF PARISIAN NOBLES IN THE EIGHTEENTH CENTURY

| Groups Sampled | Religion | Law | History | Literature | Arts and Sciences |
|---|---|---|---|---|---|
| General Survey 1750–1789 (50 libraries) | 10% | 4% | 25% | 49% | 12% |
| Dukes and Peers 1700–1779 | 20% | 3% | 49% | 19% | 9% |
| Officers of *Parlements* 1734–1795 (30 libraries) | 12% | 18% | 31% | 24% | 15% |
| Tax Farmers 1751–1797 (18 libraries) | 6% | 7% | 30% | 32% | 25% |

[25] This represents a comparison of the data furnished by D. Depraz, *Enquête sur les bibliothèques des nobles à Paris après 1750* (Mémoire de Maîtrise, Paris, 1968); J.-P. Labatut, *Les Ducs et Pairs au XVIIᵉ siècle* (Paris, 1972), 232; F. Bluche, *Les Magistrats du Parlement de Paris au XVIIIᵉ siècle* (Paris, 1960), 291; and Y. Durand, *Les Fermiers Généraux au XVIIIᵉ siècle* (Paris, 1971), 562–63.

read exactly the same sorts of history, history nevertheless provided them all with a base for their particular culture, rooting their aristocratic ambitions in the past and justifying them.

Beyond this shared taste for history, differences begin to appear, arising first from the social roles of the various groups that made up the nobility. This explains the large proportion of works on the law among the judges of the *parlement* and of books on the arts and sciences, on finance, tax structure, and commerce among the tax farmers. If the dukes and peers had fancier tastes, they were also more pious, but their libraries, in the surveys we have at our disposal, were the oldest. During the second half of the eighteenth century, Parisian magistrates and public officials detached themselves from religion even more markedly than their provincial counterparts. The proportion of works of theology among members of the *parlements* declined from 19 percent between 1734 and 1765, to 12 percent between 1766 and 1780, and to 6 percent between 1781 and 1795. Finally, literature had the largest share among the newest elite, the tax farmers, who had "arrived" through finance; but we should note that this proportion was less great than among all levels of Parisian aristocracy.

Although the two groups show some divergences, nobles in Paris and in the provinces seem to show a parallel evolution. Religious books declined, works of history and literature predominated, and books on the arts and sciences found a less enthusiastic reception. Differences between nobles *de robe* and *d'épée* continued to exist, of course, but they seem less clear than in the seventeenth century, when the culture of the *robins*, based in authoritative works, in a humanism of shared references, and in the primacy of morality and the culture of the *gentilshommes*, open to literary fashion, to the sciences, and to new thought[26] were opposed. Leaving aside the common ground among these groups, the differences we have discovered seem more closely tied to their differing roles than to truly different cultural choices. We can thus begin to see the outlines of a noble model in which elites that were allied by marriage and joined by a shared lifestyle merged within a common culture.

### The Reading Bourgeoisies

The two bourgeoisies, of talent and of commerce, were less clearly homogeneous. At the end of the seventeenth century strong contrasts

[26] Martin, *Livre, pouvoirs et société*, 1:516-51.

existed between the merchants and the bourgeoisie whose professions depended upon learning (lawyers, doctors and surgeons, notaries, attorneys, bailiffs and court clerks). In the cities of western France, although nearly two-thirds of the latter group owned books, only one-fourth of the former did so.[27] At the midcentury in Paris this difference remained true: 58 percent of the lawyers, 44 percent of the doctors, and 34 percent of the minor judicial officeholders had books, but only 16 percent of the master merchants did.[28] And in Lyons during the second half of the century, 74 percent of the estate inventories of members of the liberal professions and officeholders mentioned a library (containing 160 titles on the average), as opposed to 42 percent of the inventories of merchants and wholesalers (with an average of only 40 titles).[29]

The cities of western France give a clear picture of a threefold evolution in the reading habits of the *bourgeoisie à talents*. First, book ownership made great strides there during the second quarter of the eighteenth century: In 1757-1758, 85 percent of the inventories of this group mentioned books. Not only were there more book owners; there were also bigger collections. During the first half of the century, libraries of between twenty and one hundred volumes increased to 40 percent of the total. Between 1760 and 1790 collections of more than one hundred titles gained ground, accounting for more than 30 percent of all libraries.[30] This increase in library size was paralleled by a clear change in subject matter. Books of practical professional application—of law or medicine—remained in the majority throughout the century, but their slight decline (from 65 to 50 percent), in addition to the collapse of the category of classical erudition (which dropped from nearly 30 percent to less than 5 percent of library holdings), left room for the exercise of new interests. Historical works underwent a strong rise in the second third of the century, and literature opened the libraries to books of entertainment, to theatrical works, and, in particular, to novels.[31]

The libraries of merchants, in the cities of western France as in Lyons, were organized around two poles during the eighteenth century. The first was utility, in the form of books on commerce, accounting manuals, works on law, dictionaries and almanacs, and geograph-

---

[27] Queniart, *Culture et sociétés urbaines*, 266, 286.
[28] Marion, *Recherches sur les bibliothèques privées*, 94.
[29] Garden, *Lyon et les lyonnais*, 459.
[30] Queniart, *Culture et sociétés urbaines*, fig. 38.
[31] Ibid., fig. 43.

ical accounts and itineraries, all useful to the practice of trade. The second was escape literature. Since the merchants were latecomers to book ownership, and since they built up their libraries at a time when other groups had already solidly established theirs, they were more accepting of innovation. This means that their collections reserved more space for accounts of voyages (which might also prove useful professionally), for foreign history, and for literary novelties both in French and English. Like the *gentilshommes* of the seventeenth century, who were all the more open to new works since they were novices as readers, the merchants of the eighteenth century built up libraries that rejected both the pious and the humanist traditions. At the edge of the academic world but firmly planted in the Masonic lodges, the merchants established their cultural originality both through their intellectual sociability and through their reading, refusing to cater to the classical values of the aristocracies of the sword, the robe, or the pen.[32]

## Reading among the People

According to the inventories of their worldly goods, artisans and shopkeepers seem to have been meager readers.[33] Many of them left no books, and, among those who did, many owned only one book. In the vast majority of cases, this one book was a work of piety. In the cities of the west of France in 1727-1728, these single books were in ten cases the life of a saint; in nine, a Book of Hours; in six, a Bible; and in two, a copy of the *Imitation of Christ*. Thirty years later the situation was about the same, with twelve Books of Hours, twelve lives of saints, three Bibles, one *Imitation of Christ*, one *Histoire des Juifs*, and one *Divinité de Jésus-Christ*. In Lyons after 1750, the one book owned was also the life of a saint, sheepskin-bound and inexpensive. In slightly better furnished libraries the primacy of religious works remained pronounced. In Caen in 1757-1758, out of thirty-two artisans' libraries of two to five titles, twenty-five contained only devotional works; in Lyons the same was true of 70 percent of the collections of master craftsmen and silk workers.

Even if we look only at the estate inventories, which are even more

[32] D. Roche, "Négoce et culture dans la France du xviii^e siècle," *Revue d'Histoire Moderne et Contemporaine* 25 (1978):375-95.

[33] I am comparing here the data given by Queniart, *Culture et sociétés urbaines*, 289-90, 295-96, 301; Garden, *Lyon et les lyonnais*, 460; and Roche, *Le Peuple de Paris*, 221-22.

uncertain for the popular classes than for all other groups, however, religious materials did not make up the whole of popular reading matter. As the century progressed unexpected titles crop up more and more. In Rouen and Caen, for example, profane titles began to appear next to the Bibles, the Books of Hours, and the saints' lives as early as 1727-1728. They were such works as the *Livre des comptes-faits* of Barrême and Saint Augustine's *Confessions*, which appear in the inventory of a master tailor in Rouen; a *Cuisinier bourgeois* that crops up in the inventory of an innkeeper in Caen; *Esther*, which belonged to a master tanner, and *Télémaque* and a work of Lucian belonging to a grocer of the same city; and *Clélie*, listed for a master tailor, and Rabelais for a worker in the mint, both of Rouen. Sixty years later, although two-thirds of the libraries contained only works of piety, two facts are worthy of note. First, half the time, a person's sole book was not a work of religion. It was one of Barrême's works for a retired farmer from Caen or a *Mémorial alphabétique concernant les gabelles*, a *Tarif sur les vins,* or the *Nouveau parfait maréchal* for, respectively, a day laborer, a master vinegar-maker, and a coachman in Rouen. Second, for the first time small libraries mostly composed of nonreligious books made their appearance. Thus a merchant of Rouen owned the *Evangile*, the *Médecin du Pauvre*, and a *Dictionnaire géographique*, and the estranged wife of a master wig-maker possessed a book of piety, the *Art d'orner l'esprit*, and a French-German dictionary. Thus there were signs that popular reading habits had broadened, which can be confirmed in other ways than the chronological study of estate inventories.

## Book Storage

Once it is owned a book has to be put somewhere. According to the Parisian estate inventories, the pieces of furniture that resolved this problem varied from the humblest to the most ostentatious. Among the more modest readers, the book had no place set aside for it and could be found anywhere in the dwelling—in the one room (which was most common), in the kitchen (when there was one), or in the various small subunits, such as overhead storage areas, antechambers, and wardrobes. The book was also carried on the person, as we can see in descriptions of the victims of an accident that killed 130 people on Wednesday, 30 May 1770, the day of the festivities for the marriage of the Dauphin. Trampled and smothered to death in the crush on the Rue Royale, these ordinary Parisians were identified by their kin, and inventories were drawn up of what they had on their persons. Several books are listed among the simple objects they carried. Anne Julienne, twenty years of age and the employee of a tailor, carried an almanac; Jacques Briet, identified by his lodger, was sixty years of age and had a "church book"; Marie Fournier, also sixty years of age and the wife of a water-seller, kept on her person "an old book of piety"; and Joseph Cottier, sixty-seven years old and a merchant, carried a "Freemason's Almanac."[34]

When a few more books than this were owned, a piece of furniture in which to keep them became necessary. The humblest of these was the *tablette à livres*, which was often a little cabinet that could be locked and that could contain other objects as well as or instead of books. The same was true of the *armoires-bibliothèques*, which we occasionally encounter even when their owner had no books. When one of these larger cabinets did hold books, it could be found in any room of the dwelling—in the bedroom, the dressing room, an antechamber, even in the kitchen or under the stairs.[35] Besançon during the eighteenth century provides us with a clear hierarchy of the places in which books were kept. At the bottom of the scale were the *armoire à linge* (linen press), the *coffre* (coffer), or the *corbeille* (basket). For example, in 1730 a notary found among the goods of Jean Mignard, a professor of theology at the university, "a basket brimful of worn, old books, declared of little importance." Next on the scale came the *tablette à livres*, described in an inventory dated 1747 as "a small cabinet with two doors closing with a key." The piece of furniture most frequently encountered, however, is the small bookcase, called by various names by the notaries: *buffet grillé, bibliothèque à deux battants grillées, buffet en forme de bibliothèque, armoire à deux portes*, and so forth. In general this was a small furnishing made of walnut or beech with two glass-paned or grilled doors and shelves placed at different heights to permit the storage of books by size, the folio volumes at the bottom and the smaller books on top. In rare instances there are notices of larger pieces, such as the "library with eight doors with brass grillwork" owned in 1776 by Charles Le Vacher, a surgeon at the military hospital.[36]

[34] A. Farge, *Vivre dans la rue au XVIIIᵉ siècle* (Paris, 1979), 80-87, 103-104.

[35] Marion, *Recherches sur les bibliothèques privées*, 124-26.

[36] J. Grinewald, "L'Emplacement des livres au xviiiᵉ siècle dans les bibliothèques privées de Besançon," in *Les Espaces du livre*, vol. 2: *Les Bibliothèques* (Paris: Institut d'Étude du Livre, 1980, typescript), 13-30.

These various furnishings for book storage express various intentions. The first is conservation: The book was a precious object to be carefully preserved. This implied a trip to the bookbinder. In Paris libraries of the 1750s only 5 percent of the books were listed as merely paperbound. It also meant that even the most modest books were locked up, as in the case of the twenty-eight duodecimo and sextodecimo volumes with simple calfskin bindings that the wife of a Paris nobleman, a former captain of the king's stables, kept in a coffer under lock and key.[37] A second function of the bookcase was decorative and distinctive. Among the wealthy, the piece of furniture that held books had to demonstrate the good taste of the owner, be appropriate to his estate, make his library visible, and respect the current styles in furniture. By the end of the century, when the charms of the Louis XV style with its cabinetworked glass doors had faded, the English style had triumphed throughout Europe, and library furnishings were designed in different ways according to their destined use; those for ladies, for instance, had their own forms.[38] Also by the end of the century, a concern for ease of access led to the invention of bookcases on wheels, so that the reader could take whatever books were needed from one room to another.[39]

### Libraries

Not many book owners in the cities of France of the eighteenth century kept their collections in one or several rooms specially devoted to the conservation and consultation of these works. This occurred only among the wealthiest, who owned a *hôtel particulier*, or among major book collectors. In Lyons, for example, this was the case with the library that belonged to Pianelli de la Valette, mentioned in the almanacs of that city and in Expilly's *Dictionnaire*. We know from his account books that Laurent Pianelli de la Valette spent close to 6,400 *livres* on books between 1734 and 1740—a considerable sum, since in 1725 the entire library of a *trésorier de France* who lived in Lyons, J.-F. Philibert, was appraised at 2,300 *livres*.[40] Occasionally the library was a

[37] Ibid., 126 (n. 175).

[38] *Lesewuth, Raubdruck und Bücherluxus. Das Buch in der Goethe-Zeit* (Düsseldorf: Goethes-Museums, 1977), nos. 315, 316.

[39] Ibid., no. 317.

[40] On this collection see R. Chartier, "L'Académie de Lyon au xviiie siècle. Étude de sociologie culturelle," in *Nouvelles Études Lyonnaises* (Geneva, 1969), 206-209, 212-14; and Garden, *Lyon et les lyonnais*, 464-65.

room in the country house and not in the city residence. This was the case concerning one *conseiller* at the *Cour des monnaies* in Lyons, Antoine Trollier, who arranged for a special room, hung with maps and engravings, in his château at Lissieu in which to house the 915 volumes in his collection.[41]

In Paris one or more rooms might be set aside for the keeping of books. A primary reason for this was a passion for collecting, pushed to extremes by a collector like the Marquis Paulmy d'Argenson, who accumulated several tens of thousands of books in the seventy-two rooms of his *hôtel*, now the Bibliothèque de l'Arsenal.[42] A second reason was for social appearances: The library was much appreciated as a setting for refined sociability. In the Hôtel d'Aumont on the Rue du Cherche-Midi, the library gave onto the garden through a French door. Its walls were hung with tapestries and family portraits, and in the middle were grouped a desk and a few armchairs. In other cases the library also served as the music room or as a *cabinet de curiosités*.[43] The library could also serve as the study of a lawyer, a man of letters, a magistrate, or a scholar.[44] As a place of study, it also became an intimate retreat, the best place for communion with oneself, and a storehouse for beloved objects. The definition of the word *cabinet* in Furetière's *Dictionnaire* expresses this clearly: It is a "place of retirement in ordinary houses, where one studies, where one retires from the rest of the world, and where one keeps the most precious of one's property. The place that contains a library is also called a *cabinet*."[45] The model provided by Montaigne, retreating into his *"librairie"*—"I try to make my authority over it absolute, and to withdraw this one corner from all society, conjugal, filial, and civil"[46]—runs throughout the modern period, in contrast with the model of the library as a place for ostentation and sociability.

[41] Garden, *Lyon et les lyonnais*, 462.

[42] A. Masson, *Le Décor des bibliothèques du Moyen Âge à la Révolution* (Geneva, 1972), 139.

[43] M. Marion, "Les Livres chez les Parisiens dans la seconde moitié du xviiie siècle," in *Les Espaces du livre*, 2:31-37.

[44] D. Roche, "L'Intellectuel au travail," *Annales E.S.C.* 37 (1982):465-80, particularly 474-76.

[45] Cited in B. Beugnot, "L'Ermitage parmi les livres: Images de la bibliothèque classique," *Revue Française d'Histoire du Livre* 24 (1979):687-707.

[46] *Essays*, 3:3, in *The Complete Works of Montaigne*, trans. Donald M. Frame (Stanford, 1967).

Some of the libraries built to enhance the owner's prestige were richly decorated, in imitation of the great religious and university establishments. In 1729, Massillon, the Bishop of Clermont, had a wood-paneled library installed in his private apartments on the second floor of the Bishop's Palace. In 1740, the library of the Cardinal de Rohan in Strasbourg contained marble busts, Chinese porcelains, and Parisian tapestries, all placed above mahogany bookcases with gilded copper decorations. In 1776 Louis-Joseph Borely furnished the library in his château outside Marseilles with copies of antique statuary and allegorical decorations.[47] At the same time, members of the royal family had cozy libraries installed at Versailles as places for retirement and meditation. In 1769 the library of Madame Sophie, Louis XVI's aunt, was decorated with arabesques and floral stucco work; in 1772 a library was created for Marie Antoinette, still the dauphine; and in 1775 the king's library was completed, designed by Gabriel and decorated with allegorical paintings and reliefs by the Rousseau brothers.[48]

## COLLECTIVE USES OF BOOKS

But access to books cannot be reduced to private ownership of a library in the seventeenth and eighteenth centuries any more than it can today. A book read was not always a book owned—far from it. Between the 1660s and the 1780s institutions and practices that facilitated the reading of books not owned personally blossomed all over France. It is these practices that we examine next.

### Borrowers and Lenders

Lending books is a habit as old as the book itself. Friends have always borrowed and lent books. One example of this from the first third of the eighteenth century is Laurent Dugas, presiding officer of the *Cour des monnaies*, the senechalcy, and the *présidial* (district court of appeals) of Lyons and provost of the merchants' guild of that city between 1724 and 1729, and his friend François Bottu de la Barmondière, Lord of Saint-Fonds and *lieutenant particulier* for the *bailliage* of Beaujolais. Both of these men were members of the Académie Lyonnaise, founded in 1700, and both were bibliophiles. They were in frequent correspond-

---

[47] Masson, *Le Décor des bibliothèques*, 132-42.
[48] Ibid., 130-31.

ence from 1711 to 1739, when Bottu de Saint-Fonds died,[49] and their letters speak often of the commerce, in all senses of the word, in books. They bought rare books and newly published books; they received gifts of books; and they lent and borrowed books. When Dugas was slow to send him books, Bottu, who lived in Villefranche-sur-Saône, wrote to him impatiently: "I have read all the things you sent me and I thank you for them. I beg of you to remember always this poor exile when you hear of new works. I will not keep them too long and you will always be charmed by my punctuality" (letter dated 24 March 1716). He nagged his friend: "Either buy me or lend me the *Épictète* of Madame Dacier. Do whichever of the two you think more convenient for yourself, but do one or the other promptly, as I am curious to read the preface" (letter of 8 March 1716). Dugas was, moreover, not the only person from whom he borrowed books and manuscripts. A Doctor Falconnet was also among his lenders. In a letter of 10 January 1716, Bottu charges Dugas:

> make sure that his [Falconnet's] book and his manuscript do not get lost. . . . As for the manuscript, I will most certainly get it back to him, and just as soon as I can. Concerning the book, if another can be found in Paris I will repay him for it; if not, I will send him back his own when he has asked me for it another dozen times. For a man who has fifteen thousand volumes, one duodecimo [-sized book] doesn't amount to much!

Books circulated among friends and relations in Lyons as well, even though the city was well stocked with bookstores. Dugas borrowed books: "M. the Abbé Michel lent me three more volumes of the *Nouvelles littéraires*" (8 January 1718); "The book of M. the Abbé de la Charmoye merits reading. It was M. de Messimieux who lent it to me some years ago; I don't know why I didn't buy it" (1 October 1719). He lent books as well: "Do you know the *Pia Hilaria* of Father Angelin Gazet? It is several short pieces in iambic verse or *scazons*. I had lent it to Bois Saint-Just to amuse him. I [have] started to read it and I find it diverting" (1 October 1720). Occasionally the chain of borrowers had several links: "M. Constant, the lawyer, whom I have not seen in more than a year, recently sent me a little sextodecimo book that he pointed

[49] W. Poidebard, ed., *Correspondance littéraire et anecdotique entre Monsieur de Saint-Fonds et le Président Dugas* (Lyons, 1900).

out he had borrowed expressly to have me read and that he says is extremely rare. I found it very good and very useful, and I would love to be able to find a copy for you and for me. The title is *Méthode pour commencer les humanités grecques et latines*, by M. Le Fèvre of Saumur. As he is not sure that it can be found, and as the suggestions it gives will be of immediate use to you, I will summarize what I found singular in it" (Dugas, letter of 22 February 1722). In 1734 it was by borrowing from his daughter the book lent to her by the lawyer Brossette that Dugas was able to read the *Lettres philosophiques* of Voltaire "before returning them to M. Brossette" (letters of 22 December 1734 and 1 January 1735). There was thus a sizable part of book circulation that eluded the market and its corollary, private ownership. As in the Middle Ages or in the sixteenth century, books were highly valued gifts and were sought-after as loans.[50] Interpersonal networks based on intellectual friendship were not the only ways such practices were facilitated, however. The presence of a dozen copies of the same book in one collection—the library, which was sold in 1760, of Geoffroy, first vicar of Saint-Merri—seems to indicate a custom of lending books to parishioners, here perhaps encouraged by the vicar's Jansenist leanings.[51]

## The Libraries Open to the Public

During the course of the eighteenth century, readers who had very few books of their own or none at all had new and increased possibilities to consult books in libraries open to the public. The *Nouveau Supplément à la France Littéraire*, published in 1784, enables us to survey these "public libraries of various literary, civil, ecclesiastical, religious, and other bodies" at the end of the *ancien régime*.[52] Paris seems to have been the best endowed, with eighteen collections open to the public: the Bibliothèque du Roi; three libraries gathered by private collectors (the Mazarine, that of the Hôtel Soubise, and that of the Marquis de Paulmy at the Arsenal); two libraries of civil bodies (the lawyers' library, installed in the Archbishop's Palace, and the library of the City of Paris in the former Jesuit house on the Rue Saint-Antoine); four libraries connected with educational institutions (that of the University,

[50] N. Z. Davis, "Beyond the Market: Books as Gifts in Sixteenth-Century France," *Transactions of the Royal Historical Society*, 5th ser., 33 (1983):69-88.

[51] Thomassery, "Livre et culture cléricale," 287-88.

[52] J. A. Guiot [Guyot], *Nouveau Supplément à la France Littéraire*, Fourth Part (Paris, 1784), 1-143.

located in the Collège Louis-le-Grand, of the Sorbonne, of the Faculty
of Medicine, and of the Collège de Navarre); and eight religious libraries that belonged to abbeys (Saint-Victor, Saint-Germain, and
Sainte-Geneviève) or religious orders (the Oratorians, the Recollect
Franciscans, the Minims [Order of Saint Francis of Paola], the Augus-
tinians, and the Doctrinarians). Admission to these libraries was often
subject to clearly defined regulations. (The Bibliothèque du Roi was
"open to everyone on Tuesday and Friday mornings from nine o'clock
until noon" and, at the Bibliothèque de l'Université, "one enters Mondays, Wednesdays, and Fridays from nine in the morning to noon and
from two-thirty in the afternoon until five.") In other cases access was
left to the discretion of the librarian, as in the library of the abbey of
Saint-Germain-des-Prés, where "although the library is not intended
for public use, it is still much frequented because of the free access Men
of Letters find to it." The same was true of Sainte-Geneviève, where
the library "is not by right public," but where "the Religious make it a
point of honor and a duty to share these riches with the Learned, who
can come to do research Mondays, Wednesdays, and Fridays (unless a
feast day) from two to five in the afternoon." It was also the case in the
Collège de Navarre, where the collection "consists particularly of ancient manuscripts. They are communicated willingly, as are the books,
to known persons." The Marquis de Paulmy also welcomed men of letters to "the superb and ample library that he has had formed at the
Arsenal."

In the provinces, *La France Littéraire* lists sixteen cities, great and
small, that had public libraries. Most were the collections of religious
institutions. There were *collège* libraries in Lyons, Dijon, and Valognes; chapter libraries in Rouen, Saint-Omer, and Sens; libraries of
monasteries or religious orders in Nantes, Orléans, Toulouse, and Besançon; and libraries "of the clergy" in Vesoul and Toulouse. The public library might also belong to the Academy (as in Lyons, Nancy, and
Rouen), to the university or to one faculty (as in Strasbourg and Orléans), or to the city government (Strasbourg again). A few cities seem to
have had the privilege of several public collections: Orléans, for example, had five, and Lyons and Toulouse each had three. Depending
on the individual case, access to these libraries was less than generously
accorded. Although the library of the Benedictines of Orléans was
open three days a week from eight to eleven in the morning and from
two to five in the afternoon, the library of Saint-Euverte in the same

city was only open Thursdays from two to four p.m. from Saint Martin's Day (11 November) to Easter and only from five to six p.m. the rest of the year. The same contrast can be seen in Rouen, where the chapter library was open every day from nine to noon and from three to five, but the library of the Academy was accessible only on Wednesdays and Saturdays from two to four.

This survey of libraries at the end of the *ancien régime* (which undoubtedly is incomplete) clearly attests to the importance that "public reading" acquired during the eighteenth century. Three things combined to encourage its spread. First, some of the great religious libraries were opened to the public, often at or soon after the reorganization of their collections. For example, the library of the abbey of Sainte-Geneviève, which already had 45,000 volumes by the first third of the eighteenth century, was enlarged and its furnishing embellished between 1720 and 1733. The architect Jean de la Guépière designed the

Fig. 13. The Library of Sainte-Geneviève in 1773, copperplate engraving by
P. C. de La Gardette (305 x 455 mm)
(Bibliothèque Nationale, Paris).

library gallery, which was situated on the third floor of the abbey, in the form of a cross, with a dome ringed by windows surmounting the crossing. The painter Jean Restout decorated the dome with the figure of Saint Augustine vigorously attacking heretical books, and busts of famous men sculpted by Coysevox, Girardon, and Caffieri adorned the bays along the library walls.[53]

"Public reading" was also encouraged by the opening of the great collectors' libraries. Here Mazarin set the example. Beginning in 1644, the collection that he built up with the aid of his librarian, Gabriel Naudé, was accessible to the public one day a week, on Thursdays. First installed in the Hôtel de Clèves, the library was later transferred to the building on the Rue de Richelieu constructed by Le Muet and begun in 1646. The better part of the collection was housed in the second-floor grand gallery, where fifty-four fluted wooden columns with Corinthian capitals divided the wood-paneled walls, in which were set multishelved bookcases. Sold in 1652, but reconstituted after the Fronde by Naudé's successor, François de la Poterie, Mazarin left the library in his will of 7 March 1661 to the Collège des Quatre Nations, which he founded through the same testament. On the second floor of the new building, which was designed by Le Vau and completed by François d'Orbay, two galleries set at right angles were reserved for the books. The wood paneling from the Rue de Richelieu building was reinstalled and the library holdings were transferred in 1668. It was only in 1688, however, that the library opened to the public, "two times in every week," as the Cardinal's will stipulated.[54] The Conseil du Roi imitated this model when it decided in 1720 to open the Bibliothèque du Roi "to all scholars of all nations on the days and hours which will be regulated by His Majesty's librarian, and to the public once a week." In order to do this, it was decided to transfer the collections to the Mazarin Palace on the Rue de Richelieu. Remodeling began in 1726 under the direction of Robert de Cotte and the supervision of the Abbé Bignon, the king's librarian. The work dragged on for some time, however, and was only finished fifteen years later, by which time the other occupants of the palace (the Indies Company, the bank charged with liquidating Law's system, and the Marquise de Lambert) had disap-

[53] Masson, *Le Décor des bibliothèques*, 143-44.

[54] P. Gasnault, "La Bibliothèque de Mazarin et la Bibliothèque Mazarine au xviie et au xviiie siècles," in *Les Espaces du livre*, 2:38-56; Masson, *Le Décor des bibliothèques*, 98-103.

peared. Thus in 1734 the library was able to welcome "the scholars and the curious, [both] French and foreign," but it was not yet open on fixed days and hours.[55]

Another source of encouragement for the establishment of public libraries were the private collectors who bequeathed their books on the condition that they were to be made available to the readers of the city. In Lyons, for example, the lawyer and former alderman Aubert sold his library to the city government in 1731 in return for a lifetime annuity. Dugas gave this report of the transaction:

> M. Aubert has sold his library to the *consulat* in exchange for a 2,000-*livre* annuity on his head and [one of] 1,500 *livres* on that of M. Chol, his nephew, who is at least sixty years old. He reserves enjoyment of it [the library] for [the rest of] his lifetime. After his death, it will be carried to the city hall and probably opened to the public several days of the week [letter of 28 May 1731].

In the same year, the lawyer Brossette was named city librarian, and, two years later, he in turn sold his library to the city "for an annuity on his head and on that of his son" (letter of Bottu de Saint-Fonds of 26 December 1733). In the course of the century, the Consulat split up the city library that had been thus created between the libraries of the Collège de la Trinité and the Collège Notre-Dame "to make it more easily available to readers of the different orders." The third public library of the city was that of the Academy; it was also for the most part the result of a bequest, and a real one this time. In 1763 a harbor master and supervisor of public works for the city of Lyons, Pierre Adamoli, willed his collection of approximately 5,000 volumes to the Academy on the condition that it be open to the public once a week. The Academy had nowhere to house the collection and so was unable to open the library to the public, which resulted in a lawsuit by Adamoli's heirs. Finally, in 1777, the library was installed in one of the rooms of the city hall, was ceded to the Academy by the Consulat, and was opened every Wednesday.[56]

---

[55] F. Bléchet, "L'Abbé Bignon, Bibliothécaire du Roy, et les milieux savants en France au début du xviiie siècle," in *Buch und Sammler*, 53-66; idem, "L'Installation de la Bibliothèque Royale au Palais Mazarin, 1700-1750," in *Les Espaces du livre*, 2:57-73. See also Masson, *Le Décor des bibliothèques*, 125-30.

[56] Guiot, *Nouveau Supplément à la France Littéraire*, 78-79; Chartier, "L'Académie de Lyon," 228-29.

## *The* Cabinets de Lecture

Thus a first network of public libraries opened in the eighteenth century. As we have seen, however, there were frequent difficulties. The time was often long between the decision to open a library and the moment when the public was allowed in. Moreover, certain libraries accepted only "men of letters" or "scholars." Finally, many libraries were open for only a few hours a week. Hence there was a need for other sorts of public access to books, one of which was the *cabinet de lecture*. This one term actually covered a wide variety of forms, which need to be sorted out. In its earliest form, the *cabinet de lecture* was also a bookseller's shop. In Caen in the middle of the seventeenth century, Moysant de Brieux, formerly a *conseiller* at the *parlement* of Metz and in retirement in Normandy, reported his meeting with the future founders of the Academy in these terms:

> They and I, meeting as we did several years ago in the shop of one of our booksellers, where we went every Monday to read the gazette and look over the new books, found that we could with more comfort have this same amusement in one or another of our own houses.[57]

The renting out of periodicals thus gave booksellers a first reason to open a *cabinet de lecture*. As the eighteenth century progressed, other and stronger reasons were added.

Particularly from the 1770s on, there were many booksellers who added to their usual business a *cabinet littéraire*, to which subscribers could come and read new works. Two examples of this will suffice. In Metz in 1770 a new bookseller, Nicolas Guerlache, invested 2,000 *livres* to purchase a *brevet de libraire* (bookseller's license), set up shop, and acquired bookbinding material. He was the Metz *correspondant* (sales representative) of the Brussels publisher Boubers, who specialized in prohibited books. The two men soon quarreled, and Guerlache, to bolster his business, opened a *cabinet littéraire* stocked by orders sent to the Typographic Societies of Sarrebruck and Neuchâtel. For three *livres* a month, subscribers—officers garrisoned in Metz, for the most part—could go there to read novels, travel books, philosophical essays, political pamphlets, and erotic works. Riddled with debts, Guerlache fled

---

[57] Cited from R. Formigny de la Lande, *Documents inédits pour servir à l'histoire de l'ancienne académie de Caen* (Caen, 1854), 9.

from Metz in 1774, but his creditors, hoping to be repaid, did not bring suit, and in the following year he reestablished his *cabinet littéraire*. In December 1775 he claimed that he had "nearly 200 readers at eighteen *livres* per year and about 150 at three *livres* per month." In 1777 he had 379 subscribers. His flourishing business was badly shaken by the American Revolution, which greatly reduced the number of soldiers stationed in Metz. The second example comes from the south of France. Abraham Fontanel established a book shop in Montpellier in 1772. Business difficulties led him, three years later, to open a *cabinet littéraire*. Like Guerlache, he provided novels, travel accounts, essays of the fashionable authors, and prohibited books, which he ordered from Neuchâtel, Lausanne, Geneva, and Avignon.[58]

There were mutual advantages in such *cabinets de lecture*. The readers could read works there without having to buy them. In particular, they could find there, for an affordable subscription price, the "philosophical works" that were published in quantity at the borders of the kingdom. For their part, the booksellers' business increased. In May 1777 Guerlache noted that, during the ten previous months, book sales brought him 3,600 *livres* and subscription fees 2,654 *livres*. Furthermore, the presence of a *cabinet littéraire* attracted readers, which stimulated business by creating potential buyers. "All my subscribers make me so many customers," Guerlache writes in a letter of January 1776. Faced with the urgent demand for such reading opportunities during the last twenty years of the *ancien régime*, it was often the booksellers who were on the most fragile footing, were the most recently established, or were struggling against the hostility of their more solidly established competitors who were responsible for the growth of the *cabinets de lecture*. These establishments became outposts in the provinces for the diffusion of newspapers, new works, and forbidden books.[59]

There were other *cabinets de lecture*, however, that were in no way born of the business initiative of a bookseller. Arthur Young describes one such *cabinet* in Nantes, which he visited during his travels in 1788:

An institution common in the great commercial towns of France, but particularly flourishing in Nantes, is a *chambre de lecture*, or

[58] R. Darnton, "A Clandestine Bookseller in the Provinces," in his *The Literary Underground of the Old Régime* (Cambridge, Mass., 1982), 122-47.

[59] I should mention, for the years 1770-1790, the *cabinets littéraires* or reading rooms opened by the following booksellers: Lair in Blois, Labalte in Chartres, Beauvert in Clermont, Bernard in Lunéville, Buchet in Nîmes, Elies in Niort, and Despax in Pau.

Fig. 14. The Chambre de Lecture (reading room) de la Fosse, established in Nantes
in 1759, provided a well-lit, open room with direct access to the shelves
(india ink and wash by Hénon, 1763) (Société Archéologique et Historique de Nantes).

what we should call a book-club, that does not divide its books
[among its members], but forms a library. There are three rooms,
one for reading, another for conversation, and the third is the library; good fires in winter are provided, and wax candles.[60]

The institution Young describes was the Chambre de Lecture de la
Fosse, founded in 1759. Its regulations stipulated that the 125 members
pay an initiation fee of three *livres* and an annual subscription fee of
twenty-four *livres*. The *chambre* was administered by elected commissioners, who were to order "all the gazettes and all the periodical works
most useful to the society [the *chambre*], and to buy in Nantes or order

---

[60] A. Young, *Travels in France during the Years 1787, 1788, and 1789*, ed. J. Kaplow
(Garden City, N.Y., 1969), 97.

from Paris carefully chosen good books, preferably in folio and quarto, concerning business, shipping, history, the arts, and literature, as well as some new and interesting pamphlets."[61] From the members' point of view, the advantages of such an institution were many. First, unlike the poorly heated, dimly lit libraries with their ungenerous hours,[62] the *chambre de lecture* was comfortable, well lit, and open every day, even on feast days after services. One could read at ease there, with direct access to shelves containing new works too expensive to purchase oneself (hence the rules' insistence on large format works). And second, unlike an academy, the *chambre de lecture* required no formal ceremonial and no obligatory activities: It was a place for meeting others informally and for spontaneous exchanges. This was a successful formula, combining as it did the cooptative election of members (as in the academies, the number of members was limited) and the merchandising practices of the *cabinets littéraires*. A *chambre de lecture* of this sort was opened in Rennes in 1775. It had one hundred members "of an honest and esteemed estate," who were chosen by election. The initiation fee was twenty-seven *livres*, the yearly subscription fee was twenty-four *livres*, and it stocked a great many periodicals and 3,600 books.[63] Le Mans followed its example in 1778, as did Brest in 1785, and in Nantes itself there were six *chambres de lecture* by 1793.

The spread of the *cabinets de lecture* was not limited to the cities of western France, however, nor to commercial cities. They sprung up all over the kingdom, particularly in cities of middling size that had no academy, but also in certain cities that had such institutions (Lyons, Auxerre, Clermont) and in which the clientele could not or did not want to gain entrance to that more elegant circle. This means that there was often an imprecise line separating a *chambre de lecture* from a literary society.[64] In Rennes, for example, several members of the *chambre de lecture* founded in 1775 wanted to transform it into a true "société littéraire," since as a matter of fact it was so regarded: "Our society is dedicated to reading, but would it not be possible to justify, even in the eyes of the public, the name of literary society that it has taken on?" So

[61] Queniart, *Culture et sociétés urbaines*, 432-33.

[62] In the Bibliothèque Mazarine, for example, the account books for the eighteenth century never mention expenses for heating or light (see Gasnault, "La Bibliothèque de Mazarin," 52).

[63] Queniart, *Culture et sociétés urbaines*, 433-34.

[64] D. Mornet, *Les Origines intellectuelles de la Révolution Française, 1715-1787* (Paris, 1933), 305-12.

212

wrote Le Livec de Lauzay in 1778; two years later the Abbé Germé renewed the proposal: "Without disavowing the modest title under which we are assembled ... would it not be desirable if those of us capable of doing some research or [making] judicious reflections were encouraged to share their observations and their views with us?"[65] Even though his request was rejected, it reflects a tenacious aspiration—as in the mid-seventeenth century—to connect familiarity with books to scholarly endeavors.

The reverse was also true, however. The literary societies that proliferated from midcentury on, and particularly after 1770, founded libraries and bought new books and French and foreign newspapers. In certain of these, it was the reading itself of the books at the disposal of the members that provided matter for learned exchange. In Millau, for example, there was a literary society founded in 1751 and named Le Tripot.

> It meets every day except Sundays and holidays: newspapers furnish the matter [for discussion]. When these have been exhausted, [the members] turn to the best current works. Each academician, as he enters the hall, takes the book he finds most appropriate. If in the course of his reading he finds some subject worthy of observation, he shares it with his colleagues. Private reading soon turns into general conversation. When the academician's reflections have been thoroughly discussed, they [members] return to their reading until other observations again attract the attention of the assembly. This is the way their *conférences*, which customarily end with nightfall, are spent.[66]

The vocabulary usually associated with the academy as an institution is thus used to describe a completely different reality, in which differences between subscription reading, free conversation, and scholarly communication are abolished. Elsewhere, the literary society assumed the role of public library by opening its collections, like certain academies, to those outside the circle of its members. This was the case in Mortain in the diocese of Avranches:

> A society has recently been formed in this city composed of twenty-five to thirty of its principal citizens. They have estab-

[65] Queniart, *Culture et sociétés urbaines*, 434.
[66] J. Hébrail and J. de Laporte, *La France Littéraire* (Paris, 1769), 105-106.

lished a Library in which one finds not only the most important works, both ancient and modern, but Newspapers, Gazettes, and so forth. It is open without charge to known persons.[67]

Thus there was only a tenuous difference between the *chambre de lecture* and the literary society. Both focused on printed matter—books or periodicals placed at the disposal of all—and both reacted against the exclusiveness and constraints of the academies.[68]

### The Lending Libraries

The *cabinets de lecture*, whether they were connected with a bookseller's shop or with a literary or other society, remained the privilege of a select clientele who were able to pay a fairly tidy sum in monthly or annual subscription fees. For the less well off, however, there were other ways in which printed matter could be had for payment. As early as the reign of Louis XIV, several Parisian booksellers rented out the right to read pamphlets and gazettes on the spot, right in front of their shops. François Renaudot, who held the monopoly for the *Gazette*, complained to the Conseil d'État about this custom in 1675:

> For some time now, an abuse has been introduced, both in Paris and in some other places in the Kingdom, in which certain private persons, particularly in Paris, or some booksellers who live on the Quai des Augustins have taken it into their heads to provide all sorts of reading matter, *Gazettes, Relations*, and other pieces that they slap together or that they say come from foreign Countries. These *Gazettes* and other writings they are not content to have hawked and distributed in the streets and taken to private houses, but they repeatedly give them out for public reading to all those who present themselves before their houses and shops, because of the profit they make from this.

The text goes on to speak of another custom, of reading gazettes aloud, probably in exchange for a modest contribution: "Recently, several bourgeois have once again been mistreated by *filoux* [good-for-nothings] and other drifters who have the habit of gathering [on the Quai des Augustins] under the pretext of hearing the reading of the said *Ga-*

[67] Guiot, *Nouveau Supplément à la France Littéraire*, 91.
[68] D. Roche, *Le Siècle des Lumières en Province. Académies et académiciens provinciaux, 1680-1789* (Paris and The Hague, 1978), 1:63-66, 2:477 (map 4).

*zettes."*[69] This gave new form, on the threshold of the bookstore, to the practice of the "nouvellistes de bouche," which Matham represented in his painting, *Le Pont de la Tournelle et l'île Saint Louis* (Musée Carnavalet, Paris),[70] in the mid-seventeenth century and to whom Molière refers in the first scene of *La Comtesse d'Escarbagnas* (1671). The viscount is explaining why he is late:

> I should have been here an hour ago, if there were no bores in the world: I was stopped on the way by a pestering old nobleman, who bothered me for news of the court, as an excuse for telling me the most extravagant things imaginable; these great gossipers, you know, who seek to retail on all sides the stories they collect, are the scourge of small towns.[71]

This Angoulême *nouvelliste* read the *Gazette de Hollande* and other news sheets for news "that comes from the surest quarters."

A century later, "book renters" (*loueurs de livres*, in Louis-Sébastien Mercier's expression) were legion in the capital.[72] They kept small salons or reading rooms, but above all they functioned as fee-based lending libraries. The fees were not monthly but daily, or even less. Mercier notes, in fact, that "there are works that excite such a ferment that the bookseller is obliged to cut the volume in three parts. In this case, you pay not by the day but by the hour." Mercier cites *La Nouvelle Héloïse* as one example of a book dismembered so that it could be read by several readers at once. For him, multiple lending and hasty reading of this sort became the indisputable sign of a literary success: "Great authors, go check on the sly if your works have been well dirtied by the avid hands of the multitude." The meager collections of books we see reported in estate inventories from common folk were not by any means all that was read by the humble people. For three *sous* a day, those who had few if any books could stretch the horizons of their dreams or their pleasures with a rented book.

### From Auto-da-fé to Sacred Status

During the last twenty years of the *ancien régime*, reflection on public readings became central to reformist thought. Two contradictory de-

---

[69] Cited by G. Feyel, *La "Gazette" en province à travers ses réimpressions, 1631-1752* (Amsterdam and The Hague, 1982), 97-98.

[70] A. Monestier, *Le Fait divers* (Paris: Musée National des Arts et Traditions Populaires, 1982), no. 154.

[71] A. R. Waller, trans., *The Plays of Molière* (Edinburgh, 1907), 8:5.

[72] L.-S. Mercier, *Tableau de Paris* (Amsterdam, 1783), 5:61-64.

mands converged here, as is shown by the contradictory dreams of Mercier and Boullée. In his utopia (or, better, his "uchronia"), *L'An 2440* (1771), Louis-Sébastien Mercier visits the king's library and finds it to be most odd: "In place of those four galleries of immense length, which contained many thousands of volumes, I could only find one small cabinet, in which were several books that seemed to me far from voluminous."[73] By the twenty-fifth century, men had been liberated from the tyranny of bad books and useless knowledge by an immense auto-da-fé:

> By unanimous consent, we brought together on a vast plain all those books which we judged frivolous, useless, or dangerous; of these we formed a pyramid that resembled, in height and bulk, an enormous tower; it was certainly another Babel. Journals crowned this strange edifice, and it was covered on all sides with ordinances of bishops, remonstrances of *parlements*, petitions, and funeral orations; it was composed of five or six hundred thousand dictionaries, of one hundred thousand volumes of law, of a hundred thousand poems, of sixteen hundred thousand [memoirs of] voyages and travels, and of a thousand million of romances. This tremendous mass was set on fire and offered as an expiatory sacrifice to veracity, to good sense, and true taste.

What deserved to be saved from the flames was: "We have abridged what seemed of most importance; the best have been reprinted; and the whole corrected according to the true principles of morality."

Beside playing the familiar literary game of imagining posterity's choice among the authors of the day and using this as a way of subjecting them to severe criticism,[74] Mercier says other things that were less usual in his century. The book, he suggests, can be an obstacle just as well as a support in the search for truth; moreover, human understanding needs only a limited number of guides; thus, immense libraries serve little purpose. Mercier was less radical than the wise old man of Morelly's *Basiliade* (1735), who argues in favor of allowing only one book, which condenses all useful knowledge and is possessed by all cit-

---

[73] L.-S. Mercier, *L'An Deux Mille Quatre Cent Quarante. Rêve s'il en fut jamais* [1771], ed. R. Trousson (Bordeaux, 1971), 247-71. (Translation based on *Memoirs of the Year Two Thousand Five Hundred*, trans. W. Hooper [Philadelphia, 1795; repr., Clifton, N.J., 1973], 169-71.)

[74] R. Trousson, "Les Bibliothèques de l'utopie au xviii<sup>e</sup> siècle," in *Buch und Sammler*, 99-107.

izens. Mercier nevertheless denounced the dangers of a proliferating taste for reading, an insatiable consumption of frivolities and superstitions. The attitude he preferred was that of "men who, in love with strong ideas, take the trouble to read and then know how to meditate on their reading."

In sharp contrast to Mercier's expurgatory dreams were Étienne-Louis Boullée's projects for collection on a grand scale, which date from 1784 and 1785.[75] The first of these projects was a commission from the Superintendent of Buildings for the construction of a public library on the grounds of the Capuchin Convent. Behind a colossal portico capped by a pediment adorned with a frieze, Boullée planned a semicircular courtyard, called the Temple of Apollo, which was flanked by rooms for the print and medallion collections. Across the courtyard was a vast square building, the four sides of which were to contain books, with two halls crossing at the center to serve as reading rooms. This formed four interior courtyards, each of which was to be lined with storage space for manuscripts. This first project was abandoned, but the same monumentality can be seen in the plan Boullée proposed for the reconstruction of the Royal Library on the Rue de Richelieu. Boullée's guiding idea was to cover the long (100 by 30 meters) rectangular court that lay between the existing buildings with a gigantic barrel vault. This new gallery would serve as the reading room, and it would be the largest in Europe. On all four sides of this "immense basilica," lit only by a central skylight, there were to be four step-like tiers, each ten feet high, providing the base for a continuous colonnade. At each end of the room this colonnade met the vaulted ceiling to form "a sort of triumphal arch under which two allegorical statues could be put." The books, to be shelved on each tier of the stepped base of the colonnade and behind the columns themselves, would thus be easily accessible to readers passing before them and easily fetched "by persons placed on various levels and distributed so as to pass the books from hand to hand."

In the perspective view that accompanies the *Mémoire* describing the project and in the presentation model Boullée constructed of it, he placed minuscule readers draped in Roman togas standing or strolling among the books, stopping to read one or another of the thousands of

[75] J.-M. Pérouse de Montclos, *Étienne-Louis Boullée (1728-1799). De l'architecture classique à l'architecture révolutionnaire* (Paris, 1969), 165-67 and pls. 93-102. (*Étienne-Louis Boullée (1728-1799): Theoretician of Revolutionary Architecture*, trans. J. Emmons [New York, 1974].)

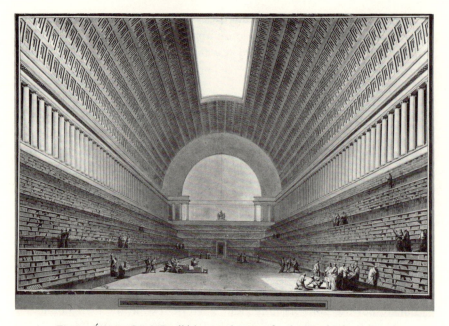

Fig. 15. Étienne-Louis Boullée's second project for the Royal Library in 1785 called for a gigantic barrel vault above a rectangular hall that would serve as the reading room. A striking skylight in the center of the vaulted ceiling would provide reading light for the books, which, arrayed in shelves on the four stepped tiers of the hall, were easily accessible (Bibliothèque Nationale, Paris).

works within reach, or else gathered around the few tables placed in the vast hall. The message is clear: The space devoted to reading takes on a sacredness that religion had lost; study is like a voyage among books, and it reflects the travelers' stops and starts. The library's function is to assemble all the accumulated learning, to be a *summa* of human knowledge, putting at everyone's disposal the thousands of works written throughout the centuries. As Boullée's avowed model, Raphael's *School of Athens*, teaches, new thoughts arise from this massive accumulation of knowledge. Classical antiquity here served as a point of reference and furnished a repertory of themes, but, even more so, it provided a guide for further progress.

## Urban Reading, Private and Public

A survey of the various ways people had access to books is a necessary precondition to an account of the history of reading, but it tells us little about actual practice—about how modes of reading differed and changed between the middle of the seventeenth century and the end of the *ancien régime*. To reconstruct this, we must turn our attention to the ways in which pre-Revolutionary society portrayed its own reading and to the printed materials themselves to see what they reveal of the uses made of them.

### Private Reading

The first and the dominant portrayal of reading showed it to be an action essentially involving the inner self, an intimate act that takes place in private and that requires the investment of intense emotional, intellectual, and spiritual efforts. French painters of the eighteenth century give us many scenes of women reading in which the heroine, alone and in private, shows discreet or extreme emotion. *La Jeune fille lisant* of Fragonard (National Gallery, Washington) shows a comfortably seated young woman reading with studious and well-mannered attention a book that she holds elegantly in her right hand. Behind her perfect immobility—she seems withdrawn from the world—we sense an inner animation, a pleasurable tension.[76] Somewhat earlier in the century and in a less limpid style, two other paintings, Jeaurat's *Scène d'intérieur* (private collection) and Baudoin's *La lecture* (Musée des Arts Décoratifs, Paris), put the act of reading in a similar setting. In these two pictures we see the homes of well-to-do people, formally furnished in Jeaurat, cozily in Baudoin. There are signs in the Baudoin that these are women's quarters: the little lap dog, the furniture of everyday use, the comfortable chair in which the body relaxes, and the disorder (discreet in Jeaurat, everywhere in Baudoin). In both paintings there is a young female reader in a morning dress, surprised at the moment her thoughts stray from her book, which she has set down, her finger marking the page, on her knees or on the sleeping dog's kennel. Moved by her reading, she abandons herself to her reveries, her head resting on a cushion, her gaze uncertain, her body languid. Her book is certain to be one of those that touch the senses and excite the imagination. Each artist uses his painting to invade feminine privacy, with reserve in Jeaurat, with more conspiratorial sensuality in Baudoin.

Even when it was not feminine and genres other than fiction were

[76] See J. Starobinski, *L'Invention de la Liberté, 1700-1789* (Geneva, 1964), 125. (*The Invention of Liberty, 1700-1789*, trans. B. C. Swift [Geneva, 1964].)

Fig. 16. *La Lecture* (Reading), by Pierre-Antoine Baudoin
(1723-1769) (gouache, 290 x 225 mm) (Musée des Arts Décoratifs,
Paris [inventory no. 26829G]).

involved, the reading generally depicted in the eighteenth century was
reading in private. The role of the book in male portraiture shifted:
Formerly an attribute of status and an indication of social condition or
occupation, it became a companion in solitude. The book is one element of decor in iconographic tradition, and a bookshelf or library signifies knowledge or power, as in the portrait of Pierre Palliot, geneal-
ogist of the Estates of Burgundy, that Gabriel Revel painted in 1696
(Musée des Beaux-Arts, Dijon) or in the glorious portrait of the Marquis de Mirabeau painted by Aved and presented at the Salon of 1743
(Musée du Louvre, Paris). Eighteenth-century portraiture added another element to the traditional iconography of the book: the act of

reading itself, which supposes an intimate relation between a reader and a book. New settings appear; reading moves outdoors into the garden or under the boughs of a tree (Carmontelle, *Le Comte de Genlis*, Collection of Queen Elizabeth II) or it becomes peripatetic, as in the silhouette of Goethe of the 1780s. In Hubert Robert's *Camille Desmoulins en prison* (Wadsworth Atheneum, Hartford, Connecticut), the representation of solitary reading reached its limit. In absolute and forced solitude, the book becomes a companion in distress, as do one's few personal possessions or the portrait of a beloved woman. Read while pacing back and forth, it brings the memory of the exterior world into the prison cell and it fortifies the soul against an adverse and unjust fate. This painting of the end of the century reworks in a secular key the iconography of spiritual reading in which a reader (often Saint Jerome or Saint Paul) in voluntary retirement pours his entire soul into the text he is deciphering with reverent concentration.[77]

Eighteenth-century furniture provided private reading with adequate accessories. The *bergère*, with its armrests and cushions, the *chaise longue* or *duchesse*, and the two-piece *duchesse brisée*, with its upholstered stool, were all new types of seats into which the reader, usually a woman, could settle at ease and abandon him or herself to the pleasures of the book. As engravings show (for example, the *Liseuse* of Jacques André Portail),[78] there was a feminine garment called, precisely, a *liseuse* that corresponded to these luxurious pieces of furniture. It was a warm but light indoor coat or dressing gown appropriate for reading in the privacy of the bedroom or sitting room. Other pieces of furniture implied a less relaxed mode of reading, such as tables that featured a movable writing desk which could prop up a book and hold a page of writing,[79] or the little writing stands called *bonheur-du-jour* that provided a writing desk and occasionally a small bookshelf.

As the century progressed a reaction began to set in against this sort

[77] The aforementioned works of Baudoin, Aved, Carmontelle, and Hubert Robert are reproduced in the catalogue by D. Sutton, *France in the Eighteenth Century: Royal Academy of Arts Winter Exhibition* (London, 1968), nos. 14, 10, 112, 594 (figs. 312, 168, 307, 335). The Fragonard painting is reproduced in *European Paintings: An Illustrated Summary Catalogue* (Washington: National Gallery of Art, 1975), no. 1653; the Jeaurat in R. Huyghe, *L'Art et l'Homme* (Paris, 1961), fig. 642; the Revel in *Catalogue des Peintures Françaises* (Dijon: Musée des Beaux-Arts, 1968), no. 104; and the silhouette of Goethe in *Lesewuth, Raubdruck und Bücherluxus*, no. 335.

[78] Forsyth Wickes Collection, Newport. Reproduced in Starobinski, *L'Invention de la Liberté*, 123.

[79] *Louis XV. Un Moment de perfection de l'art français* (Paris: Hôtel de la Monnaie, 1974), no. 423.

of furniture, which was judged too frivolous, and there was an attempt to impose more functional furnishings that treated reading more as work than as distraction. Certain of these followed a Renaissance tradition that aimed at making the consultation of books easier. Among these was the "book wheel" designed by Daudet (and depicted by him in an engraving), which adapted an invention proposed by the Italian engineer Ramelli in 1588. A series of writing desks placed along the perimeter of a wooden wheel, turned by hand, held books to be consulted. The reader could thus remain seated, consult various texts, and check cross-references without useless comings and goings and without creating disorderly piles of books.[80] At the end of the eighteenth century, English taste offered Europe a less utopian sort of utilitarian furniture: circular tables with panels that could be pulled out for use as reading desks while the larger central surface was used to consult drawings and maps. Another English introduction was a sort of *chaise longue* with a movable reading desk of an austere and geometric rigor that had no relation to the comforts of the *bergère* and its thick cushions.[81]

Does this reaction toward the end of the century indicate a consciousness that reading styles had changed, that the elites in western Europe had passed from intensive and reverent reading to a more extensive, nonchalant reading style, and that such a change called for correction? These two reading styles have been contrasted as they appeared in Germany and New England, and it is possible to compare them term for term. In the older style: (1) Readers had the choice of only a few books, which perpetuated texts of great longevity. (2) Reading was not separated from other cultural activities such as listening to books read aloud time and again in the bosom of the family, the memorization of such texts (which could then be deciphered because they were already familiar), or the recitation of texts read aloud and learned by heart. (3) The relation of reader to book was marked by a weighty respect and charged with a strong sense of the sacred character of printed matter. (4) The intense reading and rereading of the same texts shaped minds that were habituated to a particular set of references and inhabited by the same quotations. It was not until the second half of

[80] On Ramelli's machine, see Masson, *Le Décor des bibliothèques*, 110-11 (fig. 46). On the engraving by Daudet, see *Leser und Lesen im 18. Jahrhundert* (Heidelberg, 1977), 178-79.

[81] *Lesewuth, Raubdruck und Bücherluxus*, nos. 314, 318.

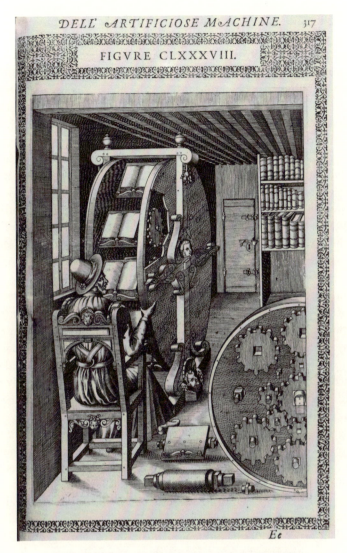

Fig. 17. Rotary Reading Desk, from Agostino Ramelli's
*Le diverse et artificiose machine* (Paris, 1588), 317r (fig. 188).
Books were so placed on the small lecterns that any one on
the wheel could be moved to the reader by a simple hand motion
(New York Public Library).

the eighteenth century in Germany and the beginning of the nineteenth century in New England that this style of reading yielded to another style, based on the proliferation of accessible books, on the individualization of the act of reading, on its separation from other cultural
activities, and on the desacralization of the book. Book reading habits
became freer, enabling the reader to pass from one text to another and
to have a less attentive attitude toward the printed word, which was
less concentrated in a few privileged books.[82]

Can this sort of shift be documented in French urban societies of the
eighteenth century? It is clear, first of all, that in France intensive reading was not bolstered, as it was in Protestant countries, by the daily encounter with the Bible—heard, read, reread, and recited. In Catholic
lands, this sort of familiarity with the Bible, far from being encouraged,
was held suspect because it deprived the clergy of its task as the obligatory mediator between the Divine Word and the community of the
faithful. In spite of this difference—which was enormous, since the
reading of the Bible provided a model for all reading in the Protestant
countries—there were several sources for the traditional sort of intense
reading in French cities. On the one hand, for many people and for
many years, as we have seen, the number of books owned remained
small, and a limited body of works made up this stock of inherited references. On the other hand, certain books were utilized intensely and
could profoundly mold minds. Almanacs served as models for the organization of account books. The narrations in *occasionnels* served as
archetypes for the first-person narratives of journals and private memoires. Books of piety, which everyone owned and read with the encouragement of the clergy, were also, in effect, just so many books that
people knew, recognized, handled, and took to heart.

As the eighteenth century advanced, the well-documented increase
in library size, the easier access to public collections, and the practice of
rental libraries no doubt influenced this older style of reading. Furthermore, although the painters' portrayals of female readers show the
book's continuing power to overwhelm the senses, they also attest to a
sort of reading that hungered for novelty, that was an act of private
pleasure, and that was set in the context of totally worldly pleasures. It

---

[82] See R. Engelsing, *Der Bürger als Leser. Lesergeschichte in Deutschland, 1500-1800*
(Stuttgart, 1974); and D. Hall, "Introduction: The Uses of Literacy in New England,
1600-1850," in W. Joyce et al., eds., *Printing and Society in Early Modern America*
(Worcester, 1983), 1-47.

224

was against just this sort of frivolous, gratuitous reading that Rousseau in France and the pre-Romantics in Germany took a stand. For them, reading should be a serious matter and should imply the active participation of the reader, whose very thoughts and existence should change. Emotion, which throws the reader into the text and inscribes the text within the reader, thus educates for life, provided that the works are read with attention again and again, meditated upon, and discussed—all of which implies, as Mercier noted, few readings, but thoughtful ones, not the accumulation of books read too fast and too superficially. Some eighteenth-century readers took such instructions literally and actually became the ideal readers Mercier imagined. Thus it was with Jean Ranson, a wholesale merchant of La Rochelle, who avidly acquired the books of Jean-Jacques Rousseau from the Société Typographique in Neuchâtel because they were for him guides to living, to be read with passion and heeded faithfully.[83]

### The Spoken Word as Intermediary

Men of the eighteenth century offer another picture of reading that contrasts with this internalized individual reading. In it, the spoken word served as "reader" for the illiterate or the barely literate. Restif de la Bretonne gives us the archetype in his *La Vie de mon Père* (1778):

> It was thus after supper that [my] father read the Holy Scripture: he began with Genesis and reverently read three or four chapters, depending on their length, accompanying them with a few observations, short, infrequent, but which he judged absolutely necessary. I cannot remember without being touched with what attention this reading was listened to; how it communicated to all of [his] numerous family a tone of good will and fraternity (in the family I include the domestics). My father always began with these words: "Settle down and concentrate, my children, it is the most Holy Spirit who is about to speak." The next day, as we were working, the reading of the preceding evening was the subject of our conversation, among the plowboys in particular.[84]

[83] See R. Darnton, "Readers Respond to Rousseau: The Fabrication of Romantic Sensitivity," in his *The Great Cat Massacre and Other Episodes in French Cultural History* (New York, 1984), 214-56; and A. Montandon, "Le Lecteur sentimental de Jean Paul," in his *Le Lecteur et la lecture dans l'oeuvre* (Clermont-Ferrand, 1982), 25-33.
[84] Restif de la Bretonne, *La Vie de mon Père*, ed. G. Rouger (Paris, 1970), 131-32.

This scene, depicted in the engraving that serves as the frontispiece to volume two of the first edition of the work, is the literary equivalent of a painting by Greuze shown in the Salon of 1755. Diderot, who refers to the painting by several titles (*Père qui lit l'Écriture Sainte à ses enfants, Paysan qui lit l'Écriture Sainte à sa famille, Paysan qui fait la lecture à ses enfants*), attests to its widespread circulation in the form of engravings: "M. de La Live, who first made known the talent of Greuze, generously consented to the engraving of his painting of the *Peasant Reading to his Children*, and there is no man of taste who does not possess [a copy of] this print."[85]

At the end of the century, some of the respondents to the Abbé Grégoire's questionnaire on "the patois and the mores of country people" described evenings devoted to reading in similar terms. A lawyer named Bernadau speaks of them in the Gironde: "The peasants' books are always in bad condition, even though carefully shelved. They hand them down to their heirs. During the long winter evenings, someone will read for half an hour to the entire assembled household from some saint's life or a chapter of the Bible."[86] The parish priest Joly mentions reading in the former *bailliage* of Saint-Claude: "Country people do [not] lack a taste for reading, but they give a just preference to works of their estate. In winter, principally, they read or have their children read ascetic books in the family circle."[87] In both of these accounts we see the same season for reading aloud—winter—the same audience— the household—and the same object—the religious book. Was this *veillée*, then, the collective and rural counterpart of individual reading among city dwellers, as many French historians have thought? Another of Bernadau's letters raises doubts:

> The books that I have most usually found in the peasants' houses are Hours, a Hymnal, a Life of the Saints (among the wealthiest *fermiers*), a few pages of which are read after supper to their workers. I remember in this connection several verses of a work on rural life that competed in the contest seven years ago against the eclogue on Ruth by M. Florian. The evening readings among

[85] D. Diderot, *Salons de 1759, 1761, 1763*, ed. Jean Seznec (Paris, 1967), 164. The painting by Greuze is analyzed in Michael Fried's *Absorption and Theatricality: Painting and Beholder in the Age of Diderot* (Berkeley, 1980), 8-11.

[86] *Lettres à Grégoire sur les patois de France, 1790-1794*, ed. A. Gazier (Paris, 1880), 143.

[87] Ibid., 210.

Fig. 18. *La Lecture du soir* (The Evening Reading), the copperplate-engraved frontispiece for the second volume of Restif de la Bretonne's *Le Vie de mon père* (Neufchâtel, 1779). After supper, his father read the Holy Scriptures aloud to the entire household, including the servants (height: 166 mm) (Bibliothèque Nationale, Paris).

227

the peasants are well described in them, as they are with no less energy in *La Vie de mon Père* by M. Rétif.[88]

First authenticated by personal experience, as seen in the initial "I," this account then blends literature and observation, as if the poetic or narrative text permitted the setting of the scene in accordance with the ideals of the time. Restif's book and poetry contest entries (probably written for the Floral Games, the Jeux Floraux, of Toulouse) were thus held to certify the existence of a social reality perceived or imagined to be identical to what he described.

The same motif builds from Greuze to Restif, from Restif to Grégoire's informants: In a rural society that was patriarchal and homogeneous, reading aloud in the evening by the head of the household or by a child taught the commandments of religion and the laws of morality to all assembled. Far from the dislocations and depravity of the urban world, peasant reading—the words spoken and listened to—cemented the household community, which included all those who worked on the farm, and at the same time instituted the reign of virtue and piety. That this representation of peasant evenings is far from the truth of the matter now seems beyond doubt. In traditional society the peasant *veillée*, when it existed, was above all an occasion for working together, for tales and for songs, for dancing and for lovemaking. In spite of the efforts of the clergy of the Catholic Reformation, the book scarcely penetrated this milieu, and collective reading seems to have been rare in it. Printed matter doubtlessly circulated widely in the rural areas of France in the eighteenth century, but this does not mean that it was massively diffused through the medium of reading aloud at night. Rather than actual rural practices, this image is most probably indicative of something else, perhaps the nostalgia of urban readers for a past form of reading. In the idealized and mythical representation of peasant life widespread among the learned elite, communal reading signified a world in which nothing was hidden, in which knowledge was shared fraternally, and in which the book was revered. There is something here like an inverted portrait of the private, individual, and nonchalant reading habits of the city dwellers. When the pictures and texts of the latter half of the eighteenth century implicitly contrapose the silent reading practices by city dwellers and notables and the reading aloud (for others, but for oneself as well) of the people and the peas-

[88] Ibid., 146-47.

antry, they demonstrate the dream of an unambiguously significant reading that brings together all ages and conditions around the deciphered book.

There were some ways of experiencing the printed word in the daily life of the cities that differed enormously from the bucolic *veillée*, but that also presupposed a mediating voice between the written word and the hearer. The song merchant was one such intermediary. Three pictures that date from the last decades of the *ancien régime* portray his commerce: *Le Chanteur de foire*, a painting by J.-C. Seckaz engraved by Romanet; *Le Violoneux*, a painting by Louis Watteau of 1785 (Musée des Beaux-Arts, Lille); and an engraving by Moreau the Younger, *La Foire de Gonesse*, which shows a song merchant and his merchandise. In all three we see the same elements. The singer accompanies himself on the violin; he points with his bow to pictures painted on a canvas that correspond to his *complainte* (song); and the booklets with the texts of the songs, hanging in a sack at his belt, are sold to the audience gathered around him.[89] Once the text had been heard and visualized, it could be recognized, with the help of the remembered melody, after it had been purchased. The song merchant wandered the countryside from fair to fair, but he was also a city figure, installed on the bridges, the squares, and the boulevards, as the Parisian Louis-Sébastien Mercier attested:

> Some squall the Sacred Hymns, others recite lusty songs; often the two are only forty steps from one another. . . . The boisterous song draws away the audience of the scapular [monastic garment] seller; he is left alone on his perch, pointing in vain with his baton to the horns of the Devil, tempter and enemy of humankind. Everyone forgets the salvation he promises to run to damnation's song. The singer to the damned tells of wine, good food, and love, he celebrates Margot's attractions, and the two *sol* coin that was balanced between the hymn and the vaudeville—alas!—is going to fall into the pocket of the worldly songster.[90]

Mercier's text gives us precious testimony about the pedagogy of the image inherited from the Catholic Reformation. It shows us the sale of

[89] These three works are mentioned in Monestier, *Le Fait divers*, nos. 166, 167 (*Le Chanteur de foire* and *Le Violoneux* are reproduced on p. 124); and in Roche, *Le Peuple de Paris*, fig. 32.

[90] Mercier, *Tableau de Paris*, 6:40-41.

songs amid all sorts of hawked knickknacks (here, scapulars, in Louis Watteau's painting, trinkets). It also shows us that the songs were purchased after the buyer had listened to a seductive spiel that taught how to decipher them.

The poster was another sort of printed matter much in evidence in the city that implied the mediating voice of someone reading aloud to those who could not read or could not read with ease. Posters had many purposes, primarily administrative, with the systematic posting of edicts and ordinances, laws and calls to assembly, *mercuriales* (lists of current food prices), and recruitment appeals. Official *placards* put out by royal, military, and municipal authorities were called to public attention by being proclaimed to the sound of trumpet and drum—permitting understanding at a first reading—and then were pasted onto walls throughout the city, where they were often deciphered in common. The same was doubtlessly true of the posters that publicized spectacles, *fêtes*, jousts, and lotteries, or that advertised the mountebanks and charlatans. A textile worker in Lille, Pierre Ignace Chavatte, copied down in his journal in 1684 a printed advertisement that had been distributed and posted in the city:

> A young boy of twelve years of age, who promises to show you marvels that you have not yet seen, has arrived in this city of Lille; he will take an iron bar three feet long, four fingers wide, and the thickness of a thumb; he will take it out of the fire red-hot and glowing and he will dance and walk on it with bare feet—a considerable thing, as the fire burns hotter than natural fire.[91]

Finally, there were all sorts of religious announcements that were posted throughout the city: episcopal decrees, certificates of pardon and indulgence, *placards* announcing confraternity affairs, and funeral notices. As the eighteenth century wore on, the posters changed their appearance, with pictures yielding space to printed texts and with texts in both upper and lower case letters or in *lettres de civilité* (cursive letters) taking the place of all capital letters.[92] Such changes, which paralleled changes in shop signs, in which text also took an increasing place, doubtlessly attest to the progress of literacy among city dwellers. The

[91] Cited by A. Lottin, *Chavatte ouvrier lillois. Un Contemporain de Louis XIV* (Paris, 1979), 325.

[92] J.-C. Perrot, *Genèse d'une ville moderne. Caen au XVIIIe siècle* (Paris and The Hague, 1975), 1:307.

practice of reading in common (with spectator-listeners gathered around the decipherer of the message), however, was far from eliminated.

In times of crisis the *placard* might become handwritten and take on a seditious purpose. In this case it served for neither administrative nor commercial purposes, but for protest. Two situations lent themselves particularly well to this shift in the uses of outdoor reading and to popular reappropriation of posted notices. Every time food scarcities arose, *placards* sprang up everywhere against those in power, accusing them of grain speculation and of starving the people. This happened in 1725 and again in 1768. Some of these *placards*, hastily scratched out and spelled phonetically, reflect only rudimentary skills of expression; others, written with a firm hand, called to action or spoke with biting satire.[93] Religious conflicts were a second opportunity for wildcat posters. This was the case during the Jansenist crisis. The lawyer Barbier noted in his journal in February 1732: "It is said that a *placard* has been found at the gate of Saint Médard on which it was written: By order of the king, it is forbidden to God to make miracles in this place."[94] These handwritten posters that proliferated in periods of tension attest in their own way to the progress of the diffusion of printed matter. They imitated the forms of printed matter and so tried to appropriate their impact. In order to do this, they set in motion mechanisms of public reading, either silent or aloud, with the more forward aiding the less able.[95]

### Among the Elites: Reading in Society

The opposition of the private reading habits of the elites and the collective reading habits of the common people must not induce us to slight instances in which these practices were reversed. Learned reading could still be reading in common or reading aloud in the eighteenth century. The correspondence between Dugas and Bottu de Saint-Fonds gives many an example of this. Two people frequently read a text together. Dugas did so with his son to teach him to reflect on his reading: "I spent considerable time with my son, reading Greek and

---

[93] S. L. Kaplan, *Le Complot de famine: Histoire d'une rumeur au XVIIIe siècle*, in Cahiers des Annales 39 (Paris, 1982), 15, 40.

[94] E.-J.-F. Barbier, *Journal d'un Bourgeois de Paris sous le règne de Louis XV* (Paris, 1963), 119.

[95] On outdoor reading in Paris, see Roche, *Le Peuple de Paris*, 229-37.

some odes of Horace. I did the same today" (letter of 28 July 1728). Or, "It is in the evening that I play chess with my son. We begin by reading a good book—that is, a book of piety—for a half hour" (letter of 19 December 1732). But reading together was also a country pastime be-tween husband and wife: "Our day was spent yesterday taking a walk. . . . We sat at the edge of a stream, where we read *Le Théologien dans les conversations* [italics added]. We were content with what we read" (letter of 14 October 1733). Between friends as well parallel reading was a pleasure because it encouraged learned exchanges afterward: "Cheinet spent the afternoon yesterday and supped with me. We read some letters of Cicero and we lamented public ignorance—I mean by that the lack of taste among our young people, who amuse themselves reading new books that are often frivolous and superficial, and who neglect the great models from which they could learn to think prop-erly" (letter of 27 March 1731).

In Lyons at the beginning of the eighteenth century, the practice of reading aloud in select society had by no means disappeared. Dugas at-tests to this in a 1733 notation on a new work of Voltaire, *Le Temple du Goût*, of which M. de la Font, *gentilhomme* to the Queen, had re-ceived an autographed copy. A first reading of the book was given in the intimacy of Dugas's family:

> M. de la Font arrived and told me that he had thought that I would enjoy hearing the reading of a new work by M. de Voltaire entitled *Le Temple du Goût*, but that if I found it to my liking, we would wait for my son, who had gone that morning to Brignais, to return that evening. He arrived a half hour later, and he was the reader; the reading lasted a good hour and a half. My wife, who arrived around seven o'clock, heard three-quarters of it.

A second occasion for reading aloud in literate society was at the Acad-emy:

> I heard for the second time the reading of this work at the acad-emy and I listened to it with pleasure. . . . M[onsieur] the Abbé Tricaut, who was to speak, did not take long, and we had the time to read *Le Temple du Goût*, but the notes that the author put at the foot of the pages were not read, and some of them are extremely curious.

Dugas planned to read the book in common a third time when he asked M. de la Font to lend him the book when his friend Bottu de

Saint-Fonds was in Lyons. He wrote to Bottu, "I feel that I will be delighted to reread it with you" (letter of 23 March 1733).

Here it is undoubtedly the novelty of the work that excited curiosity, and this sort of reading in the family circle or in public was aimed at assuaging the eagerness of other readers. There is other evidence that confirms the frequent practice of reading in society, for example the painting by Jean-François de Troy of 1728 entitled *La Lecture de Molière* (Collection of the Marquis of Cholmondeley). In a richly furnished rococo *salon*, an aristocratic company of two men and five women listen to one of the men read Molière. The women, in house dress, are comfortably installed in *bergère* armchairs, and one of them leans toward the reader to look at the text he is reading. In the background there is a low bookcase with glass doors, on top of which a clock shows three-thirty. The reader has stopped for a moment, and the gazes of the various members of the group meet or avoid the others' gazes, as though the pleasures of society that had brought them together to read aloud have sent each one back to his or her own thoughts and desires.[96]

### Printed Matter and Private Reading among the People

In the workshops and boarding houses of the cities, in the ports and in the city streets, common folk had collective access to the written word, deciphered in common. But this was not their only relationship with the printed word. Printed matter penetrated their private world, mobilizing their sentiments, fixing their memories, and guiding their habits. More often than not, this printed matter for the meditation of the common people was not in the form of books but of humbler and more ephemeral materials. Among these the *occasionnels* and the *canards* were the most important. After the middle of the seventeenth century as before, the collective imagination was fired by this sort of publication. People were fascinated by natural catastrophes, marvels and monsters, celestial prodigies, miraculous happenings, and abominable crimes. Established in the sixteenth century, these themes continued with little modification[97] until the end of the seventeenth century, when the forms of the humblest sorts of this occasional literature began to change. Their texts grew closer to awkward and confused speech, as

[96] This picture appears in the catalogue, *France in the Eighteenth Century*, no. 668 (fig. 108).

[97] See Chapter 5, "Publishing Strategies and What the People Read, 1530-1660."

if their authors belonged to the popular milieu or as if the peddlers who distributed these little booklets had penned them themselves. On the other hand, the prose morals that often followed these narrations yielded to *complaintes*, which could be sung.[98] In this way, the *canard* gradually assumed the plural structure typical of it during the nineteenth century: a picture or a series of pictures that tell a story combined with a written narration and a *complainte* or song. Thus the *canard* could bet on several modes of reception, could lend itself to various readings from the cleverest to the simplest, and could be prolonged in different ways, by developing the song, the explanation, or the commentary.

But as the example of Chavatte attests, the *canard* could also inspire an individual to an entire gamut of actions. After being read, it could be cut up and its picture pasted into a personal chronicle, as happened to one picture of a flood and the appearance of sea monsters in Flanders and Holland in 1682 and to another picture of the same year that showed the torture of "two magicians who had thrown poison in several places in Germany." Aside from being clipped, it could be copied. Chavatte, in fact, did not clip the printed texts of *canards* that he wanted to put into his chronicle but copied them. It was as if the action of writing were a condition of personal appropriation, as if transcription gave the thing he read the same authenticity as something he might have seen. And in fact Chavatte, an assiduous reader of *canards*, repeated their style and their structure when he reported the events in Lille that he saw or was told about. His own writing came to be modeled on printed formulas. He picked up their themes and their phrasing, such that a fictional narrative became in turn the guarantee of the veracity of the extraordinary events peddled about the city.[99] In this way the *canards*, sold in Lille by Prévost the bookseller, whose shop was located in the Bourse, were an intimate part of Chavatte's daily experience. He owned *canards*, clipped them, and transcribed them; in return, they shaped the way he thought and spoke, dictated his style, and imposed their definition of reality on him.

---

[98] J.-P. Seguin, "Les Occasionnels au xviiie siècle et en particulier après l'apparition de la *Gazette*. Une Source d'information pour l'histoire des mentalités et de la littérature 'populaire,'" *L'Informazione in Francia nel Seicento*, Quaderni del Seicento Francese 5 (Bari and Paris, 1983), 33-59. There is an example of a *canard* with iconographic narration and a moralistic *complainte* in Monestier, *Le Fait divers*, no. 46.

[99] Lottin, *Chavatte ouvrier lillois*, 265, 266, 329-30.

Other printed pieces, which were neither books nor booklets but simple sheets, could also be found in the houses of the people. Printed pictures—*images volantes*—are one example of this. In Paris in 1700, at a time when only 13 percent of salaried workers owned one or more books, 56 percent of them had pictures; in 1780 these percentages were, respectively, 30 and 61 percent. The same gap was true for domestic servants in 1700, but it disappeared by the end of the *ancien régime*. In 1700, 35 percent of domestics had books and 56 percent pictures; by 1780 the percentages had converged at 40 percent.[100] Among salaried workers in particular, these pictures were religious, since two-thirds of them illustrated Christian pious practices. Confraternity images accounted for the better part of these religious pictures, and they were printed in enormous quantities all the way to the end of the eighteenth century, as Jean-Michel Papillon attests:

> In 1756, about ninety years after my late grandfather Jean Papillon had cut, in pear wood alone, the large [printing] plate representing the Holy Virgin in Glory, surrounded by the Holy Mysteries of her life, for the administrators of the Royal Confraternity of the Charity of Our Lady of Good Deliverance, founded in the church of Saint-Étienne des Grès in Paris, this plate was still in use, having had five or six thousand copies pulled from it to be distributed to the brothers of that confraternity, which makes a total of more than five hundred thousand copies.[101]

Papillon says this to demonstrate the merits of woodcuts, but he also speaks to the longevity of woodblock plates (hence of the prints taken from them) and of their extraordinarily broad distribution.

Each year, in fact, all the brothers of a confraternity received a print depicting the saint or the mystery that they revered. The statutes of the confraternity of the Immaculate Conception of the Holy Virgin organized in the church of Saint-Paul in Paris, for example, stipulated that the annual membership fee gave members the right to "one candle of sixteen, an image, and a portion of blessed bread."[102] During the second

---

[100] Roche, *Le Peuple de Paris*, 226.

[101] J.-M. Papillon, *Traité historique et pratique de la gravure sur bois* (Paris, 1766), 1:423-24.

[102] Cited by the Abbé J. Gaston in *Les Images des confréries parisiennes avant la Révolution* (Paris, 1909-1910). "One candle of sixteen" refers to the candles that came sixteen to the pound.

half of the eighteenth century, this confraternity had three hundred images printed per year, along with one hundred certificates of indulgence listing those which had been granted to its membership. In Lille, Chavatte was a founding member and zealous supporter of the confraternity of Saint Paulin, founded in 1670 and open to textile workers—makers of serge and work shirts—and gardeners of the parish church of Saint-Sauveur, where it was established. There were myriad representations of the saints venerated by the faithful: a relic brought back from Rome to Lille in 1685, a silver statue melted down for a collection in 1669, but also a print like the one Chavatte inserted in his chronicle. Unlike some other more loquacious pictures, this print bears a minimal text (printed in capital letters): "S. Paulin, patron saint of gardeners" and, underneath, "The confraternity of S. Paulin is founded in the parish church of S. Sauveur in Lille, P. A. Cappon made [this print]." Distributed on an annual basis to the confraternity brothers and pasted onto the walls of their dwellings or workshops, images of this sort undoubtedly served as tangible support to the devotions demanded by the confraternity's statutes:

> The brothers and the sisters will recite three times a day the Sunday prayer and the angel's greeting in honor of God, the Most Blessed Virgin Mary, and Saint Paulin, in order to obtain the love of God and of one's neighbor and preservation and deliverance from colics and other spiritual and corporal ills.[103]

As he prayed to Saint Paulin, therefore, Chavatte also prayed to the Virgin, and she was present in effigy in his journal. The image he chose shows Our Lady of Loreto, venerated by the Dominicans of Lille, whose confraternity was established in the church of the hospital of Saint-Sauveur near his house.[104]

The confraternity images had multiple uses, offering the members a view of the saintly patron for their veneration, giving the text of prayers, and recalling the duties and services expected of them. Placed deep within the members' private lives, these images were tacked up on walls, looked at, and consulted. They were of course not the only examples of devoutly conserved religious printed matter. There were also *tours de cheminées* or *tours de lit*, which were frieze-like series of wood-

[103] Lottin, *Chavatte ouvrier lillois*, 253-57. The picture is reproduced opposite p. 256.
[104] Ibid., 239 (picture reproduced opposite p. 240).

cuts—to be mounted on mantelpieces or bedsteads—that portrayed the evangelists, the apostles, or the doctors of the Church.[105] There were images of pilgrimage to certify, for oneself and for others, the accomplishment of a pious voyage. In some dioceses (Lyons in the seventeenth century, for one), there were marriage certificates that combined the liturgical text for this ritual with a picture to give a lesson in religion.[106] In all or nearly all of these cases, the printed matter for private use among the people served to impress the memories of life's important moments. This material operated on the dual levels of image and text—thus permitting more than one "reading" of its meaning—and combined practical use with Christianizing purpose.

But religious *placards* were not the only sort of single-sheet posters printed in large numbers. As early as the end of the seventeenth century, certain of the *imagiers* of the Rue Saint-Jacques sold *almanachs de cabinet*, large tableaux for wall hanging that listed the notable events of the preceding year grouped around a central subject.[107] The distribution of this sort of publication was probably limited and cannot possibly be compared with that of pious images. Still, it shows that the repertory of images found in the estate inventories of humbler folk became diversified during the eighteenth century. The average number of images owned also increased. Among domestic personnel of greater than average wealth, average ownership grew from eight to twenty-two images between 1700 and 1780, a time when, as we have seen, the percentage of owners of images decreased by 16 percent.[108] A secular iconography of city views, landscapes, portraits, and mythological scenes carved a place for itself beside the devotional images. Thus there was a wide array of large-format, single-sheet prints, each printed on only one side and bearing both texts and pictures, to crowd the walls of the common people's houses. These sheets, produced by the thousand by printers and image-sellers (and now almost all lost), varied in their messages and their uses, but they are unanimous proof of an intimate acquaintance with print that was reading, and also something more than reading.

[105] One example is in the catalogue, *Religion et Traditions populaires* (Paris: Musée National des Arts et Traditions populaires, 1979), no. 127.

[106] P.-B. Berlioz, *Les Chartes de mariage en pays lyonnais* (Lyons, 1941).

[107] J. Adhemar, "Information gravée en France au xviie siècle: Images sur cuivre destinées à un public bourgeois et élégant," in *L'Informazione in Francia*, 11-32, and particularly 27.

[108] Roche, *Le Peuple de Paris*, 227 (table 34).

### The Diffusion of Printed Matter and the Differentiation of Reading Habits

The century, generally speaking, that separated the 1660s and the 1780s incontestably saw a broadening of the various reading publics. In the cities, in spite of moments of stasis or decline and in spite of geographical differences or differences of milieu, more people owned books and more books were owned by the owners. This advance is particularly noticeable among readers at the lower end of the social scale. As the century wore on, merchants and shopkeepers, artisans and day workers gradually increased their familiarity with books. Moreover, the proliferation of institutions that rented out books multiplied opportunities for reading, even for the humblest folk. The appetite for printed matter was thus both whetted and appeased. At the same time, the contrast between city and country reading habits attenuated. Cities, which had long figured as bastions of writing, both manuscript and typeset, lost some of their privileged position. Books circulated now in the countryside (*plat pays*) surrounding the cities, and some publishers even made a specialty of the peasant market, which, transformed by progress in literacy, was reached through the peddlers. Like the Church of the Catholic Reformation, like the school under the tutelage of the clergy and the community assemblies, the book after 1660 set off on the conquest of peoples and became one of the major aids to the process of acculturation that remodeled beliefs and behavior. The circulation of books on a scale hitherto unknown had effects that might seem contradictory. On the one hand, it encouraged the inculcation of new disciplines, whether they involved the faith, civil behavior, or trade technologies. On the other hand, it broke down mental barriers by enabling people to escape the repetitiousness of a restricted daily life by grasping information or throwing themselves into fiction.

When printed matter underwent this process of diffusion, some old distinctions became less clearly drawn. The printed work was no longer a rare possession. Consequently, it lost some of its symbolic value and became an object for a somewhat nonchalant consumption. This perhaps explains why some in the eighteenth century sought to draw new distinctions through the depictions and the practices of reading. Some attempted to categorize readers in terms of the act of reading itself, reformulating such traditional oppositions as the solitary city reader and the listeners at the peasant *veillée* or the reader in the *cabinet*

238

and the reader in the street. Others attempted to impose a way of reading that would break with the frivolity of the time and would re-create—in a secular vein—an older style of serious and intense reading. The relative uniformity brought about by the higher volume of book circulation did not by any means stifle the variety of the "figures for reading"[109] that were practiced or demanded, counseled or desired. Although the data show clearly that between 1660 and 1780 differences in book distribution attenuated, the ways in which the uses of the printed word were represented indicate, quite to the contrary, a desire for an increased differentiation in the modes of appropriation of typographic materials. It was as if the distinctions among practices had been generated by the very distribution of the objects utilized in those practices.

[109] M. de Certeau, "La Lecture absolue (Théorie et pratique des mystiques chrétiens: xvi$^e$-xvii$^e$ siècles)," in L. Dällenbach and J. Ricardou, eds., *Problèmes actuels de la lecture* (Paris, 1982), 65-80.

# CHAPTER SEVEN

# The *Bibliothèque bleue* and
# Popular Reading

THE formula of the *Bibliothèque bleue*—inexpensive books printed in large quantities and sold by peddlers—was practiced in Troyes from the early part of the seventeenth century (probably in imitation of Lyons printers such as Benoît Rigaud), but it reached its zenith during the one hundred and thirty years between the beginning of Louis XIV's personal rule and the French Revolution. During this period, the number of printers in Troyes specializing in the publication of the slim volumes in the *Bibliothèque bleue* increased, the list of works appearing in this form grew considerably, and the booklets reached an ever-larger reading public.

This phenomenon was by no means exclusive to France: In England and in Spain as well, an increasing number of books were printed in large press runs and destined for, essentially, the general reading public. In England, chapbooks (peddlers' books) were sold at a very low price (between two and four pence) and printed by the hundreds of thousands. In 1664, for example, a London printer-bookseller, Charles Tias, had over one hundred thousand books in his warehouse, which represents a copy for one English family out of fifteen. And Tias was not the only one specializing in this chapbook commerce: London had some fifteen such bookseller-printers in the 1680s.[1] In Spain in the eighteenth century, the *pliegos de cordel* found their typical format— quarto-sized booklets of one or two sheets—and achieved widespread distribution, partly due to the blind peddlers who hawked them by singing their titles or verse texts.[2] The *Bibliothèque bleue* was thus by no means uniquely French. It had its own forms and its typical con-

---

This essay first appeared in *Histoire de l'édition française*, ed. H.-J. Martin and R. Chartier (Paris: Promodis, 1984), 2:498-511.

[1] M. Spufford, *Small Books and Pleasant Histories: Popular Fiction and Its Readership in Seventeenth-Century England* (London, 1981).

[2] J. Marco, *Literatura popular en España en los siglos XVIII y XIX: Una aproximación a los pliegos de cordel* (Madrid, 1977).

tents, but it took its place among the many publications that printers in various countries throughout Europe produced for the masses.

The first generation of studies devoted to the Troyes corpus erroneously considered it specific to France. They defined it, first, by its reading public, held to be the common people in rural areas, and second, by an inventory of its texts, divided into fiction for entertainment, works of practical advice, and devotional exercises. This pioneering description still provides the foundation of our knowledge of the subject, but it now raises a good number of questions, notably, concerning the tendency to equate peddlers' literature and popular culture during the *ancien régime*.[3]

### The Corpus of the *Bibliothèque bleue*

The texts used by the Troyes printers for the low-cost, blue-covered books they published were not written solely for that purpose. The Oudots and their rivals, the Garniers, typically used texts that had already been published and that seemed to them both appropriate for the wide public they sought to reach and compatible with the expectations and capacities of that clientele. This led to an extreme diversity in their list, which borrowed from all genres, all periods, and the literature of all nations. This also led to a discrepancy between a text's original character and its final, printed form. All the texts incorporated into the *Bibliothèque bleue* were first published in formats other than the inexpensive editions intended for distribution among humbler folk, and they were written for prospective readers who had little in common with the typical buyer whom the Troyes printers had in mind. It is evident, then, that the repertoire of books published in Troyes was not in itself "popular," since it comprised texts of diverse origins, each of which had its own set of purposes, gave rise to a particular reading, and was aimed at a specific public.

The inventory of Étienne Garnier's holdings, drawn up in January and February of 1789 at the request of his widow (Marie-Louise Barry) and the tutor of his minor children, attests to the nature of this repertoire.[4] In all, 443,069 books remained in his warehouse, either folded

---

[3] See Chapter 5, "Publishing Strategies and What the People Read, 1530–1660."

[4] AD, Aube, 2E, minutes Robbin, "Inventaire de l'imprimerie, de la fonderie et des marchandises imprimées d'Étienne Garnier, 28 janvier–21 février 1789," analyzed by

and gathered (but not bound) or still in unfolded sheets. Religious books made up nearly half of these (42.7 percent), far ahead of works of fiction (28.8 percent) and manuals and practical guides (26.8 percent). A more detailed breakdown shows the relative standing of the best-selling genres. At the head of the list came books of religious instruction and edification and guides to conduct and devotion (12.7 percent of all copies). These were followed by Holy Scripture: the text of the Gospels and, even more, abridged psalmbooks and biblical tales (12.5 percent). Next came books of hymns and Christmas carols (9.2 percent), novels and comic literature (8.8 percent), saints' lives (8.3 percent), chivalric romances (8 percent), fairy tales (6.5 percent), and reports of current events and satiric pieces aimed at particular social groups or professions (5.8 percent). None of the remaining categories amounts to five percent of all copies, unless all aids to learning—ABCs, primers, courtesy books, arithmetic books, treatises on spelling, and model letter books—are considered together, which would give nine percent of all books in his stock.

This distribution of genres, established on the basis of books that were actually stored at a precise moment in one of the Troyes printshops, is quite different from the one based on surviving editions listed by Alfred Morin in his catalogue. In Morin's list, works of fiction occupy the first place with 41.4 percent of the titles, far ahead of books of instruction (28.3 percent) and religious books (28.1 percent). The bestsellers are lay works, since novels and comic literature (13.2 percent of the titles) and chivalric romances (12.7 percent) lead even the books of hymns and carols (11.6 percent). It is obvious, then, that counts of surviving titles underestimate the widely used books—religious works in particular—which had the highest press runs and which have perhaps disappeared in greater numbers (indeed, we may be totally unaware of certain publications). The inventories of booksellers' stocks correct this distortion, forcefully reminding us that the *Bibliothèque bleue* was a powerful ally of the Catholic Reformation. This remained true throughout the eighteenth century, since Étienne Garnier's stock on the eve of the Revolution was in all ways comparable to that of Jacques Oudot and his widow, inventoried in June and July of 1722.[5] In the lat-

Henri-Jean Martin, "Culture écrite et culture orale, culture savante et culture populaire dans la France d'Ancien Régime," *Journal des Savants* (1975):246-47.

[5] AD, Aube, 2E, minutes Jolly, "Inventaire des marchandises de Jacques Oudot, 18 juin–17 juillet 1722."

ter inventory, bound religious books account for 33,421 copies, to which we should add the thousands of works still in sheets but impossible to separate from sheets of secular works. Among the bound religious books, the majority were lives of saints (1,087 packets of a dozen copies), books of hours and psalmbooks (557 dozen), and books of prayer and pilgrimage songs (376 dozen). Thus, the Troyes printers published a variety of devotional materials. They published them en masse and perhaps at a better price than their competitors. Not alone in producing such materials, they nonetheless nourished the piety of the commonality of men in a France transformed into a Christian state by the Catholic Reformation.

## Texts from Lettered Culture

A review of the overall distribution of genres in the Troyes corpus needs to be accompanied by a genealogy of the texts that composed it. In the majority of cases in all categories, behind the published work lies a text that belonged to learned tradition. This is true of a large part of the literature of devotion and pious practices reprinted in Troyes from earlier works that had already enjoyed some success during the Catholic Reformation. There were, among others, *Les Sept Trompettes spirituelles pour réveiller les pécheurs et pour les induire à faire pénitence* of the Recollect Franciscan, Barthélémy Solutive, and *La Guerre spirituelle entre l'âme raisonnable et les trois ennemis d'icelle, le diable, le monde et la chair* of Louis Richeome. There were such Jesuit works as the *Accusation correcte du vrai pénitent où l'on enseigne la manière qu'il faut éviter et celle qu'il faut suivre en déclarant ses péchés au sacrement de confession* of Father Honoré Chaurend and the *Préparation à la mort* of Father Jean Crasset.

The same was true of works of fiction in the *Bibliothèque bleue*. Three examples will suffice, first among the novels. When we follow the history of five such texts, chosen both for their many reprintings and because they belong to different epochs and reflect different literary forms, it becomes clear that the Troyes printers of the seventeenth and the eighteenth centuries published texts already in print and which had circulated (occasionally for some time) in editions that, in general, can hardly be called popular.[6] The *Histoire de Pierre de Provence et de la*

---

[6] L. Andriès, "L'Imaginaire et le temps dans la Bibliothèque bleue," in *Les Contes bleus*, ed. G. Bollème and L. Andriès (Paris, 1983), 48-62.

243

*belle Maguelonne*, published in Troyes at the beginning of the seventeenth century by Nicolas I Oudot, is an anonymous novel of the first half of the fifteenth century, first printed in Lyons in 1490 and republished many times during the sixteenth century. The *Histoire des aventures heureuses et malheureuses de Fortunatus*, which entered the *Bibliothèque bleue* catalogue at the end of the seventeenth century, probably had its origins in a German *exemplum* of the Late Middle Ages that had been included in a collection of edifying tales for the use of preachers. The text was known in France through a translation from the Spanish made by Charles Vion d'Alibray and published in Lyons in 1615. It was not this edition that the Troyes printers picked up, however, but an adaptation published in Rouen in 1626. Similarly, at the end of the seventeenth century, the Oudots published the *Chroniques du Roy Gargantua cousin du très redouté Galimassue*, which was directly inspired by an anonymous booklet parodying chivalric romances printed in Lyons in 1532, two years before the publication of Rabelais's work. In these three cases, although there is no question that the texts originated and circulated in lettered circles, their first popular success during the sixteenth century came in editions that prefigured the Troyes volumes—when the widow Chaussard published the *Gargantua* in Lyons and when the widow Trepperel printed the *Histoire de Pierre de Provence* in Paris.

In contrast, two other novels had their first low-cost publication thanks to the Troyes printers. The first, *L'Innocence reconnue*, a didactic novel written by a Jesuit, Father René de Ceriziers, was published in Paris in 1634. It was introduced into the Troyes catalogue by Nicolas II Oudot in 1655 and was often republished during the eighteenth century. The second, the *Histoire de Jean de Calais*, is a novella by Madame de Gomez first published in Paris in 1723 in the second volume of her *Journées amusantes dédiées au roy*. After several reprintings in Paris, the text entered the *Bibliothèque bleue* catalogue with an edition by Jean Garnier, published with an official approval and permission of 1758. Each of these five novels, then, whether they were moralizing or entertaining, originated directly or indirectly in learned culture. The Troyes publishers took over some older texts that had already enjoyed wide distribution in Lyons or Paris; they promised diffusion on a larger scale to other books twenty or thirty years after their first appearance.

A second example from the repertoire of works of fiction is the literature of roguery, which offered the reading public the lives of noted criminals or glimpses into existence on the fringe of society. The success of two such works during the eighteenth century can be measured by their many reprintings. The first, *L'Aventurier Buscon*, entered the catalogue of the *Bibliothèque bleue* in 1657, when Nicolas II Oudot published it. Jean IV Oudot and Jean-Antoine Garnier republished it in the eighteenth century. As the complete title—*Histoire Facétieuse composée en espagnol par Dom Francisco de Quevedo, chevalier espagnol*— indicates, however, it was in fact Quevedo's novel, published in Spanish in 1626 and translated into French in 1633. All the Troyes editions used this first translation by the "Sieur de La Geneste"—who may have been Scarron—and demonstrated no awareness of the new translations that appeared in 1698 and 1776. The second work, republished several times under two official permissions, one in 1718 and the other in 1728, is the *Histoire de la vie, grandes voleries et subtilités de Guilleri et de ses compagnons, et de leur fin lamentable et malheureuse*. Once again, the text borrowed by the Oudots can be positively identified. It is a tale that appeared in Lyons in 1623 as a part of François de Rosset's anthology, *Les Histoires tragiques de notre temps*, first published (but without the chapter "Des grandes voleries et subtilités de Guillery, et de sa fin lamentable") in 1614.[7] In both cases, the Troyes printer took over a text some time after its original appearance in the literate tradition: the first, a picaresque novel that benefited from the fashion for burlesque tales, and the second, a story from the then popular genre of realistic and violent *histoires noires*.

Our last example of fiction is taken from the fairy tales. Here again, the Troyes printers made wide use of books already in circulation: the collected tales of various sorts published between 1690 and 1715, the editions of fairy tales that were published separately after 1730, and the great anthologies of the end of the century, such as the *Bibliothèque universelle des romans* of the Marquis de Paulmy (begun in 1775) or the *Cabinet des fées* (41 volumes, 1785-1788).[8] Before the Revolution, three authors assured the Troyes publishers of their bread and butter. The first, Madame d'Aulnoy, published the first three volumes of her *Contes des fées* in Paris in 1697 and the fourth in 1698, along with the four vol-

---

[7] On the *Buscon* and on Guilleri, see Chapter 8, "The Literature of Roguery in the *Bibliothèque bleue*."

[8] R. Robert, *Les Contes de fées littéraires en France de la fin du XVIIᵉ siècle à la fin du XVIIIᵉ siècle* (Nancy, 1982), 22-30 and 291-325.

umes of her *Contes nouveaux ou les Fées à la mode*. These two collections were republished separately in 1710 and 1725 (for the first), in 1711 and 1725 (for the second), and together in 1742. From them, various publishers printed extracts: Jean-Antoine Garnier took *Chatte Blanche suivi de Blanche Belle* (permission of 1758); Jean IV Oudot's widow took *L'Oiseau bleu, Le Prince Marcassin, Le Prince Lutin et Fortunée* (permission of 1758); and another Garnier took *La Princesse Belle Etoile et le Prince Chéri*. Another important compiler of fairy tales was Charles Perrault, whose *Histoires ou contes du temps passé avec des moralitez*, published in Paris in 1697 and republished in 1707 and 1724, fed the Troyes lists for some forty or fifty years after its original publication. *Les Contes des fées par Monsieur Perrault. Avec des moralités*, a republication of all the tales in Perrault's book, was published in 1734 by Jean Oudot (permission of 13 March 1723), in 1737 by Pierre Garnier (permission of 23 July 1723), in 1756 by the widow of Jean Oudot, and by Garnier the Younger (permission of May 1735). The third authorial source exploited by the Troyes publishers was the Comtesse de Murat, who compiled the *Contes de fées* and the *Nouveaux contes des fées*, which were published in 1698 by Claude Barbin, Perrault's publisher, and reprinted in 1710 and 1724. In the mid-eighteenth century, Jean Garnier republished three of her tales in separate editions: *Jeune et Belle, Le Parfait Amour*, and *Le Palais de la Vengeance*.

This strategy of borrowing continued during the Revolution and during the first years of the nineteenth century. Thanks to "Madame Garnier," who had separated from her husband, the second Jean-Antoine Garnier, and Charles-Louis Baudot, previously unpublished titles were then added to the Troyes lists. This was the case regarding Madame d'Aulnoy's *La Belle aux cheveux d'or* and her *Belle Belle et le Chevalier Fortuné*, the Comtesse de Murat's *La Fée Anguillette*, and *Le Roi magicien*, a tale from the collection of the Chevalier de Mailly, *Les Illustres Fées*, first published in 1698. The fairy tales published by the Troyes printers were thus texts from the world of letters, products of aristocratic and *précieux* circles at the moment of the genre's greatest appeal.[9] Even if their plots and motifs were imitated from or coincided with elements of peasant tales,[10] they nonetheless offered the general

[9] D. R. Thelander, "Mother Goose and Her Goslings: The France of Louis XIV as Seen through the Fairy Tale," *Journal of Modern History* 54 (1982):467-96.

[10] On this problem, see M. Soriano, *Les Contes de Perrault: Culture savante et traditions populaires* (Paris, 1968), 73-213; R. Darnton, "Peasants Tell Tales: The Meaning of

reader texts from high culture that had originated in the feminine culture of the salons and the court.

The books of practical advice in the *Bibliothèque bleue* were also new versions for a wider public of works first published in the normal manner for the Parisian and provincial booksellers' usual clientele. This was the case, for example, with François de La Varenne's *Cuisinier François, enseignant la manière d'apprêter et assaisonner toutes sortes de viandes grasses et maigres, légumes et pâtisseries en perfection, etc.* Nicolas II Oudot took over this work in 1661, on the expiration of the ten-year *privilège* granted in 1651 to its original publisher, the Paris bookseller Pierre David. Before he abandoned this work, David had put out eight editions. In the hands of the Troyes printers, it began a new and long career, with four editions in the seventeenth century and five others by the mid-eighteenth century (the last by Jean Garnier). The work became a specialty of the provincial centers: Aside from the nine Troyes editions, there were five in Lyons and ten in Rouen.[11] This publishing strategy of reprinting practical guides when their *privilège* had expired added other books to the Troyes lists: *Le Pâtissier Français* in 1662 and *Le Confiturier Français* in 1664 (first published in Paris by Jean Gaillard in 1653 and 1650, respectively) and *Le Jardinier Français* in 1723 (first published in Paris in 1651). This last was followed by a dozen editions during the second half of the seventeenth century.[12]

In all the genres of their list, then, the Troyes printers dipped into the supply of available texts. At times, there was a considerable lag between the first publication of a work and its entry into the *Bibliothèque bleue*. This cannot be taken as a general rule, however, and nothing would be more false than to see the selection of peddlers' books as comprised entirely of old works passed on to the people when the more notable members of society had discarded them. The Troyes printers were eager for novelties and were happy to take over successful titles as soon as their first publisher's *privilège* had expired. Hence their editorial policy cannot be defined on the basis of the social class for which the works they published were intended (for these books were "popular" neither in their style nor in their original buying public). Neither

Mother Goose," in his *The Great Cat Massacre and Other Episodes in French Cultural History* (New York, 1984), 8-72; and the just-published essay of C. Velay-Vallantin.

[11] J.-L. Flandrin, P. Hyman, and M. Hyman, "La Cuisine dans la littérature de colportage," in *Le Cuisinier françois* (Paris, 1983), 62-95 and "Inventaire," 100-107.

[12] *Le Livre dans la vie quotidienne* (Paris: BN, 1975), nos. 129-31.

can this policy be defined by the genre or the aims of those works which, as we have seen, came from all areas of lettered culture. Does this mean that publishing in Troyes closely resembled publishing in other provincial centers and that printers in Champagne were satisfied with merely reproducing whatever texts fell into the public domain?

## Publishers Leave Their Mark: Choices, Cuts, Editing

This was, of course, true only in part. In the first place, although they may seem heterogeneous, the texts put out as "blue" books were not left to chance. They were all chosen because they seemed likely to be bought by a wide public, and therefore to respond to widely shared expectations in the genres of piety, utility, and entertainment. Consequently, texts were chosen that fostered the most prevalent pious practices or that guided the humblest daily tasks. The works of fiction on the list indicate a preference for stories, novels, and tales that make use of certain devices to structure the narrative, which typically is both discontinuous and repetitive, is made of fragments juxtaposed one to another, and uses the same motif several times. Complicated plots that required the reader to memorize characters and events exactly were avoided. It is perhaps the similarity of such structural devices more than the subject matter itself (which shows great variety) that explains the Troyes printers' choices and that allows us to grasp, by implication, how they viewed their readers' cultural capacity.

The unity of this "library" of chapbooks and the relation of one work to another lie in just such formal resemblances. The Troyes printers offered their public texts that made up a series, sometimes by belonging to the same genre (saints' lives, fairy tales, chivalric romances, and so forth), sometimes by sharing a field of practical application (devotional exercises, recipe books, books of initiation into practical skills, and more), and sometimes by carrying the same theme through works of different sorts (the literature of roguery, discourses on women, literary and linguistic parodies, and so forth). This created networks of texts, occasionally with explicit cross-references among them, that reworked related motifs, repeating, shifting, and reversing them in essentially the same way that the various fragments of a given text were fitted together. The various series formed gradually and spontaneously. And if each of the *Bibliothèque bleue* texts can be recognized as belonging to a whole that possesses a certain unity, it is perhaps thanks to similarities in their internal structure that transcend genre.

Furthermore, the changes that the Champagne printers made in those texts worked to reinforce what they already had in common. To be sure, certain texts were conveyed unchanged into the "blue" formula. The *Cuisinier François*, for example, was identical in its Paris and Troyes editions and, for most of its editions, so was *Jean de Calais*. In general, however, the Troyes printers made adjustments in the texts they had chosen for publication, mindful of the readers they hoped or expected to reach. The changes they made were of three sorts. First, the actual layout of the text was remodeled to give a less densely printed page: The number of chapters was increased (even when the resulting divisions reflect no narrative or logical necessity) and many paragraph breaks were added. The *Bibliothèque bleue* volumes were of course not the only works to be chopped up into smaller units during the seventeenth and eighteenth centuries. The practice was more accentuated in them, however, as can be seen by comparing a text in the "blue" format with the original edition from which it was taken or with other contemporary editions.[13] The way the book was laid out, its text punctuated by chapter headings and paragraph breaks, prepared the book itself for the sort of reading the publishers thought it would receive. Neither fluent nor prolonged, such a reading would take place in fits and starts, would rely on short, easily deciphered, self-contained segments, and would require explicit signposts. Hence the many repetitions and summaries that aided the reader in picking up the thread of the narrative when his reading had been interrupted.[14]

A second editorial intervention in the publication of the "blue" texts was the strategy of reduction and simplification. Most of the Troyes editions shorten the text they reproduce, and in two ways. First, the text was pruned. Certain episodes were abridged and others cut, sometimes drastically. In the novels that entered the "blue" collection, narrative passages judged to be superfluous were dropped. In general, this "extraneous" material was descriptions of the social characteristics or the psychological states of the characters that did little to further the

---

[13] For the example of the *Buscon*, see Chapter 8, "The Literature of Roguery."
[14] G. Bollème, "Des romans égarés," in Bollème and Andriès, *Les Contes bleus*, 11-44.

action.[15] Texts were also shortened on the sentence level: Archaic or difficult expressions were modernized, sentences were tightened by weeding out relative and parenthetic clauses, and a good many adjectives and adverbs were removed. Such editorial work implies that the intended readers were capable of grasping only uncomplicated, short, and linear sentences. Textual differences between a work in its "blue" edition and the "lettered" edition from which it was taken may appear insignificant, but in point of fact they show how the Troyes printers (or the copy editors who worked for them) viewed the lexical capabilities—limited in scope and particular in application—of the majority of their potential readers.

Often, however, the process of rewriting and abridging a text obeyed other demands as well. This was true of the *Buscon*. Between the Paris editions of the Sieur de La Geneste's translation of this work and the Troyes versions, major cuts were made, but not by chance. The cuts followed two sorts of logic. First, all trace of what Mikhail Bakhtin has called "the material bodily lower stratum"[16]—scatological terms, allusions to natural functions, and evocations of sexual activities—was removed from the text. Next, all references to religion, parodic or not, were rigorously censored, and the tale was purged of all that could seem blasphemous. Ecclesiastical or pious characters disappeared or lost their religious identity, episodes describing the administration of the sacraments were cut, and comparisons and expressions that employed religious terminology were removed. Obviously, excisions and revisions on this scale profoundly distorted the meaning of the 1633 translation, since they obliterated all reference to the Spanish stereotype of exaggerated and hypocritical piety, deleted rough vocabulary, cleaned up the burlesque passages, and eliminated all parodic and ironic treatment of references to the Christian religion. The text clearly bears the mark of religious censorship, probably internalized as self-censorship, that aimed at cleansing it of all that was not proper. Due to the scatological and blasphemous violence of the original, which the La Geneste–Scarron translation respected, Quevedo's novel probably rep-

---

[15] L. Andriès, "L'Imaginaire et le temps," 62-65; A. Chassagne-Jabiol, *Évolution d'un roman médiéval à travers la littérature de colportage: La Belle Hélène de Constantinople XVI^e-XIX^e siècle* (Thesis, École des Chartes, 1974).

[16] M. Bakhtin, *Rabelais and His World*, trans. H. Iswolsky (Cambridge, Mass., 1968), 368-436.

resents the most extreme example of censorship in Troyes.[17] This same moralizing intent guided the adaptation of other texts, novels in particular, where all allusions to the body and to sex as well as overly sensual descriptions were proscribed. The printers of Troyes thus participated in the Catholic Reformation not only in the publication of manuals of devotion and spiritual exercises, but also in the purging of their fiction titles of all sacrilege and immorality.

It is not an easy task to identify who exactly carried out this adaptation and revision. The printers and their journeymen had a hand in it, as attested by the almanacs, but they probably called upon members of the clergy, men of letters, and local notables as well. Their aims were to make the texts moral, as needed, and to create a new readability for all the "blue" books by simplifying and breaking up the original text. Because this work was often done rapidly and with little attention to detail, however, the result was often anything but a simplification. The cuts rendered the stories more difficult to understand, paragraph breaks sometimes made little sense (and even cut sentences in two), and copying errors and negligence in composition made many a passage incoherent. A certain "opacity" was thus introduced into the texts by the very process that purported to render them easier to read. To explain this contradiction, we could of course recall that the commercial constraints of low-cost publishing, which suppose low sales revenues, result in little demand for care in the preparation of copy or the correction of proofs. But there was probably something else involved. The relationship between a "blue" book and its buyer was perhaps not, in point of fact, the same as the one between traditional readers and traditional books. The chapbook was not necessarily bought to be read, or at least not to be read carefully, precisely, with attention to the letter of the text. Leaving the literary books of the Troyes catalogue aside for a moment, the arithmetic books support this conclusion. If we work out the calculations that are given as examples, we find that they are quite often invalidated by typographical errors and, even more seriously, by errors of reasoning. Thus they would be totally useless as an aid to the real calculations of daily life. This limited usefulness did not, however, hamper sales. It was as if the possession and handling of a book considered to hold knowledge of numbers had more importance than its

---

[17] See Chapter 8, "The Literature of Roguery."

practicality.[18] In the case of novels or tales, a person of weak reading skills, who could assimilate only brief, elementary bits at one time, could find satisfaction in a minimally cohesive text without attaching too much importance to its incoherent aspects. Incoherences probably were seen as further instances of simple ruptures that only momentarily interrupted a linear—and not global—deciphering of the text.

## A Publishing Formula

Thus the *Bibliothèque bleue* was, first, a repertory of texts for which we need to draw up a genealogy, categorize the contents, and scrutinize certain transformations. It was also a publishing formula that gave a particular form to the objects it treated and that organized texts according to specific typographic demands. In order to understand the significance of these widely distributed booklets, we obviously must turn back to consider printed matter itself, in its most material sense. First, what was contemporary to the readers of the *Bibliothèque bleue* and to their level of expectation was not the text, which was older (in some cases considerably so), but the print format in which it was presented. And second, what was "popular" about such a series was not the works themselves, which came from all the genres of high literature, but the typographic medium that carried them, shaped by a dual demand for the lowest possible price and for a text easily read by unskilled readers.

Length is by no means the most dependable formal characteristic of the books of the *Bibliothèque bleue*. It would in fact be a mistake to equate chapbooks with short works. Novels show this well. Although the *Histoire de Pierre de Provence* and the *Histoire de Jean de Calais* were usually published in the eighteenth century in octavo volumes of 48 pages (or three printers' sheets), the *Innocence reconnue*, also published in octavo, numbered either 80 pages or 112 pages, and the *Histoire des aventures heureuses et malheureuses de Fortunatus* reached 176 pages in octavo (eleven sheets). This last approached the *Histoire des Quatre Fils Aymon* and the *Histoire de Huon de Bordeaux*, thick volumes of the *Bibliothèque bleue* that had, respectively, 156 and 144 pages in the quarto editions of Jacques Oudot's widow and son Jean. Unlike the Spanish

---

[18] J. Hébrard, "Apprendre à compter avec la Bibliothèque Bleue," in his *Lire, écrire, compter. Les Apprentissages élémentaires XVIIIᵉ-XIXᵉ siècles*, to be published.

*pliegos de cordel*, which were usually printed on one or two printers' sheets (giving 8 or 16 pages in their usual quarto format), the books in the *Bibliothèque bleue* varied a great deal in length and could reach a respectable size.

The amount of space given to illustrations varied just as much.[19] Many volumes placed a picture on the title page to substitute for the printers' marks usually found in other editions. An illustration of this sort can accomplish two things. It can reduce the amount of space devoted to identifying the publishers, as if this were not worth doing for the titles in the "blue" series; and it can clarify the title by pairing it with a fixed symbol of codified meaning and in pictorial form. Thus we have the manger scene shown in the *Grande Bible des Noëls tant vieils que nouveaux* in all of its many and varied editions; the crucifixion or the flagellation in the *Discours tragique en vers héroïques sur la Passion de Notre Seigneur Jésus-Christ selon l'Évangéliste Saint Jean* published first by Pierre and then by Jean-Antoine Garnier; and the four skeleton musicians in the *Grande danse macabre des hommes et des femmes* published by the Oudots and Jean-Antoine Garnier. Apart from these title page illustrations, which are quite frequent, the number of booklets containing illustrations is not very high. Of 332 different titles in the *Bibliothèque bleue* catalogue that can be dated to the seventeenth and eighteenth centuries, only 38 percent are illustrated, and half of these have only one picture.

When there is only one illustration, it is usually found either on the very first pages of the book or on the last page. This placement establishes a relationship between the illustration and the text as a whole, rather than between the illustration and one or another particular passage. Placed at the beginning of the volume, the illustration elicits a particular reading of the book by furnishing a key to understanding the text, either by comprehending the whole by illustrating one of the parts or by proposing an analogy to guide the reader. Thus in the seventeenth-century editions of the booklet, *Le Jargon ou Langage de l'Argot réformé*, the picture at the head of the text is focused on one character, the Grand Coesre (the king of the beggars), who is shown

---

[19] On this insufficiently known subject I am following the suggestions in F. Blondel, *Les Lieux de l'image dans la Bibliothèque bleue de Troyes aux XVIIᵉ et XVIIIᵉ siècles* (Mémoire de Diplôme d'Études Approfondies, Université de Paris I, 1983). On the high-culture models for the Troyes woodcuts, see also S. Le Men, *Les Abécédaires français illustrés du XIXᵉ siècle* (Paris, 1984).

Fig. 19. *Le Grand Coesre* (King of the Beggars) in
*Le Jargon ou Langage de l'Argot réformé* (Troyes:
Ives Girardon, 1660). This woodcut, the sole illustration
in the book, was placed on the verso of the title page
at the head of the text (height: 132 mm)
(Bibliothèque Nationale, Paris).

254

symbolically, by reversal, as either a prosperous lord or an ancient warrior. When the illustration is on the last page, it has a somewhat different function, since it enables the reader to crystallize and focus on one key image after a reading process that has been sporadic and piecemeal. In this case, the picture leaves the image in the reader's memory and points to the moral of the tale. Even when the illustration had been reused after previous publication, even when chance had a good deal to do with its choice (which depended on the wood blocks the printer happened to have in stock), the one picture that appeared in a "blue" book was enormously important to the reading of the text. Placed at the head or *in fine*, it indicated one possible interpretation.

When the Troyes books contain a series of illustrations, these images are more directly tied to the various sections of the text and are placed within the body of the book. In certain cases, as their titles indicate, the series of pictures came first in time and the printed text was merely a commentary on them. Such were *La Grande danse macabre des hommes et des femmes historiée et renouvellée de vieux gaulois en langage le plus poli de notre temps*, published with sixty woodcuts by Jacques Oudot and with fifty-nine by Jean-Antoine Garnier, and the *Figures de la Sainte Bible avec une explication très utile sous chaque figure*, printed with eighty-two woodcuts by Jean-Antoine Garnier. In other cases, such as the *Histoire des Quatre Fils Aymon, très nobles et vaillans chevaliers. Où sont adjoustés les figures sur chacun chapitre*, the pictures were added to illustrate a preestablished text that had already appeared in print. This not only increased the work's appeal, but also made the divisions in the text more explicit and more easily decipherable. Finally, in other books, the series of pictures could be independent of the text and serve other purposes than reading. It is possible, for example, that the thirty-five pictures contained in the *Exercice de dévotion contenant les prières du matin et soir, l'entretien durant la messe, et les prières pour la confession et la sainte communion. Avec les tableaux de la Passion de N.S. Jésus-Christ selon les Actions du Prêtre célébrant la Sainte Messe* (published first by Pierre and then by Jean Garnier with an approval of 1716 and a permission of 1738, then by the widow of Jean IV Oudot with an approval of 1706 and a permission of 1750) might have accompanied reflection and spiritual exercises during the mass or during devotions in the privacy of the home. Here the image, like the confraternity posters or pilgrimage handbills, became a tangible aid to pious familiarity with the teachings of the Church.

In the final analysis, what most united the products of the Troyes printing houses was their appearance and their price. For example, at his death in 1722, Jacques Oudot's stock, as inventoried by his widow, was predominantly books "bound in blue paper" or "covered with blue paper." These blue covers gave an immediate and visible unity to the titles in the Troyes catalogue. All covers were not blue, however: A certain number of publications, the *Miroirs de la confession*, the *Arithmétiques*, and the *Contes de Fées*, for example, were bound "in marbled paper"; forty dozen ABCS are listed as "covered with red paper"; and books of hours were usually bound in sheepskin. At Étienne Garnier's death in 1789, the inventory of his bindery by his widow mentions "three reams, six quires of paper colored for covers" without specifying what color. The book in the *Bibliothèque bleue* could be distinguished from other books, then, by its physical aspect: It was usually paperbound and had a cover that was most often (but not always) blue. It could also be identified by its price. In 1789, in the widow Garnier's "warehouse of paperbound books," the inventory shows 199 titles priced by the dozen: 66 of these titles (a third) cost less than five *sols* a dozen and 46 (nearly a quarter) between five and nine *sols* the dozen. The great majority of the books printed in Troyes were thus worth less than one *sol* a copy, and a large number of these cost less than six *deniers*. Even if the actual retail price realized by the peddler or bookseller was slightly higher than this inventory price, the "blue" book remained an inexpensive object within the reach of all. It was in any event a good deal less costly than even the least expensive of ordinary books, which, as the inventory of books in the widow Garnier's shop shows, were generally worth between ten and twenty *sols* a copy.

Between the mid-seventeenth century and the end of the *ancien régime*, did the printers of Troyes have exclusive control of the production of these inexpensive and widely distributed books? Probably their long experience in this sort of publishing (begun in the early years of the seventeenth century) and the size of their press runs gave them an edge. Indeed, from the death of Nicolas II Oudot in 1679 to the death of Étienne Garnier's widow in 1790, there were two generations of Oudots (first Jean III and Jacques, the sons of Nicolas II, then Nicolas III and Jean IV, the sons of Jacques) and three generations of Garniers (first Pierre, then Jean, then Jean's sons Jean-Antoine and Étienne) that succeeded their forebears in the trade. Furthermore, widows often continued the publishing activities of their deceased husbands. Anne

Havard, the widow of Jacques Oudot, often appears associated with their son Jean IV. Others were Jeanne Royer, the widow of Jean IV, and Elisabeth Guilleminot, Pierre Garnier's widow.

Although they dominated the field, the Troyes publishers had no monopoly on "blue" book production in France. In several cities, there were printers who imitated their formula and competed with them. In Rouen there were the Oursels, the Behourts, and, later, Pierre Seyer, who bought out the Behourt stock in 1763.[20] In Caen, after the middle of the century, there were the Chalopins.[21] In Limoges there were the Chapoulauds.[22] Outside the kingdom, in Avignon during the first half of the century, there were Paul Offray and Fortunat Labaye.[23] Sales tended to be divided up into areas, thus assuring a regional clientele around each center of low-cost book production. Evidence of this can be seen in the localization of the correspondents who owed money to the widow of Jacques Oudot in 1722.[24] A similar grouping of customers in debt to Étienne Garnier's widow in 1789 centered on Champagne and stretched west to Picardy, Paris, and the Loire Valley, and east to Lorraine, Burgundy, and Franche-Comté—which left the west of the kingdom to publishers from Rouen and Caen.

### READERS AND READINGS

Did the clientele of the *Bibliothèque bleue* change during the course of the eighteenth century? In its early years under the first two Oudots, its customers seem to have been largely urban (and primarily Parisian) and not immediately characterizable as only common people. Between 1660 and 1780, this sociological portrait evolved as the readers of inexpensive books increasingly became common folk in rural areas. This

[20] J. Queniart, *L'Imprimerie et la librairie à Rouen au XVIIIᵉ siècle* (Paris, 1969), 136-38.

[21] A. Sauvy, "La Librairie Chalopin: Livres et livrets de colportage à Caen au début du xixᵉ siècle," *Bulletin d'Histoire Moderne et Contemporaine* (Paris: BN, 1978), 11:95-140.

[22] P. Ducourtieux, *Les Almanachs populaires et les livres de colportage à Limoges* (Limoges, 1921).

[23] R. Moulinas, *L'Imprimerie, la librairie et la presse à Avignon au XVIIIᵉ siècle* (Grenoble, 1974).

[24] R. Mandrou, *De la culture populaire aux XVIIᵉ et XVIIIᵉ siècles: La Bibliothèque bleue de Troyes* (Paris, 1975), 41.

shift is well attested,[25] as should be clear from two examples taken from the beginning and the end of the eighteenth century. The first comes from the *Mémoires* of Valentin Jamerey Duval. Born the son of a cartwright in 1695 in Arthonnay in the *élection* of Tonnerre, Jamerey Duval, after a turbulent and errant childhood, became a shepherd in Clézantaine, a village in Lorraine near Épinal. He was almost fifteen years old when he asked his companions to teach him to read:

> I engaged my companions in the bucolic life to teach me to read, which they did willingly, thanks to a few outdoor repasts that I promised them. I embarked on this enterprise through the chance examination of a book of fables, in which the animals, which Aesop introduces in order to instruct those who think reason is theirs alone, were represented in very beautiful copperplate engravings. My vexation at not being able to understand their dialogues without the help of an interpreter made me become irritated at the ignorance in which I was wallowing, so I resolved to do my utmost to dissipate the darkness. My progress in reading was so rapid that in only a few months the actors in the apologue held no surprises for me. I went through all the libraries of the village with extreme avidity. I leafed through all the authors they contained and soon, thanks to my memory and to my eclecticism, I found myself capable of recounting the marvelous feats of Richard the Fearless, Robert the Devil, Valentin and Orson, and the four sons of Aimon.[26]

At the beginning of the eighteenth century, then, publications from Troyes had reached the villages of Lorraine. They provided material for learning to read and fostered a number of cultural practices ranging from the collective and pedagogical deciphering of a text to individual reading, from memorization to recitation:[27]

[25] J.-L. Marais, "Littérature et culture 'populaires' aux xviie et xviiie siècles: Réponses et questions," *Annales de Bretagne et des Pays de l'Ouest* 87 (1980):65-105.

[26] V. Jamerey Duval, *Mémoires: Enfance et éducation d'un paysan au XVIIIe siècle*, ed. J.-M. Goulemot (Paris, 1981), 191-93. All the titles cited by Jamerey Duval can be found in A. Morin, *Catalogue descriptif de la Bibliothèque bleue de Troyes (Almanachs exclus)* (Geneva, 1974).

[27] J. Hébrard, "Comment Valentin Jamerey-Duval apprit-il à lire? L'Autodidaxie exemplaire," in *Pratiques de la lecture*, ed. R. Chartier (Marseille, 1985), 23-60.

When by assiduous exercise I had adorned my memory with all the Gallic fictions that infect the popular spirit, I thought myself at least as learned as the village *curé*. I invited the young people who had first taught me, and, mounting a rostrum of grass, I declaimed to them, with the pompousness so characteristic of ignorance, the most beautiful passages from Jean de Paris, Pierre de Provence, and the marvelous Mélusine.

Later in his narrative, during a critical review of his adolescent reading habits, Jamerey Duval describes how peasants made use of the "blue" books:

It was one of those old books that form what is called in France the *bibliothèque bleue* and that had as a title the *Vie de Jésus-Christ avec celle de Judas Iscariote*, printed in Troyes in Champagne by the widow of Jacques Oudot. Those who, like myself, know that this pernicious novel was spread through most of the provinces of France, and that the inhabitants of the countryside knew it by heart and put it into the hands of their children to teach them to read, will perhaps ask what idea the high clergy of this kingdom had of Christianity and whether, at that time, they had ceased to be paid to prevent the people from confounding the sacred truths of the Gospel with fictions as vulgar as they were secular.[28]

Jamerey Duval began his *Mémoires* in the 1730s, when he had become a professor and a librarian. With this double distance of time and sociocultural position, therefore, the erstwhile shepherd gave his testimony on the circulation in rural areas—at least in the east of the kingdom, in regions of high and longstanding literacy—of books printed in large quantities by the printers of Troyes.

In the early years of the Revolution, the correspondents of the Abbé Grégoire who answered his questionnaire on "the patois and the mores of the people of the countryside" also attested to the presence of the "blue" books in rural areas. Some of these respondents designated them generically: "la Bibliothèque bleue" (Bernadau of Bordeaux), "les Bibliothèques bleues" (Aubry of the Duchy of Bouillon). Others listed certain titles they had encountered: the *Quatre Fils Aymon* (the Society of the Friends of the Constitution of Mont-de-Marsan and the Society

---

[28] Jamerey Duval, *Mémoires*, 195.

of the Friends of the Constitution of Carcassonne), the lives of Cartouche and Mandrin (Hennebert of Saint-Omer), the life of Guilleri (the Society of the Friends of the Constitution of Carcassonne), and "blue" tales (F.-J. de Mirbeck of Lorraine).[29] For Grégoire's correspondents, this sort of literature deserved scorn: It belonged to the sphere of superstition and credulity, and it was archaic and childish. For the Friends of the Constitution of Mont-de-Marsan, peasant "prejudices" were fortified by all such serial works: "the *Quatre Fils Aymon*, books of sorcery, fairy tales, necromancers, *Bluebeard*, etc."[30] In his report to the National Convention of 16 Prairial Year II, Grégoire himself lumped together such works, rejecting "all the puerile tales of the *bibliothèque bleue*, of gossipy old women, and of the [witches'] Sabbath."[31] Grégoire's inquiry attests to two facts: first, to the distribution throughout France, including the southern provinces, of low-cost books; and second, to a restrictive definition of the *Bibliothèque bleue*, including within it only fictional narratives, novels, tales, and histories. This echoes a definition that seems to have been shared by the Troyes publishers themselves, at least during the eighteenth century. The "Catalogue of the books sold in the shop of the widow of Nicolas Oudot, bookseller," for instance, distinguishes between "recreational books—commonly called *Bibliothèque bleue*" and all others, including little books of hours called *Longuettes*, courtesy books, ABCs and booklets of devotion to be used in schools, books of piety, books of carols and hymns, anthologies, and so forth. At the end of the catalogue, the definition of the "Bibliothèque bleue" as fictional narratives is reinforced still further by a note: "We are also augmenting the *Bibliothèque bleue* by a search for old Histories and new brief Tales."[32] Even though the range of titles put out in the "blue" format was, as we have seen, extremely wide, the expression "Bibliothèque bleue" tended in the eighteenth century to designate above all tales and novels that reached rural areas.

How did they get there? Several of Grégoire's respondents, in particular Bernadau of Bordeaux, speak of peddlers: "Those country peo-

---

[29] *Lettres à Grégoire sur les patois de France, 1790-1794*, introd. and notes by A. Gazier (Paris, 1880).

[30] Ibid., 152.

[31] Ibid., 306.

[32] On this catalogue, see H.-J. Martin, *Livre, pouvoirs et société à Paris au XVIIᵉ siècle (1598-1701)* (Geneva, 1969), 2:956-58; and Marais, "Littérature et culture 'populaires,' " 69.

ple of this district who know how to read like reading, and, all else lacking, they read the *Almanach des Dieux*, the *Bibliothèque bleue*, and other poppycock that the peddlers carry annually into the countryside."[33] Probably largely urban at the beginning of the seventeenth century, book peddling gradually conquered the countryside in the century that followed. Some of the peddlers stocked up in Troyes itself, buying directly from the Oudots and the Garniers, as indicated in a statement of the city council, written in 1760 in support of Jean IV Oudot's widow, who was having some trouble with the *parlement* of Paris:

> The greater part of the commerce in dry goods in the city of Troyes is carried on through the peddlers who come here to stock up on the *Bibliothèque bleue*. If the printshop of the widow Oudot were eliminated, this branch of commerce of the city of Troyes would soon wither and dry up, [since] the printshop of Mister Garnier, who works in competition with the widow Oudot in this sort of work, could never provide for the considerable commerce that is done every year; the peddlers, no longer finding they could stock up on the *Bibliothèque bleue* as before, would not choose to go out of their way as they do now to come only to Troyes to buy merchandise and goods they could find just as well anywhere else.[34]

But all book retailers did not stock up in Troyes, and not all of them were peddlers. Low-cost books sold in shops in cities and towns represented an important part of all sales, and the booksellers involved are listed as debtors in the inventories of the Troyes printers. Some sales came by means of less easily defined merchants: A certain Jacques Considérant sold books as a sideline to his interests as a billiard hall owner, bookbinder, and secondhand clothes merchant in Salins. The inventory of his shop, drawn up in 1759 at the request of his creditors, mentions not only catechisms and offices of the Virgin, but also "15 dozen brochures of the *bibliothèque bleue*, at two *sols* the dozen," for a total of one *livre* and ten *sols*.[35] We might well imagine that in this part of the

---

[33] *Lettres à Grégoire*, 146.

[34] Cited in Mandrou, *De la culture populaire*, 40-42.

[35] M. Vernus, "Un Libraire jurassien à la fin de l'Ancien Régime: Jean-Claude Considérant marchand libraire à Salins (1782)," in *Société d'Émulation du Jura* (Lons-le-Saunier, 1981), 133-67, in particular 149-50.

Jura there were many notions sellers and book peddlers who offered volumes of the *Bibliothèque bleue* along with the devotional books that made up the bulk of their business. Some of them bought their stocks from printers in Besançon and Dôle, in particular, the Tonnets of Dôle, who published books of piety and titles from the *Bibliothèque bleue* list. Others bought from wholesalers who, though dabbling in the book trade, corresponded with publishers in Paris, Troyes, or Switzerland— to the great annoyance of the local printers.[36] As this example shows, the distribution of "blue" books was assured by numerous retailers, stationary or itinerant, who eventually reached all possible buyers.

Thus it is certain that between 1660 and 1780 the titles in the *Bibliothèque bleue* gradually became an element of the superstitious and routine-bound peasant culture that the revolutionary elites denounced. As Bernadau indicates (in his fashion), the inexpensive book was to be found from then on at the center of an entire network of cultural practices that focused on an intensive form of reading involving both memorization and recitation:

> They are mad enough to return twenty times to these miseries, and when they speak of them (which they do very willingly), they recite to you, so to speak, word for word [from] their books. I have remarked that, when a peasant has a book at his disposal on a holiday, he prefers reading to the tavern, although the use of the latter is very familiar to him on days of rest.

When they became reading matter for rustics, then, the slim blue volumes came to be looked upon with disfavor by the elites, who condemned their out-of-date texts and scorned their rough appearance.

This contrast should not be exaggerated. To begin with, the *Bibliothèque bleue* collection did not consist exclusively of out-of-fashion, discredited old novels; it also contained many texts that waited no longer than the duration of their *privilège* to pass from their first publisher to the "blue" list. Furthermore, in the eighteenth century, books from Troyes and equivalent volumes from elsewhere were not (yet) exclusively peasant in their readership. Their city circulation, although difficult to document, must nevertheless have been sizable. It may well be true that the "notables" in the cities turned away from these books (un-

---

[36] M. Vernus, "Colporteurs et marchands merciers dans le Jura au XVIIIᵉ siècle," *La Nouvelle Revue Franc-Comtoise* 72 (1980):210-21; 73 (1980):25-33.

less they were collectors), but this was probably not the case for the entire middle level of urban society. More than in the strictly sociological portrait of their public, then, it is in the modes of their appropriation in which the specificity of the "blue" books resides. The reading that they implied or encouraged was not that of the more "learned" publications. In the acquisition and possession of these books, buyers invested a personal attachment that went well beyond the deciphering of their texts.

## A CENTURY OF STUDIES:
## SELECTED BIBLIOGRAPHY

THE CLASSIC TEXT:

Nisard, C. *Histoire des livres populaires ou de la littérature de colportage depuis l'origine de l'imprimerie jusqu'à l'établissement de la commission d'examen des livres de colportage*. Paris, 1854; repr., 1864.

THE REDISCOVERY:

Brochon, P. *Le Livre de colportage en France depuis le XVIᵉ siècle, sa littérature, ses lecteurs*. Paris, 1954.

Mandrou, R. *De la culture populaire aux XVIIᵉ et XVIIIᵉ siècles: La Bibliothèque bleue de Troyes*. Paris, 1964; 2d ed., 1975.

Bollème, G. "Littérature populaire et littérature de colportage au XVIIIᵉ siècle." In *Livre et société dans la France du XVIIIᵉ siècle*, 1:61-89. Paris and The Hague, 1965.

———. *Les Almanachs populaires aux XVIIᵉ et XVIIIᵉ siècles: Essai d'histoire sociale*. Paris and The Hague, 1969.

THE REVISIONS:

Certeau, M. de, D. Julia, and J. Revel. "La Beauté du mort: Le Concept de 'culture populaire.'" 1970. Reprinted in *La Culture au pluriel*, by M. de Certeau, 55-94. Paris, 1974.

Martin, H.-J. "Culture écrite et culture orale, culture savante et culture populaire dans la France d'Ancien Régime." *Journal des Savants*, July-December 1975:225-82.

Marais, J.-L. "Littérature et culture 'populaire' aux XVIIᵉ et XVIIIᵉ siècles: Réponses et questions." *Annales de Bretagne et des Pays de l'Ouest* 87 (1980):65-105.

Andriès, L. *Analyse diachronique de la Bibliothèque bleue et de son statut culturel aux XVIIᵉ et XVIIIᵉ siècles*. Forthcoming.

The Catalogues:

Helot, R. *La Bibliothèque bleue en Normandie.* Rouen, 1928.
Morin, A. *Catalogue descriptif de la Bibliothèque bleue de Troyes (Almanachs exclus).* Geneva, 1974.
*"La Bibliothèque bleue": Belle collection de livres de colportage du XVIIᵉ au XIXᵉ siècle.* Catalogue of a sale at the manor of Pron in Nivernois by G. Oberlé. March 1983.

The Anthologies:

Bollème, G. *La Bibliothèque bleue: La Littérature populaire du XVIIᵉ au XIXᵉ siècle.* Paris, 1970.
————. *La Bible bleue: Anthologie d'une littérature "populaire."* Paris, 1975.

Reprints:

Six volumes have appeared in Montalba's "Bibliothèque bleue" series: A. Farge, ed., *Le Miroir des femmes*; R. Chartier, ed., *Figures de la gueuserie*; G. Bollème and L. Andriès, eds., *Les Contes bleus*; J.-L. Flandrin, P. Hyman, and M. Hyman, eds., *Le Cuisinier françois*; R. Favre, ed., *La Fin dernière*; and H.-J. Lüsebrink, ed., *Histoires curieuses et véritables de Cartouche et Mandrin.*

# CHAPTER EIGHT

# The Literature of Roguery
## in the *Bibliothèque bleue*

•••••••••

*For Bronislaw Geremek*

THROUGHOUT its entire existence, from the 1630s to the mid-nine-teenth century, the *Bibliothèque bleue* offered its readers, rural and urban, portraits of society's outcasts: false beggars and real thieves, itin-erant notions sellers and swindling rogues, vagabonds living from hand to mouth and noble outlaws. The texts from this literature I shall here examine were originally published in the sixteenth and seven-teenth centuries. All were published, at one point or another in their careers, by the Troyes printshops that put out low-cost books printed on poor quality paper from secondhand type. And all were distributed among a public that was not (exclusively) the public for the more pres-tigious, well-printed, and handsomely bound books.

The earliest two works of this sort were printed by Nicolas I Oudot, the first of the Oudot family to adopt the formula of low-cost, widely distributed books, until then the specialty of the printers of Lyons. *La Vie généreuse des mercelots, gueuz, et boesmiens* ended its short publish-ing life with the Troyes edition of 1627, but, two years later, *Le Jargon ou Langage de l'Argot réformé* began a career that lasted until the mid-nineteenth century, becoming a staple in the repertory of the major publishers of peddlers' books.

Next among these "classics" of the literature of the underworld of sham beggars, thieves, and rogues of all sorts that constituted the French literature of roguery (familiar to those interested in the history of argot) came *L'Aventurier Buscon*. Published by Nicolas II Oudot and republished several times before the nineteenth century, *L'Aventurier Buscon* was a 1633 French translation of Quevedo's novel, originally published in Zaragoza in 1626. It was the only novel in the Spanish pic-

This essay was originally written to serve as a preface to the six texts reprinted in *Figures de la Gueuserie*, ed. R. Chartier (Paris: Montalba, 1982), 11-106.

aresque tradition to find a place in the Troyes publishers' lists; despite the Paris booksellers' success with them, neither *Lazarillo de Tormes* nor *Guzmán de Alfarache* nor *Rinconete y Cortadillo* (this last the most "scoundrelly" of Cervantes's *Novelas Exemplares*) were ever published in Troyes.

During the last quarter of the seventeenth century, the association between the Paris bookseller Antoine Raffle and the Troyes publishers Oudot and Febvre resulted in two other titles. The first was an inexpensive edition of a text that had already been translated and published in Paris toward the middle of the century: *Le Vagabond ou l'histoire et le caractère de la malice et de la filouterie de ceux qui courent le monde aux dépens d'autrui*. The Troyes printers here took advantage of the success of a book that had been republished many times in Italian between 1621 and the beginning of the eighteenth century (under the title *Il Vagabondo*), but was in fact a translation and adaptation of a Latin manuscript of the fifteenth century, the *Speculum de cerretanis seu de ceretanorum origine eorumque fallaciis*. The second text sold by Raffle, in contrast, was something new on the literary scene: a burlesque comedy by Claude de l'Estoile, *L'Intrigue des Filous*. The last work I will examine is a slim volume published soon after the turn of the eighteenth century and sold in Paris by the widow of Nicolas II Oudot: the *Histoire de la vie des voleurs*, the first version of a highly successful title on the Troyes lists throughout the century, the *Histoire de la vie, grandes voleries et subtilités de Guilleri et de ses compagnons*.

Although these six texts differ by date of publication, origin, genre, and style, they all appeal to the reader's imagination by introducing the secrets of an underworld of thieves and con men of all sorts—a world the public found both attractive and disquieting. These works share an underlying direction. Whether they mask fiction as truth or use the recounting of true events to support comic, picaresque, or burlesque elements of the author's invention, they all describe the society of the *gueux*. To the sedentary reader they offered a picture of vagabondage; to the law-abiding reader they presented the world of thieves; and to those who knew only the humdrum repetition of daily tasks they promised adventure. How did these books provide amusing reading and create the impression of reality? How were they understood at different moments in their publishing careers? These two questions will serve as our guides.

## *La Vie Généreuse*: SHORT STORIES AND
## THE PICARESQUE

The first work on our list is a slim volume published for the first time by the Lyons printer Jean Jullieron in 1596 as *La vie généreuse des mercelots, gueuz et boesmiens, contenans leur façon de vivre, subtilitez et Gergon. Mis en lumière par Monsieur Pechon de Ruby, Gentil'homme Breton, ayant esté avec eux en ses jeunes ans où il a exercé ce beau Mestier. Plus a été adiousté un Dictionnaire en langage Blesquien, avec l'explication en vulgaire* (The generous life of the peddlers, beggars, and gypsies, containing their way of life, tricks of the trade, and jargon. Explained by Monsieur Pechon de Ruby, [a] gentleman of Brittany, having been with them in his younger years, when he exercised this worthy trade. Also has been added a dictionary in the Blesquian language, with explanations in French). The same text, with only minor variations, was republished in Paris in 1603 and 1612; the notice "Jouxte [in conformity with] la copie Imprimée à Lyon" gave the only indication of the text's origin. The work was reprinted in 1618 and 1622, still in Paris, by P. Mesnier, and in 1627 it entered Nicolas Oudot's catalogue, where it took its place among the first "blue" books printed in Troyes: the chivalric romances and saints' lives that were the stock in trade of the inventor of the *Bibliothèque bleue*.[1] The book's title, which varied slightly from one edition to another, was a good indication of what it contained (or, rather, what the potential buyer was supposed to believe it contained): a description of the three orders of *mercelots, gueux*, and *bohémiens*. The three-part title reflects the organization of a narrative that introduces the reader to these three companies one after the other, but this title underwent slight changes in subsequent editions. The Paris editions promised a portrait of life among the "mattois, gueux, bohémiens et cagoux" (ruffians, beggars, gypsies, and beggar chiefs). The Troyes edition went back to the original three-part division, retaining *mercelots* and *bohémiens* but replacing *gueux* with *bons compagnons*. In the Paris versions, the title was enriched and rendered more exotic, even though this broke the parallelism established between title and text (the *cagoux* were the "officers of state" of the *gueux* and not a fourth society). The Troyes title aimed to amuse by antiphrasis, with *bons compagnons* echoing the adjective *généreuse*, ironically borrowed from the chivalric vocabulary.

[1] See Appendix 1 of this chapter, "Editions of *La Vie Généreuse*."

The work promises to reveal the "ways of life" (*façons de vivre*), the "tricks of the trade" (*subtilités*), and the "jargon" of the itinerant notions sellers, the beggars, and the gypsies in two different ways. There are, first, the biography, experiences, and eyewitness observations of the supposed author, Pechon de Ruby, who, presented as a Breton gentleman, recounts his early years of *gueuserie*. And second, there is a "dictionary" of *blesche*, the secret language of the peddlers and rogues. The 1596 version of the work assembled, in no apparent order, 146 words and expressions, principally argot. The dictionary was alphabetized from the Paris edition of 1603 to the Troyes edition, giving the "blesquian" equivalents of 125 French words from *bouche* to *yeux* (thus permitting the publishers to announce on the title page that the book was "better than it was in the preceding printings"). At this point the lexicon discredited the autobiographical character of the work by defining *Pechon de Ruby* as a common noun in jargon signifying "alert child."

Several traditions lay behind this combination of a first-person narrative and a dictionary of the secret language of *merciers* and *gueux*. The most important and recent in date was the Spanish "picaresque" novel, known in France from the translations of *La Vida de Lazarillo de Tormes y de sus fortunas y adversidades*, which were published in Lyons in 1560 and in Paris in 1561, some six years after the first three known Spanish editions (Burgos, Alcalá, and Antwerp, 1554). By borrowing the first words of the title from the Castilian model, by giving his tale the similar cast of autobiographical confession, and by leading his hero from company to company just as Lázaro went from master to master, the author of *La Vie généreuse* was consciously imitating the new forms of the Spanish biographical novel, which gave its central character individuality and existence by placing him in real space and rooting his adventures in a clearly defined setting.[2] Thus *La Vie généreuse*, in its first two parts at least, takes place in the woods of the Vendée and in Poitou—an area the outside limits of which are carefully drawn. Once he has crossed the Loire, Pechon de Ruby travels back and forth over this terrain. Certain places are highlighted: the fair of the Châtaigneraie near Fontenay-le-Comte, Loraux Botereau's tavern, the fair at Niort, the mill near Mortagne, and the outskirts of

---

[2] *La Vida de Lazarillo de Tormes / La Vie de Lazarillo de Tormès*, introduction by M. Bataillon (Paris, 1968), 9-69. (*Two Spanish Picaresque Novels*, trans. M. Alpert [Harmondsworth, 1969].)

Nantes. Pinned down to concrete localities, known or knowable, the narration takes on an increased appearance of authenticity.

This first-person narrative that the reader is supposed to accept as true turns out to be farcical, however, and more resembles *Till Eulenspiegel* and the tradition of *Schwankbiographie* than it does the autobiographical innovations of *Lazarillo de Tormes*. Independent episodes and brief stories taken from the traditional repertory are embedded in the author's life story. Thus we have a tale of a miserly miller who is tricked and robbed and another, more scatological tale of a gentleman with an infirmity in a most sensitive spot who is duped by a false invalid who pretends to suffer from the same ailment and a false surgeon who claims he can cure it. In the long run, the narrative, which closes with one last yarn—about Captain Charles's pretense—loses its biographical coherence and becomes a collection of light tales in which the protagonist is nothing more than an anonymous minor actor or a vague witness to the various scenes. The biography is dropped, and the Castilian model, which underlay the early stages of the narrative, becomes by the end merely a convenient artifice, permitting fragments taken from very different genres and sources to be patched together.

*La Vie généreuse* was the first French work to borrow from German-language texts warnings against the deceit of false beggars. Chief among these was the *Liber vagatorum*, which circulated in manuscript at the end of the fifteenth century and was printed in Pforzheim in 1509 or 1510,[3] to be republished by German printers several times in the course of the sixteenth century. *La Vie généreuse* took its basic intent and certain of its forms from this work. The last lines of *La Vie* say as much: "If I had had the time to write about the jolly tricks that I have seen these three sorts of people play, there would be no volume bigger. These follies mixed with cunning turns are [offered] so that all may take warning." This statement, reinforced in the editions of 1596 and 1627 by a notice "to the reader" that justifies revealing the secret language of the *gueux* by the need to avoid "gratifying this vermin," stands in obvious contrast to the parodic epistle prefacing the text, which situates the work in the tradition of joyous and entertaining stories. The

---

[3] *Liber vagatorum. Le Livre des Gueux*, introduction by P. Ristelhuber (Strasbourg, 1862), i-lxii. The German text can be found in F.C.B. Avé-Lallemant, *Das Deutsche Gaunerthum* (Leipzig, 1858), 1:165-206. (*The Book of Vagabonds and Beggars, with a Vocabulary of Their Language and a Preface by Martin Luther*, trans. J. C. Hotten and ed. D. B. Thomas [London, 1932].)

book is dedicated to an admittedly imaginary person, the lord of the *Atrimes gouvernées*—the dictionary tells us that in "blesche" an *atrimeur* is a thief and an *atrimois ambiant* is a highway robber—who in the author's opinion might benefit from the description of ruses to follow. Thus *La Vie généreuse* is presented as both a collection of comical tales and as a warning; it bears the imprint of both the tradition of *joyeux devis* (to cite the title of a collection attributed to Bonaventure des Périers published in 1558) and that of lexicons of underworld jargon.

The first of the various elements that *La Vie généreuse* derives from such lexicons is the very existence of a dictionary of a secret language as an appendix to a text. At the end of the *Liber vagatorum* there appears a vocabulary of 207 *rotwelsch* ("thieves' Latin") terms supposedly used by beggars to refer to "certain things by means of hidden words." These "hidden words," as seen in the Paris and Troyes editions of *La Vie généreuse*, turn out to be words of daily life, the familiar, the near at hand. The terms that appear most frequently in this list refer to parts of the body (22 words), the various categories of peddlers and ruffians (16), social conditions (13), domestic animals (11), articles of clothing (10), and everyday objects (8). A good many terms refer to what Mikhail Bakhtin calls the "material bodily lower stratum,"[4] further evidence of the work's close ties to the tradition of a facetious, grotesquely realistic, and often scatological literature. There is nothing exceptional in the jargon vocabulary given in *La Vie généreuse*. During these years, there was considerable interest in beggars' and rogues' argot (called *jargon*), both because it presented a danger, since it cloaked the criminal world in secrecy, and because its picturesqueness piqued people's curiosity and offered amusement. In the *Second Livre des Serées*, published in 1597, Guillaume Bouchet has one character say on the fifteenth evening:

> Someone of this company, on waking, will say that I like these ruffians, who harm no one and who only play jolly tricks to laugh with [their victims] and not to deceive [them]. But to prevent being cheated (which they call "taken in") by the thieving kind of ruffian, I would like to understand their jargon and know their language, for [then] I would understand what the Ruffians, the

---

[4] M. Bakhtin, *L'Oeuvre de François Rabelais et la culture populaire au Moyen Âge et sous la Renaissance*, trans. A. Robel (Paris, 1970), 366-432. (*Rabelais and His World*, trans. H. Iswolsky [Cambridge, Mass., 1968], 368 ff.)

Bresche-speakers [*sic*], the Peddlers, and the professional beggars say, for they help one another and use the same language among them. And to show that this language is in no way poor, that all its words have meaning, and that it can be compared to Hebrew, Greek, and Latin, I will tell you something about it.[5]

A lexicon of fifty-four words and eighteen expressions follows, of which only fifteen, incidentally, are to be found in the dictionary of *La Vie généreuse*, either because jargon itself changed (in the designation of various coins, for example) or because of differences in the list of French words for which translations are given.

The major innovation in *La Vie généreuse* was not so much its enlargement of the list of terms explained as its attempt to use this vocabulary in the text itself, thus creating (or attempting to create) a heightened sense of reality as well as offering the reader a puzzle to decipher. This technique is particularly clear in the first episode of the life of Pechon de Ruby, when he falls in with the peddlers. There is extensive use of jargon, made understandable by translation in the text itself ("*Les courbes m'aquigeaient fermy*, that is to say, my shoulders hurt") or by reference to the *blesche* glossary in the appendix to the book. Although these procedures bit by bit bring a pleasurable sense of comprehension, the meanings of many terms remain hidden—for example, when the oldest of the *merciers* harangues the group—so that jargon's secret is both revealed and kept.

*La Vie généreuse* proves itself the heir of the *Liber vagatorum* in another sense as well. Just as the German text claims it will reveal "the ruses used by mendicants and vagabonds, to the number of twenty-one and more," *La Vie* promises it will explain the deceitful "subtleties" of the peddlers, beggars, and gypsies. In the *Liber vagatorum* and the Germanic manuscripts that preceded it (for example, *Die Basler Betrügnisse der Gyler*, a document of Basel of the second quarter of the fifteenth century, or the description in Matthias von Kemnat's chronicle of 1475), this revelation took the form of a straightforward nomenclature that delineated each category of bogus beggar, characterizing his speech, attributes, and moral quality.[6] The fictional device of autobiography leads *La Vie généreuse* to another formula in which categoriza-

[5] G. Bouchet, *Second Livre des Serées* (Lyons, 1618), 109-11.

[6] B. Geremek, *Inutiles au monde. Truands et misérables dans l'Europe moderne (1350-1600)* (Paris, 1980), 187-97.

tion plays only a rudimentary role. The work is organized around successive initiations that lead the hero from one "state" to another, thus leading the reader through presentations of the various criminal milieux. In the last of these initiations, when Pechon de Ruby joins the band of gypsies, the only sign of this event is his rebaptism: "he [re]named me Fourette." The first two episodes, which take place among the peddlers and among the beggars, share traits taken from the corporative rituals of guilds and journeymen's associations. The book thus is doubly imitative: First, the rituals and texts used in real initiations in the world of the guilds are parodied on the level of beggars; and second, on the narrative level, the same procedure is repeated twice in the course of the text.

To become a master peddler or a thoroughgoing beggar, Pechon de Ruby must accomplish three deeds: He must spend money (the price of a supper in one instance, three *sous* in the other); he must prove his worth (by fighting with a staff or by responding to interrogation by the chief of the beggars, the Grand Coesre); and he must swear, with head bare and hand upraised, not to reveal the secrets of the company. The symmetry of the two descriptions is underscored by the similarity in the phrasing of the oaths Pechon de Ruby swears: among the peddlers, "*j'atrime au passeligourt du tout*, that is, I will steal skillfully," and among the beggars, "*j'atrime au tripeligourt*, I will steal three times most skillfully." The two episodes are structured identically, borrowing and combining elements from both the rites of admission to master status in the guilds and corporations—which included the presentation of a masterwork or the taking of an examination, the purchase of a meal for those who were already masters, and an oath to the community or to the king[7]—and similar rites in the ceremonies of reception into the journeymen's associations—including the interrogation of the candidate, the inviolable oath to keep secret the mysteries of the society, and the collective libations paid for by the new member.[8] The harangue of the oldest peddler and the discourse of the Grand Coesre have the same function in the narrative. They sanction the admission of Pechon de Ruby into his new estate. They also begin his instruction by revealing the tricks of the trade, just as the older masters did for the new or the sponsor of a recently admitted *compagnon* for his protégé.

[7] E. Coornaert, *Les Corporations en France avant 1798* (Paris, 1968), 29.

[8] E. Coornaert, *Les Compagnonnages en France du Moyen Âge à nos jours* (Paris, 1970), 147-73.

Two themes converge in the description of the company of the beggars, the central portion of *La Vie généreuse*. The first one—traditional—is a catalogue of the false beggars' ruses. In the Grand Coesre's discourse, this listing takes the form of a nomenclature of the various beggar specializations from which the initiates must choose. This speech is obviously modeled on the lists detailing the types of false beggars. In the course of the sixteenth century, these descriptions passed from the status of judicial documents, drawn up and used by magistrates to identify, designate, and unmask thieves and usurpers of public charity, to the status of "literary" descriptions, which offered a titillating and disquieting form of the picturesque for lively imaginations. The *Liber vagatorum* represents a transition point in this evolution. Its twenty-eight chapters inventory "the order of beggars," *Der Bettler Orden* as German editions of the sixteenth century were subtitled. The theme then passed into English criminal literature with *The Fraternitye of Vacabondes* by John Awdeley, published in 1561, which distinguishes nineteen categories of vagabonds, twenty-five "orders of knaves," and twenty-five types of cutpurses, and with Thomas Harman's *A Caveat or Warening for common Cursetors vulgarely called Vagabones*, the first edition of which dates from 1566 or 1567 and lists twenty-three types.[9] In France, *La Vie généreuse* took up the theme, borrowing from the *Liber vagatorum* the six ways to *bier* (go, operate, i.e. deceive). There is simple begging without artifice (in *La Vie généreuse*, "bier sur le minsu"; in the *Liber*, chapter 1); there is the fictional fire ("bier sur le ruffe" and chapter 21); there is the feigned loss of merchandise due to war ("bier sur la foigne" and chapter 22); and there are the false illnesses ("bier sur le franc mitou" in *La Vie* and given in detail in chapters 8, 19, 25, 26, and 27 of the *Liber*). In the course of the book, other ruses are added to the Grand Coesre's list, for example the faking of infirmities, aimed at eliciting pity (as in chapters 4 and 27 of the *Liber*), or the exhibition of false orphans.

The survey of tricks and ruses given in *La Vie généreuse* reflects a theme that was an intimate part of sixteenth-century thought. It was a tried and true technique of humorous literature. Noël du Fail used it

. [9] These two texts are published in E. Viles and F. J. Furnival, eds., *Awdeley's Fraternitye of Vacabondes, Harman's Caveat, Haben's Sermon, etc.*, Early English Text Society, extra ser., 9 (London, 1869), 1-16 and 17-91; and in A. V. Judges, *The Elizabethan Underworld* (London, 1930), 51-118. See also S. Clark, *The Elizabethan Pamphleteers: Popular Moralistic Pamphlets, 1580-1640* (Cranbury, N.J., 1982), 40-85.

to advantage in chapter 8 of his *Propos rustiques*, published in 1548 and reprinted five times before 1580. Tailleboudin, a "good and wise beggar," reveals the beggars' tricks to Anselme, one of the book's fictional rustic narrators. He lists the classic repertory of simulated diseases and infirmities, supposedly needy or suffering children, false relics, and deceitful discourses: "I took my two children, with my wench, and I put them on my donkey (the children, I mean), and I played the burgher stripped of my goods by war."[10]

This theme can also be found in medical literature. Ambroise Paré, for example, devotes five chapters (20-24) of his *Livre des Monstres et Prodiges* (1573) to "l'artifice des méchants gueux de l'ostière" (the tricks of the wicked professional beggars). His inventory begins with the simulation of gangrene through the use of a hanged man's arm, "still stinking and putrid" (also mentioned in *La Vie généreuse*), and continues with "the deception of a woman beggar feigning an ulcerous sore on her breast," "the deception of one scoundrel who faked leprosy," the description "of a *cagnardière* [a woman of the band] pretending to have Saint Fiacre's disease and pulling long, thick [animal] intestines from her backside by artifice," and the description "of a large and hearty wench from Normandy who pretended she had a snake in her stomach."[11] On each of these occasions, medical science (speaking through Paré or his brother) revealed the deceit and confounded the impostor, who was turned over to the law. Paré's tone is grave and his purpose serious. He was intent on unmasking blasphemers, who, as he saw it, odiously parodied the work of the Creator when they took on false illnesses. His second aim was to separate the "good" poor, deserving of charity, from the false beggars who abused public generosity. "I wrote [the treatise]," he declares, "to know their deceptions, which, [when] known, can be declared to the Judges. So that, under the veil of poverty, they will not steal the bread of the proud and deserving poor and, as loafers, they will be banished from the land or forced to [do] some task necessary to the public."[12] This explains why Paré goes beyond a description of cases that he had seen himself or that his brother had

---

[10] N. du Fail, *Propos rustiques de Maistre Léon Ladulfi* [1548], in P. Jourda, ed., *Conteurs français du XVIᵉ siècle* (Paris, 1965), 635.

[11] A. Paré, *Oeuvres* (4th ed., Paris, 1585), mli-mlvi; and *Des monstres et des prodiges*, critical ed. with commentary by J. Céard (Geneva, 1971), 69-79.

[12] Ambroise Paré, "Mémoire" [1575], in C. S. Le Paulmier, *Ambroise Paré d'après de nouveaux documents* (Paris, 1884), 245.

described to him to draw up a list of the deceitful tricks of the "thieving imposters" that resembles the Germanic nomenclatures but lacks their systematic organization. It should be noted that Paré drew up his catalogue with the help of a variety of printed sources he does not cite—including textual borrowings from the *Propos rustiques*—thus raising humorous literature to the status of objective reporting.

The list in *La Vie généreuse*, although less detailed than Paré's list, plays a double narrative role. On the one hand, the catalogue is part of the Grand Coesre's speech, a procedure quite unlike Paré's presentation, but one that gives it a ring of truth (at least for a reader willing to accept the book as autobiography). This appearance of truth in turn imparts credibility to the entire story. On the other hand, the feigned infirmities appear in the book itself and are necessary to the plots of the individual episodes (for example, the episode of the false surgeon entitled "Autre bon tour"—another good trick). The text of *La Vie généreuse* embodies an ambiguity typical of descriptions of beggars' artifices all through the sixteenth century, since the literary expression of these descriptions claimed to be based on observations of reality, yet, conversely, the fictional portrayals of such people became proof of an incontestable and disquieting reality.

The second theme around which the central portion of *La Vie généreuse* is organized is that of the beggars' kingdom: "In the morning, we went off to Clisson, and there we found a troop that surpassed our own in felicity, pomp, refinement, and order surpassing that of the Venetian State, as you will see." So, while the description of the ceremonies for the admission of new recruits was implicitly modeled on the rules and regulations of the trade guilds and journeymen's associations, the description of the beggars' company was based on a series of explicit comparisons with the institutions of the monarchic state. The general meeting of beggars is identified with the Estates General; their leader, the Grand Coesre, is called a "worthy prince ... having the Majesty of a great Monarch"; his lieutenants, the *Cagoux*, are called provincial governors; the *Brissart* collects taxes, ordinary and extraordinary; and those who disobey are called "rebels against the State" or traitors to the crown. Even on the level of stylistic detail, the systematic use of a vocabulary pertaining to the state (the Grand Coesre and his *cagoux* are "like a lower court of *parlement*," the *cagou* for Brittany is called General, and so forth) underscores this comparison by presenting the society of beggars as a kingdom with a hierarchy parallel to that of France under the monarchy.

By the end of the sixteenth century, it was hardly original to present the beggars as having a king. For more than a century this image had been well rooted in the minds of the dominant classes, complementing the catalogues of specialties among sham beggars and real thieves. The two themes mingle in the report of an investigation carried out in 1445 by Jean Rabustel, "clerk and prosecuting attorney of the city and commune of Dijon," of the band of *Coquillards* ("pilgrims"), which operated unrestrainedly in and around the city.

> For two years now there have lodged and still lodge in this city of Dijon a number of companions, idlers, and vagabonds, who, when they arrived and throughout the time they have remained in this city, do nothing but drink, eat, and spend large amounts of money; play at dice, cards, skittles, and other games; continually and habitually, particularly at night, they frequent the bawdy-house, where they lead a filthy, vile, and dissolute life of ruffians and rakes. ... And it is true that the said companions have among them a certain language and jargon and other signs by which they know one another; and these gallants are called the *Coquillards*, which means the companions of the *Coquille*, who, as it is said, have a King whom they call the King of the Coquille.

One member of the band, a barber named Perrenet le Fournier, later describes the secret terms for sixteen categories of thieves and robbers, then goes on to reveal the meanings of sixty words and expressions of their "exquisite language, which other people cannot understand."[13] One should note that, in this lexicon, "a Breton is a thief [*larron*]," which perhaps sheds light on the origins of Pechon de Ruby, who is presented as a "gentleman of Brittany." The Dijon document is by no means the only text to suggest the existence of criminal monarchs. The *Journal d'un bourgeois de Paris sous Charles VII* reports the punishment meted out to a band of "beggars, thieves, and murderers" who had kidnapped children and mutilated them to cripple them and so make them more pitiful as beggars.

> Of these beggars were hanged a man and a woman on Wednesday, the twenty-third day of April near the green mill or Saint

[13] L. Sainéan, *Les Sources de l'argot ancien* (Paris, 1912). The trial of the *Coquillards* (1455) is on pp. 87-110.

Denis's road in France, [in the year] one thousand four hundred forty-nine. Some of the said beggars who were in the company of those mentioned above were put into prison; for it was said that they had made a king and a queen in their mockery [*par leur dé-rision*].[14]

Like the Dijon prosecutor, this Parisian burgher leaves room for doubt as to the existence of these rumored sovereigns ("it was said," "as it is said"). He also adds a word of explanation: The supposed king and queen were monarchs "par dérision."

In the sixteenth century, this mockery became the source of a parodic character frequently seen in humorous literature. Noël du Fail makes use of such a stock figure in his *Propos rustiques*, where Tailleboudin announces to Anselme:

Just keep your mouth shut and I will make you rich if you will follow me. You must understand that among us (and our numbers are inestimable) there are trades, chapters, monopolies, posts, banks, *parlements*, jurisdictions, brotherhoods, passwords, and offices to govern, some in one Province and others in another. What! We know one another even if we have never seen one another; we have ceremonies proper to our professions; [and] admirations, oaths to keep inviolate the statutes drawn up by our late lamented predecessor, Ragot, from many worthy customs, with additions of his own wit. The which we obey just as much as you [observe] your laws and customs, although ours are unwritten. There is more: no one is permitted to pry into our affairs before he has sworn an oath not to reveal the secrets of the Council and to bring his take to a stated place at night. A (possible) place where not even the highest lord has a table better furnished or with more variety; nor does he drink fresher [drafts]. All this at the hour of midnight, for scandal is one of the chief dogmas of our Religion.[15]

Thus Noël du Fail records all the elements that later constituted both the essence and the ornamentation of the description of the beggars' assembly as Pechon de Ruby "saw" it—the oath, the rendering of accounts, the wealth of food and drink. The author of *La Vie généreuse*

---

[14] *Journal d'un bourgeois de Paris sous Charles VII*, Collection des chroniques nationales (Paris, 1827), 15:547.
[15] Du Fail, *Propos rustiques*, 633.

thus made broad use of this widely distributed literature of entertaining tales that linked fifteenth-century reports of actual cases (albeit extremely succinct and couched in dubitable terms) to the literature of *gueuserie* that furnished material to the publishers of Troyes.

Although it borrowed its themes and literary formulas from Noël du Fail, *La Vie généreuse* gave them an original coloration. The beggars' State is now presented as a burlesque gathering in which their low manners are humorously contrasted to the nobility of their titles. Nothing illustrates this better than the description of their Estates General and the supper of the prince. In both cases, classic forms of monarchic ceremony, known through *images volantes* or reports, provided the basis for a description that drew on traditional themes of the least refined material culture and the lower body zones: gross manners, grotesque bodies, and an abundance of food and drink. *La Vie généreuse* draws a purely "literary" effect from the dubious existence of beggar kings, an effect designed to amuse the reader by underscoring the contrast between the well-known references that framed the description (the monarchy, its institutions, its dignitaries, and its vocabulary) and the baseness of all that goes on. Burlesque literature is founded on just this procedure, and it makes this book (at least in this central section) one of the first French works of a genre that became the specialty of the printers of the *Bibliothèque bleue*, in particular Nicolas II Oudot, the son of the publisher of *La Vie généreuse*.

The narrative changes in tone again with Pechon de Ruby's last adventure, his encounter with the gypsies. The pace quickens and the fictional autobiography is to some extent neglected in favor of the tale of a peasant wedding near Moulins and a series of vignettes showing the customs and tricks of the "Bohemians." Here *La Vie généreuse* reacted to the increasing interest in gypsies, who appeared in Paris for the first time in 1427, and the author did his best to summarize the notions that had contributed to the frightening picture and the black legend of this foreign people. The text does not repeat the account of their origins, which usually explained their perpetual wandering as an expiatory pilgrimage, a seven-year cycle of penitence to obtain pardon for an ancient abjuration of Christianity; it speaks only of the misdeeds that were usually attributed to the gypsies—thievery, counterfeiting, and fortune telling—and that lay behind the royal decrees for their expulsion (the edict of 1539 and the ordinance of 1561). If they were feared, however, the gypsies also inspired fascination. Indeed, they had the support of the nobility: *La Vie généreuse* suggests as much in three different places, and it is the nobles' pity that brings the tale of Captain Charles to its conclusion. Gypsies are presented as masters in the arts of deception, with perfect command of ruses and disguises. Furthermore, it is related, they can predict the future, a talent mentioned in only one line of this slim volume, but a talent to which the author promises, in a final note to the readers of the Lyons edition, to dedicate another book: "I hope, with God's help, to be able to show you soon a more useful work, which will be a survey of chiromancy with a number of handsome examples and pictures of the Bohemians' staff, by means of which anyone can himself become capable of being an expert Engineer [trickster]." At the end of the text, then, *La Vie généreuse* attempts to satisfy the public's curiosity, piqued by the strangeness of these "miserable voyagers, with no assurance of hearth or home, [who] make a perpetual profession of beggary, thievery, and idleness," as Étienne Pasquier wrote of them.[16]

Thus the first of our six texts is a composite work in which the narrative technique of autobiography, doubtlessly imitated from *Lazarillo de Tormes*, serves to patch together bits and pieces from different genres and different ages—humorous tales, descriptions of curiosities, parodies, the nomenclature of categories of beggary, and lexicons of jargon. This explains the unfinished and disparate character of the work, which is surely not authentic autobiography, as has often been believed. Neither is it a literary creation in any way comparable to its Spanish model. This is not only because the work to some extent unravels as it progresses, abandoning the procedures set up at the outset, but also because its very texture reflects the way it was intended to be read. The text (in itself short) is fragmented into a great number of brief chapters (eighteen in all), each an independent unit with its own title, each designed to be read separately and slowly. It is organized around repeated motifs (for example, the two initiations) couched in identical terms. This tight, clearly labeled chapter division occasionally imposes an unnatural break in a sequence of events (for example, in Pechon de Ruby's interrogation by the Grand Coesre) or, conversely, gives a chapter

[16] É. Pasquier, *Les Recherches de la France, augmentées en cette dernière édition de trois livres entiers* (Paris, 1643), 392-94. On the gypsies, see in particular H. Asseo, "Marginalité et exclusion. Le Traitement administratif des Bohémiens dans la société française du XVIIᵉ siècle," in R. Mandrou, ed., *Problèmes socio-culturels en France au XVIIᵉ siècle* (Paris, 1974), 9-87.

more content than is indicated by its heading (as in the case of the chapters entitled "Good trick for silencing dogs" and "Form[s] of lodgings"). By the way he presents his text, the author of this work presumes it will not be read easily and from beginning to end, as people familiar with reading read books, but with more effort and requiring pauses and guidelines.

### *Le Jargon ou Langage de l'Argot Réformé*: THE CARNIVALESQUE AND THE BURLESQUE

*La Vie généreuse* was published in only one edition in Troyes (perhaps two), but the second work we will examine was one of the bestsellers of peddlers' literature between the mid-seventeenth and the mid-nineteenth centuries. At least thirty editions can be documented, half of them from Troyes printing houses, of *Le Jargon ou Langage de l'Argot réformé comme il est à présent en usage parmy les bon pauvres, tiré et recueilly des plus fameux Argotiers de ce temps* (Jargon or the language of reformed Argot as it is presently used by the good poor, gathered and collected from the most famous *Argotiers* of our time).[17] This work thus represents a small but highly important piece of the puzzle in any inquiry into the success and the modes of reading of the literature of roguery, the French counterpart of the Spanish picaresque literature. The origin of *Le Jargon* remains somewhat unclear, since the first edition has been lost, but several things can be said from a parallel reading of the subsequent editions. First, this work is clearly an offshoot of *La Vie généreuse*, since it reuses a portion of the text of *La Vie* and some other scattered expressions, crediting its source in veiled terms: "And later, they [the *Cagoux*] taught them ten thousand tricks, as Doctor Fourette [the name the Captain of the Gypsies gave Pechon de Ruby] reports in his book on the life of the beggars, wherein he tells several stories, the following among them." *Le Jargon* was written to capitalize on the success of *La Vie généreuse* by offering its readers another book on the same themes, but brought up to date. The first edition of *Le Jargon* most probably appeared in 1629, since by 1630 it was inspiring imitations and responses: A Lyons edition of 1630 notes that it is "Jouxte la copie imprimée à Troyes, par Nicolas Oudot." Also in 1630, the Parisian bookseller Jean Martin, whose shop was on the Pont Saint-

---

[17] See Appendix 2 of this chapter, "Editions of *Le Jargon*."

Michel and who specialized in the publication of burlesque works and *occasionnels*, published a *Reponce et complainte au Grand Coesre sur le Jargon de l'Argot réformé*. A historical allusion within the text, a thirty-line poem on the "Resjouissance des Argotiers sur la prise de La Rochelle," enables us to set a *terminus a quo* for the lost edition of Nicolas Oudot. This celebration in jargon, parodic in language but pious in intent, marked the taking of that city, the defeat of the English, and the glory of the king (the *dasbuche* Louis XIII, who the author hopes will have "beaux petits mions"). Since La Rochelle fell 29 October 1628, *Le Jargon* must have been printed in 1629 or, at the very earliest, during the last weeks of 1628. It is legitimate to suppose that, three years after his publication of *La Vie généreuse*, Nicolas Oudot attempted to exploit once more the curiosity that the public had already demonstrated concerning the false mendicants' secret language and purported monarchic and corporative organization.

The idea was obviously a good one, since other printers soon took over the text. In Paris, the widow Du Carroy (on the Rue des Carmes) put out an undated edition the title page of which reads *Le Jargon ou langage de l'Argot réformé . . . revu, corrigé et augmenté de nouveau par l'Autheur. Seconde Édition*, perhaps printed before Jean Martin's *Reponce*, hence in 1629 or 1630. Three editions appeared in Lyons (1630, 1632, and 1634) with title page references to "la copie imprimée à Troyes par Nicolas Oudot" and the subtitle *Augmenté de nouveau dans le Dictionnaire des mots plus substantifs de l'Argot, outre les précédentes impressions, par l'Autheur*. In Troyes itself, Nicolas Oudot's son, Nicolas II, republished the work in 1656. He was followed by Yves Girardon in 1660 and, at the end of the century, probably by Jacques Febvre, since an edition of this date bears the mention, "A Troyes, et se vend à Paris chez Jean Musier" (Febvre's correspondent after 1696). Two of Nicolas II Oudot's sons, Jean (1683) and Jacques, also reprinted the book.

The 1656 and 1660 editions placed the same quatrain but different woodcuts on the verso of the title page. Nicolas II Oudot used a print of only one person, a dagger at his belt and his left hand raised, as the caption tells us, "The Grand Coesre addressing the Argotiers." Girardon, in contrast, used a woodcut (see fig. 19) showing a man and a woman finely dressed in old-fashioned clothing, which necessitated a change in the caption: "The Grand Coesre with his marquise. To the Argotiers." The last version of the illustration before it was dropped is a woodcut in the edition sold by Jean Musier, which showed the Grand Coesre as a crowned and armored warrior leaning on an immense broadsword. In each instance, the printer used an old wood block, dating from the previous century, from his stock. The relation of the picture to the text is thus totally arbitrary and was in no way intended to reinforce the text's attempts at realism. In contrast to satirical prints, such as those in Lagniet's collection *La Vie des gueux amadouée en proverbe*,[18] which show the Grand Coesre seated on the back of a cutpurse and tend to portray this personage as he was described in *La Vie généreuse*—with a full beard, a patched coat, a "most rotten" leg, and an applewood staff—the pictures in the Troyes editions of *Le Jargon* let the imagination run free. They have little to do with the text and were taken from existing stocks of wood blocks with little care for verisimilitude, which gives an atemporal and unreal cast to the book. Instead of appealing to the picturesque qualities of the picaresque tradition, they use simple worldly or mythical signs to symbolize power.

*Le Jargon*, unlike *La Vie généreuse*, has an identifiable author. The title page describes him as "un pillier de Boutanche qui maquille en molanche en la Vergne de Tours," the proprietor of a woolworking shop in the city of Tours. Later on, an acrostic sonnet, presented as such and entitled "A la louange de l'Argot" (In praise of Argot), reveals his name: Ollivier Chereau. There was, in fact, an author of that name. A self-taught *maître-sergetier* (master serge worker), he published two works that were printed by Jacques Poinsot of Tours: the *Histoire des illustrissimes Archevêques de Tours* in verse (1654) and *L'Ordre et les prières de la très noble et très ancienne confrérie du Saint Sacrement, sous le nom des Apostres, érigée en la chapelle dite vulgairement le petit saint Martin de Tours* (1656).[19] This man thus seems to have been a pious provincial littérateur, capable of writing in genres that ranged from ecclesiastical history to the literature of piety. This cultural background helps us to better understand *Le Jargon*, which should probably be taken as literary entertainment based on the humorous effects of argot. This intention is evident in the erudite irony of the preface, which be-

---

[18] J. Lagniet, *Recueil des plus illustres proverbes divisé en trois livres* (Paris, 1657-1660).

[19] On Ollivier Chereau, see J.-L. Chalmel, *Histoire de Touraine* (Paris and Tours, 1828), 4:109-10; S. Bellanger, *La Touraine* (Paris, 1845), 577; and M. Prévôt and Roman d'Amat, *Dictionnaire de Biographie française* (Paris, 1959), 8:1007. For the attribution of *Le Jargon* to Chereau, see A. Estevanne, "Quelques recherches sur le livre d'Argot," *Bulletin du Bouquiniste* 105 (1861):246-50. The *Histoire des illustrissimes Archevêques de Tours* attests, on several occasions, to Chereau's taste for acrostic verse.

gins as a hymn to the goodness of God, protector of all creatures from kings to beggars, then drifts into a parodic paean to the Argot (the beggars' society), "compendium of all other sciences and virtues." Doubtlessly it is also because he was a zealous Catholic that Chereau ends this book with a rhymed celebration in jargon of the taking of Huguenot La Rochelle, which the Catholic party considered a brilliant victory. Another "pious" allusion is the mention of the governor of Languedoc, Henri Montmorency (inaccurately named Anne in the text), who distributed alms to all the poor who confessed and took communion on Holy Thursday. He was decapitated in 1632 after he revolted against the king.

*Le Jargon* is even more an assemblage of bits and pieces than is *La Vie généreuse*. The Lyons edition of 1630, which, we can suppose, reproduces the lost first edition printed by Nicolas Oudot in Troyes, strings together the preface, the acrostic sonnet "A la louange de l'Argot," chapters on "L'Origine des Argotiers" and the "Ordre ou Hiérarchie de l'Argot," the "Dictionnaire argotique dressé par ordre alphabétique," a central chapter on "Des Estats généraux" that describes eighteen rogue *vacations* (occupations), a "Dialogue de deux Argotiers" that includes three songs, the "Procès [lawsuit] entre Mathelin le Rechigneux [the Surly] et Collas le Souffreteux [the Needy]," the resulting "Sentence [verdict] donnée par le sieur Cagou," the description of the "Cour des Miracles ou Piolle franche où les Argotiers et les Gueux font leur retraicte" (the alleged safe retreat that rogues frequented), the "Resjouissance des Argotiers sur la prise de la Rochelle," and the "Lucque," a facetious permission to publish. These disparate pieces are tied together by two shared themes and a stylistic technique. The first theme concerns the kingdom of Argot. The author not only uses the descriptions of *La Vie généreuse* (unencumbered by its autobiographic fiction), but he also founds his narrative on the same basic situation, since it is a meeting between peddlers and beggars that leads to an explanation of the origins of the order of Argot. Thus Pechon de Ruby's observations reappear in *Le Jargon*: the portrait of the Grand Coesre with his patched coat and his sham putrid limbs, the rendering of accounts by the *cagoux*, the punishment of rebels, the oath administered to new recruits (with the left hand upraised), and the supper. This material is, however, stylistically transformed: The descriptions are no longer alleged to have come from an eyewitness and participant, but are given in the more impersonal form of objective narrative.

Into his borrowed description of the beggars' Estates General, Che-reau inserted another traditional theme: the various classes of false mendicants, "each [of whom], of whatever condition he may be, comes to give an account of his occupation." A hierarchic list of eighteen "states" follows, each identified by its argot name, its typical activities, and its amount of tribute due to the Grand Coesre. The nomenclature here is far richer than in *La Vie généreuse* and makes use of the classic repertory of denunciations of false mendicants, the *Liber vagatorum* in particular. Although we know of no French translation of this work in the sixteenth century, it was republished many times in the fifty years that preceded the publication of *Le Jargon*. We know of three Frank-furt editions under the title *Die rotwelsch Grammatik* (1583, 1601, and 1620), and the version that includes a preface by Martin Luther, which was originally published in 1528, was reprinted in 1580, 1626, 1627, and 1634.[20] Half of the classes of false beggars in *Le Jargon* duplicate or adapt chapters in the *Liber vagatorum*:

Des Orphelins = Von den Bregern (chapter 1): nonspecialized beggars

Des Marcandiers = Von den Bandierern (22): false merchants claiming to have been robbed

Des Millars = Von Stabülern (2): beggars with shoulder bags

Des Malingreux = Von den Seffern (25): beggars with false wounds

Des Piètres = Von den Klenckern (4): false cripples

Des Sabouleux = Von den Grantnern (8): false epileptics

Des Coquillards = Von Düczern (9): false pilgrims

Des Polissons = Von den Schwanfeldern (12): nearly naked, falsely destitute beggars

Des Convertis = Von Veranerin (23): false converts

Furthermore, the description of *ruffés* or *rifordés*, who begged with cer-tificates attesting that their houses had burned, reflects a description in chapter 21 of the *Liber*. And other categories of false illnesses—*callots, hubins*, and *francs mitoux*—are nothing but variations on a theme pres-ent in the *Liber*. Chereau innovates, on the other hand, when he counts among the subjects of the Grand Coesre the adepts of "le Doublage"—

[20] On the editions of the *Liber vagatorum*, see J. M. Wagner, "Liber vagatorum," *Se-rapeum* 23, no. 8 (1862):113-17; and D. B. Thomas, ed., *The Book of Vagabonds and Beg-gars with a Vocabulary of Their Language*, trans. J. C. Hotten (London, 1932).

thieves and robbers. Thus the association of beggars and thieves was added to the association of peddlers and beggars to explain the origin of the society of Argot: "[T]o be a perfect *Argotier*, you have to know the jargon of the Blesches, or Peddlers, the dissimulation [of] the beggars, and the subtlety of the cutpurses."

The originality of Ollivier Chereau's book in relation to *La Vie généreuse* (and to all the literature on *gueuserie* in Europe) lies in its systematic use of jargon. The dictionary that opens the work is considerably longer than in other works (the 1660 Troyes edition by Girardon lists 251 terms). Most significantly, however, the various sections are written in argot without the equivalents "in the vulgar tongue" in either the text or the notes. This use of a language that was secret but decipherable with the help of the dictionary is perhaps the work's chief mechanism (and the explanation of its success). It made it possible to parody several types of works, hence to create burlesque effects by twisting the sense of the most official texts (royal ordinances, judicial proceedings, permissions to print), various literary genres (dialogue, song, poetry), and even religious liturgy, as in the prayer of "the Sickly." This procedure also enabled the author to copy the descriptions and tales of *La Vie généreuse*, making these appropriations seem new and unpublished in their jargon "translation." This is what happens in the description of the Estates General, as we have seen, in the trick the beggars play on the miller, and, in abbreviated form, in the trick played on the gentleman ailing in a most sensitive part of his anatomy.

This technique, based on linguistic word play, obviously derived from the tradition of Carnival literature that accompanied the festive rituals, that parodied medical or juridical discourse, and that used macaronic languages. This derivation is even indicated in a sally in *Le Jargon*: The false permission to print that ends the book is dated "the eighth calends of February and day of Mardi Gras." Argot masks language just as Carnival costumes disguise the body, and this joking dissimulation permitted irreverent parody of legitimate discourse. This recourse to a jargon that mocked by twisting authorized forms of language was undeniably rooted in the fertile soil of Carnival culture, which was public and traditional; it can also be understood, however, as a means to literary entertainment as a form of burlesque. In point of fact, *Le Jargon* appeared at the very same time that other books, written in vocabularies hitherto excluded from accepted literature, were using unprecedented word forms to subvert rules, mock genres, and distort language.[21] In addition to informal terms, "low," technical, or archaic vocabularies, borrowings from other languages, and picturesque neologisms, argot was one of the sources from which burlesque authors could draw (as, for example, the poet Saint-Amant, whose *Oeuvres* first appeared in 1629). On the other hand, the parody of the high genres by the use of words and the development of themes normally foreign to such genres was the very mainspring of the burlesque. One good example of this is the work entitled *Les Fantaisies de Bruscambille contenant plusieurs Discours, Paradoxes, Harangues et Prologues facécieux faits par le sieur Des Lauriers, comédien,* a collection of texts that were presented orally at the Hôtel de Bourgogne and printed in Paris (in 1612) by Jean de Bordeaux and which, soon after, entered the catalogue of Nicolas II Oudot. In its contrast between base subject matter and exaggerated figures of rhetoric, the *Fantaisies de Bruscambille* provided the model for a literary genre that cast in a recognized form (in this case, noble eloquence) a text whose theme was incongruous and whose language inadequately conformed with the canons of the genre.

Ollivier Chereau took on just such a "task" in *Le Jargon*, since he used established literary and juridical forms to narrate the derisive complexities of the beggars' life in argotic language. We can place *Le Jargon*, then, at the intersection of two cultural elements familiar to all. The first was the habitual culture of public spaces of the city dwellers, still much alive at the turn of the seventeenth century, which climaxed in the Carnival festivities and the rituals and parodic texts they elicited. Chereau uses this familiar culture as a point of reference in recalling the Carnival tradition at the end of the book. Here he warns the reader not to take the work for what it is not, even if, up to that point, the reader might have been tempted to believe in the truth of the book. For the provincial man of letters who authored *Le Jargon*, however, the game of parody was undoubtedly more amusing when he used the formulas and procedures in vogue among his fellow literati—the use of disapproved vocabularies and the noble treatment of the lowly subject.[22] The kingdom of Argot was from this dual viewpoint an opportune subject, since it justified the use of an exotic and comic vocabulary

---

[21] F. Bar, *Le Genre burlesque en France au XVIIᵉ siècle. Étude de style* (Paris, 1960), 74-85 in particular.

[22] M. Soriano, "Burlesque et langage populaire de 1647 à 1653. Sur deux poèmes de jeunesse des frères Perrault," *Annales E.S.C.* 24 (1969):949-75.

and provided a repertory of grotesque and vulgar situations. Thus we can see *Le Jargon* as a provincial offshoot of the principal sort of burlesque, as one example of literature that entertained by denying or reversing the rules of legitimate writing. This combination of reference to the Carnival tradition, of a theme popularized by *La Vie généreuse*, and of a then stylish literary game allowed for a number of possible readings of the book—at varying levels of erudition, with varying conformity to standards of the picturesque, and with varying sensitivity to the inversion of codes of behavior. It was undoubtedly this possibility of plural readings that guaranteed the book a success that seems surprising, but that made it one of the most popular titles in the market of low-cost literature.

In the first Lyons (1630 and 1632) and Troyes (1656 and 1660) editions of the book, though not in the Paris edition of the widow Du Carroy, Ollivier Chereau included in *Le Jargon* a section that contrasts with the rest of the work: a description of the "Court of Miracles, or *Piolle franche*, where the Jargoneers and the Beggars make their Hideaway." Not only does he avoid jargon in this chapter, but he also returns to the half-serious, half-joking first-person voice of the preface. This theme of the retreat, where, "miraculously," false invalids and false cripples return to health and drink in company, is absent from *La Vie généreuse*, but it was not new. It belonged to the tradition of humorous literature, and Noël du Fail made good use of it in his *Propos rustiques*, where Tailleboudin tells Anselme:

> Do you not see those blind men, the ones whose faces have neither shape nor features? And those others with lightning-struck arms hanging loose (the which, however, come from hanged men, their own being strapped close to the body)? And others with withered hands that straighten out like anyone else's when they sit down to table? Others, ham hocks hanging from their belts? Or that one, faking a leper, who has tied up his throat with a string? Or that other one, who, having burned down his house, carries a long parchment we drew up for him and made look really authentic? That other one, falling down with Saint John's disease, whose wits are just as sharp as yours? That one, pretending to be dumb, craftily swallowing his tongue? And have you not seen the man who claimed his stomach and intestines were falling out, displaying a sheep's stomach? And what dupery is that? And the one

who goes around kneeling on two little pads, who in the consistory does better somersaults and handsprings than any acrobat in town? For this reason, the street to which we retire in Bourges is called Miracle Street, since those who are twisted and malformed about the city stand tall, cheerful, and ready for anything there.[23]

At the beginning of the seventeenth century, the theme of the court of miracles had become familiar enough to appear, for example, in a burlesque text published in 1616, *Le Carabinage et matoiserie soldatesque* by Richard de Romany, and, to take another example, in a perfectly serious *Mémoire* of 1612 analyzing the failure of an attempt to institutionalize Parisian mendicants. This second text mentions "the place vulgarly called Court of Miracles, behind the Filles-Dieu, at the foot of a rampart between the Porte Saint-Denis and Montmartre, where [the beggar masters] can usually be seen of a summer evening dancing, gaming, laughing, and having a good time."[24] Hence *Le Jargon* makes use of a theme that was already popular, or at least sufficiently so to have entered the terminology of Parisian topography.

Unlike the rest of the text, this report on the court of miracles is not treated in burlesque fashion; it introduces a serious subject and reflects the author's intent to avoid misinterpretation of his work. When he repeats the classic distinction between the true poor, "mentioned by our Lord in his Gospel," and the idle, deceitful, high-living, and vagabond *gueux*, Chereau places his text within the tradition that aimed to protect legitimate charity from usurpers (see Luther's preface to the *Liber vagatorum* in 1528 or Paré's explanation of his purpose). At the same time, Chereau indicated that humorous fiction was not incompatible with serious thought and took a stand in the debate on charity, widespread at the beginning of the seventeenth century. Perhaps the allusion to thoughtless people whose judgment was "wrong-side-to" and who might understand the work as an invitation to "extinguish the charity of good people toward the poor" should be read as an echo of the disputes during the 1610s and 1620s between those who favored shutting up the needy in hospices and those who remained attached to time-honored works of charity and alms, decreed by God for the salvation of the giver and the recipient alike. The little we know or can

---

[23] Du Fail, *Propos rustiques*, 633-34.

[24] *Mémoire concernant les pauvres qu'on appelle enfermés* in L. Cimber and F. Danjou, eds., *Archives curieuses de l'Histoire de France*, 1st ser., 15 (1837):243-70.

guess of the religious allegiance of the author of *Le Jargon*, moreover, conforms with an attitude of implicit disapproval toward cutting off the city's destitute from the world (as, for example, in the institution of La Charité in Lyons from 1622 on) and affirms the dignity of Christ's poor—hence the legitimacy of the charity of the "good people."[25]

Chereau's book had continued success throughout the eighteenth century; it was republished time after time and was listed in the catalogues of nearly all the Troyes printing houses. The official approval and permission to print of 1728 resulted in an edition of 1737 put out by Jacques Oudot's widow and her son Jean, one by Jean alone in 1741, and another by Pierre Garnier's widow and Jean-Antoine Garnier. An approval of 1740, which, like that of 1728, noted "the great number of times" the book had been reprinted, authorized another edition by Jean Oudot. Finally, in 1822, the widow André, "Printer-Bookseller and Papermaker [on the] Grand' Rue," put out the last Troyes edition of *Le Jargon* in its original form and under its original title. Beside these Troyes printings, we can also trace a Lyons edition (by Antoine Molin, permission of 1728) and two or three editions in Rouen. These editions are similar to each other, but in two ways they differ from the seventeenth-century editions. First, entire sections disappear: the Grand Coesre's quatrain addressed to the *Argotiers*, the preface, the acrostic sonnet, two or three songs included in the dialogue between two *Argotiers*, the lawsuit between Mathelin and Collas, the description of the court of miracles, the poem on the taking of La Rochelle, and the *Lucque*, or parodic permission. The edition by Nicolas II Oudot's son Jacques (active, 1679-1711) inaugurated this process by cutting the trial, the court of miracles, and the *Lucque*. From Jacques Oudot's widow to the widow André, the editions kept this same format: Only "L'Origine des Argotiers," the "Ordre ou Hiérarchie de l'Argot," the "Dictionnaire," the "Dialogue" (much cut), and the "Chanson de l'Argot," noted as being "good for dancing to the tune of 'Donne vos, donne vos,'" remain. There seem to have been two reasons for abbreviating the text in this manner. The desire to shorten the book is one, since eighteenth-century editions contain thirty-two pages against the sixty of the seventeenth-century versions. This accounts for the omission of the trial, the reduction of the dialogue, and the elimination of two or

[25] R. Chartier, "Le Retranchement de la sauvagerie," in G. Duby, ed., *Histoire de la France urbaine*, vol. 3: *La Ville classique* (Paris, 1981), 223-43.

three songs. Thus pieces that were perhaps redundant or thin were sacrificed to save space. Some of the cut sections also fitted poorly into the scheme of telling tales in argot (the preface and the section on the court of miracles) or were attached to a precise event (the final poem). In this way, the text was "detemporalized" and focused on the single aim of producing comic effects through the use of argot. The argot itself—and this is the second characteristic shared by the eighteenth-century editions—remained unchanged. Not only were the remaining sections untouched, but the argot dictionary was reprinted exactly as it had been in the first editions, typographical errors and all.

It was only with the editions of the mid-nineteenth century that this lexicon was changed and enlarged. In the 1830s and 1840s, *Le Jargon* became one of the mainstays among publishers of literature to be sold by peddlers. At that point, Troyes lost its monopoly on the book. It was republished by Baudot, to be sure, but it was also published by Pellerin in Épinal, Charles Placé in Tours, Lecrêne-Labbey in Rouen, Thiery in Pont-à-Mousson, and by the Deckherr brothers in Montbéliard. Three changes marked these editions. First, in all cases the title became *Le Jargon ou Langage de l'Argot réformé à l'usage des merciers, porte-balles et autres. Tiré et recueilli des plus fameux Argotiers de ce temps, par M.B.H.D.S. Archi-suppôt de l'Argot. Nouvelle Édition corrigée et augmentée de tous les mots qui n'étaient point dans les précédentes éditions.* The good poor (*bons pauvres*) were replaced by peddlers (*merciers*), a supposed "chief" of argot (*archisuppôt de l'Argot*) took the place of the shopkeeper (*pillier de boutanche*), and the announcement of the dictionary's enlargement was simplified and emphasized by capitalizing "Nouvelle Édition." The title page thus became more readable when freed of archaic references (the "bons pauvres") and now indecipherable jargon expressions. A second change was the enlargement of the dictionary. In the Baudot and Pellerin editions, it included 670 words and expressions—nearly three times its length in the seventeenth-century editions. Such an increase was accompanied by carelessness—faulty transcriptions, confused definitions, and consistently reproduced typographical errors. Moreover, this lexicon bore little relation to other documents concerning argot at the beginning of the nineteenth century and was constructed by borrowing from regional patois or bizarre definitions. Finally, the nineteenth-century editions share a parodic permission on the last page, the *Condé*, which differs from the *Lucque* of the first printings, replacing the Carnival reference with a reference to Tours (Turcan) as the book's place of origin.

Although Chereau's book was somewhat shortened and its dictionary enlarged, the remaining sections of the text were republished unchanged in the nineteenth century. This sort of longevity, which offered the readers of 1830 a book organized around themes (the kingdom of the beggars, the classifications of false mendicants) dating from the fifteenth or sixteenth centuries and jargonesque writing dating from the seventeenth, leads us to ask what kind of reception such a text could possibly have had two centuries after its first appearance. Since these readers have left no record of their thoughts on the book, the modern reader is left to his conjectures. It is certain that in the nineteenth century the book could no longer be taken for a description of external reality. The ambiguity maintained in the seventeenth century between "realistic" effects and the discreet avowal of parodic intent no longer cohered, and the reader knew immediately that the book was a humorous tale, a work of fiction written to entertain. How, then, can we explain its continued success? The list of books that "can also be found at the Librairie de Baudot," printed on the flyleaf of Baudot's edition of *Le Jargon*, attests to a continuing taste for books that parodied genres and languages. Along with *Le Jargon*, we find facetious sermons (the *Sermon de Bacchus*, the *Sermon et consolation des cocus* [cuckolds]), a parodic catechism (the *Catéchisme à l'usage des grandes filles pour être mariées*), a burlesque *Contrat de mariage*, and works in gutter language. Based as it was on similar distortions of form and language, Chereau's book could thus be presented as yet another text that played with the rules of legitimate writing. This accounts for its continued presence in the peddlers' literature of the nineteenth century—and all the more so, since it permitted the low-cost publication of a new argot dictionary not substantial enough to be published alone. (We know of only one edition of a *Supplément au Dictionnaire Argotique*, probably the work of the bookseller-printer Chalopin in Caen and published under the parodic address "At [the sign of] the Alder, by Mesière, Babbler to the Grand Coesre. With [a] *Condé* by the *Cagou* of Tours." It is twelve pages long and gives 349 new terms.) The clientele for these peddler-marketed books—largely rural by the end of the eighteenth century—could find both satisfaction at the revelation of a secret and amusement in the picturesque, metaphorical, jargonesque comical aspects in this collection of argot terms. *Le Jargon* probably seemed to the printers of such books the handiest receptacle in which to insert this updated vocabulary, enabling them to couple a modified dictionary with a selectively shortened but basically unchanged text. This may also have led to two ways of reading the work: the first taking the list of argot terms as a guide to deciphering a disquieting and contemporary language—supposedly still in existence in the France of Louis-Philippe—and the second taking as sheer entertainment the account of the beggars' Estates General, by this point as distant and unreal as the chivalric romances and tales.

## Buscón in Translation: Choice and Censorship

The third of our texts on *gueuserie* is quite obviously on a different level from *La Vie généreuse* and *Le Jargon*, since it is a translation of one of the major Spanish picaresque novels, the *Historia de la vida del Buscón llamado don Pablos* (History of the life of the Rogue named Don Pablos) of Francisco de Quevedo. This work first appeared in Nicolas II Oudot's catalogue in 1657, published under the title *L'Aventurier Buscon. Histoire facétieuse. Composée en Espagnol par Dom Francisco de Quevedo, Cavalier Espagnol. Ensemble les lettres du chevalier de l'Épargne. L'Aventurier* was republished under nearly the same title (with an official approval dated 2 November 1705 and a permission of 18 November 1728 granted to Jean III Oudot) first in 1730 by Jean IV Oudot, the inheritor of the permission, then by Jean-Antoine Garnier, who published "blue" books between 1765 and 1780. In the nineteenth century, Baudot took up the text and gave it a new cover (instead of the old title pages) bearing the title *L'Aventurier Buscon. Histoire comique.*[26] The book undoubtedly found a secure and durable place in the inexpensive literature published in Troyes and elsewhere, since it is listed in the *Catalogue de la Bibliothèque bleue* put out by Lecrêne-Labbey, a printer-bookseller of Rouen, at the end of the eighteenth century.[27]

The long career that this great Spanish classic enjoyed as a work of the *Bibliothèque bleue* poses several questions concerning the reception of picaresque literature in seventeenth-century France. If we take the edition of Nicolas II Oudot as the first Troyes edition of *L'Aventurier*,

---

[26] A. Morin, *Catalogue descriptif de la Bibliothèque bleue de Troyes (Almanachs exclus)* (Geneva, 1974), nos. 39-40.

[27] The catalogue is reproduced in R. Hélot, *La Bibliothèque bleue en Normandie* (Rouen, 1928).

the book had to wait twenty-five years after its first French translation before it appeared in the *Bibliothèque bleue*. By that point, its success was already assured. The first Spanish editions of the work date from 1626 and were published in Zaragoza, Barcelona, and, under a false Zaragoza address, probably in Madrid. Many other editions followed: two in 1627, one in 1628, one in 1629 (in Rouen, by Charles Osmont), one in 1631, and a Lisbon edition in 1632.[28] The work was translated into French in 1633 and published, under the title Nicolas Oudot was to adopt word for word, by the Paris bookseller Pierre Billaine. The publisher gives the name of the translator in a note to the readers: "le sieur de la Geneste," the translator of Quevedo's *Agréables Visions*. This new Spanish work, the preface announces, "has been fashioned *à la française* by a hand that has marvelously embellished it." La Geneste's translation was reprinted at least ten times before the Troyes edition— in Brussels (1634), Lyons (1634 and 1644), Paris (1635, 1639, 1645), and Rouen (1641 and 1645)—and it was included in the Rouen edition of Quevedo's *Oeuvres* in 1647 and 1655.[29] Its success did not diminish until 1698, when a new translation by "le sieur Raclots, Parisien" appeared.

The warm welcome the *Buscon* received in France during the first half of the seventeenth century clearly reflects French enthusiasm for Spanish picaresque fiction. Between 1600 and the appearance of the Troyes edition of *L'Aventurier*, successive translations of *Lazarillo de Tormes* went through at least nine French editions, *Guzmán de Alfarache* went through sixteen (one in 1600 in Gabriel Chappuys's translation and fifteen thereafter in Jean Chapelain's translation), the *Relaciones de la Vida de Marcos de Obregón* three, and the *Antiquité des larrons*, the French title of *La desordenada codicia de los bienes ajenos*, another three. The *Novelas Exemplares* of Cervantes, one of which, *Rinconete y Cortadillo*, presents a society of rogues ruled by Monipodio, went through eight editions in Paris. The entry of Quevedo's *L'Aventurier* into the Troyes repertoire should thus be seen in the light of

[28] See F. de Quevedo, *La Vida del Buscón llamado don Pablos*, critical ed. by Fernando Lázaro Carreter, in *Acta Salmanticensia, Filosofía y Letras* 18, no. 4 (Salamanca, 1965), xiii-xvi. (The translator has consulted two modern English translations: *The Life & Adventures of Don Pablos the Sharper: An Example for Vagabonds and a Mirror for Scamps*, trans. Francisco Villamiquel y Hardin [Leicester, 1928], and *Pablo de Segovia (The Spanish Sharper)*, trans. and intro. H. E. Watts [London, 1927].)

[29] According to R. Greifelt, "Die Übersetzungen des spanischen Schmelromans in Frankreich im 17 Jahrhunderts," *Romanische Forschungen* 50, no. 1 (1936):51-84.

other undeniably successful Spanish novels, translated and retrans-
lated, published in Paris, Rouen, and Lyons.[30]

This popularity makes it all the more surprising that *L'Aventurier
Buscon* was the only Spanish picaresque text to be published in the *Bibliothèque bleue*. Neither the *Lazarillo* nor *Guzmán de Alfarache* nor
Cervantes's tale ever found a place among the "blue" books, even
though their themes (vagrant criminals, descriptions of their techniques and of the underworld social hierarchy, and, in the case of *Rinconete y Cortadillo*, the use of jargon) made them similar—literary
qualities apart—to *La Vie généreuse* and *Le Jargon ou Langage de l'Argot
réformé*. Why, then, was the *Buscón* the only work chosen? A major
reason was its publishing history. In 1649 Nicolas II Oudot had published Quevedo's *Visions* in La Geneste's translation.[31] We can suppose
that the success of this work (later republished by Jean III Oudot and
mentioned in Lecrêne-Labbey's Rouen catalogue) persuaded him to
offer the public a second translation by La Geneste in the format he
and his father had created. There is, however, another explanation.
Quevedo's novel, at least in its French translation, could be read on the
two levels we have already seen in connection with *Le Jargon*: the scat-
ologic tradition of Carnival culture on the one hand and the parodic
and grotesque forms of burlesque literature on the other.

All the Troyes editions of *L'Aventurier Buscon* used the 1633 translation, and, throughout the eighteenth century, they continued to ignore new translations—from that of Raclots (1698) to those of Restif de
la Bretonne and Hermilly (1776). Until the Baudot edition of the 1830s
and 1840s, Quevedo's work was offered to buyers of the "blue" books
in a translation two hundred years old. This raises two questions. First,
what did La Geneste make of the novel he offered to the French public? And second, did the Troyes printers continue to publish his translation without cuts and changes? The answer to the first question
would carry me beyond my present purpose, but it may be useful to
recall La Geneste's alterations of the Spanish original.[32] In the first

---

[30] According to ibid. On *Guzmán de Alfarache*, see E. Cros, *Protée et le gueux. Recherches sur les origines et la nature du récit picaresque dans Guzmán de Alfarache de Mateo
Alemán* (Paris, 1967), 456-57. On the *Novelas Exemplares*, see G. Hainsworth, *Les "Novelas Exemplares" de Cervantes en France au XVIIᵉ siècle. Contribution à l'étude de la nouvelle en France* (Paris, 1933), 253-57.

[31] Morin, *Catalogue descriptif*, nos. 1221-23.

[32] The basic study of the 1633 translation is A. Stoll, *Scarron als Übersetzer Quevedos.
Studien zur Rezeption des pikaresken Romans "El Buscón" in Frankreich (l'Aventurier*

place, although the translator sometimes seeks adequate French equivalents for proper names (Roquille, Ragot, Le Grimpant), place names, and institutions, he delights in underscoring the "Spanish" character of the narrative, thus creating local color and picturesque distance. Various procedures contribute to this effect: the reference to known stereotypes concerning the Spanish character and customs; the explanation of idiomatic expressions (*dom, morisque, corregidor*); the citation of Spanish proverbs in the original language; the retention of many place names and proper names not necessarily familiar to the French reader; and the insertion into the text of allusions to *Don Quixote* not present in Quevedo's original (Pablos's horse is "a Rocinante of Don Quixote"; on his return to Madrid, Buscon declares, "I tailed the beard of Sancho Panza, the Esquire of Don Quixote"). This Spanish cast imparted to the text by the translator is clear from the title page, which asserts that the story was "composed in Spanish by Dom Francisco Quevedo, a Spanish knight."

The translated title also suggests a second possible way of reading the work: as an *histoire facétieuse*. In point of fact, throughout his translation, La Geneste makes use of formulas taken from the early seventeenth-century French burlesque tradition. His vocabulary includes "low" terms and obscenities, the slang of La Halle (the Paris market), and argot. His style relies heavily on the techniques of burlesque rhetoric: repetition, enumeration, periphrasis, and comparison. The translator of 1633 found himself faced with the complexity of Quevedo's writing, with all its juggling of metaphors and plays on words (the *concetti* so beloved of the time) that transform men into animals or objects and create a universe of Boschian, fantastic creatures (Bosch is cited in the text). Above all, he found himself ill at ease with a work of social significance that mocked people with ridiculous pretensions to rising in society, a work he was incapable of understanding. So he interpreted the book as a comic tale and based his translation on the vocabulary and literary formulas of the burlesque. This (and other factors) explains why it is possible to attribute the translation to Scarron, the first part of whose *Roman comique* was published in 1651.

The most important change that La Geneste (or Scarron) wrought on Quevedo's novel is undoubtedly the complete reworking of its end-

*Buscon, 1633)* (Frankfurt-am-Main, 1970). See also D. Reichardt, *Von Quevedos "Buscón" zum Deutschen Avanturier* (Bonn, 1970), chapter 2 (devoted to La Geneste's translation, which A. Stoll attributes to Scarron).

ing. In the Spanish original, Pablos's chances of marrying Doña Ana are ruined when he is recognized by his former companion, Don Diego Coronel, and, after becoming in turn a beggar, an actor, a poet, and "a nun's gallant," he returns to Seville. There he hobnobs with rogues, participates with them in the murder of two archers, takes refuge in a church where a prostitute, La Grapal (Grajales), falls in love with him, and finally ships off to America. He declares:

> I resolved—not through penitence (for I lacked wisdom), but through [the] lassitude of the obstinate sinner and after having debated the matter with La Grapal—to leave with her for the Indies to see if my fate might improve by a change of society and country. Nothing of the sort came to pass, as you will see in the second part, for a man who changes only his place, and not his life or his habits, will never better his condition.

None of this appears in the 1633 translation, which was used in the Troyes editions. Instead, after his wanderings as a beggar, actor, and poet, Pablos, back in Seville, falls in love with Rozelle, the only daughter of a rich merchant. He enters the merchant's household as a domestic and, by various stratagems, lets it be known that he is a "knight of Spain." The ruse works, and Pablos marries Rozelle. He then tells her of the trick he has played (of which she approves), pockets the dowry and the inheritance, and resolves "from now on to follow the profession of an honest man." The final sentences draw the happy moral of the tale: "All is under the Providence of Heaven and one cannot predict the future, but I can now say that there are few persons in the Universe, of whatever status or prosperity, whose happiness can be compared to mine. May Heaven long keep me in the company of my dear Rozelle." This conclusion, a total distortion of Quevedo's conclusion, seems to respond to two literary necessities. First, it ends the novel, sealing the happy fate of the protagonist. And second, it provides a moral to the tale, since Pablos's return to an upright life shows that man can improve and can recover his natural identity even if he strays. In the final analysis, the adventurous life is nothing but a temporary detour (for the hero) and an entertaining interlude (for the reader) before a steady and honest life fulfills the promise the hero showed at the start, since in the first chapter Pablos describes himself as having "had, since childhood, always the generous sentiments of a gentleman." In reversing the end of the novel, La Geneste–Scarron was attempting to make it conform with the reigning conventions of the genre in France, which demanded a happy ending, a likable hero (or a hero who did evil only in spite of himself), and an exemplary morality.

Did the Troyes editions of the work distort the Spanish text in ways other than those for which the translator was responsible?[33] A scrupulous comparison between the Troyes edition published in the eighteenth century by Jean-Antoine Garnier and the 1633 edition makes the answer clear. At first glance, the later edition seems totally faithful to the earlier one, since it repeats every word of the 1633 title (to the point of absurdity, since there is an announcement of the publication of the *Lettres du Chevalier de l'Épargne*, a work absent from the catalogues of the Troyes publishers of the eighteenth century). Furthermore, the Troyes edition respects all but one of La Geneste–Scarron's chapter divisions and chapter headings (which fitted the twenty-three chapters of the original Spanish edition of 1626 into twenty-two chapters and eliminated the original separation into two books). The text published by the Oudots and the Garniers differs from the 1633 translation, however, in three ways. First, the text was brutally abridged to bring it down to a size more acceptable to the Troyes printers. In its *Bibliothèque bleue* editions of the eighteenth century, the work has 160 pages, a good deal more than *Le Jargon ou Langage de l'Argot réformé* (which shrank from 60 to 48 pages, then from 48 to 36 between 1630 and the end of the eighteenth century). This length is not very different, however, from other "classics" of the *Bibliothèque bleue* that were reprinted many times during the seventeenth and eighteenth centuries: the *Histoire des Quatre fils Aymon* (156 pages in a quarto edition by the widow of Jacques Oudot and her son Jean), the *Histoire de Huon de Bordeaux* (144 pages in an edition by the same publishers), and the *Histoire des aventures heureuses et malheureuses de Fortunatus* (176 pages in the octavo editions of Pierre Garnier and his widow). This proves, incidentally, that publications in the *Bibliothèque bleue* format were not necessarily brief texts.

The text was not only abridged—as we shall soon see—but was also presented in shorter segments. Paragraphs were few in the Paris edition of 1633 but numerous in the Troyes volumes. For example, the chapter entitled "Buscon commençant à pratiquer la vie de ses con-

---

[33] Parallel reading of the Spanish text and the 1633 French translation (and the Troyes reprintings of it) is possible using the Carreter edition (note 28, above) or the translation of F. Reille, *Romans picaresques espagnols* (Paris, 1968), 757-880.

frères de l'Industrie, attrape une franche lipée et escroque une courti-
sane" (Buscon, while beginning to practice the life of his industrious
brothers, gets a good talking to and cheats a courtesan) is divided into
nine paragraphs in the Paris text but into thirty in the Garnier edition.
For another example, in the chapter entitled "Du traitement que Buscon ressent en sa prison, les délits, la misère et la maladie des prison-
niers, la tyrannie et mangerie des geôliers et autres officiers, enfin la
délivrance de Buscon" (On the treatment Buscon receives in prison, the
crimes, destitution, and sickness of the prisoners, the tyranny and glut-
tony of the jailers and other officers, [and] finally, the delivery of Buscon), there are eight paragraphs in the 1633 edition but thirty-eight in
the Troyes edition. This desire to make reading easier by inserting
pauses and new starts was carried to ridiculous extremes. On page 120
of the Troyes text, the separation between the second and third paragraphs cuts a sentence in two, leaving the first half meaningless and
ungrammatical. When the Troyes printers divided the texts they republished into smaller units, they were, to be sure, conforming to a
tendency common among printers of the seventeenth and eighteenth
centuries, but they exaggerated this tendency, probably in an effort to
make reading easier for buyers of their books who were far from expert readers.

This abridgement of the La Geneste–Scarron translation involved
serious cuts in the text, but they were not random; great and small, they
follow a discernible logic. The first chapter, "De l'extraction de Buscon
et des qualités de ses père et mère" (On Buscon's ancestry and his father's and mother's qualities), is a good illustration of this. Already al-
tered and watered down in the 1633 translation, Quevedo's text here
lost all touch with his original intent. The most important cuts censored passages that portray Pablos's mother as a prostitute and a witch.
Every allusion to her venal activity is omitted or transformed. For example, the end of the phrase "la plupart des Versificateurs et Poètes
d'Espagne, firent plusieurs plaisantes oeuvres sur elle" (most of the
Versifiers and Poets of Spain made entertaining works on her) was
changed to "à sa louange" (in her praise). Her complaint "c'est moi qui
vous ai fourni du pain aux dépens de ma chair" (I'm the one who has
given you bread paid for by my flesh) lost its last five words. Sorcery,
too, is barely touched on in the later text; "she bewitched all who knew
her" was retained, but the description that follows in the 1633 text, and
which is close to the original Spanish, was eliminated. It reads:

[She] knew how to fine-draw a torn maidenhead with great dexterity, make a breast like new, and disguise old age; some called her a fixer of dislocated affections and others, more rustically, called her an innocent *maquerelle* [procuress] and a *raffle de dix* [ten-sweeper] of the money of all who had dealings with her, but she only laughed at them and trapped them all the better when her chance came around. Let me tell you briefly about her penances. She had a room into which no one but she entered and which looked like a cemetery, for it was full of the bones of the dead that she kept, to hear her tell it, to remind her of death and to show her scorn for this life. The floor was strewn with wax figurines and with verbena, ferns, and other herbs of Saint John's Eve, out of which she made strange mixtures.

Likewise, the activities of Pablos's father, who appears as a barber in the later edition, are treated euphemistically. "My son," he declares in the 1633 edition, "the thief's trade is a liberal art." In the Garnier edition, however, "thief's trade" becomes "barber's trade." In the passages that follow, the cuts made in the later edition are italicized:

Why do you think the Sergeants persecute us so? Is it because one potter hates another potter? *Why do they banish us, whip us, and hang us?* I can hardly say this without having tears come into my eyes, for the good old man was weeping like a child, *remembering all the times they had lashed his shoulders*; [and he said] it is because they did not want there to be any *thieves* but themselves where they lived.

In the first chapter, the Troyes adapter also eliminated certain vulgar words. For example, the expression "il décrassait et débarbouillait le grouin de ses patients" (he wiped and cleaned the dirt off his patients' snouts) became "il débarbouillait ses patients" (he cleaned his patients up). Religious allusions, parodic in intent or not, were eliminated as well: "comment merci Dieu, vous dites que . . ." (how, thanks to God, you say that . . .) became "comment merci de ma vie [my life], vous dites que . . ." At the end of the chapter, the reference to the mother's broken chaplet was cut out of her angry speech, "She would have said more, for she was highly irritated, *if, in the violence of her gestures, she had not unstrung her chaplet, [which was] made of the molars of several dead men whose life she had shortened, and had to pick them up,*" and replaced by "if she had not been interrupted." The last sentence in this section is another good illustration of such cuts. The 1633 edition reads, "My mother began to sniffle [about] her chaplet of pulled teeth, and my father went off to shave someone, I cannot say whether of his beard or his purse," but the Garnier edition reads, "My mother began to cry, and my father went off to shave someone."

As the first example above shows, the Troyes rewriting of the La Geneste–Scarron text aimed particularly at keeping the hero from falling too low, at censoring blasphemous allusions, and at eliminating the crudely sexual and the macabre. This policy was carried through from start to finish, and it served to designate passages to be eliminated and phrases to be rewritten. The Troyes adapter of the *Buscon* scoured the text of "low," material, and corporal words that had been used by the 1633 translator. Thus words and expressions designating excrement disappeared: *tout bréneux* and *merde* became *ordures* and *montrer le caca* (to point to the excrement) became *montrer la farce* (to point out the joke). Similarly, a roll of paper "as greasy as a Cook's parts" was improved to "as greasy as a Cook"; the verb *pisser* was changed to *respirer* (breathe); and the word *cul* was either eliminated—as in the phrase "les chausses lui tombèrent sur les genoux et lui laissèrent [le cul] tout à l'air" (his pants fell to his knees and left him [his butt] in the open air)—or changed to the more delicate *derrière*. This decision to avoid scatological vocabulary also led to the elimination of two scenes of physical soiling that were kept in the 1633 translation: the scene in which the schoolboy defecates in the box of goods belonging to the merchant he meets at an inn and the scene in a chapter eliminated from the Troyes edition, "Le courtois accueil que Buscon reçut de son oncle; la bonne chère qu'il lui fît en sa maison, et comme après avoir recueilli sa succession, il quitta sa compagnie" (The courteous welcome that Buscon received from his uncle; the good food and drink that he offered him in his house; and how, after he had received his inheritance, he left his company). The censoring of the former avoided the coprophagous result and the elimination of the latter avoided a drinking scene that ends in vomiting.

The Troyes edition censored sexual allusions as well. *Putain, pucelage, maquerellage*, and *concubinage* (prostitute, virginity, pandering, concubinage) became forbidden words, as in the phrase "je crois que la conscience entre marchands, *c'est comme un pucelage dont une maquerelle trafique*, c'est ce qui se vend sans se livrer" (I think that conscience among merchants *is like virginity offered by a procuress; it* is sold without being delivered). Prudery also explains the drastic cuts made in other parts of the text, for example in the portrait of the old woman in whose house Buscon "se fait médicamenter" (gets medical attention):

> She dabbled in many trades: at times she arranged marriages and at times she pimped; she lent money at interest and on good security; her house was never empty of people; she was most skillful in teaching young girls who aimed to be courtesans. ... Aside from that, she taught how to grab a gallant's jewel: for young girls, out of profligacy and as a sort of game; for those of more mature years, as a favor; and for old women, as recompense.

Or take the answer of the overly cooperative actor regarding his somewhat venal wife:

> Do you know no way, I said to him, that one could negotiate with that tradeswoman and make twenty *écus* or so in the bargain, for she seems to me most beautiful? It would hardly be proper, he answered me, for me to show you how, since I am her husband; but I will tell you that your money would be well employed in her merchandise, for, speaking without passion, I can assure you that nowhere in the world is there flesh more delicate or more beautiful, or [a wench of] a more playful humor than she. In saying this, he descended from his carriage and got into another, perhaps to give me an opportunity to speak with her. I found this procedure highly amusing and I had to admit that, as he said, he was speaking without passion.

Earlier in the text, the portrait of the sodomite imprisoned with Buscon and his companions is only barely sketched in the Troyes edition, where it lost all but the first sentence of the original translation of the Spanish text:

> I learned that he had made love in the masculine gender. He was so fierce and so dangerous that the Jailer, a prudent and cognizant man, was obliged to give out trousers reinforced with iron parts, just like spiked dog collars, to all whom he lodged where that devil was; and if he had not been chained up, no one would have [even] dared to fart near him for fear of reminding him of their nether regions.

The Troyes adapter's retention of even the crude allusion to the imprisoned giant's homosexuality is perhaps more surprising than the censorship of the passage.

The adapter was never caught short, however, where vigilance on religious matters was concerned. The later edition made systematic cuts and changes for religious reasons in a text that already had secularized a good many Christian references. Comparisons and invocations disappear: "nous ne sommes plus que des âmes *dans le Purgatoire*" (we are no more than souls *in Purgatory*); "je vous prie de prendre garde à ce que vous ferez *car je ne suis pas un Ecce Homo*" (I warn you to watch what you do *for I am not an Ecce Homo [submissive Jesus Christ]*); "le visage triste et pâle *avec un grand per signum Cruciis de inimicis suis*" (a sad, pale face *with a great sign of the Cross for his enemies*), which was replaced by "avec un grand nez de grues" (with a big nose like a crane's beak); "ils demeurèrent nuds comme deux *figures de la Resurrection*" (they were left as naked as two *figures from a Resurrection*), which was replaced by "fantômes" (ghosts); "il passe autour de nous *puis il fait un signe de croix. Jésus, dit-il*" (he went around us, *then made the sign of the cross. Jesus*, he said), which became simply "A dit-il" ("ah," said he); and, to end the list, "encore Dieu voulut pour moi" (as God willed it for me), which became "encore le sort voulut pour moi" (as fate [or luck] willed it for me). The same sort of censorship stripped the parodic decrees against poets of their religious allusions: "comme étant chrétiens et de nos prochains" (since they were Christians and our fellow men) became "en cette considération" (in that connection); "quelque reliques" (some relics) became "quelques choses" (some things); *terre sainte* (holy ground) became *terres étrangères* (foreign lands); *anges* (angels) became *aigles* (eagles); and *divinités* (divinities) became *lumières* (lights). One last item lost its ending: "sur peine d'être exilés *aux ténèbres éternelles et abandonné aux malins esprits et aux forces infernales à l'heure de leur mort*" (on the threat of being exiled *to the eternal shades and abandoned to the evil spirits and infernal forces at their hour of death*).

The same desire to purify the text of all that might seem blasphemous mockery led to the mutilation or elimination of religious phrases placed in the mouths of the sham beggars. Thus, for the *chevalier de l'industrie*, who was a false healer, "son passe-port pour entrer partout était *un Deo Gratias, le Saint Esprit soit avec vous*" (his passport everywhere was a *"God be thanked, the Holy Spirit be with you"*) instead read

"... un bon-jour" (a "good-day"). Similarly, "Quand il nommait le dé-mon *il disait Jésus nous en délivre*, il baisait la terre *en étant aux Églises*" (when he named the Devil *he said, Jesus deliver us from him*; he kissed the ground *when he was in church*). Buscon received the same treatment:

> Je m'étudiais à user de paroles extraordinaires pour mendier: *Fi-dèles Chrétiens, disais-je, serviteurs de Dieu, ayez pitié de ce pauvre corps accablé de plaies et d'infirmités, et qui supporte patiemment sa douleur.* Voilà comme je parlais les jours ouvrables; mais aux fêtes je changeais de langage: *La foi sans la charité est inutile, disais-je, Ames dévôtes envers Dieu, qui est la même Charité, et par le mérite de Marie, cette grande Princesse, et cette Reine des Anges, donnez l'a-mour à ce pauvre mutilé et affligé de la main du Seigneur.*

> (I took care to use extraordinary words to beg. *Faithful Christians, I used to say, servants of God, take pity on this poor body riddled with sores and infirmities that patiently bears its pain.* That is how I spoke on working days, but on feast days I changed my tune. *Faith without charity is useless, I would say, Souls devoted to God, who is Charity itself, and by the merits of Mary, that great Princess and that Queen of the Angels, give love to this poor cripple, afflicted by the hand of the Lord.*)

In the Troyes edition, then, Buscon talks of "extraordinary words" of which his readers are deprived.

Religious censorship also dictated the transformation or excision of all references to the ecclesiastics Buscon encounters in his wanderings. Thus in chapter 4 the *curé de village* who Buscon meets at an inn in the Vivarais disappears completely, and the hermit who dices with (and so fleeces) Buscon and the soldier encountered at the gates of Madrid becomes simply "a man" in the Troyes edition. This completely changes the character of the episode and, since it leads to a long cut, weakens the satire of religious hypocrisy. The cut passage reads:

> We began the game, which was a game of chance with dice, and nothing could [have been] more comic than when he said he did not know how [to play] and begged us to show him what we were doing. This worthy holy man at first let us win some of his *reales*, but toward the end he turned on us so sharply that he left us bled white in no time at all and made himself our heir before we had

303

even died. At each loss, the soldier called on the Devil a hundred times and cursed interminably, and while I was eating the tips of my fingers the hermit was using his to rake in our money. The more we spoke of the Devil and raged and swore at our bad luck, the more he called on the saints and angels. After he had fleeced us, [to the extent that] the soldier had lost his one hundred *reales* and I my six hundred, we asked him if he would play for pledges [IOUs]. He answered that he was loath to play that rough a game with us, and that we were Christians and his fellow men. But another time, he said, when you play, do not swear. I took patience when I was losing, [he said,] and I put myself in the hands of God and the saints, and you can see how fortune smiled on me. And since we neither had his skillful wrist movements nor his knack for dicing, we believed what he told us; then the soldier swore, not to stop swearing, but to never gamble again, and I did the same. A pox [on him,] he [the soldier] said, I have often found myself among Lutherans and Moors, but they never treated me as roughly or with as little charity as this devil of a hermit. All this time, the hypocrite was laughing at us from behind his cowl, having already taken up his chaplet again.

The Troyes publishers found two scenes in which a dying man receives the last sacraments equally intolerable. The second of the two is a faked and mocking deathbed scene in which Pablos escapes the pursuit of the *corregidor* (the officer of the watch) and the rector of the *collège*: "I threw myself into the bed with a nightcap on my head, a candle in one hand, and a crucifix in the other, and a young priest at my side helping me to my death, while all the other companions intoned prayers." In the Troyes edition, the candle became a glass, the crucifix a bottle, the young priest a young recruit, and the litanies a drinking song. The other deathbed scene, in which one of Ragot's schoolboy boarders is indeed dying, is presented seriously in the original, but the Troyes adapter cut out the Christian rites as incongruous in a burlesque tale: "Then he was confessed, and when the Holy Sacrament was brought to him, the poor sick wretch, who had barely had enough strength to speak during his confession, cried out with all his might: 'Oh, my Lord Jesus Christ, if I had not seen you enter this house I would have believed myself already in hell.' "

A certain amount of incoherence results from these mutilations of the La Geneste–Scarron text. Some cuts make it difficult to understand episodes in the novel. For example, bereft of its "punch line," in which Buscon substitutes "Ponce d'Aguire" (a victim of their pranks) for "Pontius Pilate" in the recitation of the Credo, the tale of the tricks played by Pablos and Diego loses its point. Later, the omission of the letter in which Buscon's uncle tells him of his father's sufferings when he was supposedly hanged and of his mother when she was a prisoner of the Inquisition may very well conform with the logic of other changes in chapter 1, but it makes the allusions that follow completely incomprehensible. Such is the case when Buscon says, "if until that hour I had one foot on the ladder, as everyone knows, you must understand that my father climbed all the way up" or "on approaching the city, I saw my father by the highway waiting for company."

Other cuts weakened the intention of the translator and the Troyes publisher to present a comic work based on Spanish stereotypes. Bigotry was doubtlessly one of the best known of these traits, but the chapbook editor removed all mentions of chaplets, rosaries, and signs of the cross. For example, "the hermit was saying his Our Fathers with a chaplet whose wooden beads were so big that they would have served well as mace heads" became "the man was reciting songs." "We left the house with a grave step, holding our rosaries in our hands, as is the custom in the Spanish nation" was transformed into the absurd ". . . holding a bowl in our hands, as is the custom in the Spanish nation." Similarly, there was the elimination of one of the portraits that in the 1633 translation best expressed the well-known Spanish stereotype of the exaggerated and hypocritical piety of a female bigot who is also a procuress (think of La Celestina, the heroine of Fernando de Rojas). In the Troyes edition, Doña Cypriana, the wife of Pablos and Diego's host at Alcalá, is deceitful, but no longer falsely religious when all the following is omitted:

> She always wore a chaplet around her neck which had so much wood on it that someone less pious than she might have preferred to shoulder a load of firewood. It bore many different medals, pictures, crosses, and indulgence beads, with which she prayed (so she said) for her benefactors. She counted more than a hundred patron saints, and, as a matter of fact, she needed that many intercessors to excuse the sins she committed. She slept in a room above my master's, and she said more Prayers than the wisest

blind man in the [Hospice of the] Quinze-Vingt of Paris, for which she made up Latin words never known to Cicero that had us dying of laughter. Aside from these virtues, she had a thousand other skills; she was a reconciler of opposed parties and a medicator of voluptuosities—which is the same profession as the pimp's—but when I quarreled with her about it, she made excuses, saying "un bon chien chasse de race" [it runs in the family].

There are several ways to interpret the Troyes publishers' cuts and revisions of the translation of the *Buscón*. In the first place, the text bears evident marks of religious censorship, perhaps internalized into self-censorship, which aimed at cleansing the work of all its immoralities and blasphemies. The liberties permitted to the Parisian translator of 1633, who was writing above all a literary novelty for a limited public, were no longer judged appropriate in a text for wider distribution and less-informed readers. When the Troyes publishers removed everything that seemed a threat to the dignity of priests or that ridiculed religious beliefs, they functioned as vigilant auxiliaries to the Catholic Reformation, which no longer permitted parody and burlesque concerning the mysteries of the faith. The Troyes expurgation of the *Buscon*, which removed an essential element of the original that the 1633 translation had preserved—the travestied and ironic religious references—was responding to the same sort of motivation that led to the censorship of festivities (particularly those that profaned consecrated places and parodied liturgy), to the control of theatrical productions (think of the prohibitions of *Tartuffe* and *Dom Juan*), and to the persecution of blasphemers. France at the high tide of the Catholic Reformation was not Spain in the Golden Age, and the Church could no longer tolerate a treatment of religious matters it considered sacrilegious.

On the other hand, the Troyes adaptation of the text exhibits few marks of an antiquated style. This explains the expurgation of the "low" material and bodily vocabulary, judged to run counter to the conventions of good writing, even—indeed, particularly—when the work was aimed for the public at large. It also explains the abandonment of some of the characteristic formulas of burlesque rhetoric, for example picturesque enumeration, which was reduced to one term alone. Of the triad in "Il faut que ce soit quelque bardache, quelque bourgeron, quelque Juif" (Some whoremongering cuckold of a sodomizing Jew proposed that[34]), the Garnier edition retained only "quelque Juif." Of the litany of assonances in "[the names] lined them up behind [the Dons] like Coridon, Bourdon, Gaillardon, Gueridon, Randon, Brandon, and several others of like termination," the Troyes publishers retained only a limping "like Brandon." The translation thus lost all its now improper vocabulary, used in jest in the 1633 edition, as well as its translation of figures of speech that had become antiquated.

With the original Spanish text sadly distorted and the 1633 translation severely censored, the *Bibliothèque bleue* version of the *Buscon* wrenched the thematic organization that underlay Quevedo's work badly out of joint. For the reader of Oudot's or Garnier's versions, the tale appeared primarily as a series of meetings and anecdotes. Even more than in the original text, the personality of the protagonist pales, and his continuing presence serves the primary function of patching together a series of independent portraits and genre scenes in which the characters encountered are never seen again. A loose narrative structure of this sort, which piles up independent incidents, demands no recall of characters or their relationships to one another and no attention to a plot unfolding throughout the novel. This was well suited to a mode of reading in fits and starts that seems to have been the habit of the public for the Troyes books. The reader is thus led from one milieu to another—from the school to Ragot's boarding school in Segovia to the *collège* in Alcalá to the company of the *chevaliers de l'industrie* in Madrid to the actors' troupe in Toledo to Rozelle's family in Seville. The trips from one place to another give opportunities for extraordinary encounters. Between Alcalá and Segovia, for example, the hero meets, one after another, a man who gives him advice, a swordsman, a poet, a soldier, a man on his ass (a hermit in Quevedo and La Geneste), and a Genoese trader. As it jumps from one place to another, from one group to another, and from one character to another, the narrative is in no way governed by necessity; it can be taken up, dropped, picked up again, and read in snatches, a little at a time. This is doubtlessly one reason why the Troyes publishers chose to put out the *Buscon*.

Another reason lies in the themes treated in the book. Even with its watered down vocabulary, the Troyes version of Quevedo's novel contains a good bit of scatology, particularly at the beginning. Discharged enemas, expectorated spittle, and soiled beds belonged to the tradi-

[34] The Villamiquel y Hardin translation (see note 28), 93.

tional repertory of Carnival celebrations and to the bodily, excremental comedy characteristic of the culture of the public square. This remained the basis of comedy in the *Bibliothèque bleue* text, which often refers to bodily functions in contrasting, for instance, the meager fare of Ragot's boarding school with the overeating and drinking that takes place at the inns. The reference to Carnivalesque festivities at the beginning of the book is maintained: "It was then the time of the [feast of the] Kings [Epiphany], and the master, wanting to provide some amusement for his students, decided to create a kingdom: we shared out the cake and, without cheating, the Kingdom of the bean [the favor in the cake] fell to me." A note of this sort, which is also found in Quevedo, undoubtedly had the same effect as the date given in the false permission in *Le Jargon*. Placed at the beginning or the end, it situated the text in a comic and festive tradition founded on a grotesque and scatological realism. The meaning of the reference to Carnival perhaps lost some of its essence and its function as a framework to the book when it passed from Quevedo to the French translation,[35] but what remained permitted the book to be read with a festive amusement at the setting and the repeated references to what the body ingests and expels.

The public found the *Buscon* entertaining, coming as it did after the publication of *La Vie généreuse* and *Le Jargon*, because it too portrays a beggars' society: the company of the *chevaliers de l'industrie*, as the 1633 translator put it. The description of this community of gentleman beggars and thieves, which stretches over five chapters and thirty pages, is one of the most important episodes of the book. This society, first mentioned by the gentleman Pablos meets on the road to Madrid and then described by Buscon himself after his recruitment into the company, is based on the same principles as the kingdom of Argot. There is, first, the authority of a leader, here Dom Torivio (in Quevedo, Don Torribio), the master of the house in which the "knights" meet. The exercise of various specialties by the members is another: "Les uns se nomment Égrillards, les autres les Matois, les autres Filoux, les enfants de la Mate, les Remparts, les Agrippes et plusieurs autres noms qui dénotent leur profession," which is an approximate translation of the nomenclature in Spanish—"caballeros hebenes, güeros, chanflones, chirles, traspillados y caninos" (Nobody, Addle-pate, Crookshank, Lackwit,

---

[35] See E. Cros's brilliant demonstration in *L'Aristocrate et le carnaval des gueux. Étude sur le Buscón de Quevedo* (Montpellier, 1975).

Pinchguts, or Starveling[36]). Third, there is the respect for rules held in common. And fourth, there is an inexhaustible store of lies and deceptive stratagems. As compared to the "objective" and anonymous taxonomy of *Le Jargon*, the *Buscon* introduced two innovations that gave new life to the genre. First, the image of *gueuserie* is inverted, since the thieving ruffians no longer give themselves false illnesses and misfortunes but an assumed wealth, in which their actual destitution is hidden behind their appearance as gentlemen. And second, the novel embodies, in a series of particularized characters, what hitherto had been no more than a list of "the various manners of robbing." Thus there is the "governor" given to Pablos, who turns out to be the gentleman he met on the highway, the hypocrite claiming to cure scrofula and chancres, and the "other brother named Polanque," who begs and steals at night while crying out, "remember death and give charity for the souls of the departed." Thus *L'Aventurier Buscon* gave flesh and life to a theme that had become classic in the Troyes repertory.

The Troyes publishers of the seventeenth and eighteenth centuries picked Quevedo's novel, which they knew from the La Geneste translation, over the *Lazarillo*, which was by then antiquated, and the *Guzmán de Alfarache*, with its complicated structure and complex aims. The reasons for their preference are clear: The text was highly scatological; the plot freely alternated between picturesque portraits and short comic tales; and the narrative made use of mockery and parody—think of the entire chapter devoted to "Ordonnances contre les Poètes de Balles, Muses verreuses, mécaniques et de louage comme les chevaux" (Ordinances against Mule-pack Poets, Pox-ridden Muses, Common Workers and [those] for Hire like Horses). Furthermore, it repeated in a new form one of the most successful themes in the *Bibliothèque bleue* catalogues: the description of the society of beggars. But, in the context of the triumphant Catholic Reformation, when such widely distributed books were tightly controlled, the very reasons that led to the choice of the *Buscón* were those that led to its censoring. In the Troyes version, therefore, burlesque scatology is no longer expressed in its own vocabulary, scabrous tricks and practical jokes are no longer appropriate, and mockery must necessarily spare clerics and religion.

---

[36] The Villamiquel y Hardin translation (see note 28), 120.

## *Le Vagabond*: Nomenclature and Entertainment

The *Bibliothèque bleue* versions of the *Buscon*, from Nicolas II Oudot's edition to Baudot's, constituted one episode in the life cycle of the novel, but the Troyes publication of *Le Vagabond* was the last French edition of that work. The title entered the Troyes catalogue at the end of the seventeenth century, with the publisher's address given as "At Troyes, and sold in Paris by Antoine de Raffle," which indicates that it was one of the publications the Troyes printing houses put out primarily for the Parisian market. Antoine Raffle, whose estate inventory bears the date 15 April 1696, printed some works destined for wide distribution himself, but above all he was the *correspondant* and sales representative for the Oudots and the Febvres.[37] When he ordered a reprinting of *Le Vagabond* from them toward the end of the century, he was adding to the Troyes repertory a title that had already been published twice in Paris in 1644, by Jacques Villery and by Gervais Alliot. The work was a translation by Des Fontaines of an Italian text published in Viterbo in 1621 and republished at least five times before its first French edition (in 1627 in Venice and Milan, in 1628 in Pavia, and in 1637 and 1640 in unknown cities). Just as the title page of the French edition fails to note that the work is a translation, the Italian title page disguises the origin of the work. First, the author, a Dominican monk in the monastery of Santa Maria in Gradi at Viterbo named Giacinto de Nobili, hides under the pseudonym Rafaele Frianoro. And second, there is nothing to indicate that the book is the translation and adaptation of a Latin manuscript entitled *Speculum de cerretanis seu de ceretanorum origine eorumque fallaciis*, probably written in the 1480s by the cleric Teseo Pini, a "decretorum doctor" and Deputy Bishop at Urbino and then at Fossombrone, where he served under the man to whom the work is dedicated.[38]

Even more than for the *Buscon*, the Troyes edition came at the end of a chain of translations and adaptations of this work. The first of these, from the beginning of the seventeenth century, transmitted from Latin to Italian a text that was already some one hundred and fifty years old. The translator, Frianoro–de Nobili, who most probably dis-

---

[37] On Raffle's bookstore, see H.-J. Martin, *Livre, pouvoirs et société à Paris au XVIIᵉ siècle (1598-1701)* (Geneva, 1969), 2:956-57.

[38] The basic study is P. Camporesi, *Il Libro dei Vagabondi. Lo "Speculum cerretanorum" di Teseo Pini, "Il Vagabondo" di Rafaele Frianoro e altri testi di "furfanteria"* (Turin, 1973), 79-165 on *Il Vagabondo*.

covered the manuscript of Teseo Pini in an ecclesiastical library, changed the text, both cutting it and adding to it, and gave it a new title, *Il Vagabondo*. He also attempted to disguise its source by changing the names of the characters, veiling concrete references, and transposing to a third-person narration what had originally been given in the first person. The second stage of translation and adaptation occurred with the Paris editions of 1644. Although these French versions gave no hint that they were translations—the name of the translator was dropped—they remained close to the Italian text, kept the same foreword, and maintained the organization of chapters treating the various classes of outlaws (*bianti e vagabondi*, in the Italian text). Des Fontaines did, however, rearrange the text. In the first place, he changed the order of the work. The French and Italian versions both give the nomenclature of the various sorts of vagabonds in chapter 1, but, subsequently, the chapters describing them are distributed differently, with no very evident reason for the changes. Furthermore, the translator used discreet touches to create an Italianate character for his text: He established a specific setting for the anecdotes that are told and created a picturesque effect to whet the curiosity. He kept the Italian (by doubling the translation), for instance, to designate certain things: "The *Beates* are a certain sort of beggar that the Italians call *Bianti*," "the *Fourbes*, about whom I wish to speak here, are called *Felsi* by the Italians," and so forth.

Above all, Des Fontaines changed the title and the conclusion to the book, thus giving it a sense that it did not have (or not to the same extent) in de Nobili's version. The first part of the French title closely follows the titles of the Italian editions of 1627 and thereafter: *Il Vagabondo, overo sferza de Bianti e Vagabondi. Opera nuova, nella quale si scoprono le fraudi, malitie e inganni di coloro che vanno girando il Mondo alle spese altrui* (The Vagabond, or [the] whip of Vagrants and Vagabonds. A new work, in which are discovered the frauds, evil deeds, and tricks of those who go around the World at the expense of others). But what follows—*Et vi si raccontano molti casi in diversi luoghi e tempi successi* (And there are related here many cases that have occurred in different places and times)—takes on a different cast in French: *Avec plusieurs récits facétieux sur ce sujet pour déniaiser les simples* (With several comic tales on this subject to edify simpletons). This designation of the work as a series of "comic tales" places it in the tradition of entertaining and diverting literature, which claimed not to present its inventions

as reality, but only to amuse by describing clever stratagems and credulous dupes. Falsely addressed to the "simple," the book was in reality
offered to whoever was entertained by sly tricks and enjoyed laughing
at those taken in by them. This departure from realism, in which the
text is presented as a series of short tales, is better evidenced by chapter
38—"Des diseurs de contes" (On storytellers)—which the translator
himself added at the end of the book. This chapter, which to all appearances completes *Le Vagabond*, is actually the announcement of a
sequel, to be devoted to those who deceive, not by their appearance or
their ruses, but by their fine words and their tales. In the Villery edition
of 1644, *Le Vagabond* is in fact followed by yet another text, also written
by Des Fontaines, the *Entretien des bonnes compagnies*, which was typeset and paginated separately and which contains a series of very brief
stories and jokes.[39] These added sketches seldom feature beggars or
vagabonds, so the two works thus joined (*Le Vagabond* and the *Entretien*) have only the vaguest relationship as far as themes and subject
matter are concerned. Thus the chapter "On storytellers," which ends
one work and introduces the other, seems to be merely an artifice to
justify the juxtaposition of the two works. In its last sentence, however,
Des Fontaines suggests a connection between them and hints at how
they should be read: "I will limit myself to remarking on some of their
most comic traits, since the ridiculous is the object of this book rather
than the reasonable." *Le Vagabond* and the *Entretien* required the same
sort of deciphering; in both cases, the reader took pleasure in amusing
tales, was not overly concerned with the veracity or falsity of the events
reported, and was amused by practical jokes and witty sayings.

The Troyes publisher changed nothing in the Villery and Alliot editions when he republished the translation of *Le Vagabond*, but he
added the *Entretien des bonnes compagnies*. This retained its own page
numbers, but was joined with the first work and printed in ongoing
signatures, proof that the two texts were composed together to make
one book.[40] This combination did not last. *Le Vagabond* was not reprinted in another Troyes edition in the eighteenth century, but the
*Entretien* was reprinted several times by the Oudots (by the widow of

[39] The copy in the BN, Paris, has signatures and pagination as follows: *Le Vagabond*,
8° a⁴ A-M⁸, [I-VI] 1-192; *Entretien des bonnes compagnies*, A-I⁸, 1-144.
[40] Bibliothèque Municipale, Troyes, Bibliothèque bleue 588 and 589: *Le Vagabond*
... *Ensemble l'Entretien des bonnes compagnies*, 8°, A⁴ B-L⁸; *Le Vagabond* [I-VI] 1-98,
*Entretien des bonnes compagnies* 1-74. The *Entretien* begins on leaf G⁴.

Nicolas II in 1716 and by the widow of Jacques and their son Jean) and by Pierre Garnier before being brought up to date and published by Baudot under the title *Sans-chagrin ou le Conteur amusant. Recueil de contes récréatifs*. The separate career of the *Entretien* and the abandonment of *Le Vagabond* in the eighteenth century show that this combination of texts under the cover of humor was not lastingly "new," doubtlessly because a text translated from the Italian (although not published as such)—a vehicle for themes two centuries out of date—resisted the entertaining and recreational cast with which the translator and the French publishers of the seventeenth century tried to endow it.

The entry of this work into the *Bibliothèque bleue* is easily explained: It presents, one after another, thirty-four classes of beggars and vagabonds, which echoes and amplifies the organization of *Le Jargon ou Langage de l'Argot réformé*. This theme is stated, more clearly than in the Italian original, in the very first chapter: "But we will see better the ruses and the advantages of our vagabonds in describing their sorts. There are various degrees of beggary just as there are of grandeur." This implicit reference to *Le Jargon*, presenting *Le Vagabond* as a work on the same subject but in a different key, is repeated on the following page. When he translated the expression, "il loro gran padre sacerdote di Cerete" (their great father, [the] priest of Ceres), Des Fontaines dropped the reference to Ceres' priest and invoked the kingdom of the beggars: "their great master (I fear they will be offended that I do not give him the august title of monarch)." The relation between *Le Jargon* and *Le Vagabond* goes further than their comparable overall organization, however, since a certain number of the "sects" among the vagabonds are similar to the "occupations" (*vacations*) of the beggars—thus the Sickly and the Ulcerous (*Accapponi*), the Jostlers and the Epileptics (*Accadenti*) or the Tremblers (*Attremanti*), the Rabid and the Bitten (*Attarantati*), the Converts and the Rebaptized (*Ribattezzati*), and the Scamps and the Rascals (*Coccini*). Even though he employed a different vocabulary, the translator of *Il Vagabondo*, like his publishers, probably was attempting to exploit the similarities between this work and *Le Jargon*, a proven bestseller.

Each chapter, except the last (on the storytellers, who by their very nature use artifice), presents one category of vagabonds. And each follows the same pattern: A label designating each type is given in French and Italian, often etymologically justified; then the activities and attributes of the type are listed; finally, one or more stories involving one or more of the impostors being discussed are told. This structure is close to that of the *Liber vagatorum*, which relates in the same way the definitions and exempla, then adds conclusions to guide the reader's charitable activities. Chapter 6 of *Le Vagabond*, "Des Encapuchonnés, ou des faux frères" (On the hooded ones, or false friars), can serve as an example of this organizational structure, even if all its elements are not necessarily found in the other chapters. At the outset, there is the designation and the etymology: "I style these vagabonds *Encapuchonnés* because they go throughout the world in the guise of monks and believe they make their idleness believable by hiding it under hoods, in imitation of the many great servants of God." Next comes a touch of Italian local color that sets the scene for the anecdotes and creates a picturesque distance: "The Tuscans call them *Affrati*, which is to say, false friars, or *frères Frapards*." Once they have been named, the *Encapuchonnés* are characterized by listing their "indignities": illicit celebration of the mass, illegitimate exercise of confession, collection of alms under fallacious pretexts, and false miracles. Next come four short tales. The first, which concerns the multiplication of eggs, is not given a precise setting, but the author authenticates it, saying he has heard it told "by persons worthy of belief." The second, about a sham announcement of the end of the world, is situated in Urbino. The third, in dialogue form, is presented as the confession of one of the *Encapuchonnés*, Tomaso de Valle ("You must know that we more easily fool those who profess to know the intrigues of our sect," and so forth). Finally, the author declares he has heard the last story, which concerns the unmasking of a false hermit in the diocese of Volterra by "several ecclesiastical doctors," from "an eyewitness." *Il vagabondo*, then, made use of the old formula of a classifying nomenclature as the framework for a collection of short stories, which are treated much more as humorous fables than as cautionary tales. It is perhaps this association of the taxonomy of *Le Jargon* and the tales of the *Buscon* that gave Des Fontaines's translation its entry into the Troyes catalogue.

Why then was it not kept in the catalogue like the *Entretien des bonnes compagnies*? First, the text clearly belongs to a learned literature that relies on erudite references, etymologies, and cultural allusions. This trait, already present in the Italian original, is even more pronounced in the translation. In the first chapter, "De l'origine des gueux vagabonds" (On the origin of vagabond beggars), for instance, Des Fontaines's translation contains many things not in contemporary Italian editions, and all the additions derive from more literate culture. There is a passage on a Pyrrhonian philosopher, an allusion to Homer, and sayings credited to Saint Augustine or to the beggar philosopher who spoke with Alexander the Great. Thus the text played on references and procedures (for example in its speculation on the origin of the word *Cerretani*) that were most probably alien to the better part of the usual readers of the "blue" volumes. This learned discourse formed a sort of screen between the tales to which it gave expression and the readers, rendering entertainment difficult. We can understand the preference for the *Entretien*, which strung together a series of witty sayings and amusing rejoinders without moralizing or a show of erudition.

On the other hand, censors and publishers at the height of the Catholic Reformation had every reason to be disquieted by *Le Vagabond* and its listing of a large number of religious deceptions. It is undeniable that Teseo Pini, and Frianoro–de Nobili after him, rooted their vagabonds' ruses in the improper use of religious institutions and the devious solicitation of credulous piety. Unlike *Le Jargon*, which for the most part treats sham infirmities, the nomenclature of *Il vagabondo* is by and large a listing of religious dupery. For that very reason, the text might confuse those unable to sense the clear borderline between the licit and the superstitious, the fake and the real, true belief and credulity. The French translator felt this danger and so redoubled his precautions and distinctions—to a much greater extent than had the Italian author—in order to unambiguously separate the "good religious" from the false and faith from superstition. This prompted him to add a number of commentaries on the original text. Thus in chapter 2, there is a defense of begging "for the honor of God" and of giving alms to the needy. Likewise, in chapter 6, the first paragraph underscores the radical difference between true monks and the hooded impostors who wore the same habit. This scrupulous care to avoid confusion between legitimate religion and the fraudulent activities it might inspire, however, was not enough to save the work.

We can suppose that the work was a victim of the same thinking that led to the censorship of the *Bibliothèque bleue* version of the *Buscón*. In fact, *Le Vagabond* parodies actions that are the very essence of religion. In chapter 6 alone there are bogus absolutions, water changed into wine, and a multiplication of eggs. To be sure, the text condemned such activities and denounced them as deceptions that honest people should guard against, but at the same time it dramatized them in tales written to make people laugh. This ambiguity, which also marks the foreword where we find two explanations of the text's purpose—the warning against deception but also the amusement for "some winter evening"—may well have seemed intolerable, for it transformed blasphemy and sacrilege into entertainment. The playful treatment of religious questions may have been accepted at the beginning of the century, but it was no longer acceptable when the Catholic Reformation imposed an unreserved respect for what it held most sacred.

## A RETURN TO THE BURLESQUE

After Nicolas II Oudot, who was always on the lookout for new burlesque texts, had published *L'Intrigue des Filous* (The Intrigue of Thieves) in 1661, it was printed in Troyes[41]—just like *Le Vagabond*—by Jacques Oudot (perhaps) for distribution by Antoine Raffle. *L'Intrigue* was a play written by Claude de l'Estoile that had been published in Lyons in 1644 and in Paris in 1648 before it entered the Troyes catalogue. If to some degree it deserves a place in the "literature of roguery," it is because several of the characters in the play are out and out scoundrels: three thieves, a fence, a woman seller of stolen goods, and a counterfeiter who for a time is taken for an upright citizen. Claude de l'Estoile, the youngest son of the chronicler, Pierre de l'Estoile, was by no means the first to introduce such shady characters to the stage. As early as the beginning of the century, authors of plays and ballets made wide use of this criminal cast of characters. In 1606, a *mascarade* at the fair of Saint-Germain had presented the farcical scene of a *mannequin* (a large puppet) giving birth to four astrologers and four painters, but also to four cutpurses. In 1653, ten years after l'Estoile's comedy was written, the fourteenth *entrée* of the *Ballet de la Nuit* by Benserade presented "the Court of Miracles, where all sorts of Beggars and Cripples go at night [and] emerge, healthy and hearty, to dance their *Entrée*, after which they sing a ridiculous serenade to the master of the house."[42] Thus both *mascarades* at fairs and court ballets, in which the king and courtiers danced, made use of such fascinating but terrifying criminal figures.

[41] Morin, *Catalogue descriptif*, nos. 650-51.
[42] See J. Silin, *Benserade and His Ballet de Cour* (Baltimore, 1940), 214-28.

L'Estoile's comedy incontestably belongs to the genre of court drama, since it was presented in Fontainebleau before the Queen Mother in 1647. The author's preface, dedicated to the Captain of the Watch of Paris, contrasts the stage thieves, for whom he begs the captain's protection, to the real ones, who would do well to fear his enforcement of the law. Fiction thus served as a warning here: "These are enemies unmasked, who, displaying their skills to the People and the Court, teach the Court and the People to prevent themselves from being deceived by them." Above all, however, the fiction was presented as entertainment: "The terms in which they express their thoughts are grotesque, the way they trap the smartest [people] is even more so, and the fence who serves them is not mad, but he is hardly less comic than if he were so." Thus comic theater and court ballet made inoffensive buffoonery of figures who in real life were dangerous people, criminal or insane (Claude de l'Estoile also wrote a *Ballet des fous* [Ballet of the mad], now lost). There were two reasons for the success of works with underworld characters. First, social fears could be defused by turning them into laughter, even though such fears were put on view in grotesque form. And second, putting beggars and thieves on the stage in a court *divertissement* was a way to present one of the most popular forms of burlesque—the presentation of low subject matter and vulgar characters—in a noble genre (here, as court ballet or verse comedy). If we can believe the letter that one of l'Estoile's friends wrote him shortly after the 1647 performance, the comedy's reception conformed with this dual intent on both the psychological and the literary levels. The friend wrote:

> You must indeed be an enemy to your own glory, since you did not come last Thursday to Fontainebleau. You were afraid of being upset by the clapping of hands, the noise of which, however loudly it rises, always charms the heart. The handsome words you put in the mouths of your thieves, as they unveiled their artifices, taught us to defend ourselves, and [here] in a region of forests and rocks we saw them close at hand with no danger. They did us no greater harm than to oblige us to love our enemies, so much pleasure did they give us.[43]

[43] Cited from E. Fournier, *Le Théâtre français au XVIᵉ et au XVIIᵉ siècle* (Paris, 1874), 524.

The inclusion of this comedy in the Troyes repertory enlarged the audience for the work and made it available to the habitual public, Parisian for the most part, of the *Bibliothèque bleue*. L'Estoile inserted the play's riffraff, who provided a picturesque element, into a classical plot based on the difficult course of a love affair (Florinde's love for Lucidor). A series of confusions and mistaken identities ensues when Clarisse, Florinde's confidant, mislays Florinde's portrait, but a happy ending is reached after Lucidor's rival has been recognized as a counterfeiter. The originality of this work—and what made it merit reprinting in Troyes—does not lie in the plot but in the roles of the three thieves: Le Balafré, Le Borgne, and Le Bras-de-Fer (Scarface, One-Eye, and Iron-Arm). They appear only intermittently on stage (not at all in act 2 and only in the last scene of act 3) and seem more an afterthought in the plot than a necessity, but they introduce two sorts of comic effects. The first derives from the use of a humorous language that borrows from several burlesque vocabularies, for the most part from "argot" (or terms given as argot). Thus we have *jouer de la harpe* (play grab-and-run), *jouer du couteau* (use knife-play), *filer la laine* (hold up people for their clothing), *se barbouiller l'armet* (to worry your head about something), to be *rond comme une boule* (drunk as lords [literally, round as a ball]), *battre aux champs* (hit the road), *branle de sortie* (give the boot to), *moule en pourpoint* (belly; body), *engueule-bouteille* (bottle-guzzler), and so forth. I might note that this argot has no relation to the language of the *Argotiers* in *Le Jargon* and that for the most part it relies on a picturesque and image-oriented colloquial language with a broad use of coarse terms and proverbs—hence its appropriateness to ruffians and outlaws.

The second sort of comic effect emerges from the dramatization of the life of the thieves. In act 1, scene 1, for example, the three thieves complain about the fence: "There is no faith among fences; they are tricksters, evil men, and they rob the robbers." Act 4, scenes 4 and 5, give another example: Le Balafré, Le Bras-de-Fer, and Le Borgne, lying in wait at a street corner, "filent la laine" (leap out and cry "Your money or your life"), but then recognize their victim as the fence, Béronte. At his suggestion, they decide to burgle the house of Clorinde's mother, Olympe, the widow of a money-changer. This brings up the subjects of thieves' lore (how to put a guard dog to sleep with an "admirable drug"), their *engins* (tools) and *instruments* ("We will bring some to file the ironwork, and passkeys that open all locks"), and their strategy ("And then like wolves we will lope back to our ambush to see who goes, who comes, and both stand watch"). The high point in this portrayal of criminal activity occurs in the first two scenes of the last act. As l'Estoile writes in his preface, "Stealing in secret was permitted in Lacedaemon, but here they are permitted to steal in public." The play here deals with two motifs. The first is immediate, visible, and "real" and concerns the preparations for the theft: "Are our tools ready? Here is all we need—lockpicks, passkey, muffled file, pliers, and many other tools our hands work with." The second motif concerns the punishment of thieves, and it enters the text as remembered experience (in Béronte's case) or as a premonition of fate (by Le Borgne). There is, first, the pillory ("I was not yet fifteen when the theft of a coat led to their tying my back to a post, where, my neck in irons and my feet in the mud, I glared at the passers-by for some time"). There are also mentions of branding with a red-hot iron ("the king's mark"), the scaffold, the question, and the wheel ("This blow received, our broken limbs, exposed on some major road, are the horror of passers-by and the target of storms; they serve as an example to the people and as food for wild beasts"). Thanks to Lucidor's courage, the attempted burglary fails, and Olympe, her eyes opened, grants him her daughter's hand.

Even though the thieves appeared in l'Estoile's comedy only to wind up the plot, it was received as a play about the criminal underworld. The innovation it brought was that it gave people something to see or read about that concerned the stratagems of real robbers, burglars, and highwaymen, not just the tricks of false beggars, as in *Le Jargon* or *Le Vagabond*.[44] Although the activities of the cutpurses are treated comically and the thieves are totally defeated when Lucidor intervenes, they are still presented as dangers not only to goods but also to people. Le Balafré boasts, "And anyone who comes to grab me by the collar will see himself greeted with a pistol shot," and Le Borgne adds, "The barber's [surgeon's] pity is cruel to the wounded man; and that of the thief is cruel to himself and often plunges him into highest misfortune. We never leave witnesses to our crimes [since] we are pursued too energetically." This is why the many beggars and thieves who appear in these ballets and comic plays should be understood as the "grotesque" (a

---

[44] See also J. L. Alonso Hernández, "Le Monde des voleurs dans la littérature espagnole des XVIe et XVIIe siècles," in J. L. Alonso Hernández et al., *Culture et marginalité au XVIe siècle* (Paris, 1973), 11–40.

word that appears often in l'Estoile) caricatures of well-founded fears and were inseparable from the measures taken to purge the city of its "dangerous classes." When the police spoke of such criminals, they used terms much like the ones that described the entertaining characters in the literature of roguery. Evidence of this can be seen in the deliberations of the Conseil called by Colbert in 1666 and 1667 to reform the police, at which the chancellor, Pierre Séguier, declared, "cutpurses are joined into a corps in Paris; they have officers and respect a degree of discipline among themselves." The lieutenant charged with criminal matters at the Châtelet (court of royal justice and police headquarters) added, "they have much correspondence among them."[45]

Putting robbers and robbery on the stage was, moreover, a good way to inject new life into the satirical formulas. Often these jokes were at the expense of those who went along with thieves ("But let the Provost watch out. We run few risks. Surrounded by knights errant, he takes the petty thieves and lets the big ones go") or even their social superiors, for example the *partisans* (tax farmers): "There is a woman, the widow of a *partisan* who stole in one day more than you in a year, and who, thanks to a tax he had imposed on the grape harvest, made their house into a second Pont-au-Change. Could one pile up more goods on top of each other? Everything is of silver, even the chamber pots." This passage belongs totally to the burlesque tradition, and it contains notions that the Troyes publisher of the French translation of the *Buscón* felt it necessary to cut. The play also has strongly worded descriptions of torture and of exposed and broken bodies as well as the figure of the *entremetteuse* (go-between), who resells stolen goods, arranges rendezvous, and runs a "maison de joie" (brothel). Why did the character of Ragonde (and thus the play itself) find a place in the catalogue of the *Bibliothèque bleue* at the same time Quevedo's novel was so severely mutilated? There are perhaps two reasons for this. First, l'Estoile's text stays within the boundaries of prudence, and Ragonde is only a procuress in the deluded mind of Béronte, who wrongly believes "that she sells fewer suits than girls." Furthermore, the very form of a comic play in verse, like its vocabulary, which steers clear of any sexual crudity, euphemizes a theme that was otherwise judged intolerable in publications destined for wide circulation. In spite of this, however, the play

---

[45] BN, Paris, MS français 8118, fols. 114-15.

did not have a successful career in the *Bibliothèque bleue* catalogue, and the edition printed for Raffle was the last Troyes printing of the work.

## Toward a New Stock Character:
### "The Noble Robber"

The last of the texts in the six under consideration had a more brilliant success. The *Histoire de la vie, grandes voleries et subtilités de Guilleri, et de ses compagnons et de leur fin lamentable et malheureuse* (History of the life, great thefts, and wiles of Guilleri and his companions and their lamentable and unfortunate end) went through many editions during the eighteenth century under two different permissions. The first, given in Paris on 1 July 1718, covered an edition put out by the widow of Jean Oudot, with an approval dated 26 June 1716, and another by the widow of Nicolas Oudot, with an approval of 22 June 1718. The latter bears a slightly different title, substituting *voleurs* (thieves) in general for Guilleri. The second permission, given in Troyes (on 12 August 1728, with an approval of 7 August 1728), covered the various editions put out by Étienne and Jean-Antoine Garnier.[46] The book was still popular at the turn of the nineteenth century: It was republished in Caen by the Chalopins under a made-up address, "à Lelis chez Goderfe, rue de Nemenya," that was also used by Deforges, a bookseller of Sillé-le-Guillaume whose books were printed in Le Mans.[47] It was also republished in Troyes by Baudot, who reproduced Jean-Antoine Garnier's edition with a new pink cover.

When it entered the corpus of "blue" volumes, Guilleri's story already had had a long and varied career in print. Behind it stood attested historical fact: the criminal activities of a band of robbers under the leadership of the Guilleri brothers who plundered Poitou between 1602 and 1608. The most informative document on their exploits is probably a *mémoire* written by André Le Geai, the Sieur de La Gestière and Provost of Poitou at the time, requesting reimbursement for the expenses he had incurred in the pursuit and capture of the Guilleris

---

[46] Morin, *Catalogue descriptif*, nos. 516-20.

[47] A. Sauvy, "La Librairie Chalopin. Livres et livrets de colportage à Caen au début du XIX^e siècle," *Bulletin d'Histoire Moderne et Contemporaine* 11 (Paris: Bibliothèque Nationale, 1978), 95-140.

and their henchmen.[48] This text describes the band's activities: "The said robbers broke into the houses of gentlemen and others, robbed on the highroads to the royal fairs at Fontenay and Niort, extorted ransom from merchants and rich peasants, [and] taxed them sums of *deniers* that they forced them to pay [out] of fear of being killed." It also relates the various confrontations between the bandits and the royal troops commanded by the Sieur de La Gestière and the Count of Parabère, the lieutenant general for Haut-Poitou, and lists both the robbers hanged and the archers wounded or killed. In 1606 a younger Guilleri brother, "young Mathurin," was taken prisoner and broken on the wheel in Nantes. Two years later, Philippe Guilleri, who had retired to Gascony as a wine merchant, was denounced by "someone named Crongné," was captured near Bazas, and was broken on the wheel at La Rochelle "for the aforementioned murders, robberies, and ransomings." At the end of his *mémoire*, the Provost of Poitou lists his expenses for "these chases, voyages, captures, and judgments of the said robbers," which amounted to 7,000-8,000 *livres* for his own expenses, 12,000-15,000 *livres* for the horses, and 3,000-4,000 *livres* for the upkeep of his archers from July 1604 to March 1606 and for the fee paid to the informer.

This historical episode gave rise to a series of texts dramatizing the exploits of the Guilleris and their companions. Two *occasionnels* (sixteen-page pamphlets) that attempted to capitalize on the newsworthiness of the elder Guilleri's trial in 1608 lie at the base of the tradition, but they have different titles and seemingly refer to two separate events. The first, printed by Jean de Marnef in Poitiers, is entitled *La Prinse et lamentable desfaite du Cadet Guillery lequel a esté prins avec quatre vingt de ses compagnons auprès de Talmon et roué à Nantes le 13 mars 1608. Avec la complainte qu'il a fait avant que mourir*. The second, which was printed twice in Paris in 1609 (once at the address of Abraham de Meaux), was "jouxte la copie imprimée à La Rochelle pour les héritiers de Jerosme Hautain" (in conformity with the edition printed at La Rochelle by the heirs of Jerosme Hautain) and was entitled *La Prinse et défaicte du capitaine Guillery qui a esté prins avec soixante et deux voleurs de ses compagnons qui ont esté rouez en la ville de La Rochelle le*

---

[48] A. de Barthélemy, "Les Guillery, 1604-1608," *Revue de Bretagne et de Vendée*, 2d ser., 6, no. 2 (1862):126-33. See also Vicomte X. de Bellevue, *Les Guillery, célèbres brigands bretons (1601-1608)* (Vannes, 1891).

*25 Novembre 1608. Avec la complainte qu'il a faicte avant que mourir.*[49] In point of fact, except for a few short cuts in the Paris editions, the text is the same, relating three or four "subtle inventions" of Guilleri, then his capture, his torture, and his last words before his death. The 1609 *occasionnels* differ from La Gestière's account in two ways. First, Guilleri is called the "younger son of a great house of Brittany (the name of which I will not report, for fear of offending someone)," instead of the son of a mason. Further, the fate of the two brothers is inextricably confused. In both the Poitiers *occasionnel* and the one printed by Abraham de Meaux, it is "the younger Guillery" who is captured and broken on the wheel—at Nantes according to Marnef, at Saintes for de Meaux— whereas in the other Paris edition of 1609 it is Captain Guilleri himself who is broken, and at La Rochelle. The latter was more in conformity with what actually happened, since it was Philippe, the elder of the brothers, who was tortured at La Rochelle in 1608.

Other texts' reliance on these *occasionnels* is incontestable. Pierre de l'Estoile, who reported the torture of Guilleri in his journal, followed the Paris *occasionnels* closely, copying from them liberally. Other elements found in the *occasionnels* and in l'Estoile's journal are the signs that the Guilleris posted "along the roads," in which "they made it known that they wanted the lives of the Men of the Law, money, pillage, and ransom from Gentlemen."[50] Also in both the *occasionnels* and the journal are: the king's order to capture them, the siege of the bandits' stronghold, the capture of Guilleri and eighty of his men, and his torture at Saintes and that of his companions "in various jurisdictions."[51] Another indication of the popularity of Guilleri's story was a brief *libelle* (pamphlet) printed by Antoine du Breuil in 1615 that attacked the princes who had revolted against royal authority at Condé's instigation. The pamphlet, which bore the title *Reproches du capitaine Guillery faicts aux Carabins, picoreurs et pillards de l'armée de Messieurs les Princes*, assails the exactions of the troops levied by the princes, making use of the hero and some portions of the text of the *occasionnels* about Guilleri.[52] The polemic of the *libelle* is simply organized: For

[49] These *occasionnels* can be found in the BN, Paris, under the catalogue numbers Res G 2873 (Marnef), Ln[27] 9354 A (Abraham de Meaux) and Ln[27] 9354 B.

[50] *La Prinse et défaicte* (de Meaux ed.), 10.

[51] *Mémoire et Journal de Pierre de l'Estoile*, in J. F. Michaud and J.J.F. Poujoulat, *Nouvelle collection des Mémoires pour servir à l'histoire de France*, 2d ser. (Paris, 1837), 1:475.

[52] BN, Paris, Lb[36] 570. On the pamphlet literature for and against Condé, see D. Richet, "La Polémique politique en France de 1612 à 1615," in *Représentation et vouloir*

each of the ten episodes drawn from the life of the bandit (and introduced by such formulas as "When Guillery I was . . ." or "For all that
I was Guillery . . ."), there is a corresponding denunciation of the
princes' soldiers as cowards, thieves, and murderers.

The figure of Guilleri takes on a new image in this presentation. In
the *occasionnels*, the robber is portrayed in a fairly bad light: "He advances his murderous hand on the passer-by and [assuages] his desires
in pillage." The Poitiers version declares its intention to relate only
"one or two deeds of his wickedness and of his subtle inventions, which
served him so well in finding ways to snatch the money of the poor
people who fell into his nets." Only the *complainte* of the tortured bri-
gand facing death redeems him by spelling out the moral of his tale:
"The best natures can be corrupted, like mine, which, letting itself be
flattered by the persuasions of my brother, whom despair had wrapped
in its veils, also let itself be swept into a debauchery that now makes my
hair stand on end when I contemplate my error." Repentant and constant under chastisement, Guilleri was supposed to deter others from
crime: "Since I must here serve as an example, in order to bridle the
courage of those who might want to become attached to the disorders
that enveloped me, may it please [God] to open the gate to his Paradise
to my soul."

In the 1615 pamphlet, Guilleri remains a bandit, but he is infinitely
less criminal than the princes' soldiers of fortune. Furthermore, he is
portrayed quite differently. The author emphasizes his courage and
loyalty as a soldier in the service of the Duke of Mercoeur, excuses his
crimes as due to the despair of a forced retreat, and underscores his humanity toward his victims. The character thus sketched is a generous
bandit, an enemy of murder, merciful in his robberies, and quick to aid
the unfortunate: "When I found someone on the roads . . . if I found
he did not have enough money to complete his voyage, I gave him some
of mine; if he had more than he needed to reach his destination, we
counted it and shared it out like brothers, and when that was done, I
let him go without doing him any harm or injury." Thus as early as the
beginning of the seventeenth century, soon after the execution of the
"real" Guilleri, the texts tell two differently formulated versions of his
story: one that paints him as terrible and redeemed only by his ultimate

*politiques. Autour des États Généraux de 1614*, ed. R. Chartier and D. Richet (Paris,
1982).

remorse and courage during the trial, and the other that outlines, with polemic intent, the figure of a "conscientious, faithful, and approachable" robber whose crimes are nothing compared to the cruel deeds of the princes' soldiers.

Literature at first chose the first of these images. It was a cruel and detestable Guilleri whom François de Calvi portrayed in his *Inventaire général de l'histoire des Larrons. Où sont contenus leurs stratagèmes, tromperies, supplices, vols, assassinats et généralement ce qu'ils ont fait de plus mémorables en France*, published in Rouen in 1633. This sizable anthology aimed both to protect the public by outlining the robbers' methods and to show their "most tragic acts" and "bloodiest councils." At the beginning of book 2, Calvi inserted three chapters on the tragic life of Captain Lycaon that repeat the subject matter of the *occasionnels* on Guilleri, sometimes even using the same phrases. The narrative recalls the "noble relatives" of the bandit and his courage in the service of the Duke of Mercure (Mercoeur), but from the outset it emphasizes his inclination to evil: "Everyone said that this was not a man, but rather a monster that Hell had vomited up from the depths of its abysses to make him commit one day an infinite number of robberies and brigandages." When he becomes chief of the band, Lycaon-Guilleri commits one cruel act after another: His troops "spared the life of not one of those whom they happened to meet and who they thought had money"; seven archers, stripped of their clothing, are hanged on the branches of trees, still wearing their hats, "a hideous spectacle to see"; and the hangman, who they meet near Pontoise, is ill treated and "attached with a garter to the branches of a tree, where they put him to death." Lycaon is a sorcerer as well as a murderer. This trait was already present in the *occasionnels*, where "he had a familiar spirit, by whom he had himself carried in no time at all wherever he wanted to go," but it is accentuated here: "He was thought to be a sorcerer," "he had a familiar spirit with him." Moreover, the band's robberies and murders arouse the anger of the people, who are as delighted with the capture and death of Lycaon's brother—"broken on the wheel in view of all the nobility of the countryside, and to the great contentment of all the people, who wished a thousand times more for him"—as they are with his own death: "It is impossible to relate how joyously all the neighboring Provinces received news of this execution, for one might say that a monster such as this had never before been seen." As in the *occasionnels*, only his end redeems him: "He died with admirable constancy, and no heart—although all were unanimously against him—failed to be touched with pity at seeing his resolution before death and [hearing] the beautiful words he spoke before breathing his last. This teaches us that a good beginning is not all; one must also end well."

Calvi took the *occasionnels* of the beginning of the century as the framework for his narrative, but he transformed the name of the evil protagonist and added several episodes (the archers stripped and hanged, the meeting with the Provost of Rouen, the murder of the hangman of Pontoise). Furthermore, he constantly bolsters his narrative with mythological comparisons and references to classical antiquity, which give the text a literary dignity that the occasional pamphlets lack. In so doing, he plays on the amusing contrast between the criminal adventures of Lycaon and the nobility of the ancient heroes with whom he is compared. It was not in this somber but learned version of the Guilleri story that the Troyes publishers found what they were looking for. Their text lay elsewhere, in one of the many sequels and republishings of a work by François de Rosset, a poet, translator, and compiler: *Les Histoires tragiques de nostre temps. Où sont contenues les morts funestes et lamentables de plusieurs personnes, arrivées par leurs ambitions, amours déréglées, sortilèges, vols, rapines, et par autres accidents divers et mémorables.*

In 1623 a Lyons edition of this work, which had first been printed in 1614, added a new story to the text in chapter 19, "Des grandes voleries et subtilitez de Guilleri, et de sa fin lamentable." Here Rosset adapted Guilleri's story in ways compatible with the expectations of the *Bibliothèque bleue* readers (or at least as the publishers saw them) by stripping the tale of all its antique paraphernalia, limiting the story to a few (abridged) episodes, and adding a conclusion closer to historical reality, since it tells of Guilleri's retirement. From this point on, the text led a double life in print. On the one hand, it was often republished as a part of the *Histoires mémorables et tragiques de ce temps*, which was reprinted in Lyons in 1662 and 1685, in Rouen in 1700, and again in Lyons in 1701 and 1721.[53] On the other hand, it entered the "blue" catalogue by itself, where it met with continued success up to the nineteenth century. There are only minimal differences between the texts of the Troyes editions and the *Histoires mémorables*, and these are limited to

---

[53] *Des grandes voleries et subtilités de Guilleri* can be found on pp. 356-79 of the Lyons edition of 1662 and on pp. 349-79 of the Rouen edition of 1700.

stylistic adjustments: the elimination of difficult or antiquated expressions, the simplification of the writing by abridging the tale and tightening the sentences, and the omission of relative clauses and adjectives. The only formal difference of importance concerns how the text is divided. The Troyes editor created ten chapters (nothing like Rosset), of which only the last, "Comment Guilleri devint amoureux" (How Guilleri fell in love), runs to any length. The tale is thus clearly broken up into a series of short sketches, each telling a brief adventure, that lend themselves to episodic readings. The Troyes editions also broke the text up into more paragraphs than in previous editions of the tale. The Rouen edition of 1700 by Antoine Le Prévost, for example, divides the story into twenty-two paragraphs, and the edition of Nicolas Oudot's widow has thirty-seven paragraphs. Less densely printed, the text was thus more accessible.

The *Guilleri* of the *Bibliothèque bleue*, which was based on Rosset's version, represents a turning point in the history of the stock characters of the literature of roguery. It borrowed time-honored formulas that go back, for example, to *La Vie généreuse*. Indeed, it is a biography (although not an autobiography), in which the adventures are set in a particular locality—the same region, by the way, as the one haunted by Pechon de Ruby. Like Pechon, Guilleri is a Breton gentleman; like him, he ranges over the region around Niort, Fontenay-le-Comte, and La Rochelle before he retires to Saint-Justin, "a town removed from the world" in the wilds of the Landes, and is then imprisoned in Royan. Also like Pechon, Guilleri relies on a number of ruses the author refers to as *subtilités*. Other elements common to the two texts are their brevity and their division into extremely short chapters. The author speaks of the need for such brevity three times: "If I wanted to describe all the evil deeds that he did during the nine or ten years that he led such an execrable life, I would need a fat volume, instead of which I intend to write only a short story. I will thus be content to recite briefly the most remarkable *subtilités* that he perpetrated during the time he led the life of a robber"; or, "If I wanted to go on describing the ruses and *subtilités* that he did during the time he led the life of a robber, I would need an entire volume, and not the abridged one to which I obliged myself at the start"; or, later, "I will be content with what I have written of his life, so as not to be too prolix." These excuses, which recall those with which *La Vie généreuse* closes, place the book within the tradition of joking tales, short works that were easy to read and easily deciphered by those who would find too long a text discouraging.

The work is composed, then, along the lines of much older books that were present when the Troyes catalogue was founded. It also makes use of the techniques of burlesque literature, in particular of disguises and recognitions, just as in *L'Intrigue des Filous*. Thus Guilleri "disguises himself in the garb of a messenger," is "dressed as a hermit," and is then "disguised as a gentleman." In contrast, he is unmasked twice, by a merchant from Bordeaux during his retirement in Saint-Justin and by a merchant from Saintes on the boat taking him to Rochefort. By thus contrasting disguises with discoveries, the story also gives the hero successive fortune and misfortune. Just as Guilleri's robberies have assured him glory and money, he is struck by the death of his brother, and just as he has chosen the path of upright living, he is recognized and denounced by one of his former victims. Twice the author underlines this chaotic element in human destiny: "Then, since good fortune had always shown him her smiling face, she wanted to let him see a turn of her habitual inconstance"; and "He was bathing in his delights, believing that no one would know him, but the miserable man did not consider that God knew all his secrets." Thus burlesque techniques were linked to a moral judgment of inconstant fortune, since it is under the appearance of honesty that Guilleri fools everyone, and, in contrast, he is recognized as a robber when he no longer is one.

But the novelty of *Guilleri* lies elsewhere: It is the first text in which a new stock figure, the generous bandit (later to find its full incarnation in Cartouche and Mandrin), made its appearance in the *Bibliothèque bleue*. All the various traits held to be characteristic of the "noble robber" in the collective imagination of preindustrial societies, as outlined by Eric J. Hobsbawm,[54] apply perfectly to Guilleri in this short tale:

> 1. The noble robber is not a criminal at the outset. Guilleri, who is of noble extraction, is "forced" into banditry by the demobilization of the army levied by Henry IV against the Duke of Savoy. He thus loses a chance to make amends for his turbulent youth as a student, and, given his "little revenue," peace compels him "to choose another expedient to earn [his] miserable living."

[54] E. J. Hobsbawm, *Bandits* (New York, 1969), 35-36.

2. He rights wrongs and takes from the rich to give to the poor: "To those he met who had no money, he gave some, and to those who had some, he took half." Guilleri thus redistributes wealth, substituting himself for the rich who fail to fulfill their charitable responsibilities.

3. He is not an enemy of the king, but of local oppressors. In this book, Guilleri never appears in rebellion against the sovereign (nevertheless, the indirect cause of his indigence), whose fury is qualified as "just." All of Guilleri's victims are men who dominate and often exploit the common people. Thus a rich peasant who hides his wealth is held up and stripped of all he has, the provosts and their archers are made to look ridiculous, and the city merchants are plundered. Thus also the robber is in turn robbed and those who thought to take prisoners are themselves captured.

4. He kills only in self-defense: "He hated murderers, and if any of his people had committed some murder, he punished them severely." The "subtleties" of Guilleri always leave his victims with their lives and, more often than not, with their purse as well. The peasant is robbed of only half his wealth, the archers are tied to trees "without doing them any other harm" and then released, and Guilleri makes his men "give back all that belonged to them." Mockery is more important here than robbery, and criminal activity is above all the derision of usurped authority or ill-gotten gain. This is why the narrator usually speaks of a crime without reprobation, emphasizing the ingeniousness of the ruses or the "subtlety" of the tricks.

5. He becomes a respected member of the community. Converted to the upright life, Guilleri marries a rich widow, is "raised to one of the highest degrees of fortune," and enjoys his marriage and retirement to his château. Here, however, Guilleri differs slightly from the canonical portrait of the social bandit: Having left the scenes of his youth never to return, it is by hiding his past life that he spends his happiest days.

6. He is invisible and invulnerable. The provosts and their archers are powerless to harm Guilleri, both during his career as a robber and after they surprise him in his château:

"He ran off to the thickest part of the wood, and it was impossible to take him." As is often the case, this invulnerability is considered of magical origin, but the Troyes text prudently underplays this notion, which might alarm religious orthodoxy: "Some claim that he had a familiar spirit who guided him in his enterprises; I will leave judgment on the matter to their discretion and will remain silent on this point."

7. He dies only through betrayal. Here the merchant from Saintes and the Provost of La Rochelle, intent on revenge for, respectively, a robbery of 80 *écus* and a trick played on him, surprise a trusting Guilleri, who then confesses his crimes and is "broken alive in punishment for his robberies."

This work paints a portrait of Guilleri that emphasizes his moral qualities: He is courageous, generous, liberal, courteous, and gifted with "beautiful qualities" and "rare perfections." Somewhat like the French version of Buscón, who returns to his true identity at the end of the novel, Guilleri's life after his retirement and marriage fulfills the early promises of his character and mind. Morality demanded that he be punished, however, and that he expiate his crimes by his execution. It is here that the book betrays internal tensions. On the one hand, it offers a "positive" picture of a social bandit and elicits sympathy and compassion from the reader; but on the other, it is obliged to teach the moral lesson of just punishment for crimes committed. This explains the inclusion of a series of traits that are not part of the normal image of the "noble robber." Overwhelmed by the death of his brother, Guilleri hopes to change his life, and so acknowledges the sinfulness and guilt of the life he has led: "He dreamed only of retiring to some unknown place to spend the rest of his days in the fear of God." As his discourse to his companions shows, moreover, God's punishment, like the king's punishment, is legitimate in his eyes, and the sinner must accept it—as Guilleri does after his capture: "I see that God wants to punish me for my errors."

*Guilleri* thus has an ambiguous status. The work was built upon themes that it shared with the *occasionnels*, but it also anticipated the books and pamphlets devoted to Cartouche and Mandrin. It used motifs that were present in the popular imagination to fashion the character of a beloved and admired social bandit, which, in the form of an amusing biography, assured it a place among the works destined for a wide public. This character, often attested in the oral traditions and collective memory of traditional societies, gave rise to a wealth of poems and ballads, and in Guilleri it found its first incarnation in the catalogue of the *Bibliothèque bleue*. But it found that place and that incarnation during an age and in a form subject to the strict control of Christian morality. The book was thus obliged to turn its readers away from evil, to teach that punishment was ineluctable, and to encourage a life different from Guilleri's. This explains the unevenness of a text that both lauds and censures its hero, that sympathizes with his tribulations yet celebrates his punishment, and that humorously presents his "subtle" robbing techniques but then holds them as culpable behavior. The theme of the social bandit is thus forced to come to terms with a morality of respect for order and obedience to law, such that the admired hero is at the same time a sinner to be punished. The book's last words speak to the combination of compassion and severity that this figure should inspire: "Thus we see the end of this unfortunate robber, who thought to avoid the just chastisement of God by his flight," and Rosset adds, "but in the end he had to pay the penalty for his wrongdoing." A contradictory text, *Guilleri* clearly illustrates how themes that sprang from popular culture could be reformulated and reinterpreted by those who gave them written form and then returned them, transformed, to the common people.

## ROGUERY: SOME CHARACTERS AND SOME READINGS

Undeniably, the *Bibliothèque bleue* books on *gueuserie* had an immensely successful career. Their prices, often ridiculously low, were a primary reason for this. At the end of the eighteenth century, Lecrêne-Labbey in Rouen sold the *Guilleri* to booksellers and peddlers for 12 *sous* for a dozen copies, *Le Jargon* for 15 *sous* a dozen, and the *Buscon*, more expensive because it was a larger book, at 3 *livres*, 12 *sous* the dozen.[55] The account books of the Caen bookseller Chalopin attest to the size of the stocks and the regularity of the sales of books on roguery thirty or forty years later. Around 1820, Chalopin had in stock 4,500 copies of *Le Jargon*, which he sold for 30 *centimes* each. In 1822, he had

---

[55] Hélot, *La Bibliothèque bleue en Normandie*.

3,400 copies, in 1825, 3,300, and around 1829, 2,700. The *Dictionnaire argotique* or, more accurately, the *Supplément* published under the imaginary address, "A la Vergne chez Mesière," was just as popular: Chalopin had 3,068 copies in stock around 1820, 2,468 two years later, and 1,900 around 1829.[56] These examples, which concern only one provincial distributor of the "blue" books, should suffice to demonstrate the steady demand for books on argot and on the beggars' kingdom. How are we to understand the attraction of works that offered disquieting but entertaining deceivers of all sorts among a public that was large as early as the seventeenth century and probably even larger later?

Two collective experiences seem to lie behind this success, both of which created a fearful but fascinated interest in people living outside society's rules and at the expense of others. The first of these experiences was urban life, and it took root at the turn of the seventeenth century when consciences began to be troubled by what was held to be an extraordinary increase in the number of beggars and vagrants in the cities.[57] Texts proliferated that denounced the invasion of the cities—and particularly the biggest city, Paris—by itinerant beggars. The authorities and leading citizens amassed horrified descriptions of the typical refuges of these rootless people, who came to the city to beg or to steal: the *faubourgs* just beyond the city gates and ramparts or the courtyards, alleys, and dead ends that abounded in medieval cities and that provided lairs for *larrons de nuit* (thieves of the night), as one *mémoire* of 1595 called them. In the capital, one of these concentrations of indigents struck imaginations more than all the others: "The place vulgarly called Court of Miracles, behind the Filles-Dieu, at the foot of a rampart between the Porte Saint-Denis and Montmartre." Documented from the beginning of the seventeenth century, this *cour des miracles* first figures as a topographical designation in the Gomboust map of 1652. It probably dates, however, from the last decades of the sixteenth century, not, as Victor Hugo would have us believe, from the end of the Middle Ages. These many pockets of beggars and ruffians within the city, which put honest citizens in close proximity with rogues and criminals and created a certain familiarity between the groups, were certainly perceived as an intolerable threat to the security

56 Sauvy, "La Librairie Chalopin," 126 (n. 45) and 129 (n. 61).

57 R. Chartier, "La 'Monarchie d'Argot' entre le mythe et l'histoire," in *Les Marginaux et les exclus dans l'histoire* (Paris, 1979), 275-311.

and moral health of the city. They were also seen, however, as pools of picturesque characters whose immorality was reprehensible but attractive and whose ruses were found captivating.

This first social experience created a demand for books that brought these figures to the forefront but that also toned down their real features. A second and rural experience may help to explain the continued success of the dictionaries of argot. Such works were always presented as keys to the peddlers' language, and we must not forget that in the nineteenth century the title, *Le Jargon ou Langage de l'Argot réformé*, exchanged its former subtitle, *comme il est à présent en usage parmi les bons pauvres* (as it is now in use among the worthy poor), for a new one, *à l'usage des merciers, porte-balles et autres* (as used by notions sellers, pack-carriers, and others). This substitution clearly shows that both the figure and the language of the peddler disconcerted but intrigued people. For the rural readers of the "blue" books, the notions seller was a dangerous con man, but also an amusing and wily figure. Half merchant and half thief, the *porte-balle* took advantage of his clients' good faith, but his wit and skill usually made them forgive his guile. This ambivalence is reflected in the literary tradition from the sixteenth century on and can also be found in the tales on peddlers' reputed craftiness collected during the nineteenth century and still in circulation.[58] To decipher their secret language could be considered revenge for their ruses and clever tricks; thus *Le Jargon* helped the fooled become the fooler. This undoubtedly contributed to the success, which continued into the eighteenth and nineteenth centuries, of a book that gave the illusion of a more equal match between the itinerant peddler and the sedentary communities he served.

In order to satisfy the demand created when urban and rural readers of the *Bibliothèque bleue* discovered such marginal figures, the Troyes printing houses made use of a repertory of texts that seemed to them the most apt to nourish their readers' imaginations. The result was a mélange of French works and translations, first editions and republished texts, the picaresque and the burlesque, biographical tales and taxonomies. As was their habit, the Oudots and Garniers used texts that were available; at the most, they revised them either to avoid re-

[58] E. Besson, "Les Colporteurs de l'Oisans au xix^e siècle. Témoignages et documents," *Le Monde alpin et rhodanien* 1-2 (1975):7-55, in particular pp. 38-39. On peddlers, see L. Fontaine, *Le Voyage et la mémoire: Colporteurs de l'Oisans au XIX^e siècle* (Lyons, 1985).

ligious censorship or to render them more readable to a public they knew to be relatively unfamiliar with books. The literature of roguery thus serves as evidence to corroborate the notion that the *Bibliothèque bleue* was not a series of texts proper only to a culture that can be designated as "popular";[59] rather, it was above all a publishing formula quick to make use (with some reworking) of all written material that appeared to satisfy a widespread demand.[60]

When common social experiences were transformed into the stock figures of literature, it was possible for the books on beggars and rogues to be evaluated as literal truth, etching motifs into the imaginations of the dominant classes that were taken for real. There is perhaps no better proof of this than the description Henri Sauval put in his *Histoire et recherches des Antiquités de la ville de Paris* (1724).[61] In a chapter on the "Cour des Miracles" (volume 1, book 5), Sauval describes what he himself had seen on visiting this place after it had been emptied of its customary inhabitants by the lieutenant of the city police, La Reynie. He then recounts the better days of the community of beggars and rogues by citing *Le Jargon ou Langage de l'Argot réformé*, which thus takes on the status of an objective description of a past reality still present. Sauval took from *Le Jargon* its basic theme of the kingdom of Argot: "Concerning the *Argotiers*, they are the poor whom you see at fairs, at pardons, and at the markets. There are so many of them that they make up a great Kingdom; they have a King, Laws, Officers, Estates, and a language of their own." He also adopted the nomenclature of the older book: "Their Officers are called Cagoux, Archisuppôts de l'Argot, Orphelins, Marcandiers, Rifodés, Malingreux and Capons, Piètres, Polissons, Francsmitoux, Calots, Sabouleux, Hubins, Coquillarts, Courteaux de boutanche."[62] Furthermore, he appropriated nearly word for word the description of the beggar king in *Le Jargon*: "Their

[59] R. Chartier, "Culture as Appropriation: Popular Cultural Uses in Early Modern France," in S. L. Kaplan, ed., *Understanding Popular Culture: Europe from the Middle Ages to the 19th Century* (Berlin, N.Y., and Amsterdam, 1984), 229-53.

[60] H.-J. Martin, "Culture écrite et culture orale, culture savante et culture populaire dans la France d'Ancien Régime," *Journal des Savants*, 1975:225-82; J.-L. Marais, "Littérature et culture 'populaire' aux xviiᵉ et xviiiᵉ siècles. Réponses et questions," *Annales de Bretagne et des Pays de l'Ouest* 87 (1980):65-105; R. Chartier, "La Circulation de l'écrit," in Duby, *Histoire de la France urbaine*, 3:266-82. See also Chapters 5 and 6 of this book.

[61] H. Sauval, *Histoire et recherches des Antiquités de la ville de Paris* (Paris, 1724), 1:510-16.

[62] For definitions of some of these titles, see pages 284 and 290.

king usually takes the name of Grand Coesre [and] occasionally [that] of King of the Thunes, because of a scoundrel of that name who was King three years running and had himself carried in a little cart drawn by two large dogs, and who later died in Bordeaux." This description is followed by a free résumé, in which Ollivier Chereau's jargon is returned to normal French, of the portions of the older work that list the various occupations (*vacations*) of the *argotiers*. Sauval's book dovetails two levels of reference. The first is topographic—the circumscribed space of the court of miracles that had been swept out by La Reynie but that still existed, although with other denizens, at the time Sauval was writing: "I have seen a mud [brick] house half buried in the ground, tottering with age and rot, which was hardly four *toises* [7.8 meters] square, but in which nevertheless there lodged more than fifty couples in charge of an infinite number of small children, legitimate, natural, and snatched." The other reference—one that Sauval hides from his readers—is to a text: A literal reading of *Le Jargon* furnishes the material for a description of the society of the Grand Coesre's subjects and officers. Whether Sauval himself was ensnared by the "blue" book, or whether he intended to "trap" his readers by presenting fiction as reality,[63] his text indicates one way in which books on roguery could be read: Their "literary" character annulled, the stock figures they portrayed could be taken literally as representing reality.

In point of fact, one of the aims of these works on beggars and ruffians in the catalogue of the *Bibliothèque bleue* was to seem real. This explains the Troyes printer-publishers' preferences for biographical accounts, for stories with clearly established settings, and for straightforward lists of nomenclature. As narrative techniques, these share the goals of leading the reader to believe what is told and to accept what is read as true. At the same time and in the same texts, however, there is clear parody that reveals the text's traps to anyone capable of reading on this other level. This fiction can be established directly, as in the plot of a comic play, but generally it is indicated more subtly—by setting the text in the Carnival tradition or according to the rules of the burlesque or by establishing it as entertainment through use of the humorous or the picturesque. Belief in what is read is thus accompanied by a laugh that gives it the lie; the readers' acceptance is solicited, but a certain distance shows literature for what it is. There is a subtle equi-

[63] L. Marin, *Le Récit est un piège* (Paris, 1978).

librium between the fable presented as such and realistic effects. This delicate balance permits multiple readings that fluctuate between a persuasion by literal interpretation and an awareness of and amusement at the parody. Is it impossible to read with both belief and disbelief? To accept the veracity of the narrative and still refuse to be duped into thinking it authentic? And can we not characterize as "popular" this relation with texts that ask to be taken as real even as they show themselves to be illusory?[64] This was perhaps the most fundamental expectation of the readers of the "blue" volumes. It is also the reason for the success of the literature of roguery, which gave written expression to fragments of social experience even as it parodically denied them. Thus the reader could simultaneously know and forget that fiction was fiction.

## APPENDIX TO CHAPTER EIGHT

*Line endings in the original are indicated by solidi.*
*The hyphens at the ends of lines in this transcription indicate*
*word divisions made in typesetting.*

### I. EDITIONS OF *La Vie Généreuse*: A DESCRIPTIVE BIBLIOGRAPHY

1. Lyons, 1596:

LA / VIE GENEREUSE / DES MERCELOTS, GVEVZ, / ET BOES-MIENS, CONTE- / nans leur façon de vivre / Subtilitez & Gergon. / Mis en lumière par Monsieur Pechon de Ruby, / Gentil'homme Breton, ayant esté avec eux / en ses ieunes ans, où il a exercé / ce beau Mestier. / Plus a esté adiousté vn Dictionnaire en / langage Blesquien, avec l'expli- / cation en vulgaire. / A LYON, / PAR IEAN IVILLIERON, / 1596, / Avec permission.

8°: A-E⁴; 40 p. paginated [1-2] 3-39 [40]. BN, Res Li⁵ 64 B

2. Paris, 1603:

La vie genereuse des / Matthois, Gueux, Boesmiens, / & Cagoux, contenant leurs / façons de vivre, subti- / litez & gergon. / Avec un Dictionnaire en langage Blesquin, / avec l'explication vulgaire, mieux qu'il / n'a esté aux précédentes impressions. / Mis en lumière par M. Pechon de Ruby, / Gentil'homme Breton, ayant esté auec / eux en ses ieunes ans, où il exercé ce / beau mestier. / A PARIS. / Iouxte la copie Imprimée / à Lyon. 1603.

8°: A-D⁴; 32 p. not paginated. Collection Heilbrun, no. 179

---

[64] See R. Hoggart, *The Uses of Literacy: Changing Patterns in English Mass Culture* (Fairlawn, N.J., 1957; London, 1967).

3. Paris, 1612:

La vie genereuse des / Mattois, Gueux, Boemiens, / & Cagouz, contenant leurs / façons de vivre, subtilitez gergon. / Avec un Dictionnaire en langage Blesquin, avec l'ex- / plication vulgaire, mieux qu'il n'a esté aux precedentes impressions. / Mis en lumiere par M. Pechon de Ruby, / Gentil-homme Breton, ayant esté avec eux / en ses ieunes ans, ou il a exercé ce beau mestier. / A PARIS, / Iouxte la copie Imprimée / à Lyon. 1612.

8°: A-D⁴; 32 p. not paginated. BN, Res Li 64

4. Paris, 1618:

La Vie genereuse des Mattois, Gveuvx, Boemiens et Cagovx, contenant leurs Façons de viure, Subtilitez et Gergon. Avec un Dictionnaire en langage Blesquin, avec l'Explication vulgaire mieux qui n'a esté aux precedentes impressions. Mis en lumière, par M. Pechon de Rvby, Gentil-homme Breton, ayant esté auec eux en ses ieunes ans, où il a exercé ce beau mestier. A Paris, Par P. Mesnier, Imprimeur et Portier de la Porte Sainct Victor, 1618.

8°; republished by Techener in *Les Ioyevsetez, Facecies et Folastres imagina-cions . . .* (Paris, 1831)

5. Paris, 1622:

La Vie generevse des Mattois, Gvevx, Boemiens et Cagoux . . . Paris, P. Menier, 1622.

8°; 31 p. British Museum, C 38 c 17

6. Troyes, 1627:

LA VIE GE / NEREVSE DES MER- / CELOTS, BONS COMPA- GNONS / & Boesmiens, contenant leur fa- / çon de viure, subtilites & gergon / mis en lumiere par Maistre Pe- / chon de Ruby; Gentil-homme / Breton, ay-ant esté auec eux en ses / ieunes ans, ou il à exercé ce beau / Mestier. / Plus à esté adousté vn Dictionnaire en / langage Blesquien, auec l'explication en / vul! gaire, mieux qu'il n'a esté aux / precedentes Impressions. / A TROYES. / Chez Nicolas Oudot, demeu- / rant en la rüe nostre Dame. / 1627.

12°: A-D⁸⁴; 24 p. not paginated. BN, Res Li⁵ 64 A

II. Editions of *Le Jargon*, 1630–1822: A Descriptive Bibliography

1. Lyons, 1630:

LE / IARGON, / OV LANGAGE DE / L'ARGOT REFORME: / Comme il est à présent en vsage / parmy les bons pauures. / Tiré & recueilly des plus fameux / Argotiers de ce temps. / Composé par vn pillier de Boutanche, / qui maquille en mollanche en la / Vergne de Tours. / Augmenté de nouueau dans le Dictionnaire, / des mots plus substantifs de l'Argot / ontre les precedentes impressions / par l'Autheur. / A LYON, / Iouxte la copie imprimee à Troyes, / Par Nicolas Oudot. / M. DC. XXX.

12°: A-D⁸⁴ E⁴ F²; 60 p. paginated [1-2] 3-60. Collection Heilbrun, no. 321

2. Lyons, 1632:

LE / IARGON, / OV LANGAGE DE / LARGOT REFORME: / Comme il est à présent en vsage / parmy les bons Pauures. / Tiré & recueilly des plus fameux / Argotiers de ce temps. / Composé par vn Pillier de Boutanche, / qui maquille en molanche en la / Vergne de Tours. / Augmenté de nouueau dans le Dictionnaire, / des mots plus substantifs de l'Argot / outre les precedentes impressions, / par l'Autheur. / A LYON, / Iouxte la copie imprimee à Troyes, / Par Nicolas Oudot. / M. DC. XXXII.

12°: A-D⁸⁴ E⁴ F²; 60 p. paginated [1-2] 3-58 [59-60]—the sheet C⁷ is signed D I A-. Bibliothèque Municipale, Lyons, 804 988

3. Lyons, 1634:

Bibliothèque Carnavalet. Edition cited in L. Sainéan, *Les Sources de l'argot ancien* (Paris, 1912), 179

4. Paris, n.d.:

LE / JARGON / OV LANGAGE DE / l'Argot reformé, comme il est / à présent en vsage parmy / les bons pauures. / Tiré & recueilly des plus fameux Argotiers, / de ce Temps. / Composé par vn Pillier de Boutanche, / qui maquille en mollanche, en la / Vergne de Tours. / Reueu corrigé & augmenté de nouueau, / par l'Autheur. / Seconde ÉDITION. / A PARIS. Chez la veufue du Carroy, rüe des Carmes.

12°: A-D⁸⁴ E⁴ F²; 60 p. paginated [1] 2-58 [59] 60. BN, Res X 2038

5. Troyes, 1656:

LE IARGON / OV L'ANGAGE DE / l'Argot Reformé. / COMME IL EST A PRÉSENT EN / vsage parmy les bons pauures. / Tiré & recueilly des plus fameux Argotiers de ce temps. / Composé par un pillier de Boutanche, / qui maquille en molanche en / la Vergne de Tours. / Augmentè de nouueau dans le Dictionnaire / des mots plus substantifs de l'Argot outre / les precedentes impressions par l'Autheur. / A TROYES, / Chez Nicolas Oudot, rüe nostre Dame, au / Chappon d'Or Couronné, 1656.

12°: A-D⁸⁴ E⁴ F²; 60 p. paginated. Collection Heilbrun, no. 9

6. Troyes, 1660:

LE IARGON / OV LANGAGE DE / l'Argot Reformé. / COMME IL EST A PRÉSENT EN / vsage parmy les bons pauuvres. / Tiré & recueilly des plus fameux / Argotiers de ce Temps. / Composé par vn pillier de Boutanche, qui maquille en molache en / la Vergne de Tours. / Augmenté de nouueau dans le Dictionnaire / de mots plus substantifs de l'Argot, outre / les precedentes impressions, par l'autheur. / A TROYES, / Par IVES GIRARDON, Rue nostre / Dame, au Chapon d'Or, 1660.

12°: A-D⁸⁴ E⁴ F²; 60 p. not paginated. BN, Res X 2037

7. Troyes, 1683:
Le Jargon

Troyes, Chez Oudot, à la Bonne Conduite, 1683.
Edition cited in Morin, *Catalogue descriptif*, no. 671

8. Troyes (and sold in Paris), n.d.:
LE / IARGON / OU LANGAGE / DE L'ARGOT REFORME / Comme
il est à présent en usage / parmi les bons pauvres. / tiré & recueilly des plus
fameux Argo- / tiers de ce temps. / Composé par un pillier de Boutanche, / qui
maquille en molanche en la / Vergne de Tours. / Augmenté de nouveau dans
le Dictionaire / des mots plus substantifs de l'Argot, ou- / tre les precedentes
impressions par l'Au- / teur. / A Troyes, & se vend /A PARIS, / Chez JEAN
MUSIER, Marchand / Libraire, ruë petit-Pont, a l'Image / Saint Antoine.
12°: A-D⁸⁴ E⁴ F²; 60 p. not paginated. BN, Res X 2036

9. Troyes, n.d.:
LE / JARGON / OU LANGAGE / DE L'ARGOT REFORME / comme
il est à present en usage / parmi les bons pauvres. Tiré & recueilly des plus
fameux / Argotiers de ce tems. / Composé par un pillier de Boutanche, / qui
maquille en molanche en la / vergne de Tours. / Augmenté de nouveau dans
le Dictionai- / re des mots les plus substantifs de l'Ar- / got, outre les préce-
dentes impressions / par l'Auteur. / A TROYES, / Chez JACQUES OUDOT,
Imprimeur / & Libraire, ruë de Temple.
12°: A-D⁸⁴; 48 p. paginated [1-6] 7-48. BN, X 14026

10. Troyes, 1737 (approval of 7 August 1728, permission of 12 August 1728):
Le Jargon
Chez la Veuve de Jacques Oudot et Jean Oudot fils, Imprimeur et Libraire
rue du Temple, 1737.
Bibliothèque Municipale, Montpellier, L 2874

11. Troyes, 1741 (approval of 7 August 1728, permission of 12 August 1728):
LE / JARGON / OU LANGAGE / DE L'ARGOT REFORME / comme
il est à présent un usage / parmi les bons pauvres. / Tiré & recüilli des fameux
Argotiers / de ce tems. / Composé par un Pilliere de Boutanche / qui maquille
en molanche en la / Vergne de Tours. / Augmenté de nouveau dans le Dictionaire / des mots les plus substantifs de l'Argotier, / outre les précédentes
Impressions, par / l'Auteur. / A TROYES, Chez JEAN OUDOT, Impri-
meur- / Libraire, ruë du Temple. 1741. / Avec permission.
12°: A⁸ B-C⁴ D²; 36 p. Bibliothèque Municipale, Troyes, Bibl. bleue 475;
Collection L. Morin (with variant titles, cf. A. Morin, *Catalogue descriptif*, no.
670)

12. Troyes, n.d. (approval of 6 August 1728, permission of 12 August 1728):
LE / JARGON / OU LE ŁANGAGE / DE L'ARGOT REFORME /
comme il est à présent en usage / parmi les bons pauvres. / Tiré & recueilli des
plus fameux Argotiers / de ce tems. / Composé par un Pillier de Boutanche /
qui maquille en molanche en la Ver- / gne de Tours. / Augmenté de nouveau

dans le Dictionnaire / des mots les plus substantifs de l'Argot / outre les pré-cédentes impressions, par / l'Auteur. / A TROYES, / Chez la Veuve P. GAR-NIER, Imprimeur- / Libraire, rue de Temple. / Avec Permission.

12°: A⁸ B-C⁴ D²; 36 p. not paginated. Collection L. Morin

13. Troyes, n.d. (approval of 6 August 1728, permission of 12 August 1712 [*sic*]):

LE / JARGON / OU LE LANGAGE / DE L'ARGOT REFORME, / comme il est à présent en usage / parmi les bons Pauvres / Tiré & recueilli des plus fameux Argotiers / de ce temps. / Composé par un Pillier de Boutanche, / qui maquille en molanche en la Vergne / de Tours. / Augmenté de nouveau dans le Dictionnaire / des mots les plus substantifs de l'Argot, / outre les pré-cédentes impressions, par / l'Auteur. / A TROYES, / Chez Jean-Antoine GARNIER, / Imprimeur-Libraire, rue du Temple. / Avec permission.

12°: A⁸ B-C⁴ D²; 36 p. paginated [1-2] 3-36. bn, X 26 675

14. Troyes, n.d.:

LE / JARGON / OU LANGAGE / DE L'ARGOT REFORME, / COMME IL EST A PRÉSENT EN USAGE / PARMI LES BONS PAUVRES. / Tiré & recueilli des plus fameux Argo- / tiers de ce temps. / Composé par un Pilier de Boutache, / qui maquille en molanche en la Vergne / de Tours. / Augmenté de nouveau dans le Diction- / naire des mots les plus Justantifs de l'Argot, outre les précédentes impres- / sions, par l'Auteur. / A TROYES, Chez J. A GARNIER, Imprimeur / Libraire, rue du Temple. / Avec Permission.

12°: A⁸ B-C⁴ D²; 36 p. paginated [1-3] 4-36. Collection Heilbrun, no. 110

15. Rouen, n.d.:

Le Jargon ou Abrégé de l'Argot ormé. Comme il est à présent en usage parmi les bons pauvres. Tiré et recueilli des plus fameux Argotiers de ce temps. Composé par un pillier de Boutanche qui maquille en Molande en la Vergne de Tours. Augmenté de nouveau dans le Dictionnaire des mots les plus substantifs de l'Argot, entre les précédentes impressions par l'Auteur, A Rouen, chez la Veuve de Jean Oursel, rue Saint-Jean.

12°: 36 p. Edition cited in Helot, *La Bibliothèque bleue en Normandie*, no. 138

16. Rouen, n.d.:

Le Jargon
Rouen, Jean Oursel l'Aîné.
Helot, *La Bibliothèque bleue en Normandie*

17. Lyons, n.d. (approval of 7 August 1728, permission of 12 August 1728):

LE / JARGON / OU LANGAGE / DE L'ARGOT REFORME / comme il est à présent en usage / parmi les Bons-Pauvres. Tiré & recueilli des plus fameux Argotiers / de ce Temps. / Composé par un Pilliere de Boutanche / qui maquille en molanche en la / Vergne de Tours. / Augmenté de nouveau dans le Dictionnaire / des mots les plus substantifs de l'Argotier / outre les précédentes Impression, par / l'Auteur. / A LYON, / Chez ANTOINE MOLIN, Libraire, / rue Quatre Chapeaux. / Avec Approbation / Permission.

12°: A-C⁶; 36 p. paginated [1-2] 3-36. bn, X 26 674

18. Troyes, n.d. (approval of 7 August 1740, permission of 12 August 1750):
LE / JARGON / OU LANGAGE / DE L'ARGOT REFORME / Comme il est à présent en usage parmi / les bons pauvres. / Tiré & recueilli des plus fameux Ar- / gotiers de ce tems. / Composé par un Pilliere de Boutache, / qui maquille en molanche en la Ver- / gne de Tours. / Augmenté de nouveau dans le Diction- / naire des mots les plus substantifs de / l'Argotier, outre les précédentes Impressions, par l'Auteur. / A TROYES, / Chez Jean OUDOT Imprimeur- / Libraire ruë de Temple. / Avec Permission.

12°: A⁸ B⁴ C⁶; 36 p. paginated [1-2] 3-36. Bibliothèque Municipale, Troyes, Bibl. bleue 474

19. Rouen, n.d.:
LE / JARGON / OU LANGAGE / DE L'ARGOT REFORME, / COMME IL EST A PRÉSENT EN USAGE / PARMI LES BONS PAUVRES. / Tiré & recueilli des plus fameux Argo- / tiers de ce temps. / Composé par un Pilier de Boutanche, / qui maquille en molanche en la Vergne, / de Tours. / Augmenté de nouveau dans le Diction- / naire des mots les plus substantifs de / l'Argot, outre les précédentes impres- / sions, par l'Auteur. / A ROUEN, / Rue Martainville, n° 128.

12°: A¹² B⁶; 36 p. paginated [1-3] 4-36. Slatkine Reprints, 1968

20. Troyes, 1822:
LE JARGON, / OU LE LANGAGE / DE L'ARGOT REFORME, / Comme il est à présent en usage parmi / les bons pauvres; / Tiré et recueilli des plus fameux Ar- / gotiers de ce temps; / Composé par un Pillier de Boutanche, / qui maquille en molanche en la / Vergne de Tours; / Augmenté de nouveau dans le dic- / tionnaire, des mots les plus subs- / tantifs de l'Argot, outre les pré- / cédentes impressions, par l'auteur. / A TROYES, / Chez Vᵉ ANDRÉ, Imprimeur-Libraire, / et Fabricant de Papiers, Grand'Rue. / 1822.

12°: 36 p. paginated [1-4] 5-36. Collection L. Morin

III. Editions of *Le Jargon* in the Nineteenth Century

1. LE JARGON OU LANGAGE DE L'ARGOT REFORME, A L'USAGE DES MERCIERS, PORTE-BALLES ET AUTRES; Tiré et recueilli des plus fameux Argotiers de ce temps; par M.B.H.D.S. Archi-suppôt

de l'Argot. NOUVELLE ÉDITION. Corrigée et augmentée de tous les mots qui n'étaient point dans les précédentes éditions, 48 p.

- A Troyes, Chez Baudot, Imprimeur-Libraire
  Bibliothèque Municipale, Troyes, Ancienne Collection Niel; Collection L. Morin; Collection J. Darbot; Collection Heilbrun, no. 153
- A Rouen, Chez Lecrêne-Labbey, Imprimeur-Libraire, Grande-Rue n° 160
  BN, X 14029
- Tours, Ch. Placé, 1838
  Edition cited in C. Nisard, *Histoire des livres populaires* (Paris, 1864)
- Épinal, Chez Pellerin, Imprimeur-Libraire
  BN, X 14027
- Montbéliard, A la Librairie de Deckherr Frères
  BN, X 14028
- A Pont-à-Mousson, Chez Thiery, Imprimeur-Libraire
  Edition cited in R. Yve-Plessis, *Bibliographie raisonnée de l'Argot* (Paris, 1901), no. 79

2. LE JARGON OU LANGAGE DE L'ARGOT REFORME Pour l'instruction des bons Grivois. Recueilli des plus fameux Argotiers de ce nom. Augmenté dans le Dictionnaire des mots plus substantifs de l'Argot, A beaucaire, Chez Ragotin, Rue des Escargots, à l'Enseigne du Vin Tourné, 28 p.

Bibliothèque Municipale, Troyes, Bibl. bleue 469

3. SUPPLÉMENT AU DICTIONNAIRE ARGOTIQUE, Contenant tous les mots qui sont en usage parmi les bons grivois, et qui ne sont point contenus dans le Dictionnaire de l'Argot, par M.B.H.D.S., Archi-suppôt de l'Argot, A La Vergne, Chez Mesiere, Babillandier du Grand Coëre. Avec Condé du Cagou de Turcan.

Collection Heilbrun, no. 381

The last two titles are probably the work of the Chalopins, printers and booksellers of Caen, who liked to use made-up addresses.

# CONCLUSION

......................................................................

THIS book contains a series of case studies centering either on specific practices or on one or another particular corpus of texts. What remains to be done is to attempt to tie them together and to propose a reading of the whole. There are, to be sure, certain propositions that underlie them all.

The first of these concerns written culture in French society from the sixteenth to the eighteenth centuries. This culture has long been gauged by only two methods of measurement: the counting of signatures to establish literacy rates, thus giving an indication of variations in the ability to read and write according to period, geographical distribution, sex, and socioeconomic status; and the scrutiny of library inventories to estimate the circulation of books and evaluate reading habits. Obviously, the present book relies heavily on the results of inquiries such as these. Nevertheless, it aims at shifting their conclusions somewhat. Access to printed matter cannot be reduced to book ownership alone: All books read were not necessarily privately owned, and all printed matter that a reader absorbed was not necessarily a book. Furthermore, writing was present at the very heart of an illiterate culture—in festive ritual, in public places, and in the workplace. Thanks to reading aloud and to the image that reiterated its message, the written word was accessible even to those unable to spell out its letters or to those whose unaided comprehension was rudimentary. Thus literacy rates are an inadequate measure of familiarity with the written word, and particularly so in traditional societies, where reading and writing are dissociated and learned sequentially. There were many individuals (women in particular) who left school knowing how to read at least to some extent, but not how to write. Similarly, private ownership of a book is, in itself, an inadequate indication of acquaintance with the plural uses and many effects of printed matter. It is impossible to know how many people incapable of signing their names were nevertheless readers and how many readers possessed no books (or at least none worthy of being appraised by the notary who inventoried their goods) but read posters, broadsides, *canards*, and the chapbooks of the *Bibliothèque bleue*. Still, we must postulate the existence of people such as these—and in great numbers—if we are to comprehend the impact of printing on the traditional forms of a culture that continued to be largely based on the spoken word, on gesture, and on pictures.

This first affirmation elicits others. In the first place, it accounts for the importance which all who attempted to regulate behavior and fashion minds attached to written objects. This in turn explains the role that widely distributed texts played in pedagogy, discipline, and acculturation: The works on preparation for death told how death was to be considered, how to make ready for it, and how one's last moments were to be lived; the treatises on *civilité* stated the prescriptions and prohibitions necessary to live in this world in a Christian and civil manner. This also accounts for the control exercised over printed matter, in particular over works that reached the greatest number of readers and the humblest, works which were subject to imposed or self-imposed censorship to prune away all that might offend religion, morality, or decency. Thus it was with the same will that both festivities and texts were expurgated, that both human bodies and reading matter were controlled, and that conduct and thoughts were dictated. Two major developments lay at the base of this motivation and lent it strength. First, there was a tenacious and lasting effort by the Catholic Church to impose on all of society (on its own clergy first, then on all the faithful) norms that distinguished true beliefs from illicit superstitions and reverential acts from reprehensible excesses. Second, within the new social forms that had been engendered by the absolutist state (in court society, for example), censures and constraints were elaborated. Gradually, these were seen as appropriate for the molding of all individuals, whatever their estate. The present essays, taken together, attempt to identify evidence of this twofold fundamental process, which profoundly transformed the society of the *ancien régime*, in small-scale phenomena—in such texts as the guides to a good death, the Christianized and socially oriented *civilités* for children, and the books of entertainment.

With all the possible uses of the written word and from the various ways of treating print, the texts of this period established representations and images in which we can recognize the divisions that people of the *ancien régime* held to be the most decisive. They illustrate contrasting levels of cultural competence, differing reading abilities, and various styles of reading. At times obviously, as in the *artes moriendi*, but more often simply in the format of the printed page, text and image joined to permit plural "readings" of the same object by its appeal to

344

literate and illiterate alike. But all who read a text did not read it in the same fashion. Publishers of peddlers' books, for example, did not suppose their public had a great familiarity with books. Thus they offered repeated opportunities to find one's place, numerous headings, and frequent summaries. Brief and self-contained sequences were better suited to this sort of reading; only a minimal coherence was required in texts composed of disjointed textual units (chapters, fragments, or paragraphs). This elementary, segmented, and discontinuous reading is reflected in the revisions made by the printers of the *Bibliothèque bleue* as they adapted texts for inclusion in their catalogue destined for their humbler readers. This editorial perception of differences in the reading abilities of various groups parallels another series of representations in literary and pictorial form: the opposition of an individual style of reading—alone, in private, and involving personal thoughts or emotions (generally presented as the reading of the elites)—to the "popular" use of print, in which the spoken word mediated for the printed word as someone read aloud to a household gathered during the evening, to a religious assembly, in the workplace, or on the street corner.

These major cleavages, present in thought and image in the texts and pictures of the period, can be approached in different ways. First of all, it is clear that they underlay writing and publishing strategies, since they describe implicit methods of reading and possible uses of the written materials put into circulation. By the same token, they acquired an efficacy, traces of which we can find in typographic objects, in protocols for reading that make them explicit, and in the changes in a text when it was offered to new readers in a new editorial formula. It is thus from this starting point—the various representations of reading—and with the dichotomies created in the modern period (between the reading of a text and the reading of a picture, between literate reading and rudimentary reading, and between reading in private and reading as a community) that I have attempted to examine the manipulations and uses of printed texts—humbler but more continuously present and a good deal more influential than books—ranging from the *images volantes* and *placards* (always with their accompanying texts) to the *canards* and booklets (often illustrated) of the *Bibliothèque bleue*.

Because it quickly attracted the interest of French historians in search of ancient popular culture and because it constitutes the most homogeneous and longest lasting corpus of printed works destined for a broad-based reading public, I have reserved a prominent place for the *Bibliothèque bleue*, defined here as a publishing formula identifiable by its material and economic characteristics, not on the basis of the "popular" nature of the texts it offered. Its texts all had earlier careers in print, either brief or lengthy, before their publication in the *Bibliothèque bleue* series, and they came from all genres, all epochs, and all styles. Every book put out by the Troyes printer-publishers and their imitators was the result of a search through the repertory of already published texts for works that seemed compatible with the expectations and abilities of the public they aimed to serve—a broad public of readers not restricted to the cultivated elites alone. The particular corpus of the literature of roguery has enabled me to test the hypotheses that concern the distinction between the history of texts and the history of editions and that therefore are focused on the typographic and textual differences between the *Bibliothèque bleue* edition of a given title and its earlier versions. This restricted and readily handled corpus illustrates the cultural crosscurrents characteristic not only of the *Bibliothèque bleue* catalogue as a whole, but also of each of its titles. In the specific case of roguery literature, each title emerges from the interrelationship of several cultural traditions. At the bottom, there is the Carnival tradition, which is followed by the moralizing literature of exposure and warning, the repertory of facetious tales, and, finally, the new forms of the picaresque and the burlesque. The complexity of these interlocked traditions invalidates any overall social definition of such material, and it invites reflection on the plurality of the readings it authorized, ranging from a belief in the veracity of the descriptions to a grasp of fiction as fiction. This plurality of readings does not necessarily distinguish different classes of readers, but it can indicate contradictory or successive attitudes on the part of one and the same reader.

Representations of reading (and of differences in reading) during this period, as revealed on the practical level in the printed works themselves and on the descriptive and normative levels in the literary or pictorial settings, thus constitute essential data for the archaeology of reading practices to which this book hopes to make a contribution. But such representations must not mask other distinctions that people of the time perceived less clearly. There were certainly many practices that invert the classic opposition between solitary reading in the bourgeois and aristocratic homes and reading in common among humbler folk. Reading aloud, for instance, remained one of the pastimes that cemented elite sociability, either in the privacy of the *salon* or, in public, in learned assemblies. But then printed matter also penetrated to the heart of the "popular" home, where it imbued modest objects (which were not by any means always books) with the memory of an important event in the owner's life, recalled strong emotions, and served as a sign of personal identity. Contrary to the accepted image, "popular" reading was not always reading in common; we need to look to the secret solitude of humble folk for the simple practices of those who cut out the pictures in *canards*, who colored the printed engravings, or who read the "blue" books on their own.

In order to understand the variety of ways in which people related to the printed word, one contrast seems to me fundamental: city versus country. It returns like a leitmotif in these essays, for it is a constant in the separation of the two cultures of the written word. In the cities, print was everywhere present, posted, exhibited, cried in the streets, and highly visible, which, through a patient apprenticeship in customs and uses, created a familiarity that was the beginning of literacy. In the *plat-pays* around the cities, however, writing by hand had long remained the monopoly of the notary or the cleric, and printed matter was scarce. To be sure, in the eighteenth century (earlier in the north, later in various areas of the south), the titles in the *Bibliothèque bleue* catalogue, which had long been sold in the cities, began to penetrate the countryside. Here they attenuated the major and longstanding discrepancy between city and country and so prompted city dwellers to search for a new way to distinguish urban life in what was read and how it was read. But, as attested by the grievances expressed and drafted on the eve of the Revolution, the gap continued to exist as the two contrasting cultural formations produced two different sorts of discourse in their demands for redress of grievances—one abstract, general, and reform-oriented, the other specific and concrete.

This book has attempted, *à sa façon*, to consider a few of the essential questions concerning the cultural evolution of France from the sixteenth century to the eighteenth. These include the strategies employed in the work of Christianization both before and after the high water of the Catholic Reformation, the diffusion of new norms of behavior that were elaborated in the cauldron of court circles but imposed on an entire society, the penetration of the corpus of ideas proposed by the Enlightenment, and the variations in the apportionment of sociocultural differences. For each of these problems, the basic terms of which have been formulated in works that have now become classics, I have followed the same method, choosing a particular corpus, mobilizing serial data and statistical measurements for a preliminary approach to the subject, then investigating the differences or the shifts in the discourses, the notions, or the uses under consideration.

In so doing, I have on more than one occasion attempted to include in my analysis reflections on its chances of success or its obligatory limits. If I have referred to how historians of the present day interpret certain objects of historical inquiry (festivities, for example) or if I have pointed out the limits of one historical approach or another (the history of ideas practiced in Germany or the quantification of cultural objects dear to the French), it was not in an attempt to negate the value of the working knowledge gained through these investigations or approaches, but, perhaps through an explicit statement of choices made or constraints involved, to avoid false debates and vain quarrels. From the same set of texts, various readings can in fact be proposed, and no one analysis can claim to exhaust all the possible ways in which the texts can be understood. May the essays in this volume be taken, then, as valid attempts to account for the various bodies of literature I have treated, using approaches and concepts that seemed helpful and not contradictory, but that are not the only ones that might serve to study the *cahiers de doléances*, the works on preparation for a good death, the *civilité* treatises, or the volumes in the *Bibliothèque bleue*.

Library of Congress Cataloging-in-Publication Data

Chartier, Roger, 1945-
The cultural uses of print in early modern France.

Includes index.
1. Books and reading—France—History—18th century.
2. Books and reading—France—History—17th century.
3. Books and reading—France—History—16th century.
4. France—Intellectual life. 5. France—Popular culture.
6. Popular literature—France—History and criticism.
7. Printing—France—History. I. Title.
Z1003.5.F7C47    1987    028'.9'0944    87-45515
ISBN 0-691-05499-1 (alk. paper)

Roger Chartier is Directeur d'Études
at the École des Hautes Études
en Sciences Sociales in Paris.